MW01293895

THE ANALYST'S ANALYST WITHIN

THE ANALYST'S ANALYST WITHIN

LORA HEIMS TESSMAN

THE ANALYTIC PRESS

2003   Hillsdale, NJ   London

Published by
The Analytic Press, Inc., Publishers
Editorial Offices:
101 West Street
Hillsdale, NJ 07642

www.analyticpress.com

Designed and typeset by CompuDesign, Charlottesville, VA.

Library of Congress Cataloging-in-Publication Data

Tessman, Lora Heims
    The analyst's analyst within / Lora Heims Tessman
    p. cm
    Includes bibliographical references and index
    ISBN 0-88163-351-8
    1. Psychoanalysis. 2. Psychoanalysts--Psychology.
  3. Psychotherapist and patient. I.
    Title.
    RC506.T465 2003
    616.89'17—dc21

2003050204

Printed in the United States of America

10 9 8 7 6 5 4 3 2 1

CONTENTS

Acknowledgments   vii

1   Overview   1

2   Conversations and Process   20

3   Satisfaction and the Analyst   28

4   In the Mind's Eye   65

5   Gendered Desires: An Introduction   83

6   Women with Male Analysts   87

7   Men with Male Analysts   114

8   Men with Female Analysts   132

9   Women with Female Analysts   158

10   Theories of Thought   183

11   The Training Context   198

12   Evolving Identity as Analyst   210

13   Analysis Ending and Unending   223

14   Mourning   235

15   Leave-Taking   248

16   Self-Analysis   258

17   Dilemmas of Posttermination Contact   270

18   The Analyst Imagined   297

19   Concluding Reflections: The Future of a Collusion   307

     Appendix A   319

     Appendix B   323

     Appendix C   325

     References   329

     Index   343

ACKNOWLEDGMENTS

$\mathcal{E}$njoyable interchanges with friends and colleagues inspired me to transform a longstanding interest in how the analyst's analyst inhabits memory over time into the research project described in this book. In particular, I would like to acknowledge the following:

The 34 psychoanalysts who participated in the research project have my gratitude and admiration for their generous involvement, the depth of their introspection, their wisdom, and their trust. I feel honored to have been allowed to accompany them in revisiting the memories of their analysts. I have been enriched personally, and in my analytic work, by the opportunity to know the Participants in this way. Finding myself delighted and also pained by what I heard, they often moved me to deep respect and lingering fondness. Each time I sifted through their narratives, I found myself in internal dialogues with the Participants.

The members of the workshop "Changes in How the Analyst Is Experienced Intrapsychically over Time after Termination," which has met monthly at my home since 1995, became valued friends and companions in ideas. Many of them contributed further by reading early drafts of some chapters and making extremely helpful suggestions. These colleagues include Alan Bateman, Stanley Cath, Toni Greatrex, Jim Herzog, Judith Huizenga, Gerald Lazar, Jeremy Nahum, Alan Pollack, Kenneth Reich, Steven Sands, Maurice Vanderpol, Anna Wolff, and Judith Yanof. Additional friends and colleagues who read some chapters or made insightful comments are Leon and Carola Eisenberg, Eleanor Herzog, and Benson Snyder. I am thankful to all of them. Their encouragement, which lightened the writing, meant a great deal to me.

I am appreciative of the Boston Psychoanalytic Society and Institute and of the Research Advisory Board of the International Psycho-analytic Association for granting the funds that made it possible to transcribe the research interviews.

Working with my editor, John Kerr, included the distinct pleasures of being treated to his original and multilayered associations, his unusually good aim in pinpointing just where the issues lie, his free-dom to delve into unexpected territories to discover their harvests, and his editorial talent in honing the writings into publishable form. At The Analytic Press, Nancy Liguori, with knowledgeable kindness, shepherded the work to actual publication. Thanks also to Wendy Gelberg for her excellence in transcribing the interview tapes and assisting in the analysis of data.

I am always grateful to my daughters, Debora Bolter and Lisa Tessman, and to my grandchildren, Jessica and Nathaniel Bolter and Yuval Tessman-Bar-On, for their astounding ways of bringing joy into life. Much love goes to my husband, Arnold Modell, who was sup-portively patient while the writing occupied me.

William Blake, the poet, said: "No one has ever measured how much the heart can hold." Somewhere, within that region, my former analyst still frolics.

OVERVIEW

Memory believes before knowing remembers.

—William Faulkner, *Light in August*

A psychoanalyst was asked how he felt about the termination of his own analysis. His answer was, "In a word, fine. In two words, not fine!" The research comprising this book explores the worded and wordless in such layers of "fine" and "not fine." Empirical data about how analysis is experienced by the analysand have been sparse. A barely tapped resource lies in what psychoanalysts discover—what "memory believes"—when they recall their intrapsychic experience of their own analysts over time.

A number of questions have intrigued me about how one's analyst remains memorable over time after termination, and these questions form the basis for each of the topics explored in this book: How is the analyst remembered differently when an analysis has been deeply satisfying from when it is experienced as beneficial, but with major limitations, or from when, in retrospect, it is judged to be highly unsatisfactory and even damaging? What surmised attributes of the analyst are viewed as linked to the potential for or the obstacles to mutative change? How do the analysand's conjectures about the analyst's view of him or her affect what is internalized and what is memorable about the analysis? How does the gender of the analyst and analysand, housed in like or unlike bodies of desire, affect what transpires between them? What changes in how the analyst is experienced intrapsychically take place over time after termination, and why might these changes matter? How does posttermination contact, or its absence, acquire meanings that affect future developments in positive or negative ways? How are analyses influenced by the sociocultural context of a Psychoanalytic Institute as representative of prevalent theory and practice? The research I describe aims to illuminate these questions rather than to test specific hypotheses.

My interest in these issues led me to talk with a sample of 34 analysts (30 members of the Boston Psychoanalytic Society and Institute and four from other parts of the country) about how their own analyst became memorable in ways that have made themselves felt over postanalytic time. My primary concern was not with training per se, but was—and is—to explore the processes of remembered engagement and internalization as general phenomena. Nevertheless, issues derived from the training context also could be expected to make their presence felt.

I wanted to note differences that might correlate with the decade during which the training analysis took place, that is, while paradigms in theory and practice were changing. I also wanted to sample each of the four possible gender combinations. Thus, sample selection was based on the variations in time and gender. An additional salient dimension is the unique dynamic within each particular analytic dyad. For the study of qualities related to the particularity of each analytic dyad, comparison pairs of two kinds were constituted: pairs of two analysts for the same analysand and pairs of two analysands for the same analyst. Of the 34 Participants in the research, 28 had two or more analyses. There were six instances in which two Participants had shared the same analyst. The Participants portrayed a total of 64 analyses, and the sample comprised 11 training analysts and 23 nontraining analysts.

The research was designed around internal rather than external validity, namely, the subjective judgments of the Participants about their satisfaction or dissatisfaction with their analyses, the ingredients that went into those judgments, and the consequences of the experience. By external criteria, such as the opinion of a spouse or Rorschach scores, the value of the analysis might be judged differently. Verification about whether the analyst felt toward the analysand as he or she was portrayed was also not attempted. I now briefly introduce some considerations that shaped the research process and the theoretical controversies in which it was couched and then proceed to preview the parts of the book that follow.

Embarking on the research forced me to struggle with a number of quandaries in methodology: I had found myself attracted to what might be learned about the analytic process by talking to analysts about their own experience, a population unique in having experienced analysis from two positions, on the couch and behind the couch. This population is probably distinctive in other ways as well, such as having a penchant for introspection, the urge to articulate what is usually unspoken, some familiarity with anguish, a belief in the possibility of change, and the myriad motivations that led them to choose psychoanalysis as a career. Any distinctive sample calls for care in what the generalizations are about.

The choice of analysts as the study population also had the disadvantage of some stringent restrictions, which I considered worth their yield. Privacy and confidentiality were essential for the Participants, as well as for the analysts portrayed in their recollections. Protective measures are spelled out in the letter of invitation to the Participant (Appendix A). Nobody knew who was a Participant unless the person chose to divulge it. Several people stated that if anyone else—with the exception of the secretary who transcribed the tapes—would have access to the material, they would not be willing to participate. The secretary, who later became a research assistant, had to be someone with no current or likely future connection to psychoanalysis. Each Participant was sent his or her transcript for consent and to edit out passages that were not to be quoted. One eloquent Participant asked that the total narrative of his analyses be sealed. Of course, material vetoed for public quotation was not lost to the research findings, because it was still tabulated and counted in the aggregate comparisons of categories. Participants were invited to make up their own pseudonyms. The tapes, with possibly recognizable voices, were destroyed once transcribed. Although I was surprised that Participants rarely vetoed quotations, there are a variety of specific instances in which they did, including charged comments about Institute politics and ambience, about colleagues or supervisors, about certain revealing aspects of family background, about particular fantasies associated with shame, or about criticisms of their analysts that they feared might cause hurt feelings. There was also reluctance to release certain passages for a very different reason—namely, a sense of privacy about precious interchanges with the analyst during periods of profound erotic feelings. I agree that privacy is an essential component of such erotic experience and that public display might alter it in some way. Therefore, I opt to limit some of its elaboration, generally, in these accounts. Most of the excerpts quoted here appear under the pseudonym of the Participant to allow for cross-referencing of material about that person. When a Participant preferred delinking a particular quotation from the pseudonym, the citation is given anonymously from "an analyst."

To further protect anonymity, presented excerpts are primarily process material (although parts of excerpts may be edited, summarized, or juxtaposed to different sections of the interview). Biographical details are kept to a minimum. I concur with Gabbard's (2000) recent writings on "Disguise or Consent" that biographic detail is more revealing than process material. I noticed, however, that certain recognizable details about the analysts portrayed were nonetheless earmarked with consent for presentation. In such cases, I let the Participants choose what would be divulged rather than let my sense of discretion trump theirs. Among the hidden pleasures of citing the narratives in a form as close to verbatim as possible might be this: I often feel moved by exactly how a patient communicates, so deeply emblematic of his or her essence, but of course I can't act on my urge to share it with others. Preserving the Participants' voices may gratify the same urge. When people wanted their message to remain undisguised, I was mindful of Winnicott's adage that "it is a joy to be hidden but disaster not to be found" (1963, p. 186).

A further reason for preserving the experience-near process material lies in its potential use as raw data for others to come to their own, perhaps different conclusions.

I chose to focus largely on Participants who are fellow members of the same Institute because I came to feel that the accretion of views, for instance, of Participants who had the same analyst and who shared the same history of Institutional practices, added more than it lost. Involving colleagues meant that I considered them to be Participants rather than research subjects. Without a frame for working through such issues, I did not want to include personality measures or attachment interviews or ask for self-described categories of character problems, which might have eventuated in Participants' self-criticisms or self-assigned diagnostic categorizations, potentially adding needless iatrogenic factors to whatever issues of self-esteem were already operant. There is enough of that in Psychoanalytic Institutes already. Nevertheless, references to diagnoses made their appearance. For instance, several women made asides such as, "being a good hysteric, I reacted this way," and several men referred to their ex-wives as "definitely borderline." While ignoring the question of diagnoses, it did, however, seem relevant to reflect on the role of a quotidian attitude, namely, the Participant's theory of thought, an emotionally charged belief about whether one's own thinking is primarily dyadically or autoevoked. This variable, associated with other traits, bears on how termination is metabolized, because it involves moving from dyadic communication to the soliloquy of self-analysis.

The taped interviews lasted between 2 and 8 hours per Participant according to the Participant's choice of how much there was to be said. They included both spontaneous narrative and responses to 13 lines of open-ended questions. The questions are included in the letter to Participants in Appendix A. In approaching the interviews, a priority was to provide a context that might maximize communicative freedom for candid personal responses in some depth. The interviews, planned in two-hour segments when possible, usually opened with an unstructured narrative about each of the Participants' analysts, which tended to last at least through the first session, followed by those questions that had not been responded to spontaneously. The conversations were not begun with the questions because it seemed important that the material be cast in the Participants' metaphors rather than in my own. The questions had been sent to the Participants before the interview, however, to allow for the development of associations over time, rather than privileging instant reactions. One aim was to evoke the momentum of memory in such a way that the Participant would have the possibility, if so inclined, to make self-analytic use of whatever emerged.

I was to learn that most of the Participants had either two analyses or another extended therapy with an analyst. Whether the second treatment came before or after the training analysis was about evenly divided. That the absence of a second analytic experience did not necessarily signify satisfaction in the aftermath of the first was highlighted by the finding that the proportion of Participants who felt their analysis was unsatisfactory was highest within the minority who never returned to another analytic experience. I have come to regard second analyses as denoting an affinity for analytic process and its yield, rather than dissatisfaction with a first experience.

Each Participant's narrative in toto, as well as the response to each of the 13 lines of questions, was grouped by degree of retrospective satisfaction with the analysis, by gender combination, and by the decade during which the analysis took place. The interaction of those distributions is summarized separately for the total number of analyses described and for training analyses specifically. These findings are found in Appendix C. Their elaboration in the form of excerpts from the narratives can be found throughout the book.

It became evident that a crucial dimension of the Participants' recalled experiences were based in their feelings about how the analyst experienced them. Commonalties in each of the three categories of satisfaction did not reside in specific behaviors or techniques of the analyst (such as amount of silence, self-disclosure, interpretation of defense or of the transference), but rather in the meanings attributed to the affective messages through which interpretations and other interchanges with the analyst took place. The presentation of the findings revolves around such meanings.

The conversations with Participants did not purport to assess the veridical experience of the past analysis, that is, what "actually" happened. My working assumption was that the historical encoding of the past is affected by the mind-set of the present, but that affective memories evoked about the analyst express important influences on the present. Any time period chosen for study during or after analysis has its singular features. A retrospective view of the analyst reflects a choice to highlight the dynamics of memory in current experience. It takes into account the observation that the analysis is far from over when it ends, that postanalytic developments occur in the wake of what the actual analysis has started. Changes in retrospective satisfaction, and in associated views of the analyst, occur over long time spans. Guntrip (1975) advised: "Analysts are advised to be open to post-analytic improvements, so presumably we do not expect 'an analysis' to do a 'total' once for all job. We must know about post-analytic developments if we are to assess the actual results of the primary analysis" (p. 145).

The Participant's memories, with whatever highlighting of meaning, emphasis, or evaluation may have been set into motion during the interviews or in prior self-analysis, thus stand in a parallel relation to a more familiar phenomena, namely, the constant retranscription of childhood memories by the time they emerge within the transference–countertransference context of analysis. In general, it is this constellation of desires, adaptations, and self-protective compromises from childhood, already retranscribed (or having resisted retranscription lest there be retraumatization), that make up the issues brought to treatment. There are, of course, also important differences between parent and analyst as remembered, because much of the impact of early childhood experience acquires its patterns of organizing anticipations from times when the psychic organizers of affects, with their associated metaphoric, embodied imagery, are nonverbal. Still, the changing balance in the controversies over the past five decades about the analyst's contribution to verbal and nonverbal enacted communication seems reflected in the following: In many analyses of earlier decades, in addition to whatever transference phenomena were interpreted and discussed, a pattern of enactment of unconscious expectations from early relationships seemed to dominate the affective ambiance of the analysis, apparently without at that time any articulation by either the analyst or analysand. Nonetheless, the therapeutic action or disaction of these analyses decades ago seems to have hinged on the dynamic in these patterns. To attempt to illuminate the impact of both what was said and what was enacted without being said, this study explored how the Participants linked their views of the analyst's role as actualized in communication, with the eventual sense of benefit and satisfaction with the analysis.

In the psychoanalytic ambiance of today, there is great diversity in formulations about therapeutic action. Some emphasize that the analysis of ego resistance through which the analyst helps the analysand observe in the self what was previously taboo allows for a reduction of intrapsychic conflict and defense, permitting parts of the self previously unknown to be integrated (Gray, 1973, 1986, 1990; Weinshel, 1992; Busch, 1995). Others (Loewald, 1960, 1962, 1979; Greenberg and Mitchell, 1983; Hoffman, 1983, 1996; Mitchell, 1988) underscore the impact of the new object relationship established with the analyst. For example, Fonagy (1999) holds that "psychic change is a function of a shift of emphasis between different mental models of object relationships." He proposes further that "the therapeutic action of psychoanalysis is unrelated to the recovery of memories of childhood, be these traumatic or neutral." In this connection he argues explicitly that "the experiences contributing to representations of object relations will have occurred mostly too early to be remembered, that is in the conscious sense of experiencing recovering a past experience in the present" (p. 216). With regard to the potential implications for technique, Joseph (1981) noted that "interpretations dealing only with the individual associations would touch only the more adult part of the personality, while the part that is really needing to be understood is communicated though the pressures brought on the analyst" (p. 448).

If the analyst engages with the analysand in mutative responses to such early and unmentalized anticipations, the process may call forth a different range of skills, satisfactions, and limitations than if the analyst's primary role is that of interpreter of repressed impulse with its layering of defense and transference attitudes. Analogously, if the analyst's own transferences are viewed as playing a role in the analytic interchange, then his or her involvement is imbued in a positive way with potential for changes in the analyst, but this opportunity also confers an added, perhaps disturbing, responsibility to acknowledge that not every turbulence in the analytic relationship stems from the patient's "projective identification." Once engaged, the affective meanings of an analyst's communication will affect the alchemy between the analysand's reexperience of the past in the present and the hope for pursuing a more satisfying future.

Deeming the nature of the analyst to figure importantly in how the analysis is experienced rests on a premise, among others, of the beneficial interplay of the fantasies and the actuality of the analyst. Freud depicted psychoanalysis as "conversations" rather than as soliloquies of free association. He said of the patient–analyst couple, "Nothing takes place between them except that they talk to each other" (1926, p. 187). So he assumed that interchange between two individuals could create an effect. But because he saw fantasy as distorting and leading away from reality, fantasy had to be renounced for reality to be accepted. To my mind, this goal would constrict, mute, or deaden the freedom for fantasies that vitalize play, love, and work. I prefer to concur with Loewald's (1975) assertion:

> Reality testing is far more than an intellectual or cognitive function. It may be understood more comprehensively as the experiential testing of fantasy—its potential and suitability for actualization—and the testing of actuality—its potential for encompassing it in, and penetrating it with, one's fantasy life. We deal with a task of reciprocal transposition [p. 368].

I believe that the analyst is experienced as that crucially tested "actuality" for retranscribing intrapsychic realities that have been foreclosed. The alchemy between the analyst as subjectively created object and his or her "actuality" as evoked by the particular analysand is key. What is meant by the analyst's actuality? *Webster*'s defines actual as "being in existence or action now." During analysis, the actuality of the analyst involves those expressions of self that emerge in relation to the particular analysand, selectively evoked by who and what the analysand brings. Thus, the analyst is *actually* different with different patients. Fonagy et al. (1995) believe that the way the capacity for self-reflective mentation and for understanding mental states of the other develops is that "the child gets to know the caretaker's mind as the caregiver endeavors to understand and contain the mental state of the child" (p. 256). Similarly, as the analysand attempts to know the analyst's mind, aspects of the analyst's actuality emerge whether or not he intends to make deliberate self-disclosures. Such interplay contributes to the *affective knowledge of the nature of the connection*, which sows what "memory believes, before knowing remembers."

How the function of termination in itself is understood is influential in how it is metabolized by both the analyst and analysand. For some decades, there was considerable stress on the analysand achieving "independence" from his or her attachment to the analyst as the sign of having resolved, through the transference, the remnant dependence on past attachments to parents. The valued heir to the analytic relationship putatively was the self-analytic function, a result of the identification with the analyst. Consonant with the ideology of this understanding, it was deemed important that the analysand renounce the remnant wishes for gratification with the analyst. Concurrently, the capacity to mourn the ending of analysis was increasingly viewed as one of the indicators of readiness for termination. The notion that resolving the transference neurosis entails the further task of mourning for the relationship to the actual analyst moved the fulcrum of thinking and practice in the field toward the assumption that the relationship itself had importance.

More recently, a different set of assumptions has underlain a view of what termination is about. These assumptions involve the very nature of internalization. In this view, what is internalized are transformed anticipations, in the form of representations, verbal and nonverbal, of both dyadic interchange and self-contained states in the presence of the other. Sander (1997) speaks of inner states of "being together with" and yet "distinct from." Geller and Farber (1993) refer to the internalization of an "internal dialogic partner." It is not the interaction in itself that remains memorable, but the intrapsychic representation of that interaction. As the analysis progresses and self-protective maneuvers lend less coloration to the image of the analyst, the analysand increasingly experiences the actuality of the analyst. Although eternal asymmetry is inevitable in this relationship, constructed as it is around the intrapsychic world of the analysand, a growing sense of mutuality may characterize the termination and post-termination period. S. Cooper (2000) posits a mutual containment of affects between analyst and analysand rather than it being solely the analyst who contains the affects of the patient. In this process the analysand has come to know the quotidian aspects of the analyst's ways intimately, including his or her limitations. Cooper notes:

> There are elements of our personalities that most analytic patients will get a feel for, albeit filtered through whatever he or she brings to the situation. In particular, patients get a sense of how the analyst deals with specific affects, conflicts and transference attributions. . . . One of the really good outcomes of analysis is the patient's heightened ability to get a sense of the analyst's functional person, his strength and weaknesses, not through revelation, but by working through. In so doing, the patient can get out of a more infantilized, idealizing position in relation to the analyst. Many of these observations are in the background during analysis and move to the foreground during postanalysis years. Yet these dynamics are always operating—it is just a question of if the patient and analyst are able to look at the elephant in the room [p. 101].

In such models of analytic process de-idealization can occur through intimate knowledge rather than distance, free-spirited observation rather than adaptation to surmised taboos about articulating certain perceptions of the analyst. Posttermination autonomy would not depend on detachment from feelings about the analyst, but rather on the transformation of the kind of idealization that diminishes the self to enlarge the other. Nonetheless, other aspects of the feelings previously attributed to idealization, such as admiration, a ready flow of cherishing the person of the analyst with some felt excitement, or memories imbued with pleasurable, including bodily feelings, may remain.

Some of the ideas I have just advanced influenced my choice of focusing on the nature of the intrapsychic presence of the analyst, rather than on the more usual attempt to evaluate the "success" of the analysis in terms of intrapsychic changes during and after the process. It seems to me that as the affectively salient patterns begin to emerge in the transference, the form in which they emerge is already affected by the particular communicative ambience being sustained with the analyst. The analysand's surmises about the analyst affect how memory is experienced; what kind of bodily states, in desire, can be tolerated; what forays in imagination beget what meanings. Neither memory nor enactments are true to the alleged "repetition compulsion" because they arise in a new context. Furthermore, the way they are remetabolized, again, includes the dialogue of affect between analyst and analysand. Thus, it makes sense that the actuality of the analyst, in his or her affective communications, is key and that therefore the same analysand may have a very different analytic experience with two different analysts.

This view of how internalization involves the analyst requires a reconsideration of the relationship between past and present. For Freud, the patient's experience of the analyst is, importantly, not real, not contemporary; it is a wholesale temporal displacement of past onto present. This understanding has been the basis for the traditional interpretation of transference as, by definition, a distortion of the real analyst, functioning as a blank screen. Countering the theory of temporal displacement, the contention of Mitchell (2000, pp. 17–18) and others is that the categories established in past experience are brought to bear in response to new, very real, contemporary experiences through which they may be transformed. Criticizing the view that in the transference "salient affective unconscious memory" is "mapped onto the here and now as a conscious experience," Mitchell points out that although cognitive psychologists contend it is new perceptions that revive early memories through metaphor and metonomic triggers, they are ignoring the knowledge that the memories are dynamic. He quotes Edelman's statement that memory "is a form of re-categorization during ongoing experience rather than a precise replication of the previous sequence of events." This assumes that memory is not simply repeated, that affective categories from the past are not just mapped onto the present, but rather that they are relived and transformed in the context of the current situation. This differs from the repetition compulsion with its automaticity. It alters our premises about how transference develops. Loewald (1975) has said

> reliving the past is apt to be influenced by novel present experience. Inasmuch as re-enactment is a form of remembering, memories may change under the impact of present experience. . . . It is thus not only true that the present is influenced by the past, but also that the past . . . as a living force within the patient . . . is influenced by the present [p. 360].

As Loewald (1988) elsewhere noted, the symbol and the symbolized mutually enrich and reciprocally transform each other; the snake cannot be reduced to simply mean the penis, for once so symbolized both are transformed forever in psychic life. So, too, in psychic life, is the analyst transformed. Still, some compelling templates of early self-states and interactions may elude the analytic engagement and its experiential access to memory, whereas others are evoked but thereafter remain latent for reemergence under particular affective conditions. I regard memory as "a complex, dynamic, recategorising and interactive process, which is always embodied" (Leuzinger-Bohleber and Pfeifer, 2002b, p. 3).

This different understanding of the relationship of past to present has clinical implications. Mitchell (2000) speaks to these: "In this newer more distinctly interactive model, the mind would be responding to very real qualities in the analyst, in the present, through categories developed in, and metaphorically linked to the past" (p. 20). He adds that "the past isn't passively triggered by a trivial feature of the present, but, rather, as Loewald understood it, memory is actively seeking sites in the present, by locating and actually creating deep similarities, so that the past can be properly memorialized" (p. 22).

In this framework, a revised view of the meaning of the analyst by the end of analysis and during the postanalytic phase may be in order. Termination involves three dimensions of relinquishing of the analyst and the mourning evoked by each has different qualities. The first dimension requires forgoing the analytic function of the analyst while fortifying a self-analytic function with autonomous momentum. This dimension of mourning is familiar in psychoanalytic theory, as is the liberating pleasure of more autonomous mastery in self-reflection that is said to accompany mourning and may be felt as rewarding. The second dimension is to renounce the intimacy with the analyst, a loss that may evoke considerable grieving. Although the psychic energy of the analysand becomes more richly and productively centered in intimate relationships outside the analysis after termination, based on templates learned with the analyst, traditional notions about the transfer of such energy from the analyst to the outside world neglect the truism that people cannot be substituted for one another (why they cannot is another question). Hence, the feelings for the analyst may continue to be unique. The third dimension invites transformations in the image of the analyst as person. This dimension, not often explored or anticipated, is of particular interest. It can be highly beneficial, enriching the analytic gains, or it can be fraught with such complexity or disappointment that the changes are felt to "ruin" the previous good results. Some de-idealization of the analyst may reap benefits for the analysand when there is a parallel process of self-acceptance without having to be perfect. The analyst may be transformed from a benign power to a less benign but more interesting and more fully human being.

The analyst also faces complex challenges prior to termination. The analyst, too, must deal with whatever feelings of loss or rents in his or her psychic economy are tapped by the departure of the analysand (Viorst, 1982). In addition, there are optimally transformations in his or her self-image vis-à-vis the analysand, a kind of relinquishing of authority that has been likened to becoming the parent of an adult child. Unlike the parent, the analyst must maintain those boundaries of intimacy, which provided safety for the emotional power of the analysis itself. Simon (1995), alluding to Shakespeare's *The Tempest* as a tale of transformation, notes:

> The parent must relinquish (and the child must complementarily relinquish) the vision of mother and father as magicians who can control and shape the life and character of their children. Prospero's turning in his magic tools (breaking his magic wand) and his asking for forgiveness is emblematic of that process of relinquishing. But relinquishing is part of a transformation that allows a new level of relationship, a new form of connection.

Many of us were attracted by Freud as the original "analyst within" who still sits in our imagination, available for inspiration and/or heated debate. Freud was at a particular disadvantage, however, because he did not have the opportunity of having an analyst with whom to experience what fuels deep analytic change. Hence, we cannot expect him to know about that. Since his time, analytic training instills the dual vision of having been on the couch and also behind the couch (Simon, 1993). Looking at the accounts of Freud's analysands who wrote about their analyses clarifies and vivifies their experience of his personal directness. It also demonstrates that he treated his various patients in extraordinarily different ways (Lohser and Newton, 1996). He had an affinity for H.D. the poet. In addition to interpretations, he introduced transitional objects and literature into her treatment. For example, he showed her his bronze statue of Pallas Athena, declaring, "This is my favorite—she is perfect—only she has lost her spear!" At the end of the first month of analysis, H.D. wrote of Freud to her companion Bryer, "We are terribly en rapport and happy together." In contrast, Freud was contentiously disapproving with Joseph Wortis. Analyst and analysand constantly said terrible and belittling things to each other. Nor did Freud's involvement seem determined by symptom array or degree of illness. Wortis presented as a defended neurotic, whereas H.D. had emerged from a psychotic episode and today would be considered borderline; the issue was not that Freud avoided sick patients, as is sometimes said of him. He did seem to favor patients inclined toward avid collaboration in discovering their unconscious life, such as dreams, as well as toward compliance with his ideas. Likewise, when he pitted himself against the patient's resistance, as with Wortis, it was not a matter of analysis of resistance (or defense analysis, a later, ego-psychological stance) but rather a matter of chiding the patient for resisting the unconscious. It is often pointed out that Freud practiced very differently from what he advised in his series of technique papers. He could be opinionated, interactive, self-disclosing, and gossipy, while also highly insightful. He was not ordinarily reserved, neutral, or cold like the proverbial surgeon he invoked in theory. Yet there is actually nothing contradictory about this, if one puts his practice in the context of his theory of cure (Lohser and Newton, 1996). Lohser and Newton (1996) point out the following:

> Since in Freud's view the work of analytic treatment was to make the unconscious conscious through free association, other aspects of technique considered essential by contemporary standards were of lesser significance to him, in particular, those having to do with neutrality and transference analysis. The reliance on free association allowed Freud to be spontaneous and real with his patients and to engage in a number of behaviors that would now be called unanalytic by many. "What was subsequently called 'classical' Freudian technique grew out of later ego psychology and doesn't resemble Freud's approach." This meant that Freud was able to use his person and associations much more actively in the work [p. 160].

But it also meant

that Freud tended to underestimate certain implications of his patients' attachment to and admiration of him. Judging from his analysands' memories, Freud did not act as though he felt that termination of the analysis, or his own failing health and recurrent references to his own death had a bearing on his patients' reactions [Lohser and Newton, 1996, pp. 170–171].

In addition, Freud was candid about the character of his own discomforts, which might have made him averse to sticky attachments. For example, Freud chose to represent himself to H.D. as abhorring maternal aspects of the analyst's role. She wrote:

> He had said "And—I must tell you, you were frank with me and I will be frank with you, I do not like to be the mother in the transference—it always surprises and shocks me a little. I feel so very, very masculine." I asked if others had what he called this mother-transference on him. He said ironically and I thought a little wistfully "O, very many" [Doolittle, 1956, p. xxxvii].

In his mind, Freud seemed to separate the "real relationship" to the analyst from the transference and believed the appearance of transference from the past to be so robust and inevitable that the "real relationship"—as long as it was of the "unobjectionable" kind (that is, not interferingly hostile or erotic)—would not hold it at bay. He was already aware, however, that the analyst needed to "overcome" various personal inclinations and temptations that might obstruct the analyzing role. Freud advised that the only way for a psychoanalyst to protect himself against expressing "countertransference" was to undergo analysis of his neurotic tendencies himself. First (Freud, 1910), he recommended that erstwhile analysts undergo self-analysis, as he himself had done. But soon he felt it important that the analyst undergo a training analysis so that he might resolve his resistances and thus "become aware of those complexes of his own which would be apt to interfere with his grasp of what the patient tells him" (Freud, 1912, p. 116). By 1937, he doubted the likelihood that neurotic propensities could be sufficiently eliminated in the course of the analyst's own analysis and proposed that one of the main functions of a training analysis is to prepare the future psychoanalyst for the ongoing self-analysis that must enduringly be a central part of his work. In addition, he advised that the analyst undergo periodic reanalysis, every five years or so, "without feeling ashamed of taking this step" (p. 249).

In recent years, there has been a great deal of promising research, internationally, about the process and outcome of psychoanalysis (Shapiro and Emde, 1993; Fonagy, 1999). Sophisticated methodologies have been applied to quantify dimensions in the patient, in the analyst, and in the transactional process that correlate with a variety of results of the treatment. Objectives have included the attempt to define which sort of patient (diagnostic category or character style) does best with what sort of treatment (psychoanalysis or psychotherapy of a particular theoretical persuasion), which attitudes on the part of the analyst affect outcome, the role of match between patient and analyst, and so on. Some suggestive findings have relevance to our topic. In a study of the prognostic relevance of a working alliance as seen by patients and therapists, for example, Rudolf and Manz (1993, p. 139) observe, "The therapist's own perspective on the working alliance was most predictive of eventual outcome." Kantrowitz (1993), focusing on "when matches of conflict areas or blind spots foster or impede treatment," similarly notes: "The particular character of the analyst and analysand overlap in a manner that potentially influences both the depth and the limits of the analysis" (p. 893). Freedman and Lavender (1997) studied videotapes of therapists' nonverbal behavior during "difficult" and "not so difficult" sessions with patients. Three modes of experiencing the patient were posited as covarying with variations in nonverbal behavior: empathy marked by rhythmicity, a symbolizing countertransference marked by transitory arrhythmicity, and a desymbolizing countertransference marked by continuous arrhythmicity. Particularly interesting is the authors' distinction between "transitory arrhythmicity," associated with the analyst's state of generating a symbolizing countertransference response, from "continuous arrhythmicity," which involved "protective shielding" from reception of the patient's transference. Jones (2000), using operational definitions of "interaction structures" in the communication between patient and therapist, identifies patterns of change via Q-sort analysis of process material. He posits that "interaction structures are likely to be shaped by the patient's implicit, procedural memory, along with the therapist's countertransference" (p. 115). The Boston Change Process Study Group (Nahum, 2002) notes that "a great deal of the information that both analyst and patient gather about each other and their relationship derives from the implicit domain." The group studied the microevents of the analytic process to assess changes in the patient's "implicit relational knowing." The working assumption was that "implicit relational knowing is permeated with affective 'valuations' regarding how to proceed with others" (Nahum, 2002, p. 1060). Some dynamics of progressive interaction are also described in a study in progress comparing the psychotherapy or psychoanalysis of "improvers" and "nonimprovers" at the Anna Freud Centre. The treatments are described as "strongly transference focused" regardless of whether they were formally classified as analysis or psychotherapy. "Preliminary scrutiny indicates that 'improvers' in terms of psychiatric measures could be differentiated from 'nonimprovers' on the basis of aspects of the analytic process."

> Transference in successful cases is characterized by anxiety, guilt, fear of rejection, idealization and projected aggression. By contrast failed treatments are typically associated with shame, humiliation, existential anxiety and a sense of boredom and 'cut-offness' on the part of the analyst. . . . Of great importance was the observation that unsuccessful treatments showed differing trends as the analysis unfolded. For example, in poor outcome treatments, the quality of the analytic material gradually deteriorated, affects decreased in intensity, immature mental functions increased with primitive transferences, and the use of sexual fantasy to support identity. Sadly, there was evidence for the analyst responding by increased disengagement [Fonagy, 1999, p. 158].

A large-scale study of the long-term effects of psychoanalysis and psychoanalytic therapies (for 120 analysands and 70 therapy patients) is currently being conducted through the German Psychoanalytic Association, via interviews with both patient and analyst. The interviews include inquiring into the patient's representation of the analyst in successful compared with less successful treatments (Leuzinger-Bohleber and Target, 2002a). An interesting initial finding was that in successful treatments, narratives about what transpired in the treatment showed agreement between patient and analyst, whereas major discrepancies in accounts characterized unsuccessful analytic pairs.

The present study of the analyst's analyst within is framed by the juncture between restrospective satisfaction and dissatisfaction with one's analysis and the dynamic changes in how the analyst has remained memorable over time. Taken in aggregate, the narratives of Participants suggest that the optimal use of the inner presence of the analyst to further positive development after termination is preceded by satisfaction with the analysis.

The book is arranged in the following way: Chapter 2 describes some features of the research conversations. Chapter 3 elaborates how the analyst is experienced in satisfying and unsatisfying analyses. Chapter 4 is focused on the Participant's view of the analyst as person and the Participant's surmises about how the analyst viewed the Participant.

The chapters that follow ponder how gendered desires infuse and affect the analytic relationship. After an Introduction, a separate chapter is devoted to each of the four possible gender combinations: chapter 6, "Women with Male Analysts"; chapter 7, "Men with Male Analysts"; chapter 8, "Men with Female Analysts"; and chapter 9, "Women with Female Analysts." Chapter 10 offers conjectures about a confluence between the analysand's theory of thought and how the dyadic aspects of the analytic relationship are psychically metabolized. It bears on the transition from dialogue to inner soliloquy, experienced at the time of termination. Then come the chapters that seek to address the training context. Chapter 11 briefly sets the training analysis, with its controversies and conundrums, into its social-historical context. Chapter 12 inquires into the Participants' evolving identity as analysts, by asking where, when they are analyzing, sit the manner, the matter, and the mind-set of the training analyst?

I then turn to other issues bearing on how the analyst resides in memory and is, or is not, a continuing influence. Chapters 13 through 18 take up how the Participants' narratives bore on the topics of approaching termination, mourning the loss of the analyst, taking leave of the analysis, as well as on the nature of ongoing self-analysis and its connection to the remembered person of the analyst, the dilemmas of posttermination contact, and the vicissitudes of how the analyst might still be engaged as either a generative or a problematic inner figure. In each of these chapters, there are comparisons of the Participants' responses according to their level of satisfaction with the analysis. The final chapter, 19, comments briefly on the major findings of the research, nests them in the controversies to which they speak, and ponders implications.

The Appendixes contain the letter to the Participants, the procedure for sample selection, and the tables containing the distribution of findings about the interaction of the Participants' satisfaction with the gender combination and the decade during which the analysis took place. There are separate tables of tabulations for the 64 analyses described and for the training analyses alone.

In the tension that existed in me about whether to present the material as a systematic research report or to make selections geared toward a focus on the excerpts from the Participants' narratives and the ideas they generated, I opted for the latter, with the hope that readers interested in more methodologic detail might contact me.

CONVERSATIONS AND PROCESS

It was when I said,

"There is no such thing as the truth"

That the grapes seemed fatter

The fox ran out of his hole.

You . . . You said

"There are many truths,

But they are not parts of a truth."

Then the tree, at night, began to change.

—Wallace Stevens, "On the Road Home"

Before proceeding to the findings, some account of the interview process is in order. In this chapter, I describe certain qualities of mind and feeling that the Participants brought to the interviews and reflect on some after-reactions. The conversations with the Participants wandered between being refreshingly engaging and profoundly moving. It was a privilege to come to know them more deeply than colleagueship usually invites, with an added view of what about psychoanalysis had attracted them. A number of the Participants evoked my admiration for the inner resources they brought to overcoming multiple hurdles on the way to becoming the particular analyst they turned out to be. Moreover, it became evident that the generation of training analysts the Participants described, some of whom had not crossed my mental horizons, had had their own hurdles as well. Not surprisingly, some among this previous generation also elicited in me a new respect for or awareness of their talents. In instances that left the analysand feeling damaged by the analysis, I was more apt to feel sad and sometimes angry. The size of the reputation of the analyst turned out to be no measure of the impact on his or her analysands. Nor did the analyst's public beliefs, as evidenced in published writings, necessarily jibe with descriptions of what he or she communicated in practice.

The degree of positive or negative feelings toward the former analyst did not appear to be a primary determinant of willingness to participate in the study. Both valences in feeling were represented in roughly the proportion of their representation in more anonymous surveys of analysts' satisfaction with their analysts (Shapiro, 1974, 1976; Craige, 2002). The interviews were explicitly beneficial to me because they provided data for the research. However, the Participants suggested that they could also derive some benefit when engaging the memories of the analyst stimulated further understanding of his or her intrapsychic significance.

Throughout the interviews, I was impressed by the familiarity with which most Participants traveled along a self-analytic road, but with eyes open to multiple new byways. Yet many were surprised by those memories of the analyst that arose while we talked that had not emerged in posttermination self-analysis. It seemed that the dyadic analytic process, which, by definition becomes self-analytic soliloquy at termination, was once more tapped in this two-person (or three-person, counting the inner presence of the analyst) frame. Given the time-limited nature of the conversations and the multiple topics to be covered, my own participation differed from how I approach psychoanalysis or psychotherapy in that I more often interrupted the Participant's train of thought with questions and comments.

Participants' expressed wishes about the overall privacy of the conversations varied. Several gave me blanket permission to "quote anything," declaring trust in my judgment. **Dr. Cecco Angiolieri** added that seeing a copy of his transcript was unnecessary because "both of my analysts are long dead and I'm not ashamed of what I said, it's nothing to be hidden." Remembering the analyst sometimes also revived a sense of fidelity to privacy for the dyad, however. **Dr. Veronica Clark** conveyed, with care for her analyst, that she had no problem with telling me all that she had, but "while I have given permission, he hasn't and I know how private he is, so I have some conflict about that."

At the beginning of the second meeting, I was apt to ask about "after-reactions" to the first. Most, but not all, Participants also made spontaneous comments about the experience. The reactions most often mentioned follow. Participants expressed surprise about their access to the freshness of memory and feeling about the analyst. For instance, **Dr. Henry Lewis** astonished himself with tears of still missing his second analyst 10 years later. This analyst had at the time tapped a wellspring of feeling in him, in contrast to his intellectualizing, humiliating experience with the first. **Dr. John Deere** observed: "When I thought about my experience last week talking with you, I was surprised at the intensity of my feeling, how it welled up, because I wasn't aware that it was so close to the surface. I realized that for me, change takes place not as intellectual construct or experience but very much as an emotional, affective experience first, which comes about in some focused way, but then leads to a lot of thought, a lot of pulling apart and exploration." **Dr. Jay Glenn** explained, "My reaction is that, as it always has been since I first started analysis, things that I even knew well and thought plenty, if I told them to someone, in this case the analyst, I felt them more than if I didn't tell them. It's interesting to me that I gave you so much detail about what I thought was wrong with the analysis and learning from the negative examples. So in reviewing with you the things I reviewed, I was feeling them more than I do ordinarily, by quite a lot. It doesn't mean the feelings aren't there. But they come out more in relating them." **Dr. David Lawrence** also commented, "I was surprised by how much the fighting between us came out, the kind of the negative feeling about the way he treated me. But in looking back like this, I'd say he wasn't an intuitively gentle or loving man with me, though I think he liked me." **Dr. Raphe Lieberman** ended the interviews with: "I'm surprised at how much got tapped. This obviously touches a lot of bases. Do others get fairly emotional, too?" A number of women, with remnant longings of love for their analysts, mentioned the absence of place and opportunity to express this except in the privacy of the interviews.

Some noted that as they recalled their analysts, issues with parents also rose willy-nilly to the surface. Said **Dr. Gary Thomas:** "I told myself beforehand, 'so I'm not gonna say a word about my mother.' (Laughs.) I'm kidding, of course, but I was struck by her presence to that extent."

Participants conveyed a sense of melding inner developments that had been disparate in time or meaning and were realigning in a different way. They seemed to construct a sort of life time-line in relation to changes in their experience of their analysts. **Dr. Bob White** remarked, "As I've gone over these questions again, I feel my feelings. It's just amazing to me, thinking about this, that my feelings about my first analyst have changed so." **Dr. Francesca Emon** stated, "I felt very good about the whole discussion and was aware that I said things even that I hadn't thought of before, but can think now." **Dr. Mozes Nounous** mentioned a sense of surprise and added:

MN: I found it very enlightening. It's an organizing sort of interview that you're doing. I have all sorts of pieces here, and the way, by my telling you, which you would expect in an analytic kind of setup like this is to some degree, I do a lot of free-associating. You put the pieces together and it turned out they fit, and you helped me with that. That's how I feel about it. I looked forward to coming today, because when I came the first time, I didn't know what was going to happen. What am I going to say about my analysis? But, it's amazing! It has been good. And I guess I'm also at a point in my life where I trust myself more, and my feelings, and what I do. So it can all be put together now. I have a little more confidence, so it is very helpful to me now.

Several Participants stressed that during the interviews, they evolved a new perspective on unarticulated aspects of the transference–countertransference configurations that had been unconscious organizers of communicative parameters in the analysis. These are so complex that I reserve their illustration for the longer narratives in other chapters.

Although many Participants generously expressed appreciation during or after the interviews, I was struck by the ways in which they brought their own resources to bear on generating self-observations, which they then put to use. **Dr. Jack Robinson** wrote a note: "I thought I'd let you know how personally valuable I felt the experience was. When I finished reading the transcript, I was a little aghast that I put the episode where I seem so proud of my ability to fire that person on the staff, because then I felt more in charge, next to my apparent accommodation to my analyst and my mother. What I did about firing that person had to be done, but I certainly feel differently about it now, not proud of how I acted." **Dr. Stuart Laraphil** said, "Participating in the project has been a gift to me, though I probably won't be able to bear looking at the transcript. But, one of these days, actually, my thought is, with your response to my response, I may look at it again, with you sitting beside me in my mind, you know?" **Dr. Zelda Fisher** noted, "The experience of telling about termination has been important to me for memorializing and working it through, since it is natural to talk with others about becoming separate from the relationship with one's parents, but not about terminating with one's analyst." Some pointed to the role of our interaction in their experience of the interviews. **Dr. Henry Lewis** remarked, "There is something about the way that you frame things and stay with important moments that moves things back and forth." **Dr. Steven Zeller**, referring to what he viewed as a facilitating ambience within the interview, concluded, "And so it's a complete pleasure to indulge myself in talking about me, for so long." I wondered whether many of the Participants' crediting attitudes reflected an enduring quality that had infused their analytic approaches as well, namely, a readiness to sustain dyadic interchange by observing positive potential in the face of also needing to confront profound ambiguity and pain.

There were comments about continuing absorption in the process, between the first and second conversation. **Dr. Veronica Clark** relayed the following:

VC: I found myself thinking about and remembering a lot about the first analyst and found myself back in that analysis affectively, which was something I suppose I should have realized was going to happen, but hadn't realized was going to happen. I spent hours and hours thinking about it to the point where my family would say, "what is going on with you just sitting there, you've been sitting there for half an hour staring into space," and I'd say, "I'm thinking." (Laughs.) So I was spending a lot of very active thinking time back in that first analysis, which was interesting, and talking to my husband about it, too, because he was with me during that analysis and his memories also were that it was not a pleasant time with me.

Two Participants, **Drs. Heather Rodine** and **Emma McClinton**, who had each suffered from unresolved issues with women analysts they experienced as difficult, were distressed by "regressive feelings," in **Dr. McClinton's** phrase, after the first interview but found subsequent meetings more integrative. **Dr. McClinton** specifically asked for an additional meeting because "I felt it important to have one in order to sort of put things back together again. And it was very useful for me in a therapeutic way." **Dr. Heather Rodine** is cited at the end of this chapter to illustrate how she metabolized the process.

A few individuals expressed the hope that with participation in the project they might complete "unfinished business" with their analyst or find a way to heal hurt. As **Dr. Zelda Fisher** mentioned, "I feel something unfinished about the relationship to my analyst. I've tried to work out the competitive components on my own, but it hasn't worked, so I wanted to use these interviews to arrive at some peace about this." **Dr. Elizabeth Light** noted that "my reason for doing this, other than I think that the project is very worthwhile and interesting, is primarily to help me to heal because I have not yet healed." Beginning the second interview, she added, "The one talk with you has made me feel a lot better and I'm grateful to you—it has started a healing process for me."

Dr. Saul Green, tearful about his deceased analyst, as well as the mother who died in his childhood, spoke painfully of his lifelong sorrow about the impermanence of those one risks loving. During the interviews, he arrived at a sense of difference about his relation to the death of his mother and the death of the analyst—namely, that the constraining guilt he felt about his mother's death was not repeated with his analyst: "So I think what we are saying is that with my analyst, guilt is over." As the interviews ended, he mused, "Something that just occurred to me as you were talking, maybe nothing ever disappears! It's hard to give it a spatial sort of place, but it just occurred to me about our conversation, maybe that gets placed somewhere, too, and doesn't disappear."

Finally, an important dimension, or vector, for the Participants' use of the interviews related to whether the interviews evoked psychic *disengagement or reengagement* with the analyst. This seemed to vary according to where, in the dance between needed individuation and connection, the analytic pas de deux had left the analysand. I illustrate each direction with an example.

Dr. Heather Rodine *(Toward Disengagement):* She had told me of having to protect herself from impingements, first by her mother and then by the analyst, who, Heather felt, had spoiled a good analysis, posttermination, by oscillating between initiating intimate communication, and then fending it off with "chilling schizoid walls of withdrawal." Heather came to believe that the analyst was a better analyst than person. The schizoid retreats thereafter made the analyst humanly inaccessible in ways that felt cruel. Posttermination Dr. Rodine struggled alone with some depression about this irony, a sense of having lost access to a previously sustaining introject. Her reactions to the first and later interviews differed a great deal. She felt the ending of the first was too abrupt, and, while collecting herself, said, "We've been in a different space." Later she observed, "I was in it, didn't have perspective on it, and felt great fatigue." But after the final meeting, she told me, "I felt wonderful afterwards, I don't know exactly what happened, but something I had lost for years was in reach again." A year later she contacted me to say, "I have come many a mile in letting go of the disappointment in my analyst that was still affecting my life." She was trying to understand why, what got set into motion. She told me her theory about it.

HR: I realized that during our meeting my analyst was not in the room, that you were interested *in my experience, not my analyst's*. I think it allowed me to loosen the unconscious identification with her, it was a way *out* of that dyad. I somehow found myself with more freedom to do things my own way.

LT: That fits with your comment that you couldn't have written your original paper if your analyst were still alive, that you feared she would have seen it as invading her territory.

HR: Yes, and I felt permission for doing that because the interview was outside the dyad. I've always needed fresh air. It was not substituting a new dyad but rather pointed to pathways to move ahead. **Dr. Rodine** feels that it is easier posttermination "to face that the person of the analyst is disappointing because in essence it is a fantasy." She spoke of "being allowed to give up the unconscious identification. I needed a reworking of that which I didn't or couldn't have done on my own."

Dr. Kathryn Maxwell *(Toward Reengagement):* At the start of our second meeting, Dr. Maxwell spoke of the process as revivifying her memories.

KM: I felt a lot after last time. I was back into what it felt like having a wonderful analytic hour. I don't mean that they were all enjoyable, but just recreating it, by talking to you about it, brought it back in a way that was, really, wonderful for me. Even now as I think about it, I remember what it felt like to feel that connection in the hour with somebody. It's just such an incredible feeling. Recreating it and feeling that you understood exactly what I was talking about from your comments. It felt like going back and revisiting, not so much wanting to be there again but just looking at it because it'll have meaning, like photographs of a wedding or whatever. So in that way it felt great. And then last night, it was funny, 'cause I didn't know consciously I was thinking, "today I'm coming back to talk about it," but last night I had a dream about him, and I don't dream about him that often anymore.

I regard a flexible rhythm between the analysand's engagement and disengagement with the analyst as propitious for analytic process. It speaks to a freedom to move between self-experience as distinct from and as joined to the analyst. In the context of retrospective perspectives about the analyst, however, reengagement and disengagement appear as a barometer of where the Participant, given his or her experience, now locates the place of constructive connection or distance.

3

SATISFACTION AND THE ANALYST

You must be he I was seeking, or she I was seeking.

(It comes to me as of a dream.)

I have somewhere surely lived a life of joy with you. . . .

You give me the pleasure of your eyes, face, flesh as we pass,

You take of my beard, breast, hands, in return.

I am not to speak to you, I am to think of you when I sit
    alone or wake at night alone

I am to wait, I do not doubt I am to meet you again,

I am to see to it that I do not lose you.

—Walt Whitman, "To a Stranger"

Dr. Raphe Lieberman had three analyses. He judged the first, while
he was in medical school, as having been moderately satisfying but
quite limited; the second, his initial training analysis, as highly dissatisfying; and the third as deeply satisfying. Following is his nutshell
description of how he experienced the three analysts.

The First Analysis

RL: That first analysis during medical school was I would say—of
analyses I have known—neutral. It wasn't terrific, it wasn't harmful.
I liked him well enough. He wasn't mean, bad, or judgmental. But
somehow he wasn't a mensch. It was a control analysis, fundamentally an ego-conflict kind of thing, fairly traditional analysis. It cleaned
out some pockets of oedipal competition and anxieties about my
father, but an awful lot just didn't get touched. So though he wasn't

attacking or putting me down as my second analyst certainly did, I never felt deeply understood or connected to him, although it was pleasant. Afterward, I didn't miss him.

The Second Analysis

RL: It was a disastrous analysis and a disastrous experience. Dr. X was very judgmental, very harsh, very opinionated about what I should or shouldn't be doing with my life and saying things like, "Narcissism can't really be analyzed," blah, blah, blah, so it was really a very, very painful experience—which stayed that way. I had a dream fairly early in the analysis with him, of walking down a green glade toward a lovely garden following him, clearly looking for a father and idealizing the father, and he said, "You can't follow me, this is no garden path" completely missing the chance to analyze but rather putting it punitively and critically. . . .

[At a later point in the analysis] He said, "Let's take the summer to think about whether to continue this analysis or—I think it was explicit—"whether you should continue at the Institute." So as you can imagine I had a very anxious summer. To his credit, he said in the fall, "Look, this analysis isn't working, you should get another analyst," but he didn't toss me from the Institute. When he said, "this analysis isn't working" he meant in a one-person way that I wasn't up to it—and I said, "What do you mean?" He said, "Doctor, if you were a third-year surgical resident and all you could do was an appendix, wouldn't you think that there is something wrong with the way that it is going?" And I remember sitting up, turning around and saying, "This is not surgery."

The Third Analysis

RL: My final analyst certainly helped me to feel good about myself, accepting of myself and who I am. She's got a way of putting reality in your face, which leads to the sense of having options. At first she seemed rather formal, very respectful, quite proper, but increasingly I felt just very accepted, very safe, very cared for, cared about in a wise presence, someone who saw behind the formulas. Although her language at that time was fairly classical, it was never used as a club.

Some people find her removed and formal. I think that's a facade, that there is tremendous warmth. I was very lucky to be with someone who was warm and smart and liked me. It's all of the qualities, that clearly she is so much of a person. So after we stopped there was a real loss, the loss of relationship as well as of the analysis.

The analytic venture, usually begun with excitement, hope, and anxiety, can be profoundly affecting, remain too perfunctory, or experienced as wounding. When the analysand is also an analytic candidate, en route to becoming an analyst, it has even greater risks and allure. In a sense, it is a "play within a play" because the passion to be an analyst is entwined with the passions of the analysand. In this chapter, the focus is on the following questions: What attributes of the analyst, as experienced, foster the likelihood for an analysis to be experienced as satisfying? How do the analysand's acts of imagination (like Dr. Lieberman's garden search) directed toward the analyst fare in satisfying and dissatisfying analyses?

None of the Participants portrayed themselves as wanting analysis only for didactic rather than personal purposes. They spoke of entering analysis with some awareness of those strengths and vulnerabilities, urgencies and desires that, in the past, had posed obstacles to happiness in love, work, or the life of the imagination. Some Participants described close or supportive family relationships having sustained their development, albeit with complicated expectations. Others had transformed difficult childhood years into an appreciation for life in impressive ways. Rather than taking good things for granted, they had a special compassionate hopefulness in supporting the struggle to get there. For example, three Participants had suffered World War II as children in Europe; several had suffered from the absence of a parent through death, divorce, or intermittent hospitalizations; two had suffered chronic, serious physical abuse from their mother; and so on. One Participant, who called his analysis "a developmental experience" said the following about his own analytic skill: "It sure doesn't come from my life history because it was a very discouraging life history, but it's not been discouraging to me. Often, as you listen to histories when analyses begin, you say, 'Oh, my God, that was really a very tough series of experiences to digest and progress from.' It turns out that it isn't so much the experience as it is, but the capacity of other people around me, and myself, to deal with it, which really has made the difference. In analysis it's what the two of you make of it."

It is worth noting that within the research sample a difficult child-hood did not appear to limit satisfaction with the analytic results nor with the quality of functioning as an analyst. Our usual theories of trauma or developmental deprivations do not adequately account for this. It once more raises the issue of how the development of intrapsy-chic resilience is fostered or stymied by the potential in relationships with others. Within the research perspective the "other" is the ana-lyst. An elaboration of how the analyst is experienced is presented in the series of narratives in this chapter to facilitate fathoming the dynamics of how the analysands' emergent desires and their deriva-tives in fantasy are forged in the crucible of analytic interchange. This involves a focus on the alchemy between the subjectively created ana-lyst and his or her actuality within the analytic process.

I have continued to be impressed by how powerful, in feeling and in consequences, a good analysis can be. Deeply satisfying analyses seem memorable in resoundingly different ways from those experi-enced as unsatisfactory or wounding. Participants ranged from the majority, who recalled their analyses as instrumental in transforming their lives in positive, needed ways, to those whose analyses, as remembered, were at best disappointing and at worst deeply wound-ing. For those who felt moderately satisfied, most often the benefits gained were felt to be worth having tolerated the limits posed by what had been omitted or untapped or by surmised obstructive aspects of the match with the analyst, which were not worked through during the analysis but struggled with either in later self-analysis or with another analyst. None of the Participants expressed a fantasy that his or her analyst should have been perfect, like an imagined perfect parent, although this may have been experienced differently during the analysis. They expected some disappointment in the analyst, which naturally always occurred, but stressed the consequential importance of how such disappointments were processed by the ana-lytic dyad.

Participants' narratives were categorized according to their retro-spective satisfaction with the analysis. If the category was not obvi-ous, the Participant was asked whether he currently considered himself deeply satisfied, moderately satisfied, or highly dissatisfied with the analysis. The categories are based on the subjective experience of the Participant, without attempts at external corroboration. The three cat-egories of satisfaction are used throughout for comparison of all the other dimensions discussed. Some characteristic configurations in how the analyst was recalled in each of the three categories emerged. I contour the features of each category first, somewhat simplistically, and then proceed to narratives about two analytic dyads in each category to fill in the complexities. Each individual analytic dyad was characterized by several, but not all, of the features listed. Within a framework of some key attributes, happily for those with affinity for being in the analyst's role, there seem to be as many individual ways of being analysts in satisfying analyses as there are of being satisfying friends, lovers, spouses, children, parents, or analysands.

Deeply Satisfying Analysis

In deeply satisfying analyses, given all their particularity, one common feature stands out: In one way or another, the analysand felt a deep affective connection with the analyst within a palpably intimate distance of analytic process. Such felt connection went beyond "attachment" or "dependence" to include a sense of shared rather than unilateral engagement and discovery, while the analyst continued to analyze (and not just relate) no matter what. This did not mean that the authoritative aspects of the analysts' emotional power were minimized, but rather that the analysands felt their analysts' willingness to accompany them in exploring their inner worlds. For instance, one Participant said, "I always felt he was with me." Another muses, "He sort of trots to keep in step with me." Although the analysts might have been loquacious or quiet, more interpretive or experiential, reserved or interfering, they conveyed that the analysis and analysand were meaningful and important to them. Progressively the analysands felt deeply known and cared about, with a sense of acceptance of their individuality.

A feature of this affective connection in satisfying analyses was that the analyst was open to dealing with intense and vehement feeling. This included tolerance for affects directed toward her, including intense feelings of love, and hate (with various affectolibidinal aims) terror and sorrow.

Another feature was openness of a different kind: The analyst did not evade processing his own contribution in shaping the transference–countertransference configuration. He explored rather than disputed correct observations on the part of the analysand. This seemed to signify to the analysand that it was not his task to protect the dyad from surmises about the dynamics between them, that dyadic collusion to disavow untoward perceptions was not needed by the analyst.

The analyst was seen as a complete "Other," able to live a vital life, to stand up for what was important, for herself and her values, and not desirous of the analysand to repair her self-regard. The analyst's personhood was frequently stressed: "She was her own person" or "He led with such integrity and humor—I never felt I had to complete him." The analyst appeared capable of "the analyst's act of freedom" (Symington, 1983) in the service of the treatment. The meanings of this quality, helpful in withstanding pressure to enact a particular role, are elaborated in the final chapter.

The analytic interaction was not constricted by preconceptions about what material or which psychic level would be emphasized or whether inner or outer reality would be privileged for attention, response, or interpretation. This meant to the analysand that the analyst was not invested in imposing a preconceived theory but instead was ready to respond to whatever emerged from the analysand.

Analytic interventions were not confined to one kind of responsiveness, such as only offering "attunement" or only injecting "otherness," but flexibly involved both. The optimal rhythm between attunement and otherness differed for different analytic dyads. Surprise about the analyst's response could function to foster the projective–introjective flow. Often this took the form of the analyst's assertively questioning or altering self-defeating or otherwise immobilizing frames of assumptions in the analysand. A pleasurable meeting of minds through the analyst's distinctive sense of humor was frequently mentioned.

The analysand believed that, after the analysis, he or she would be viewed as a person beyond being a patient and would maintain some intrapsychic residence in the analyst.

When analysands felt that an analyst was dedicated to being helpful, various foibles were perceived—and seemingly forgiven. For example, **Dr. Mozes Nounous** was traumatized in adolescence, having had to live in hiding in Europe during WW II. When he expressed his terror of Nazis, early in analysis, the analyst interpreted this fear as just his projected hostility and seemed not to understand his war trauma at all. Our theories would hold that successful treatment of a survivor requires sensitive understanding of what survival involved. She was, however, helpful in other ways in a good analytic alliance, steadying him through a period of frighteningly profound depression without attempting to rush him through it. He felt fond and grateful to her for all the benefits of the analysis and considered his analysis to have been deeply beneficial.

None of the analysts in deeply satisfying analyses were lauded as having been "perfect," and the work of some postanalytic deidealization was evident in most, almost as a preference for the less ideal whole human being. Analogously, Participants seemed to take for granted that not all the important issues had been taken up or worked through but would continue to evolve through self-reflection and life experience. Although self-analysis was seen as heir to the analytic process, it often also evoked conscious or preconscious connection to the image of the analyst, who remained affectively accessible within. For most, but not all, the image became less salient over time.

Moderately Satisfying Analysis

This category included several different patterns, with dissimilar dynamics. For some there were intensely helpful components but at a high psychic cost; for others the crux of problematic issues stayed relatively untouched. In the latter (and larger) group were those who emphasized the limited emotional connection to the analyst; those who adapted to a perception of the analyst's preferred approach by consciously or unconsciously censoring communication about taboo desires; those who felt chronically misunderstood by the analyst in some area of interpretations to which the analyst seemed attached; as well as those who struggled with some trait in the analyst that they could not like or respect (such as surmised anti-Semitism) but with which they managed to work.

Several Participants' comments suggested an interesting interplay between prevailing theory and practice. They regarded oedipal issues as favored in interpretive focus but also noted that the analysis was most helpful around these issues. They viewed the analyst as less inclined as well as less able to deal with preoedipal issues. They mentioned other candidates, whom they regarded as having primarily preoedipal issues, as having fared badly with the same analyst. Still, important beneficial aspects of these analyses were noted, and the analyst was pictured as liking or respecting the analysand. Idealizations were not absent in Moderately Satisfied Participants. Several people in this group recalled fantasizing varieties of greatness in the analyst, retrospectively recognized by them as a reaction to disappointments.

Highly Dissatisfying Analysis

In unsatisfactory analyses, the obstacles attributed to what the analyst actualized led to four kinds of configurations that seemed to prevent mutative, affective engagement in the analysand:

In one configuration the analyst was experienced as having had chronically hostile (rather than just aggressive), envious, or enacted competitive motivations toward the analysand, which were neither acknowledged nor analyzed, but tended to be automatically blamed on the patient. Although analysts' persistent competitive motivations and behavior were also identified by a number of "moderately satisfied" analysands, in those dyads the issue was more openly confronted within the analysis.

A second kind of obstacle involved an intrusive agenda on the part of the analyst, eventuating in two opposite dangers for the analysand: being absorbed and also being expelled as inadequate. I regard this form as a "Pygmalian countertransference" in which the analysts seemed convinced that they were sculpting a candidate into a future form of themselves and felt betrayed by either different developments or rebellion. For those who could not rebel, because of inner or external constraints, such patterns encouraged a masochistic compliance. Ironically, although such analysts supplied a flow of interpretation to which they attributed change, they were actualizing the ambivalently desired parental power and authority over the analysand without analyzing the consequence for stalemating inner development.

The third configuration involved analysts who seemed so emotionally insulated, detached, or aloof that a genuine dialogue of affects could not be sustained, despite the analysts' also having attractive and admirable traits. It is important to differentiate such emotional insulation from the analyst being reserved or having inhibitions in some particular area in ways that were not problematic. For instance, **Dr. Phil Langer** spoke of appreciating his analyst's "caring without impingement," a warmth and interest within formality. **Dr. Harold Koestner** sensed some mutual affection: "As much as two reserved Englishmen can" (neither was English). Yet although a reserved nature could be a positive, a protective psychic retreat from emerging affects had consequences of polarizing disowned attributes within the dyad. Steiner (1993) calls attention to the value of "the reversibility of projective identification" within the analytic dyad in order for the patient to regain parts of the self that have become unavailable because they have been split off and protected. Steiner postulates that when mourning is avoided (and projections cannot be returned to the self), the internal situation gives rise to "psychic retreats," states of mind that serve as places of refuge. Emergence from the psychic retreat involves the same processes as mourning after bereavement. An analyst's reliance on psychic retreats should not be assumed as indicative of schizoid pathology per se, because periods of withdrawal from the interaction, to the analyst's own inner world, or "private self" (Modell, 1993), are essential to analytic process. When research Participants experienced the analyst as habitually communicating his need for psychic retreat, however, there was a profound sense of rebuff, aborting revisions in how traumatic affects might be experienced. Interpretive processes might proceed, but the analysand remained insecure about being basically welcome.

When the analyst was experienced as depressed, the dynamics of the treatment seemed different and more variable when it was an object-seeking depression, for this kind of depression could be accompanied with tolerance for periods of sadness or despair in the analysand, without having to rush to solution. By contrast, when a withdrawing, insulating depression in the analyst seemed to pervade, the locus of pessimism and negative affects tended to include both analyst and analysand, with untoward consequences.

A fourth configuration included a dissonant perception of obvious vulnerabilities in the analyst, resulting in the analysand's being unable to bring observations into the analytic dialogue and in the freezing of energy required for the disavowal of perception. This fourth dynamic tended to overlap with one of the other three, but also occurred in some analyses judged to be moderately satisfying. For example, **Dr. Gary Thomas** never discussed the meaning of having a frail and limping analyst who suffered from Parkinson's disease, unable to meet him in the downstairs waiting room because the analyst said nothing about it. "I felt disabled on the couch, and he did nothing to enable me," **Gary** recalled. Aside from the workings of guilt, constructive identification is stymied when the analyst models an extreme counterdependency that does not lend itself to being either effective, or affective in this case leaving **Dr. Thomas** feeling abandoned: "In retrospect, he probably shouldn't have started analysis with me. I think this is the first time I've had that thought, actually."

The generalizations about dynamics in each of the categories of satisfaction do not capture the complexities of interaction described by individual Participants. Because so much is determined by the particularity of the dyad, I offer two rather than a single example within each category of satisfaction.

Deeply Satisfying Analysis: Examples

The two examples selected here underscore that different character traits can distinguish the analyst in a deeply satisfying analysis. For **Dr. White,** the imprint of his forcefully assertive (second) analyst's nature was crucial to his satisfaction; for **Dr. Maxwell,** her analyst's resonant receptivity, without assertive intrusiveness, became transmutative. In both cases the analyst was experienced as well matched to the analysand. Both Participants highlight their sense of the analyst as person.

Dr. Bob White

Dr. White protected the internalized benefits of a rich second analysis by declining invitations for posttermination social contacts that might "tamper" with the momentum of its continually growing impact. Prior to analysis, the knack for being able to do that already seemed in place: He had identified strongly with the positive influence of his father, who had died while Dr. White was a baby but who had left a legacy in the form of a reputation of being "a fine man" as mentor and community leader. The bereft family remained hopeful, and industrious, with high expectations for the son's achievements. **Dr. White** became known for the very qualities that were attributed to the father he did not know. He speaks of family members who have died:

BW: I mourn for these people, as I do for my analysts, in a way which is that I think of them as alive. They're alive inside of me. And I don't feel that degree of sadness and missing that some people do.
LT: Are you saying that you were used to the presence of the absence, it was a lively force in you?
BW: That's right. And to living with memory and, internalization.

He views his first analyst as kind but silent, "taciturn and not terribly related." He was more apt to deflate than appreciate Bob's achievements. This dimension silently actualized a mother transference involving his assumption that more and more heroics of performance were required for her approval. For example, when he was eager to marry his fiancée, the analyst insisted on a very prolonged "analytic engagement," until the analyst decided that he was fit to marry. Dr. White felt, "Who was he to run my life? He was supposed to stay in my head." But at termination he felt "immensely grateful to him, first that we finished, second that I had such a good result, getting married, and that my career was going well." Much later he became aware of unexpressed anger about the degree to which it had been a "do-it-yourself-analysis, because the analyst didn't talk enough, wasn't present enough." It echoed having to construct the absent interaction with the dead father on his own. In that vacancy the analysand had "made up a lot of myths" about the analyst of an idealizing kind. Although he felt consciously satisfied with his analysis as complete at termination, a clue to other layers of feeling lay in his attitude that he could see no reason for a second analysis, other than that it was required for training. Now he realizes that stance meant he did not look forward to repeating the pain. When many years later Dr. White received a "very complimentary" letter from this analyst, saying he'd been following my career with great interest, Bob felt surprised and gratified, but would have preferred the signs of such interest during the analysis. He notes what was "in general disappointing: He expected too much from me, expected too much self-analytic ability without having even an interpretive process to spell out the conflict, what was going on in the process between us. I didn't lack participation. But I didn't raise enough hell. If I had, I think I would have been raising hell by myself." Nevertheless Bob felt that "part of him was very good, that caring, kind part. I've carried that with me in the feeling and desire that I wasn't going to run out of strength or kindness or heart in treating in analysis a sick and challenging patient. I trusted that part of me, but basically in my practice, I could never be as standoffish as he was. It just wasn't in my nature, and I didn't think it was right."

A poignant story captures the ambivalence about knowing more about the actuality of the first analyst:

BW: I was really quite curious about his life. At the same time I saw T.S. Eliot's play *The Confidential Clerk*. Claude Raines played a member of the House of Lords who has a bastard son whom he's very interested in, whom he hires as his confidential clerk, to see after him, but maintaining the secret. At one point Raines says to his son, "Would you like to know who your father was?" And the answer was surprising to me and clicked. The son said, "No, I wouldn't. I don't think I could put up with his difficulties." I brought them into the analysis—the father–son issues—my wanting to know about him but feeling that if I knew more, I might be crushed to discover that he was less than I wanted him to be.

When **Bob White** and I return to this memory during our second conversation, he adds, "So, come to think of it, the bastard son business *was* the first analysis. I could analyze that right now this way: You don't want to talk to me, who the hell wants to know about you?!" He muses:

BW: I never really thought we were compatible as people—unlike my second analyst, who, fortunately for me, couldn't have kept his mouth shut for an hour. Well, he might have. But he didn't. And he said plenty. He was a buttinsky if there ever was one. But lovable, persistent, actively caring. He was a man you could fight with, very important for me. I think *that* analysis helped me decide I didn't want to be a bastard son. I would rather go mano a mano with my analyst. And he helped me go my own way too, to say, "What do I want to do? What do I like to do that feels right?" Rather than, "What's out there that needs to be done?"

The second analyst "brought out a lot of vitality in me. I've never since been troubled with depression." His mode of relating was "nourishingly vital and with it aggression worked out very well." The analyst seemed active both in interpreting aggression and wrestling with it when directed at him. When **Bob** reported an incident involving a quarrel with his wife, "he lit on that, and said, 'Look what you're doing here, you want to hurt her.' So he was very active about sadism. First analysis I felt that it wasn't in my nature. The second analysis I found out it could be stirred up. But when I told him that I was embarrassed by his teaching, that it was uninspired, he didn't seem to be in control of the direction that things were going, it was as if he was reading somebody else's notes—it turned out he was reading someone else's notes—he analyzed this. Rather than taking it personally. And I was impressed with that as one of the measures of him as a person." **Bob White** comments:

BW: Considering his two-person way of working, he was a modern analyst in the sense of participating in the process. He wouldn't be a bit surprised now about how important the analyst would be, in the shared process, with the analysand. He did some things, the questioning, getting-in-your-face kind of business, which meant that he wasn't gonna put up with my not being involved with him. He's much more with me than my first analyst is; thank God for that second analysis. And it's had much more to do with the way I am as an analyst. I don't think I'm as buttinsky as he was. Nor do I need to be in charge the way that he did. But I certainly need to be involved.

Knowing the analyst as his own man did not feel elusive:

BW: He sort of needed to be himself. I never thought that I was getting a party line, that he was speaking orthodoxy to me about what was going on. These were his thoughts. And a lot of them were cooked up with me. He was a character, authentic, not a pale copy of anything. And his life seemed easy to visualize. I saw him as a paterfamilias.
LT: That way of being together and communicating so directly that you found between you and your analyst—I wondered where that then came to roost, if it came?
BW: It came to roost partly in my marriage, but partly with my kids who thanked me and are angry at me for my expectations of them and how much I butted into their lives, so to speak, how much I expected from them and how much I would do for them and be with them. A huge difference from the aloneness with my first analyst.

Dr. White portrays a rich termination phase in terms of "a very good set of interactions late in analysis, around an assertion that I wanted to do things my way and I felt that he was holding me down."

BW: So we got into aggression between us, we struggled, and then in the last six months there was a shift, and it was that wonderful time when he felt that he was saying almost everything that came to his mind and I was saying almost everything that came to my mind, and free association was truly going on, and there was something that we were sharing. I was getting the best of him, and he was getting the best of me. So the termination phase was so powerful and positive that I didn't feel the sadness at the end of analysis, as much as I felt a sense of accomplishment: This is marvelous. I'm really graduating, now I'm really gonna do it. And, now I have an indelible feeling about what it is like to finish an analysis.

The analyst, a tennis buff, was known to play tennis matches with his own candidates after termination.

BW: I said, "I do not want to do that." It felt to me that, as much fun as it might be, it was a different game, it wasn't gonna be tennis! I want to keep knowing you as my analyst. It isn't that analysis is a fragile process, or that what is done can be that easily undone, but it can be tampered with. So I've been vigilant about keeping boundaries, I think, with both analysts, from my own side. . . . But when I'm analyzing, my memories get reevoked as I'm listening to everybody else. It's a pleasure to have him in my mind. He's with me every day. And he's forever hopeful about the future. And I join him in that. When people quip about psychoanalysis maybe not surviving into the next century [the interview took place in 1999], I can't imagine a world without psychoanalysis. It has always seemed to me like a huge difference between termination and death. And a huge difference between death and nothingness. Death is not nothing. You carry away from it an enormous amount. Just like you carry away from the analysis an enormous amount. My analysis continues to grow.

Dr. Bob White had needed the inner resources for a "do it yourself" identification with a father, whose actuality had eluded him through death, when **Dr. White** was a baby. During his first analysis, with an analyst who opted to be silently elusive, neither his vitality nor anger had their full play, Thus he came to feel like the "bastard son": Knowledge of the analyst could only be disappointing, bringing with it the imposition of dealing with the analyst's "difficulties" in interacting with him. The second analyst, an involved *pater familias*, effected a shift from the contingencies of the bastard son to the pleasures of going *mano a mano* and thence toward a rich associative freedom between them, a mutual affinity for vitality and hope. As he chose the pseudonym **Bob White**, while making reference to the bird's cheerful call, I was reminded of a dream he mentioned, while in the first analysis, of having to sing in multiple languages, some of them impossibly unknown, before being allowed to marry. Wanting to sing of love for his future wife had become an analytic obstacle course. The second analyst might have heard his song differently. Perhaps he would be humming along as he listens to **Bob White's** hopeful voice in life and for psychoanalysis.

Dr. Kathryn Maxwell

Dr. Maxwell increasingly came to love the actuality of her analyst; the analysis yielded indelible change in the kind of man to whom she was attracted, and hence in her self-experience in loving. Initially, she resented having to switch to a training analyst. An extended analytic therapy with a male analyst with whom she was comfortable was going well, although she sensed "there were levels of feeling I didn't get to."

Choosing the training analyst was conflictual. She interviewed with one analyst she experienced as very confidently sure of himself but felt "that the reason I wanted to see him was because he was like an extreme version of my Dad." She worried, "Would I ever feel comfortable just being me, not trying to be what he'd want me to be? It felt very eroticized and overstimulating. I was really attracted to that, and terrified of it. I felt overpowered by him. As it turned out I spent years talking about him in my analysis."

She settled on a different analyst because "talking with him was quieter, safer, deeper, and about my own agenda." She recalls her first dream:

KM: I was a wild horse, like I'd seen on my honeymoon, that was going to be destroyed and broken in and tamed, instead of this wonderful thing, of feeling free, and in your own world, your own decisions. My fear was that analysis, and particularly a training analysis, was gonna rein me in and take me over. Even though I knew my analyst was flexible and empathic, I had this worry nonetheless.
LT: Was there also, and this may not be so, some connection of the dream to choosing between the two analysts—that you had struggled not to choose the exciting attraction and now felt like, "I've lost it," that is, what would be renounced if you yielded? You used the word *tame*. That the freedom of self and capacity for wild feeling would be taken over by someone, if you lie down with the wrong person?
KM: That's true, because a lot of what I talked about that first year was the loss of that excitement and that part of myself I felt I would never feel with my analyst, because the transference felt so safe and so good, like a good mother.

Luckily analysis did not stay safe but encompassed the levels she had not reached in her therapy. **Kathryn** recalls the analyst as "incredibly agile in going wherever I was. The analysis went to different territories and was able to come in and out of different levels. He was very respectful of exactly where I was and was not a person to insert himself into the center of a situation."

As the analysis became more intense and deepened, she felt immersed in a profoundly erotic love for the analyst, infused with the wish to know as much as she could about his intrapsychic and actual life. Attuning herself to the kind of information easily gleaned in analytic circles, she learned of his ways with his family, in his teaching, and so on. She treated this knowledge as a gift of experiencing another dimension of him, rather than as something she insisted on or to which she was entitled. In turn, the analyst was unflappably receptive to its exploration. His response to her erotic fantasies, as well as to her aggression, was of a piece: They were not something to be feared within her, or between them, but to be trusted as enriching emotional life, as clues to the past in the present, and as resources in the present to change her experience of the past.

The analyst, in his "un-narcissistic" ways of being with her, became more potent and powerfully exciting than the "phallic narcissistic men" who had previously attracted her. Erotic fantasies of becoming pregnant by him were bathed in her knowledge of the kind of man he was with his own children.

KM: He never got afraid of the fantasies, never had to inject reality. Because he knew I knew the reality. He went wherever I needed to go with it in fantasy, about not just his impregnating me, but literally what kind of man he is and was. He didn't make a lot of transference interpretations; he didn't need to, because that's where we lived through most of the analysis. I was constantly finding out about his life, and he never got defensive, just allowed it all into the analysis, but tried to look at what it brought up for me with my own family. I so admired who he was as a person and analyst, and what he meant to me.

The analyst's interventions were not confined to interpreting her intrapsychic life, but extended to new ways of considering her options in vertical life. Examples she gave seemed dedicated to the message that it was possible to pursue her own agenda without either losing herself, or renouncing the connection to the person she desired. Once when she felt it impossible to deliver a report by the deadline, while meeting her commitment to patients and children, he suggested, "send the report in a taxi," surprising her and saving the day because in doing that she needn't short either her family or career. "So he would very concretely tell me these things," she recalls.

Because she had assumed, "that if the man is center stage, there's no room for me and my agenda, in a lot of the classes I just felt like I shouldn't even speak" The analyst often affirmed the value of her ideas directly. His input on parenting her rambunctious toddler, now a delightful child, was crucial. While others pressured her toward stricter discipline, her analyst said, "But aren't you delighted to have a child who's not afraid. Who's really willing to live? And who's really willing to be the wild horse?"

KM: I'm so grateful, because I felt like my job as mother was gonna be, ironically, to tame him, to make him be a good boy, like I was, a compliant, good girl. And my analyst, who I see in some ways as a good boy himself, was completely into my allowing my son to be himself. It was the parallel process of allowing me to be me, as opposed to having to squash feelings, which was certainly the message in my family. My analyst was like, "Come on in, welcome to these feelings."

Near termination the affect-laden issues of possible postanalytic encounters was explored. The first year posttermination, the dyad exchanged a couple of cards. After three years, when she met the analyst at a meeting, she said, "It just is so bizarre that this is the only way we see each other." He suggested she call to set up a time to meet. There was an awkward moment while she asked whether they would just meet somewhere for lunch: "He said, 'Actually, no,' and I was totally embarrassed that I had seemingly suggested it." He stressed that he wanted to meet at the office, where their conversation could be totally private. "So, that was sweet, 'cause he's not saying it has to be the office because, after all, I'm your analyst and you're my patient." They met during lunch hour, however, and the analyst had brought lunch for both.

KM: It was funny to be back in the office in a different way, having lunch instead of lying on the couch, more like with a friend. What was so nice was there was nothing analytic about it. There wasn't a denial of the analytic relationship, but, at the same time, it felt like a really wonderful interaction. He updated me on his life, but I could see he was going to be boundaried. For a long time, I had fantasies that I could be his friend and that he would want to be mine, postanalysis. But he made it clear that he wants us to be able to have ongoing contact because he wants to know how I am, but he doesn't want to do anything that would make it impossible for me to come back as an analytic patient. What I've noticed is, I have not had the desire to get together again. Like, it met some need, but I also saw what the limits are.

I asked where her feelings of loving him are now.

KM: I still feel like that's true, but not like it can be recreated in the same way any more. One way I thought about it after the lunch, it's like when you look back on an old lover. It was an incredible experience, but if you were to meet each other now, you'd feel a twinge of it, and you'd feel memories, but you can't recapture that moment or that feeling in quite the same way. I will always remember the love I felt then, to the point that when I talk about it now, I ache, because it feels so close to me. But I don't feel it in the same way now.

LT: Might there be that lingering closeness to ache, but also a kind of liberation from loving him? Or not?

KM: Yeah. That's true. It is a liberation. I feel like something was put to rest in a nice way. That's the liberation from loving him in some ways. Maybe it's like growing up. You leave home and you're separate. It fuels you and it was really great, but now it's inside of you and you move on. I feel more of that, not even since termination but since this posttermination lunch. But it's sad to me that we're not in each other's life, that one of the most important relationships *ever* ends.

Toward the end of analysis, **Kathryn Maxwell** discovered that her husband shares many of the qualities that she vividly cherished first in her analyst. In her own functioning as analyst, her interpretive style differs from her analyst's according to her nature and beliefs, although it is similar in offering her affective presence. She believes him supportively to value the differences between them and never doubts his valuing her.

Moderately Satisfying Analysis: Examples

The two moderately satisfied Participants portrayed here emphasized their confidence that the analyst liked them and had their interest at heart. The analysts had expressed their friendliness in manifest ways (the gift of a mint plant for **Dr. Miller,** symbolically rife; a collegial relationship with **Dr. Brown**). It was during an epoch of psychoanalysis, when progressive interpretation of unconscious fantasy constituted the essence of analytic process. Yet both Participants felt that the deepest affective issues, with the associated underlying fantasies, had eluded the analysis and thereby limited its benefits.

Dr. Eleanor Brown

Having had some psychotherapy with a man, **Eleanor Brown** wanted a woman analyst. She felt her analysis was quite helpful, yet that some deep components of herself had not emerged. In Institute policies at the time the reporting analyst had an actual role in the career progression of the candidate, but other interactive boundaries were unclear. **Dr. Brown** linked the limits of what she could experience in the transference to the analyst's inhibitions, buttressed by prevalent theory.

While waiting for analysis to begin, the pair met at a meeting.

EB: I had some reaction to seeing her there, and her interpretation was that I was ready to form a transference without even getting quite into the analysis and she was both right and wrong; she picked up the intensity of the transference, but filtered through a classical interpretation, which didn't sound quite right, but came through as critical. Later my sense was that she was so uncomfortable with preoedipal transferences, I think that's what she was hearing. At the time all I picked up was discomfort. She did have a formal aspect. Others criticized her about that and a lack of affect. Once I picked up that regressive things and fantasies were looked on with criticism, I censored, although not consciously. So what got inhibited would probably have been there had it seemed like a more legitimate thing for a young analyst to be experiencing. Now our candidates, as you know, will talk about all kinds of things like homosexual transferences, that would have been totally out of line then, just never openly discussed. It felt like it wasn't permitted. That was the biggest failing in the analysis, she just couldn't really—she and her theory, about how you were supposed to be—so that just never opened up in the transference. I was resentful of her reporting role; but there was nothing I could do so I did a lot more unconscious censoring than I then realized, the effect was quite subtle.

Nevertheless **Eleanor** was engaged by certain interpretations:

EB: I remember an interpretation that struck me as right, stereotyped as it may have been, so I used it as confirmation that this person at least could speak to your unconscious. I thought, "she's on to something" with some relief. So, some interpretations about oedipal acting out and the defensive use of action felt usefully correct. There were a lot of interpretations she offered that I just couldn't see or feel but the occasional thing got through. So that, plus the fact that I wanted to graduate, made me not make too much trouble. She did have a very conventional side, like anything you did to please your husband was assumed to be all right! I once pointed this out to her, but couldn't get anywhere with it. I think it was her own character that was then fitted with the theory. Most people who were put together enough to be analysts had problems on an oedipal level, but it was a big impediment for me because a lot of my issues just didn't get dealt with. So actually, many of the gains I made, especially since then, have been pushed by patients not by my analyst.

But one thing she did that I thought helpful was, in spite of her classicalness, very early on, she told me about when she got married and the grief she'd gotten from her husband's family, because my family was giving me a hard time about that, so she said, "I know what you are talking about. I went through that too; eventually it dies down," and I appreciated that.

Eleanor always felt the analyst was well disposed toward her, but while in analysis, extraanalytic contact was fraught with tension. Both were staff members at the same hospital, "so often we sat in the same small meeting, which was uncomfortable. There were periods when the transference was intense enough, a kind of ambivalent angry set of reactions, when I could barely stand running into her in the Institute, never mind those meetings." Prior to termination, **Eleanor** and the analyst agreed about the positive changes achieved, such as a greater awareness and comfort with aggression.

A few months posttermination the analyst invited **Dr. Brown** to her house for tea and cookies, presenting her with a gift for her baby. Their relationship continued on a different footing: "She was courteously warm, and I saw her once or twice a year. We then developed a collegial relationship."

An important turning point took place several years postanalysis when **Dr. Brown** told the analyst she was going to have another baby, and the analyst exclaimed, "What do you want all those children for?" After feeling quite upset, **Eleanor** phoned her and said, "I have to stop taking you so seriously!" They both laughed, able to shift the bond to emphasizing a mutual recognition of the other's individuality and aiming to relegate the asymmetry of power to the past.

I asked about Institute teachings on termination at the time. "Certainly you were to have a self-analytic function. . . . Posttermination

contact was inevitable if you were a candidate, and the issue of boundaries was very fuzzy. But the internal—you were expected to have
resolved the transference, whatever that means."

Dr. Harold Miller

Dr. Miller appreciated the person his analyst was but alludes to certain crucial omissions from the analysis: "On the whole the analysis
with her was good and productive, but left the important things not
sufficiently resolved, did not deal with real-life, three-dimensional daily
problems. So I did not confront inside myself the fundamental difficulties."
He believed his analyst to have been supportive, nonjudgmental,
and able to hear skepticism, although he could not criticize her
directly. He felt the analyst liked him, and he liked and trusted her.
One year she brought him a pot of mint plants from her summerhouse
after the August vacation, saying, "There was a lot of mint, it was
very good and can be transplanted." Her attitude seemed to be that
good things that grow (in analyses or gardens) could take root with
him. Although he viewed her as an "old maid," he associated this
image in a positive way with his image of Anna Freud for whom he
had admiration. While appreciating being listened to and respected,
he felt the analysis could not "get to actual problems" because she
seemed to overlook the terrible "reality" of his marriage while she
interpreted his inner life. In her stance toward inner life, "She was
observant, did not put theory in the way of what was emerging, was
open to a real dialogue, was not doctrinaire." He felt the analyst's
desire to be helpful, but at times "there was advice which missed the
underlying issues. "For example, in response to **Harold's** avoidance
of sex with his wife, by complaining about her "vaginal odor," the
analyst suggested, "Tell her to take a douche," rather than dealing
with "the troubled relationship" or helping him to explore the underlying fantasies about vaginas, odors, and anxieties about women.
Ironically, in this example, the limitation was an avoidance of inner
life rather than tunnel vision focused on its meanings.
Dr. Miller notes that the analyst did not self-disclose, even when
she was quite ill. For example, approximately six months before completing the analysis, he smelled feces midway through an hour. She
terminated the session saying there had been an accident and she
would call about the next appointment. He surmised that she had a
colostomy bag which had broken. They did not meet again for two

days. She seemed better, but her illness and this incident was never discussed between them, "even though I asked and expressed concern," other than in the form of **Dr. Miller's** associations to his mother's serious illness in his childhood when she had a colostomy after a ruptured appendix.

Retrospectively **Harold Miller** is aware that throughout the analysis, his erotic energy stayed contained and muted, while outside the analysis he maintained a bad marriage. He recalls that soon after termination, he decided to be less sexually renouncing in ways not anticipated during the analysis and quickly began a sexual love relationship with another woman, whom he then left to return to his wife. During the research interview, he suddenly wondered whether the timing of this love affair suggested it was an "acting out" of the erotic needs and fantasies that he had not sufficiently brought into and faced in the analysis. He was not in treatment almost a decade later when, despite considerable turmoil, he found himself able to end his marriage and then to remarry, making a much happier match with a richer kind of emotional connection.

One dimension of **Dr. Miller's** appreciation of the analyst pivoted on her undogmatic approach, which contrasted to what he experienced in the Institute during training. As far as he remembers, concerning the dogmatism, the resultant transferences evoked by analyst and Institute were not analyzed. He described some of the constraints of the Institute as echoing the constraints of church, from which he had turned at age twelve when he had doubts about being a believer. When I asked for an example, he recalled that when he raised questions about Freud's sources in a seminar at the Boston Psychoanalytic Society and Institute, he was shocked that the teaching analyst became angry and said, "Are you with us or against us?" That seemed all the more startling in view of the fact that five years before, in a very different setting, **Harold Miller** had been asked by this analyst if he could arrange a liason for him with a woman. At the time, his supervisor had warned him not to pick fights with senior analysts, which might result in his progress as candidate being halted.

Dr. Miller felt much more negative about his experience with another woman analyst whom he consulted for therapy many years later about problems with his grown children. Although this analyst seemed initially sympathetic to his distress, as treatment continued, she appeared to him to be dogmatic, leading with what he felt were preconceptions about his contribution to the difficulties with the children, and being chronically angry rather than supportive. Treatment was discontinued, and his disappointment with her stance remained unresolved. Reviewing his experience of the two analysts during the interview revived for **Dr. Miller** once more his appreciation of the undogmatic, benign interest he had felt from his original analyst.

Highly Dissatisfying or Damaging Analysis: Examples

The two Participants exemplified here had the same analyst. Although this analyst, as portrayed, showed none of the egregious behaviors attributed to some other analysts of dissatisfied Participants, I select these narratives to highlight the subtle sequence of dynamics that seemed to insulate the analyst from his analysands. In **Dr. Levy**, we can see the unfolding, unfortunate fate of his intensifying attachment to the analyst, whereas **Dr. Lewis** felt stymied in experiencing such attachment at all. **Dr. Lewis** is able to contrast this state with his affective experience of a second analyst.

Dr. Noah Levy

Dr. Levy taught me about what he termed *iatrogenic narcissism*, a response to his perception that the analyst did not "want anything" in the relationship to him. He entered analysis with dissonance between his family's style of "getting on with life" by ignoring feelings of loss or vulnerability and his own need and capacity to hold sorrow in shared introspection. He had lacked support for fully mourning the father, who had died while **Dr. Levy** was still adolescent, temporarily derailing his inner sense of purpose. Although internal time had stopped, he was still expected to march to its beat. As his analysis progressed and his analyst came to mean more to him, summer separations brought this dilemma to the fore, and he feared the analyst was disgusted by what he would judge as regressive. The analyst, endearing and admirable in many ways, was known to be particularly shy and often seemed in "psychic retreat" from direct wishes for intimacy with him. Disavowal of his own dependency needs was legion, and his mourning (when his wife died) was concealed. It seems that the candidate contained all the so-called regression between them. During termination, the sense of loss painfully evocative of the loss of his father was short circuited and reactualized without acknowledgment, and perhaps without awareness in the analyst. The incom-

municable sense of loss of the analyst at termination still lingers, sur-
rounded by the haunting question, "Could he have ever liked me as
I am?" **Noah Levy** expects that when his now quite aged analyst dies,
he will experience an "irreconcilable loss."

In the initial interview the analyst asked only for the barest details
of his emotional history or distress: "He said, 'Do you like to read
and think about things?' It was like a job interview. I was shocked,
and it set a tone away from feelings." **Dr. Levy** pictures the analyst as
"fitting my family, the "chin-up" quality of 'what's the big deal, get
over it, get a life, enough is enough' feeling. That was so strongly the
ethos of my childhood, the basic philosophy. If my mother was upset
about something, she baked a bubke. You do not lie in bed or daw-
dle; you get on with it. And I'd learned to value that."

NL: During the first year, the analysis was pretty controlled. I mean
it was in my head. But the second year, toward summer, I acquired
lots of symptoms. In anticipation of his going away, was I aware of a
desperate missing? But I started to develop a lot of panicky anxiety
that I haven't had since the summer my father died. And this was not
from my childhood. I started stuttering and got migraines. It never
happened before in my life. I was completely in psychosomatic agony,
driven by panic, while whatever was behind it was unreachable at that
time. I'm sure he meant to be helpful when he said that "if you could
get in touch with your anger you could get rid of that headache." That
felt like being told I was failing this treatment and that I had another
thing to do on the spot that I couldn't do. I was scared that this guy
doesn't like this stuff. He's not sympathetic with anyone. He is terse;
I kept hearing the impatience. I was with somebody who said, I
thought, "I took you cause you thunk good now look at you—a completely regressed rat. Yuck!" And, granted, we were all locked into
some aberration of classical theory, but I didn't think that even if you
were going to look at the unconscious derivatives at the moment,
that the pay dirt was in anger. I was more panicked, that was all over
me, and he wasn't a person who could be patient with what I would
go through in missing him. I needed permission and couldn't protest.
So maybe that's where anger did come in. It was a horrible summer,
with incapacitating symptoms, migraines all the time. When my wife
and I gave a ride to a very elegant classmate of hers, she turned with
this look at me in the back seat like—"why did my friend get this
buffle carp?"

LT: So that's what you felt your analyst felt?
NL: You got it. This feeling of complete disgust and humiliation and all these symptoms and I was unable to get out of it. Meanwhile I had a very idealizing transference. I was intimidated, so I actually couldn't understand things like that during analysis, 'cause I thought that was his province. I saw him as an incredibly brilliant guy who knew many things. I didn't question that.
LT: Was part of not questioning a sense that *whatever* he said—it *must be* so?
NL: Yeah, holy is the name—it was part of the bible. I would go to analytic conferences and not understand a word. I would just love the music, the idea that these people were so far above me. It was a defense against accessing—it was a defense against many things—but partly against accessing any kind of criticism, and I suppose I just kept myself invalidated so I couldn't really get in touch with anything else I was feeling, which was totally upset.

   We come to the issue of the analyst not wanting anything: The analyst's wife became suddenly ill and died within weeks. Two days later, he was back at work.

NL: I knew something was wrong, had been aware that his wife was ill. When you don't know how to talk to somebody about things and then not picking up the ball on the other end, what do you do? But in terms of today, you might recognize interpretively that I was spending a lot of time worried about how he was. But the message was, "Do your thing, just ignore me." Which, of course, I couldn't, and if I said, "How are you," I was afraid he would interpret that as a defense. So the idea that I was not going to be able to at least discuss with him how I was going to handle being anxious about his wife, and being told to just go on, I was probably being seduced into, maybe he's fine, maybe he doesn't *have* feelings. That's what I mean by iatrogenic narcissism, with the idea of a nonperson because he won't let me deal with him as a person, so what am I supposed to do here? I think in retrospect, knowing him, he just wanted to be left alone. That was probably enough for him. Anyway, he would never accept help from any of us. The whole analysis was pervaded with a sense that if you just touched too closely, he was jumping back—very palpably—if you crossed some threshold of the personal, come from beyond his ability to deal with it, the feeling was literally, physically, backing off. He would be fidgeting with his shoes, and I was always aware of that.

Eventually the analyst proposed reducing appointments to "three times a week, with the idea that we were going to terminate. I was far enough along."

NL: He needed to lighten his load. I was clearly a good candidate to go. At that time I wasn't wounded by it. I figured I'm closer to being ready to graduate. But the thing we forgot is that I had a major relationship with a man [that was] ending. My father dropped dead. So, in retrospect, it was a very bad idea. Because, again, I'm not saying that pointedly at him, but it's just a regular two-person problem, saying I didn't speak up, and he didn't catch it. It's happened before, and I was taking away again an injunction that this is the right way to do it, and certainly the message was, "Don't hold on, don't become a drag and be bothering me." And he said none of this. To be fair. But, this is the leftover: In my accommodation for others, I don't pay attention to certain things, like the fact that he liked me or didn't like me never was settled. So, the same profound doubts that I went into analysis with, the result of his standoffishness, left all the doubts intact, and, I was always trying to rationalize it in some way, well, he's this kind of guy, and I drive him crazy in that way, and—
LT: Like your mother always excusing how your uncles were treating you sort of thing?
NL: Yeah. Exactly. I have a repertoire of indulgences that I learned from my mother that still go on about how to forgive people, and the one thing you're never allowed to mention is the damage assessment, what it takes out of you. For me that damage isn't over. I don't feel bitter, because I admired him a great deal and took something important away about how to lead a life and hold yourself in midlife. And he brought me back to taking myself seriously, taking ideas seriously. But that came at the expense of this other more basic thing that never changed, where his nonresponsiveness was definitely a clue. Any patient who asks me, "would you say more?" I'll say more. But [I] also try to get them to tell me, and to say, "We're going to need to say something, because it would help you." I wish there'd been something from him on the order of that.

Unbeknownst to **Dr. Levy**, the analyst did value him, praising his qualities of mind and recommending him to colleagues. What might have interfered with such a message to the analysand? The wish for direct emotional intimacy regularly sent this analyst into a psychic retreat (literally, in space), which fortified barriers rather than connections. The less the analyst responded, the more urgent these wishes became, now in disguise, only to be rebuffed. Such feelings could have been rich soil for reworking those pained inner states that had registered the death of his father with mourning incomplete. But the analyst seemed closed to mourning, to dwelling on sadness at loss—either in his own life or during his candidate's termination. Perhaps he believed that his gift to **Noah Levy** would be to transmit what had worked best for himself: his self-contained, "anti-regressive" proclivities to live a good life. And all this **Noah Levy** did, but a fertile opportunity had been missed. When after the interviews I mused about his choice of the pseudonym "Noah," there rose the image of having been called to survive the storm, to remember, and not to discount the turbulent sea of tears in transforming ways, to bear it so that future generations of analysands might not be bereft "irreconcilably."

Dr. Henry Lewis

Dr. Lewis saw the same analyst as **Dr. Levy**, but a decade earlier, a time when the reporting training analyst still excercized the power to influence decisions about the candidate's progress toward graduation. Although there are differences in the course of the analyses, and the eventual feelings toward the analyst, striking echoes emerge in the ways the analyst was experienced as blocking affective interchange. Wishes for emotional intimacy and attachment again eventuated in shame and humiliation. Affects associated with potential mourning, both at the death of a parent and at the termination of the analysis, were once again short-circuited. The analyst's seeming need for self-contained autonomy, while avoiding the kind of grieving at loss in which projections can be returned to the self, resulted in distancing, transmitting a value on boundaries, on "independence," and on isolation of affect rather than connection. The affective ambience stymied potentials for internalization. The interpretive process within the analysis at times felt to **Henry Lewis** like it "went on independently of me and I went on independently of it." Within this frame empathic communication seemed aborted, and the analysand treated as the carrier of the disavowed attachment wishes within the dyad. Some years after termination, **Dr. Lewis sought** out a second analyst, with whom the previously dormant possibilities became a "wellspring" of affective experience.

When **Dr. Lewis** began analysis, prior to his acceptance as candidate, the analyst made no bones about the power of his opinion in the admissions procedure, thereby concretizing anxieties about his being judgmental.

HL: He told me, "If I say that I don't think you should be an analyst, then you won't be accepted, so you have to understand that. If you are gonna apply, they are gonna want my opinion and as a training analyst my opinion will carry." So, you know, this seemed like a challenge.
LT: Like he started baring his horns of your dilemma?
HL: (Much laughter.) That's a very wonderful way to put it—especially the pun on the horn. But, I thought, if it's gonna be decided that I shouldn't be an analyst, I might as well find out. So I started with him. Of course I was accepted. I think that the fact that I felt very indebted to him had a profound influence on how I was with him. At first I felt very much like a little boy with him and felt a sense of benign tolerance from him that I think for the most part I avoided trying his patience. He was a strict classical analyst. Everything was interpreted in terms of the oedipal dilemma and narcissism. He often talked disapprovingly about the state of my "narcissism."

Dr. Lewis describes his experience of the analyst further:

HL: I repeatedly asked for appointments before rush hour because essentially it meant an extra half-hour of commuting time. Since he was totally unbending about this, and there were people who had those hours, I said, "fine, when you finish with them." What happened was that he did finish with them, but still I was not granted the hours of my choice. It felt punitive and rigid, and it felt like he was trying to teach me a lesson.
LT: What was the lesson?
HL: That I shouldn't be demanding, that I should get used to the idea that you have to adapt, that you have to compromise, that you should roll with the punches. He made me feel like a baby for requesting, demanding these considerations. There was a lot of shaming. My mother used shaming and contempt a great deal. All this business about appointments, and the money, felt like things where I was supposed to learn how to not become distressed with frustration. And I think that this was very much the analytic model.
LT: You mean the general analytic model or his?
HL: Well, his specifically.

LT: Did his talking about your narcissism, and all the oedipal interpretations feel hurtful, or feel clarifying, or feel true?

HL: No, it just felt like his interpretations went on independently of me and I went on independently of them.

Dr. Lewis recalls the interaction with the analyst the day of his father's death. His wife called the analyst's office "to have them tell me to call home. When I called, it turned out that my father had died. I knew it was coming, but, when I finished the phone call, I was quite stunned and I walked by his office and his next patient hadn't come yet, and the door was open. He was standing and so I decided that I wanted to tap on the door and tell him. I did, and he just said, "It wasn't unexpected" and that was it, not anything about "Sorry."

LT: You can adapt to it? Or I must be cautious not to tamper with your associations by showing any feeling?

HL: Yeah.

LT: Did it make it harder to cry in the presence of that?

HL: Well, I didn't cry much in there, I didn't cry either with joy or with anguish with him. It was really a kind of an empty experience. I think from his perspective I had gone through the various stages that were supposed to occur in the course of an analysis and that I was finished.

The termination date was set in accordance with the "requirements at that time."

HL: You were supposed to be in analysis for at least six months after beginning a control case, so after I began my first control case I was obligated to be in analysis for six more months. In March, I said, "I guess we can think about termination," and I figured we would go until the summer break, and he said "April 12," something like that, and I was shocked. I experienced it very much as his having had it up to here with me and wanting to get rid of me because I was still complaining about silly things.

Dr. Lewis recounts an evocative incident in the waiting room. The wife of a good friend was waiting for her husband who was having his final hour with the analyst. But until her husband came out of the office, it "didn't register that she is her to me or I am me to her. It was an out of context experience, like someone we only see in the showers and the locker room when they're naked, you don't recognize them when they've got their clothes on."

LT: (Laughs.) But may be you're implying something else, that there's something about isolating affects.
HL: Yes.
LT: That you felt was taught in there and that also existed in the waiting room.
HL: Yes, yes, right.

Once **Henry** told the analyst that he and an analytic sibling had "joked around about put-downs of each of us by the analyst."

HL: The put-downs about me involved my complaining, demanding, something that he felt was unwarranted, unmerited consideration. When I told him that, he started laughing a little bit, and I got upset about that and said something about it, and he then said, "I'd better be careful, you may take a bite out of my couch," referring to my oral greediness.
LT: When you wanted him to say my couch is here for your biting? It could be replaced.
HL: (Laughing.) Right, right.
LT: Something registers and raises a question in me about his way of putting you off. You're describing him as highlighting oedipal interpretation very classically. And as not wanting his couch bitten. Did you feel he fends off dependent longings or closeness in a way that makes the oedipal level more comfortable for him, or not?
HL: Oh yes, yeah, yeah. One analytic sibling had lost his mother at a very early age and the analyst never dealt with that. I think that he had a very firm belief that you just don't touch those things, and he didn't. Another example was his remark to Clyde [another analytic sibling]. When Clyde was saying something about "Gee I don't know how I'll ever be able to leave you, oh God, what if this went on forever?" the analyst started to laugh and said, "Don't worry I wouldn't be able to stand it."

Henry Lewis comments that joking may have been an attempt on his part to experience "some closeness to this guy whom I couldn't get close with. But at that time, although I didn't accept it emotionally, I had the assumption that this was what analysis was supposed to be, that this was the cold detached, distant observer."
He was aware of wishes to have a more intimate bond with the analyst:

HL: But my response to that was always to distract myself. It was something I've learned from my mother's knee. My mother was an incredibly flighty, distracted person. But my mother was a wonderful character; she was a force of nature with immense energy.

LT: Do you mean that was one of the reasons her knee was moving when you were at it?

HL: Yeah. No. (Laughs.) Yeah. Her knee was moving. I guess this is interesting, the way these things get reenacted, without realizing it. My mother had already had her children and didn't want any more. It was always clear that she loved her first set of children more than her second set, and this was something that was never interpreted. I mean it was enacted between me and my analyst.

LT: You touchingly brought out a couple of things. He loved the first set of patients, and their hours could not be violated (HL laughs hard) and secondly you thought he'd had enough of you.

HL: Right, and this was all mutually enacted. In other words, I was the bratty kid who complained about not getting enough love, and he was the parent who was tired and didn't want to put up with that kind of shit.

Some years posttermination **Dr. Lewis** made a pioneering contribution in areas that demonstrate the importance of issues that the analysis had not tapped. At this time, the analyst and he were on ostensibly friendly terms in social situations, to the point where they could stand together smoking cigars at a party. **Henry** gave the analyst a copy of the paper he had written, aware that part of his message was, "Why don't you learn from me for a change?"

HL: I gave him a copy of my paper and thought he would be interested in terms of his own work. And he never responded. When I saw him again months later in the corridor, I was pushy and I said, "Did you ever have a chance to look at that paper?" He said, "Yeah, it was very interesting." And that was it, that was all.

LT: I'm struck by something—that most of what you describe about him was disappointing, and yet something still mattered, because you take the trouble to offer him something very self-expressive. So there's a puzzling question of what still matters and how?

HL: Well, (long pause) that's a very astute observation that you're making. He comes across as a thoughtful person, I mean thoughtful not in the sense of humanly thoughtful but somebody who thinks about things and is willing, or tries, to think about things. I suppose it reflects a feeling that I'm trying to think about this in terms of who's winning and who's losing but that I won't take no for an answer.

(Laughs.) And even all these years later, I'm still intent on trying to get my point across.

LT: What are your notions about how he experienced you during the analysis and now?

HL: I don't think I'm on his radar screen.

LT: So are you're saying it doesn't feel like you have any sort of home in his psychic world?

HL: Yeah, that would sum it up: I don't think he emotionally entered into the process in the way that I think probably most people do now if they can.

LT: When you say now, do you see that as also in sync with the main teachings in the Institute at that time, and people see it differently now, or do you see that more in terms of particular people?

HL: I think that position was much more in line with how it was taught then. Some of the good analysts didn't adhere to that in their practice but that's how it was taught.

LT: As you practice analysis, where is he in your inner life?

HL: Nothing of him. I can't think of any ways that I operate similarly except that I'm prompt and he was prompt. I give people the bill and things like that.

LT: So just the frame remains.

HL: Just the frame.

Dr. Lewis contrasts his first with his second analyst, about whom he speaks warmly. He introduces his feelings about the second analyst into the conversation by mentioning two of that analyst's supervisees who "both really cherished" him. One of them "was very upset and angry with him" when the analyst retired. The supervisee would recount the story of "how the analyst said to him, 'come on, it's not the end of the world' and the supervisee said, 'yes it is,' and that was the kind of feeling about him."

LT: So he was precious enough to be a great loss to them.

HL: Yeah and to me. (Long pause.) Ahh. (Crying.)

LT: So you still miss him (said very gently).

HL: Yeah. This takes me by surprise. (Long pause, sounds very tearful, eventually clears throat.) And it's funny because I've cried, I laughed with him, I never felt awkward or uncomfortable. I guess this sums it up. I felt with him access to a wellspring of emotion that was unlike anything with my first analyst. It's funny I think it's the first time I've really had a good cry about him.

LT: It sounds like he made it possible for the wellspring to become a well . . . that in turn . . .

HL: A well to inform and permeate the work. So, it was a real emotional experience and, it was you know (pause) because it's funny, I really felt loved by my second analyst. You know, I think that (still or again crying—pause) other than my wife, I can't think of anybody who I felt as loved and accepted by. I would feel profoundly touched or moved by something that he said.

Having chosen the second analyst to be different, **Dr. Lewis** had begun by risking potential discord in the following way. He immediately raised questions about the analyst's relation to the Institute and to his ethnic allegiance, which he wanted "on the table" lest it "interfere." The analyst was "receptive with 'I'm so glad you told me. We'll have to figure out some way to deal with those things.' He wasn't put off."

LT: It sounds like you were able to start with a challenge that with your first analyst you found unnegotiable.

HL: Yeah, take it or leave it, and so that was how we began. At any rate (long pause) as far as feeling loved. Of course, love is something that—I fell in love with my wife, I went mad for her, and of course I came to love her in many other ways as time went on, but, with my second analyst it was not falling in love, it was coming to love and to feel loved. My father had a hard time expressing affection and my second analyst, he's a very sweet man and funny with it, too. I remember when I had broken my collarbone and I walked in for the next appointment and he took one look at me and he said, "Oh my God, some people will do anything not to have to go jogging" (both laugh) knowing that, for me, a day without jogging is like a day without love or sunshine. It was a wonderful sense of humor with a sweetness—

LT: A sweetness of knowing you so well?

HL: Yeah and a playfulness, too, making it into a sort of paradoxical reversal. And it was funny because he was in the interaction. I always felt that he was a very sweet man, and yet I never felt he was a Pollyanna. I always felt that he knew exactly what the story was and he didn't have to cover anything up.

The Interaction of Satisfaction with Gender and Decade

A key to retrospective satisfaction with analysis turns on what is actualized in the analyst's communications as evoked and perceived by the particular analysand. This particularity of characterologic match, or mutual influence within the dyad, has its own dynamic, altering over the course of the analysis. If and when the analysand is able to become increasingly emotionally engaged, previously unexpressed erotic, masochistic, sadistic or regressive wishes, despair and hope, make their appearance and engender an altered range of responses from the analyst. Not infrequently the unforeseen dynamics either turn a good match into a mismatch or, alternatively, create a more felicitous fit.

What other factors play a significant role? In planning the research, it seemed likely that the gender combination of the analytic pair and the decade during which the analysis took place would have a significant impact. Sampling was accordingly based on variations in these variables to make comparisons possible. Consequently, each analysis described by a Participant was tabulated according to the decade in which the bulk of it took place and the gender combination of the analyst and analysand, in addition to its category of satisfaction. Although one's gender and a historical point in time are very different in experiential primacy as well as origin (in terms of internal versus external) they turn out to intersect surprisingly in their relation to satisfaction. Comparisons of the Participants' qualitative portrayal of their analyses, as well as their specific responses to the 13 lines of questions are elaborated in later chapters according to the variations by gender combination and by the decade during which the training analysis took place, but a brief comment is in order here as perspective on the results of the tabulations.

While the importance of gender—housing the analysand and analyst in like or unlike bodies of desire—seems self-evident, the role of the particular decade during which analytic training took place does not. Concentric circles of influence must be considered. Beyond the analytic pair lies the ethos of the Psychoanalytic Institute of the training analyst, including that analyst's experience with his or her own training analyst. Then, too, like analytic dyads, Institutes themselves have a particularity in terms of their offerings and their strife. It has been said that "Every Institute is unhappy in its own particular way" (Kirsner, 2000, p. 226). Moreover, beyond the particular Institute lies the point in time in terms of the controversies that have continued to animate psychoanalytic theory and that have resulted in particular values and taboos in psychoanalytic practice, and in collegial relationships between psychoanalysts as well.

The analyses explored in the current study occurred over five decades, from 1945 to 1995. Over that time, and particularly in the last two decades, we have seen and participated in a sea change in attitudes toward authoritarian versus more egalitarian practices. In a parallel development, recent decades have seen a turn toward conceptual premises that locate therapeutic action less often in the analyst's authoritative access to the "truth" and more often in the reflective exploration of both members of the analytic dyad. Such sea change, with contending personalities and leaders armed by diverse theories, is evidenced in the tumultuous history of many Institutes (Kirsner, 2000). The Boston Psychoanalytic Institute's version of the storm did not abate until after intense power struggles with turmoil for everyone; it resulted in a split into two Institutes (The Boston Psychoanalytic Institute and The Psychoanalytic Institute of New England) in the early seventies. Since then, both Institutes have flourished, each in their own way, increasingly encouraging cross-town debate and collaboration (Gedo, 1997, p. 129; Kirsner, 2000). This piece of historical context is mentioned here because a disproportionate number of troubling analyses occurred in the decade of the "split." It would be spurious to generalize to other institutes about this particular decade, because its timing was individual. Nonetheless, relevant generalizations about what makes for satisfying or dissatisfying analyses in general remain pertinent, although necessarily also informed by the dynamics of how this time of trouble was visited on the conduct of analyses, especially those of male candidates, perhaps as a manifest derivative of the power struggles within the Institute. In any case, it seems that at that time, certain aspects of the analyst's character, such as toughness, were apt to be actualized at the expense of others.

The 34 Participants in the study presented narratives about a total of 64 analyses. Of these analyses, 35 were training analyses (35 rather than 34 because one Participant, **Dr. Lieberman,** officially transferred during the training analysis to another training analyst). References to additional, briefer therapies were not counted, both because the material was incomplete and because the different time range and nature of the process were not easily comparable.

The sample contained 21 men and 13 women. Eleven are now training analysts. Some of the 23 who are not have graduated too recently to be eligible for training analyst status. One training analysis took place during 1945–1955. Nine took place during 1955–1965, nine during 1965–1975, eight during 1975–1985, and eight during 1985–1995. There were 16 men with male training analysts and six with female analysts. Seven women were analyzed by male training analysts, six by female analysts.

Sample selection was not based on an attempted random or stratified representation of variables characterizing currently practicing American analysts, although it may turn out to approximate these. Because the focus of the study revolves around the various fates of posttermination internalizations under conditions of different affective contexts affecting termination, the population was selected to sample those variables most likely to be relevant to these issues rather than replicating the composition of a particular group. Therefore, the sampled analysts were distributed along each decade during which the training analyses took place and along the four possible gender combinations and included both training analysts and nontraining analysts. The sample size (n) in each cell of this distribution is too small for numerical generalizations, even when comparative numbers are dramatic. In addition, the sampling is inevitably skewed by whichever factors correlate with a willingness or interest in being interviewed about one's experience with one's analyst. Openly gay Participants were unfortunately absent, because their acceptance into candidacy occurred too recently for them to have graduated by the time of the study. Candidates whose experience led them to leave the field (or who were asked to leave the field) are not represented.

Given these features of the population, I regard the numerical distribution of the findings as a highly suggestive marker of various dynamics rather than a basis for generalization to other populations. The meaningful units for comparison between data cells could not be arrived at through counting or otherwise quantifying specific behaviors or techniques of the analyst (such as amounts of silence, self-disclosure, interpretation of transference) without taking into consideration their meaning, to the analysand, within the affective structure within which the analytic communication took place.

Tables 1–4 in Appendix C record the distribution of satisfaction category according to decade and gender combination. There are separate tables for all analyses described ($N = 64$) and training analyses only ($n = 35$). The overall distributions of satisfaction turn out to be more similar than not for total analyses and for training analyses only. The category of highly dissatisfied accounts for 22% of all analyses and 23% of training analyses, but the proportion of deeply satisfied analysands is 12% higher for training analyses (51% compared with 39%).

There are dramatic differences by decades. There were six times as many unsatisfactory as deeply satisfactory analyses for men with men during the decade 1965–1975, contrasting with the high proportion of deeply satisfying analyses during 1985–1995 for both men and women with men; that is, when Participants judged analyses that took place between 1965 and 1975, 67% were dissatisfied with the training analysis, and only 11% were deeply satisfied. In contrast, no Participants reported being dissatisfied with training analyses taking place between 1985 and 1995, whereas 87.5% were deeply satisfied. The corresponding satisfaction rate for total analyses was 59% dissatisfied in 1965–1975 and 12% deeply satisfied. For 1985–1995, only 7% were dissatisfied, and 67% were deeply satisfied. Because the training analyses make up slightly more than half of the total analyses, these figures are not independent of each other.

In considering the impact of the gender combination, it should be noted that men with male analysts make up almost half of the total analyses and of the training analyses explored. For both training and total analyses, men with male analysts were most likely to be dissatisfied with the analysis (37% of training, 30% of total analyses), whereas deep satisfaction was more likely for men with female analysts (67% of training, 56% of total analyses) and even more so for women with male analysts (86% for training, 47% for total analyses). Moderate satisfaction occurred for women with women in 50% of both training analyses and total analyses and for 25% of men with men in training analyses and 40% of total analyses. Thus, in this particular study, analyses across gender lines tended to be more satisfying. It must be remembered, however, that these figures are skewed by the effect of the decade. No man with a male analyst in the decade 1985 to 1995 was dissatisfied, and 75% were deeply satisfied, so how male analysts treat men appears to have changed considerably.

The proportion of analyses experienced as deeply satisfying has risen significantly. Although one Participant was deeply satisfied by his training analysis in 1945–1955 ($n = 1$ for that decade, nonsignificant), for the next decade the rate was 44.5%; it then slipped to an all-time low of 11% in 1965–1975, but rose again to 62.5% in 1975–1985. It rose yet again to 87.5% of training analyses by 1985–1995. The direction of the trend, should it be maintained, is encouraging.

4

IN THE MIND'S EYE

How can I say this? I think my psychiatrist
likes me: he knows
The most terrible things I've done, every stupidity,
Inadequacy, awkwardness,
Ignorance, the mad girl I screwed
Because she once again and again
Teased and rejected me, and whose psychic incompetence
I grimly greeted as an occasion for revenge;
He greets my voice
With an interest, and regard, and affection,
Which seem to signal I'm worth love;
—you finally forgave me for being your son, [. . .]
but the way
you eyed me: the bewilderment, unease
the somehow always
tentative, suspended judgment . . .
—however much you tried (and clearly you did try)
you could not remake your
taste, and like me: could not remake
yourself, to give me the grace
needed to look in a mirror, as I often can
now, with some equanimity. . . .

—Frank Bidart, "Golden State"

This chapter concerns itself with how analysands believe themselves to be seen or unseen in the mind's eye of the analyst, as well as how they, in turn, view their analysts. Such perceptions accompany affectively powerful attractions, or aversions, to imagined intimate connections of all sorts and create convictions about the optimal emotional distance between the analysand and analyst. This is a dynamic process, prone to quixotic shifts over time. Verbally articulated representations of the self with the other person are but the tip of the proverbial iceberg or volcano.

Views of self and others, and self with others are organizers of anticipation and can date from early in life. Based on conscious and unconscious assumptions about human interaction, some of these representations can be articulated verbally, whereas others, already powerful by the time language develops, can only be deduced through the affective self-states that embody them. A complication is that self-representations are highly responsive to how one is perceived by a significant other. The eye of the beholder reveals which self becomes available to be interiorized with the interaction and what that is already internalized is available to be actualized in the here and now.

In the analytic process, old and new assumptions vie to shape the analysand's images of how he or she is beheld by the analyst. These perceptions are not only relevant to self-esteem, but also to developing the revised understandings needed to deal more effectively with the complex actuality of others. As psychoanalysts we always have an interest in the question of what flexibility exists for altering self-representations through the analytic process.

It was usual for the research Participants to enter analysis with self-doubts about their worth, even when they presented a self-assured veneer. They feared that the analyst would see into them and judge them to be inadequate, filled with intractable badness or anxiety, secret lust, selfishness, and anger. In satisfying analyses, such negative self-regard was slowly ameliorated over time as the analysand progressively came to feel known and valued through the eyes of the analyst. In satisfying analyses, the sense of the analyst's regard was felt as a precursor to increased self-acceptance. Such change also allowed these Participants to tolerate a comfortable retrospective appraisal of probably having appeared as "brittle," "anxious," "narcissistic," or given to "acting out" when the analysis began.

In contrast, those who felt damaged by their analysis described the negative self-images as frozen in the mind's eye of the analyst. The analysand felt that the value of his or her personhood was unseen, useless, ripe only for being disdained or discarded. It is important to distinguish messages that were more or less continuously conveyed by an analyst about the negative features of the analysand from an analyst's aggressively assertive confrontation of negative or self-defeating qualities in the analysand; in this case, when the analysand experienced confrontation in an overall context of respect for his or her individuality and it was subjected to analysis of its meanings, such discourse could be highly beneficial.

To a remarkable degree, Participants who encountered both a dissatisfying and a satisfying analyst emerged with different self-representations from the two encounters as attributed to the minds of the two analysts. The differences between such surmised reflected appraisals of the self are large enough so that if they were taken at face value, they would be associated with divergent diagnoses and prognoses. There was a convergence between those reflected self-representations signifying that the Participant was able to feel seen for herself, valued or liked, without her difficulties being minimized and the range of affecto-libidinal engagement risked in the analysis.

When the analyst was experienced as having a very negative view of the analysand, Participants varied in their capacity to extrude this damaging perception. Fonagy et al. (1995) attribute this capacity for extrusion to being able to "mentalize" the state of the disappointing object: "A child who has the capacity to conceive of the mental state of the other can also conceive of the possibility that the parent's rejection of him or her may be based on false beliefs, and therefore the child can moderate the impact of negative experience" (p. 254). Among the Participants who surmised chronically negative perceptions emanating from the analyst, these perceptions were least resistible for those who in childhood, had needed a stance of emotional surrender to a parent as the only way to maintain that relationship.

In Participants' portrayals of their analysts, meanwhile, the attributes highlighted tended to be those that either fostered or prevented the analysand's trustful engagement. Matching proclivities between analyst and analysand, such as a shared sense of humor, were welcomed. Such matching was typically experienced as pleasurably facilitating a "meeting of other minds"(Winnicott). Such matching might also entail resonating problems, however, resulting in "blind spots" that affected the analysis. The presence of shared difficulties was also eventually surmised, as the analysis progressed.

In satisfying analyses, those initial impressions that tapped wishful idealizations or complementary strengths, became elaborated and modified by the end of the analysis, but not reversed. Such Participants felt they saw what they got. Needless to say, unsatisfying analyses were marked by disillusionment. In several such cases, the analyst's apparent need to shore up his or her own self-regard through the analysand's admiration became a grating preoccupation that was experienced as blinding the analyst to the personhood of the analysand. An unfortunate process, but rare within the sample, resulted from instances in which the analyst remained idealized while the self remained devalued.

The following two questions were intended to access the manifest quality of reciprocal gaze, which the Participants experienced with their analysts:

What are your notions about how your analyst experienced you during analysis, around termination, shortly afterwards and now?

What sort of person did you sense your analyst to be at various times during the analysis, at the time of termination, during subsequent years and now?

Excerpts from these two questions are combined for the illustrations. First, I present some contrasts between how the same Participant perceived himself or herself as seen by two different analysts associated with different levels of satisfaction.

Dr. Raphe Lieberman

The dissatisfying analysis: I think he would have described me as someone not interested in analyzing his conflicts, as someone who was narcissistic and entitled. I think he would have described me as politically dangerous. I didn't think he was right. I thought he was off. I thought he misjudged and didn't value me or didn't like me, which in fact repeated some of the core childhood issues that needed to be worked on. He was extraordinarily conservative and critical, harshly critical about what I was doing with my life.

The satisfying analysis: My second analyst was temperamentally very, very different. She has a tremendous warmth, and she is so much of a person. Initially, she seemed rather formal and proper. But with it went being deeply respectful so I just felt totally different with her . . . I felt very accepted, very safe, and very cared for, cared about, in a wise presence; someone who saw behind the formulas.

Dr. Emma McClinton

The dissatisfying analysis: I think that she would say that I was shallow, defended against, superficial. Unable to be intimate. . . . If I imagine having a conversation with her now, I would be angry and say, "You couldn't see who I was. Why didn't you, why couldn't you even know that and let me be?" When I was talking to friends I sometimes called her a witch, because she was always blaming others. . . . I thought she thought her parents didn't love her because she wasn't a boy, and she couldn't help me with that. She denied that. And, mostly I thought the trouble was me. It was how I failed to engage her. . . . When she had cancer, she denied there was anything wrong with her. But her hand was swollen. She kept disputing whatever I noticed about her. I saw her as very authoritarian. . . . My sense of her certainly was that she was depressed way before the cancer started.

The satisfying analysis: My second analyst would say I am resourceful, very helpful, to my patients and family. I do what's right, in terms of fulfilling what I consider my obligations. He would say I've a good sense of the future. I help people with theirs. He pointed out that I am chosen by patients, and that was helpful. There is a way I have of denying that piece of me, but I felt that he had a belief in me and a sense of me, even if I couldn't always show it.

I felt he was very observant, and very supportive in an ego way. He's very intelligent, much smarter than she was. Although, when she might have been bright, I never saw it. He thinks about people, about his patients, after they're gone. That was very important, and he's very good at that. So there's a sense of occupying a place in him. And a desire to be helpful. Because we don't see this as just a job. He's talked a little about himself. He's careful about what he reveals about himself, but he doesn't deny when I see something.

Dr. Henry Lewis

The dissatisfying analysis: I found him rigid and unbending. I don't remember myself as an astute observer of him at all. He came across in the way he presented himself as self-contained, soft spoken, quiet in a way that I think belied what he was actually like. Unlike my brash, loud, say it and face whatever, he was more adroit at, and felt that it was more important that he attend to how he was being received. . . . He comes across as a thoughtful person, thoughtful not in the sense of humanly thoughtful, but somebody who tries to think about things. But beneath that there was a lot of sarcasm and isolation induction. . . . There were a lot of put-downs of me, of what he thought I was like, too demanding and orally greedy and narcissistic. I had the assumption that this was what analysis was supposed to be, that this was the cold, detached, distant observer.

The satisfying analysis: My second analyst is a very sweet man with a wonderful sense of humor . . . and a playfulness too. . . . There was a feeling of kind of a person to person exchange. . . . There was a sense of real meeting and of his being able to stand, address, respect my anger in ways I never felt with the first analyst. . . . It wasn't just that I felt moved by him, but he was moved by me too, I have no question in my mind about that. . . . I always felt that he was a very sweet man and yet I never felt he was a Pollyanna. I always felt that he knew exactly what the story was and he didn't have to cover anything up.

Dr. Phil Langer

The dissatisfying analysis: While my first analyst didn't quite fire salvos, he was rather caustic and depreciatory, and it was the caricature of the neutral analyst, quote–unquote neutral, meaning that he wasn't involved with your mishegas and was totally uninvolved with his own mishegas because he didn't have any. It was very important for him to be met with open-mouthed awe. And I think that he became trapped in this kind of relationship with people where he was required to be more and more obscure and consequently profound. And they were required to be more and more awestruck by that kind of obscurity that masqueraded as profundity. I'm not sure that it was so profound. I think it was just obscure. And, at times he was utterly unintelligible. One couldn't make out what he said as having anything to do with what one had just said. I never thought about how he viewed me. I don't really think he liked me. I think he just tolerated me. He was more or less indifferent. Just another candidate. Four hours free after I stopped. But I didn't have the sense that I made any significant difference to him. I have a lot of patients who I feel, many, most of them, all of them, in one way or another, I'm different as a consequence of having been with them. That's not the way he was. I don't know what the truth is, but that's my fantasy—

The satisfying analysis: My sense of her from what she conveys is of someone who lives the way I think I would like to, who had very intimate relationships, who has a dignity, has that quality. One day a friend of mine and I were having dinner and, as it happened she was there having dinner with a couple. She didn't see me, but I watched her. And what was striking to me is how seductive and playful and tender she was with this man, who I thought was probably the other woman's husband. But there was just this very nice, warm, close quality. I thought, "Now there's a woman I could fall in love with." There was just something very genuine and very nice about it. And that's my picture of her. . . . She made it clear, and I feel she likes me. And I feel she truly has my interests in mind, in terms of helping me understand things.

Dr. Elizabeth Light describes the analyst with whom she had a satisfying analysis. This judgment reversed itself painfully (to dissatisfying) when his sexual boundary violations with other patients came to light, resulting in the loss of his license.

The satisfying–dissatisfying analysis: He's a very charismatic person, not for everyone—I know of some people for whom it didn't happen—but for many people, people just seen in consultation, he has the ability to make a person feel very understood. I think there is nothing more precious to most of us than that feeling. When I started analysis, my sense was that he was one of the most powerful people at the Institute. He was unpretentious, and warm. And I absolutely loved the man. I idealized him. I thought his nonintervention style was perfect. I felt I was very special to him (long pause). I felt I could trust him with anything (pause). That was the cornerstone for me of change, the feeling that I could trust him with anything and that he really did value me very much. He did care about me in his way, I'm convinced of it, of course he did. I don't question that. I don't think one is capable of falsifying that kind of affective connection. I think that he, however, with his craziness, is capable of replacing it very quickly, of not honoring it, of distorting it, of down the road denying it, all kinds of things like that, but in the moment it's very true. This is one of the dangers of this kind of affective availability, that it can feed the analyst too much. It was feeding him too much. That was his problem ultimately. He used what his patients gave him as his own emotional fuel. The man has an inordinate need to be special. If he had been Napoleon, literally, or a sultan, perhaps not today, but at the turn of the century and he had had affairs with *x* number of women to whom he was related or not in whatever fashion, people might have written a glorious biography about him and he would have been thrilled. If he were in another profession, in another lifetime. He has an enormous need to be admired. There is just a way he had of alluding to the people with whom he associated that gave him an elevated sense of, you know, that this guy travels in high circles, this guy gets a lot of respect, this guy is important. His denial of reality is amazing. I don't know if he would fall into the spectrum of mood disorders. He needed his patients. It is the manner in which he derived gratification from his patients that I began to see as troubling. Even before I terminated I thought he was fed by his patients rather than his family, his wife, his children, his friends, his colleagues. I could leave my practice and travel around the world and be perfectly happy, but the sense I got from him is that he would wither and die. These aren't his words; this is my fantasy, that he could not survive without seeing patients. The greatest punishment to him, but not because of shame or economic loss, would be to cut him off from a supply of patients, male and female, the admiration, the sense of being so special to his patients.

Changing Self-Representations

The following excerpts illustrate the change in the reflections of self as surmised by the analysand. The qualities attributed to the analyst during the analysis tend to become more elaborated, but not radically reversed.

Dr. Francesca Emon

The satisfying analysis: I didn't feel a self-absorption, which was something I would have been sensitive to, or a sadism, which I also was sensitive to, which is a way my father could be. He also came across to me as very wise. And pithy. . . . Apart from the transference, I sensed him to be a decent, loving man and that just got elaborated. That never got discounted. I didn't see him differently at the end. I saw him with more of that, and maybe fleshed out more. I still see him basically as a very well-intentioned, kind person, with enormous capacity for listening and, actually, nonnarcissistic. Almost unambitious. There's a way that he has such a quiet touch about his need to assert himself and, his self-promotion. He doesn't put his needs ahead of the need of the group. I've always had the fantasy that he was a wonderful parent. To be his child, I think would be fabulous, because he's so nurturant. He likes to help things grow, and people. He's really good at it. He's very facilitative, and his way, his style is to be in the background. He's like the soil, as opposed to another plant vying for the sunlight. You don't feel you have to compete.

How he experienced me really did change a lot in my mind. I think it's an indication of my changing view of myself, and now I think I'm an enjoyable person. I think I have a good sense of humor. But I thought he found me narcissistically preoccupied a lot, in the beginning. In fact, I think I was. And, that changed, as I stopped putting myself down in a lot of ways and got a handle on that self-criticism, which I externalized a lot and felt criticized by people a lot. I think I was probably more enjoyable over time. He would say that I am very optimistic about life, and about the opportunity for loving. He has said this to me, that I see every occasion as an opportunity for love, which is true, I do. But I get deeply disappointed when it's not like that. And he would say that. I think he would say I'm really funny and smart and I've got an enormous amount of energy and I'm very loving, aside from hoping to be loved. He definitely sees me as a very loving person. And I became more loving through the analysis, because I was neurotically bound up in some ways. And I think he would say that I'm sexy, also. And I really like that! (Laugh.)

Dr. Jill Tulane

The satisfying analysis: I had a feeling from the get-go that he was very kindly. Kindly and gentle. And that remained throughout the course of my work with him and since. I think as time went on in the analysis and subsequently, I've come to see him as more conservative than I had experienced in analysis, in terms of theoretical orientation and technique. I think he liked me. I think he liked me all along. But, I think he would have said I was difficult and not particularly obedient. I use that loosely, in my being late so much of the time and a lot of "acting out," as they used to say. He probably would have said that a large part of the treatment was to "get me in the office," so to speak, and that by the end of it I had become a lot more comfortable. I think he felt reassured about my future because he had had such an enormous exposure to my work as an analyst. Prior to that, he might have been worried that I was too much of a live wire to be an analyst myself.

Dr. John Deere

The satisfying analysis: I don't know him except from my experience, my fantasies of him, which, is a real way of knowing him, one piece of him. But who he is in the rest of the world I just had glimpses of. My colleagues, they loved him as a supervisor, and they really liked him in clinical courses. But who he is to me and the transformation he helped me achieve, that I do know and feel grateful for. He was instrumental in that. His way of seeing the world, seeing me, in some way I incorporated. I've taken him in. I'm a much less harsh and judgmental critic toward myself. I really liked him. I thought he was a decent person. A real mensch, a good analyst. . . . I experienced him as being a warm and available person, well versed in analytic technique but not imprisoned by it.

At the beginning I was frightened of the process and him, not because he was particularly frightening by his behavior, but rather immediate transference. That he would see who I was and what I was about, and would not be able to stand it, that I would not be able to stand it. I was so vulnerable to disapproval. Ashamed. That formed the initial experience I had. That changed over time, in the course of the analysis. I stopped feeling that way, inadequate . . . with my experience of him as an accepting, in some ways validating, person, but who would challenge me, but in ways that I felt comfortable with.

I think at the beginning he must have seen me as scared, intimidated, and very cautious, very, very closed off from myself. Over time, that changed. I could see the change in me and, by the end I think he saw me as much more in touch with my feelings, my inner experience, my life experience, my family history. I talked a lot about my sexual feelings and fantasies, my relationship with my mother, I really was able to talk about that and enjoy it and laugh about it and be enraged by it and also to talk about my father, to get at the rage I felt toward him for abandoning me to her, for leaving me saddled, for not being responsible for us financially, for not being responsible for us emotionally, a sadness of what I wanted, lost, never had.

I could wish to inflict pain on others in an angry way without having to do it, and being able to see other options. I think some piece of it also was his accepting that side of me, and not thinking it so awful. I came, even within the course of the analysis . . . it wasn't just subsequent to the analysis . . . that I really came to believe that I was a valued and valuable person. That he saw things about me that he respected and liked and some things that he admired about me, that he thought I was better at than he was. He admired my capacity to stick with really sick patients in an empathic, understanding way and to absorb some of what they struggled with.

Reciprocal Views in Connection

The following excerpts portray the harmony or dissonance between the surmised traits of analyst and analysand. One excerpt is selected for each level of satisfaction.

Dr. Steven Zeller

The satisfying analysis: I think he was very self-possessed. That meant to me a very strong person that was a type of father figure I really longed to have for myself. No buckling there. I instantly appreciated a sense of humor in him, which was sort of necessary for me to play with. I think I already was a bit of a young old fart as far as psychoanalysis goes. When I complained about the outrageous things my sister did, what he picked up was why I was still involved with her in this way and what was I looking for? That is what I mean by the integrity of it. It's not that he was unsympathetic. He had found a way not to be tormented by such things or to put in perspective what he wanted for himself. I had a sense of him as someone who called his own shots with greater freedom than I did. Once I heard some scuttlebut about him and I brought it up with him. He shrugs this stuff off. All of that reinforced the notion of somebody who'd been in positions of authority, did that well, was good at protecting himself and keeping his eye on the ball with what he wanted to do, both for himself and for whatever job he had. He enjoyed people, but basically had been a bit more of a pain in the ass in some of the committee settings than I would aspire to be. It was important to me that he was really funny. He told me jokes in the analysis. I still repeat jokes that he told. And he listened to mine. And he whined that I remembered details better than he did. We had a sort of mutual admiration society, which persisted, throughout, and continues. The business of details actually happened after the analysis.

I think of him positively for something he once mocked himself to me about, after the analysis. I think of him as one of those people who was able, with very few words, like a diamond cutter, to communicate a great deal and to choose his timing and stay out of my way in a big way, and then say the right thing at the right moment and was purposely a bit cryptic in the sense of being open-ended. That's why I said that he mocked himself for it. He later phrased that as, "as an analyst, it's too easy to hide behind being cryptic and not spell out what you know." I think that he was making a point but being unfair to himself. Obviously you don't spell out what you know, 'cause the person may not want to hear it in that way or be able to absorb it in that way. I think he was particularly judicious. I think of him like the Japanese novelist who wrote the book about Stevens, the butler, in England. He's someone who's famous for the precision of writing extremely clear, declarative sentences as a way of driving the narrative and, there's something very elegant about it. I think of my analyst as doing very elegant analysis.

I think he would have taken me initially as someone who was on the one hand a sort of bright, gift-of-gabbish type but on the other hand was quite serious about getting analyzed, whatever that may mean to me. I was quite intent. I like believing, and I think it's true, that he had a sense that I had the potential for what I needed to have a good analytic experience, meaning I was serious about it, I had a capacity to love and be loved, and tended to think in a way that makes for a good analytic patient. I think that I had the sense quite quickly, that I was okay, and as I'm spelling out what was okay, I think it was the cultural harmonies, the sort of personality style harmonies, and, then, on top of it, that I was quite intent on trying to get the same things that he was trying to give, so that it was a suit we could play in.

Dr. Heather Rodine felt that the mixture of qualities she portrays in her analyst first facilitated significant benefits from the analysis, but subsequently limited it and required of her that she find ways of distancing herself from some of her analyst's reactions.

The moderately satisfying analysis: I sensed that she could function on nonverbal and visual levels and I later learned that she had in fact painted and had been involved in theater. I needed that level. I think I meant a lot to her because we shared that. There was an intuitive sense of what I was talking about and a willingness to accept whatever meager conceptualizations I could make, and to allow for the open space for me to fumble in until I found the language that was going to get us there. But because putting things into words only skimmed what I was feeling, and not much was coming from her, it was massively frustrating for a long time. An image that I had of her, and we had arguments about it years later, was of her in a little black dress with a little white collar. Very uptight and very cold. When I made some reference much later (laughing) to that dress, she said "I never had a dress like that" and it was such a striking image in my mind. Do you remember Schraft's? Schraft's waitresses wore these little black dresses with white collars. There was something about the tea room coldness that I linked with her. I thought it was a projection of my feelings, but long after the analysis I realized she was a lot like that.

After we had become friends and colleagues, there were terrible times when she was going through her own crises. She then shut me out completely, didn't answer my phone calls until the time came when she became ill and really needed my help. I think the shutting out of me during that time was because I meant too much to her. But there was a piece of her character where she could suddenly freeze over and withdraw in a rather scary kind of schizoid retreat, worse than I had ever experienced with anyone in my life before. I gathered that her own analyst had not been able to work toward a level of mutuality with her, and without that, the schizoid shutdown stayed in place. After she went back into treatment with someone else when she became ill she admitted that to me, and I felt vindicated, but by that time a lot had already been lost.

Dr. Jay Glenn portrays the dissolution of his initial hopeful view of the analyst, as the analyst conveyed his negative views of the analysand. Dr. Glenn felt disdained by his analyst for being "too emotional." In contrast, his analysands find his emotionality beneficial, commenting on the positive power of his capacity to help them distill and intensify affects.

The dissatisfying analysis: Initially I thought he was very straightforward, in a friendly way, also kept his distance. Anyone who was an MD he called "Doctor." He never called us by our names. It was "Hello, Doctor. Goodbye, Doctor." It was always that certain formality, at the same time a kind of surety about himself. My initial impression of him from all that was that he would be okay, he would feel good to me to work with. And that was the beginning of four and a half years that were very rough. He was certainly classical in his orientation. But he had a tremendous emphasis on narcissistic entitlement and belief in stamping it out. I was there to validate his theory because he was deeply invested in it. It was so clear that he felt the need for validation. Certainly in the first three years of the analysis, I experienced him as very powerful. And he did take the power position of deciding when I could start seminars. He exercised that power over my training and certainly had a lot of power for a long while over how I saw myself. He didn't think terribly much of me and left me convinced for a while that I was somewhere in the lower rungs of capacity, in character and quality, as compared to other candidates. He thought I was too emotional for a real man. For a long time I was feeling very low for the way I felt myself seen there. I think I said something about not knowing whether I could be an analyst. I meant it. And he said, "Well, Doctor, what about your being an analyst? What do you think?" And I really could not answer him. I had no way of mustering anything that I felt qualified me. One day, I, with desperation, thought of an analyst who I considered not very good. I said, "Maybe I could be as good an analyst as he." And he said, "That's right, Doctor. Yes. You could be as good an analyst as he." (Laughs.) This is a really important question, to ask people who've been through analysis, what they believe their analyst felt towards them as a person, and did they like them? I think all analysands do develop a very strong experience about this that is not simply subsumed under transference.

Reflections

I would like to discuss how representations of self and other are internalized, their action from within, and the question of change. The interactive component of inner representations can be demonstrated very early in life. Beebe and Lachman posit that "Patterns of experience are initially organized in infancy as expectancies of sequences of reciprocal exchanges, and associated self-regulatory styles" (2002, p. 13). Such patterns become the basis for later symbolizations of self and object representations. Once organized, representations may resist reorganization to varying degrees. Although the influences are bidirectional, symmetry is not implied, because each partner may influence the other in different ways and to unequal degrees (p. 28). But matched specificities between the dyad, when attuned to each other, yield awareness of the state of the other. During attuned moments, "the way one is known by oneself is matched by the way one is known by the other" (p. 32).

We don't know the answer to the following questions: Can the internalization of analytic process with the analyst change basic representations of self with other, self with self, so that maladaptive assumptions are deleted? Or, do independent representations, generated in different object interactions exist side by side, to selectively emerge under different affective conditions—for instance, with two analysts who communicate different feelings about the analysand?

A number of models have been posited about the connection between self and other representations. The models carry with them different implications for development and also have consequences for treatment. One view would hold that core patterns of attachment and representations are increasingly ingrained as the child develops and that the task of treatment is to transform the maladaptive to more healthy patterns. Field (1992), Suomi (1995), Norman (2001), and others posit an optimal period during which early pathological relationships can be affected, reversed, and superseded. Norman (2001, p. 83) posits that "the infant has a unique flexibility in changing representations of itself and others that comes to an end as the ego develops." But other investigators stress that throughout the life span plasticity characterizes intrapsychic patterns of representations.

A second model assumes that there are multiple dyadic templates, each belonging to the history of early object interaction with a significant other. Thus, the dyadic template tapped by one analyst may differ from that tapped by another. Kernberg (1980) refers to "the patient's predominant unit of self- and object representations" finding nonverbal expression in the transference (p. 188). Attachment studies (Fonagy et al., 2002), however, suggest that "the infant develops independent models (self-other schemata) for his major attachment relations, based on his history of interaction with each of those individuals"(p. 42). These findings are confirmed in our everyday observations, clinically and developmentally, that different affecto-libidinal states are evoked by mothers and fathers (Tessman, 1982, 1989; Herzog, 2001), as well as by other, differently significant relationships in child and adult life. Sullivan (1964) believed that a person has as many identities as human relationships. If satisfying analyses draw on the potential for a useful dyadic template and further strengthen and enrich it, the problem then becomes how to transfer the benefits to more dreaded templates, which also inhabit memory and anticipation. Representations of old introjects remain ready for emergence in times of emotional peril.

I would argue for an additional possibility—namely, that the relationship with the analyst, when affectively compelling, has a specificity that imbues the transformations not only with unpredicted patterns of change, but also with newly created templates of anticipations. The kaleidoscope, shaken a particular way, settles into an unforeseen configuration of representations. If the analyst could not be imagined by the analysand according to any familiar template but turns out to have his distinctive actuality in relation to his patient, then something quite new may happen. As Suomi (1995) has established, resilient individuals may develop particular areas of strength and proclivities, which are not the mirror opposite of their earlier characterologic adaptation to privation. What opens the window to change? Are there affective conditions that either constrict or foster learning? What makes interactions with the analyst memorable in a useful way? I cite two experimental, nonanalytic interventions intended to produce change.

Suomi, working with rehsus monkeys, addresses specificity as an ingredient of dyadic match, as well as in resilient change. "Different matches between infant temperament and characteristic foster-mother maternal style, yield differential short and long term developmental outcomes" (1995, p. 197). Suomi's laboratory demonstrated that peer-reared (maternally deprived) infants grow up to be socially anxious, to have a reactive temperament, easily becoming aggressive, impulsive, and fearful and that they tend to drop to the bottom of dominance hierarchies (Suomi, 1997). With poor early attachment experiences, their neuroendocrine functioning becomes highly abnormal, which in turn affects the activation of genetic vulnerability. Yet such "reactive infants," when assigned to especially nurturant foster mothers, appeared to become behaviorally precocious, unusually secure, and, when moved into larger social groups, were particularly adept at recruiting and retaining other group members as allies. They rose to and maintained high positions in the dominance hierarchy (Suomi, 1991). So these individuals develop special capacities of resilience, with a distinctive affective–cognitive organization. Such findings suggest that there are distinctive pathways of development, rather than fitting a paradigm of "more" or "less" developmental progress. Such distinctive pathways have different implications for treatment goals than would a preconceived theory that holds universal developmental lines as ideal.

A different intervention was designed by Field (1992) in an attempt to reverse the effects of depression in mothers on the development of their babies. Infants of depressed mothers develop a depressed mood style as early as 3 months. It persists over the first year if the mother's depression persists, and negatively affects developmental scores by the end of the first year (p. 49). Infants are typically physiologically aroused during interaction with the depressed mother, as manifested by elevated heart rate and cortisol levels (p. 53). Infants change their behavior when the adult's behavior is modified, however, as if the infant's behavior was very much affected by the "mood state" or type of behavior displayed by the adult (p. 50). Field suggests a contagion effect of negative mood. Several depression researchers have found that the depressed person interprets experiences in light of a negative cognitive orientation that activates perceptual distortions. Consequently, all stimuli, regardless of their characteristics, are seen in a mood-congruent fashion. "The depressed woman may interpret even a baby's smile negatively" (p. 60).

Depressed mothers have more negative perceptions and attributions of their infants' behavior than other observers do. To alter "the mother's negative perceptions," an intervention was devised in which mother and a trained examiner together viewed videotapes of the mother–infant interaction and were both asked to rate positive, negative, and neutral behaviors. It would thereby become evident to the mother that the examiner saw the infant in more positive terms, a demonstration intended to be useful in efforts to revise the mother's perception.

What bearing does this treatment have here, because the analysands are neither baby nor rhesus monkey, the analysts most often are not depressed, and cognitive therapy is not being advocated? Field's work demonstrates wide differences in consequential perceptions of the same human qualities by two observers. Two analysts may also have very different views of the same analysand. It is difficult to picture how an analysand can manage to thrive if he or she is among the small, but troubling, minority of cases subjected to an unchanging negative gaze of the analyst's mind's eye. Fortunately, in recent decades, there is a much greater likelihood than previously that an analyst who finds himself stranded in chronically negative feelings about his patient, will make a "Field-like" intervention, by finding a collegial consultant with whom he can revise and work through his views.

Loewald spoke of the analyst's "analytic love" and respect for the patient (1970, p. 297), while incubating a conveyed vision of the patient's potential in the future, and keeping "his central focus on the emerging core" to "avoid molding the patient in the analyst's own image" (1960, p. 229). He likened this to the parent's ability to picture the child's development while the child is struggling with the sense of inadequacy. He reflects that "it is impossible to love the truth of psychic reality, to be moved by this love as Freud was in his lifework, and not to love and care for the object whose truth we want to discover" (1970, p. 297).

GENDERED DESIRES: AN INTRODUCTION

It is almost impossible to understand the extent to which this upheaval agitated, and by that very fact had temporarily enriched, the mind of M. de Charlus. Love in this way produces real geological upheavals of thought. In the mind of M. de Charlus, which only several days before resembled a plane so flat that even from a good vantage point one could not have discerned an idea sticking up above the ground, a mountain range had abruptly thrust itself into view, hard as rock—but mountains sculpted as if an artist, instead of taking the marble away, had worked it on the spot, and where there twisted about one another, in giant and swollen groupings, Rage, Jealousy, Curiosity, Envy, Hate, Suffering, Pride, Astonishment, and Love.

—Marcel Proust, *Remembrance of Things Past*

The following four chapters inquire how the gender combination of analyst and analysand, housed in similar or different bodies of desire, affects what transpires between them. The classical psychoanalytic position has been that all significant transferences will emerge in an analysis, if the analyst permits and facilitates their emergence. In practice, however, we assume there are good reasons for referring an analysand to a man or to a woman. In tandem, we assume that there are meanings in the analysand's free choice of a male or female analyst.

Gender infuses every crevice of mental life. Psychic positions of attunement, or disconnection, of being receptive and penetrated, or penetrating, and so on, are each embodied in particular experiential associations with sexual arousal or with wishes to love or to be loved in gendered ways. Each of these mental proclivities needs to be freely accessible to the optimally functioning analyst of either gender, and, by the end of analysis, to the analysand as well.

The analyst is naturally affected by the gender of the analysand. On one hand, there is an immediacy of empathy when confronted with a same-gendered patient. There are gender-specific desires and anxieties that resonate deeply and automatically (Bernstein, 1993, p. 147). On the other hand, a patient of the other gender may evoke an equally deep, complementary "role responsive" (Sandler, 1976) resonance, in addition to identifications with latent other-gender aspects of the self. In either case, conscious and unconscious desires toward the analyst will emerge, and further influence his or her way of being with the analysand. The research material suggests that the particular analyst's response to the desires of the analysand greatly affects what the analysand will risk, and hence still further complicates understanding of gender differences. Here I note my regret that gay and lesbian analysts were not among the Participants, because their acceptance into candidacy occurred too recently for them to be graduate members of the Institute during the years of the study. Their absence results in an important omission in the exploration of gendered desires in the four chapters on this topic.

Erotic love is matchless as a magnet for feeling. Its daunting personal force, as generator and organizer of fantasy life, can make it pivotal to the primary experience of the analysis. Yet, more than any other wishes, the analysand comes to know well that desires toward the analyst, as beloved, must be given up or replaced by the wish for a different kind of connection. There are aspects of erotic love for the person of the analyst (regardless of gender) that are profoundly private in a way that could be altered by sharing it with others, and in this way it differs from other feelings. Therefore, I omit some elaborations of such material from the excerpts quoted, while still trying to preserve the tenor of the expressed feelings.

It seems to me that whatever transpires in the state of desire for the analyst is most deeply interiorized, becoming indelibly imprinted into psychic life. Concurrently, desire is a state unequaled in creating vulnerability to the analyst's communications, as they signify the analyst's affective response and self-regulation in the presence of the analysand's love, sexual arousal, or both. Passionate excitement (when not manic) and intimate repose each provide fluid access to a changing imagination about the nature of the self and the interplay between self and other. Of course, sexual arousal has multiple forms and func-

tions in analysis and can serve variously as a link to love, to knowledge, to power, to being desired, to competition, to defense against
depression or feelings of deadness, and so on. But desire stirs reactions in both members of the dyad.

The analyst learns an odd dance in relation to the analysand's desire.

Laplanche (1992) alerted us to the child's alternations between an
intimate libidinal exchange with mother and being the "excluded
third" as mother withdraws from the child to turn libidinally to her
adult partner. He views the mother's erotic interest as represented by
"enigmatic messages" the child cannot decipher until later in development, but which are essential for his erotic health. Green's work on
the "dead mother syndrome," which he regards as emanating from
childhood experience with a "psychically dead" or depressed mother,
elaborates the disturbances associated with the absence of a viable
libidinal interaction (Kohon, 1999). I believe these erotic interactions
to be reproduced in the deepest levels of transference and countertransference dispositions. If the analyst withholds herself from this
level of interaction, can value the analysand with head but not heart,
dead space makes their interaction infertile. To surmise the erotic strivings in the analysand, the analyst lends herself to receiving the enigmatic messages of desire evoked by her care. But then, finding herself
in the erotic life of the patient, the analyst must take the lead in a
rhythm of repositioning herself as "excluded third," with all the attendant feelings. The analyst tolerates this position as it alternates with
needed periods of intimate involvement. A dialectic tension ensues
between these pulls to mutuality and the need for asymmetry. Analysts,
analysands, and analytic dyads vary in which side of the dialectic is
highlighted, is avoided, or is clung to defensively at various times during the analysis. If the dialectic isn't dynamic the analysis isn't moving.

Being an analyst combines profound satisfaction with frustration
in a piquant chemistry of unusual, erotically tinged intimacy with
unusual exclusion. One feels fortunate to have the analysand become
able to bring a privately experienced erotic imagination to the analytic relationship, trusting what will transpire. One's responses may
tap surprising pockets of self (not always good news). It is also a
bonus, however, that, unlike interactions with a spouse, young children, or some friends, one doesn't feel unfaithful toward one analysand
by virtue of intimate work with another. One is glad that the intimacy
inhabits its analytic space, yet one can go home to make dinner or
indulge in outrageous repartee with one's spouse. The cost, in turn, is

the essential self-exclusion from intimacy in the patient's personal life, albeit with myriad feelings toward the analysand. Within each analyst's quotidian balance between protecting boundaries and receiving the analysand's desire, there is value in recognizing the mutative potential in the analysand's enhanced experience of desire, generated within. Access to the power of desire, unrequited but not scorned, may then be fully explored in its relation to "genuine love, with all its attendant risks" (Mitchell, 1997, p. 13). Gabbard (1994) posits that:

> For many analysts the experience of being loved intensely may be far more disconcerting than being lusted after sexually. Most of us pride ourselves on being able to discern the negative aspects of erotic transference, perhaps because we find anger, envy, and hatred more tolerable than naked expressions of love and affection. Those of us who become analysts have chosen a field in which we spend the greater part of our day in a posture of professional distance from the most intimate disclosures of others. The intimacy and affective charge entailed in transference love may threaten to break down that carefully constructed distance. The term "erotic transference" has a reassuring clinical ring to it. By contrast, to hear a patient say "I love you" sounds too personal, too close for comfort. Our obsessional dissection of the difference between transference love and real love may, in fact, reflect a wish to be reassured that the feelings are somehow not "real," not truly intended for us [p. 402].

6

WOMEN WITH MALE ANALYSTS

If I had never met him I would have dreamed him into being.

—Anzia Yezierska, *Red Ribbon on a White Horse*

Women with male training analysts had the highest rate of deeply satisfying analyses: 86%. In the decade 1985–1995, it was 100%. Corresponding rates for nontraining analyses were somewhat lower.

Women Participants spoke about prolonged periods of loving and/or erotic wishes toward their male analysts; of the intensity of painful sexual longings; and of an eventual freeing sense of selfhood if it became possible to absorb the longings into life and imagination. Turmoil was accepted as part of the process. In some cases, however, the analysand did not feel safe enough in the relationship to allow erotic or loving feelings to emerge. In two such analyses, during the seventies, the analyst's insistent interpretations of penis envy became the bones of contention. For both these women a second analysis had a very different reach.

How the analyst surmised and received loving feelings affected their development, and the fates of desires directed toward the analyst varied. One Participant regarded herself as an "oedipal winner" in her analysis. Another was driven to an anguished expulsion of her love for her analyst, when he subsequently became a "noxious introject" by losing his license because of sexual boundary violations. More often the women continued to cherish the analyst for an extended period of time after termination, however, with bouts of painfully missing the man more than the analysis.

A second prominent theme, elaborated by several women seen in recent analyses, was the importance of the analyst's determined support of the analysand's autonomy and aggression. His active role in this was portrayed in distinctly different terms from those used by women who had sought out female analysts on the basis of wanting to identity with a "strong" and successful woman. Among the women who saw male analysts, Drs. Maxwell, Clark, Emon, and Tulane all emphasized that their analyst was unusually "unnarcissistic for a man," contrasting with their experience of either a "narcissistic" father who required admiration or of a vulnerable mother who would be too easily hurt by the daughter's aggression for her to have been able to express it. Additionally Drs. Emon and Tulane each felt that the analysis evoked and allowed them to work through an intensely negative mother transference. Both felt that this was what they most needed, given that an erotized relationship to men was already part of their repertoire. Both mentioned that the analyst made some statements at the end of the analysis about his own pleasure and learning in having worked with the analysand.

Person (1985) has observed that empirically "women patients, more than men, have a greater propensity to exhibit overt and sustained expressions of the erotic transference toward the analyst, whether male or female, and to experience the erotic transference as such" (p. 166). She posits that "the erotic transference utilized as resistance is more common among women, while resistance to the awareness of the erotic transference is more common among male patients." She traces the difference to a confluence of social and developmental determinants:

> In women, the preoccupation with pair-bonding, both establishing and preserving it, has social determinants that are self-evident. . . . The female pre-occupation with pair bonding may be best understood in the context of the female oedipal constellation, involving the father as primary libidinal object, while her erotic rival, the mother, is also a source of dependent gratification, leading the girl to experience dread of loss of love, a fear that is displaced from mother onto all subsequent love objects [p. 175].

In this context, Person views erotic longing as "compensatory against the fear of loss of love."

I concur with Person's view of the centrality of pair-bonding for women as providing a template for the analytic relationship, but I want to extend the developmental reach of gender further, to infancy. Certain female propensities that make themselves known from earliest infancy on may favor the development of particular libidinal and defensive configurations. Observed infant gender differences have to do with the average degree of openness to, rather than self-protectiveness from, affect contagion in a context of attending to relational interests. For examples, beginning at 1 to 3 days, infant girls appear to be more intensely involved in the "gazing dialogue" with their caretakers than are boys, whereas boys exceed in their use of "gaze aversion" when looked at by the caretaker (Hittleman and Dickes, 1979). Gender differences in seeking and maintaining eye contact versus gaze aversion continue from the first weeks of life through childhood into adulthood (Haviland and Malatesta, 1981). One need not—indeed cannot—conclude, therefore, that such differences occur on a sex-linked "genetic" basis. The less mature state of myelinization, on average, for boys at birth may require greater initial protection from arousal. The continuation of the pattern in later years, meanwhile, may reflect other factors.

Here I focus on the girl's development as an affective partner. Newborn girls (mean ages 66 to 72 hours old) are more apt to cry in response to another infant's cry than newborn boys, the mean cry duration is longer, and the autonomic level of arousal higher, correlated with the likelihood of crying (Simner, 1971; Sagi and Hoffman, 1976). The responsiveness to affect contagion thus has physiologic correlates, affecting the earliest schemata of attunement in relation to body experience. Silverman (1987) has suggested that "the female infant has more awareness of her mother's inner need states than does the male. Thus, her mother's various feeling states may be dimly experienced by the female infant, setting into motion her reactivity" (p. 210). Other data (Weinberg, 1992) suggest that an internalized representation of the affectively connected dyad may, on average, happen earlier with girls than boys. This interpretation of early differences has implications that diverge from the standard formulations that attribute the girl's well-known interest in relatedness either to socialization (which may cement the pattern) or to incomplete differentiation from the mother, reactive to the mother's clinging to a symbiotic tie. The point I make is that very early proclivities in seeking out an affectively responsive dialogue with another are more often, although not always, demonstrated by little girls. The implication is that this urge is propelled by affect states belonging to libidinal connection, a value with high priority, rather than denoting deficiencies in differentiation. I do not mean that boys are less libidinally impelled, only that the pathways to experiencing the other may configure differently.

The girl's involvement in these affect states, in turn, may favor early internalization, or presymbolic mental representation, of the dyadic interaction. Later aspects of female experience, such as heterosexual desire, may become assimilated to the libidinal framework of these early gender propensities. In the analytic situation as well, these predilections may make the female more prone to relate to the analyst through the sustained experience of erotic transference, which, in turn, may be more familiar to the female patient than to the male analyst. Cherishing the intrapsychic life of the analyst as person may be an intrinsic component of this tendency. The question remains as to what can make the affective intensity bearable enough to both patient and analyst to allow for its elaboration in ways that are most useful to the analysis.

Freud (1915) stressed the "unmistakable element of resistance in this 'love' of the woman patient for her male analyst," and advised the physician "to treat it as something unreal" (p. 166). He propounded that this path led to the necessary capacity for sublimation. "She has to learn from him to overcome the pleasure principle . . . to achieve this overcoming of herself . . . to acquire that extra piece of mental freedom" (p. 170). We need to entertain the question of whether this would be beneficial.

It seems to me that the goal of transformation of libidinal impulse into sublimated aim is misguided, because sublimation is predicated on the underlying drive connection becoming *newly* unconscious, its energy "neutralized." For women, this involves a detachment from bodily desires, associated with a loss of pleasure in bodily sensations of both interiority and prowess, and with self-devaluation in regard to loving freely in womanly ways. Within the analytic dyad, the goal of transforming erotic into "aim-inhibited wishes" stems from a particular confusion. Psychic representations of male and female genitals and their much fantasized interplay are developmentally early, although ever-changing organizers, in how the child makes sense of relating her sensual and affective experience to the people to whom she is emotionally attached. Such organizers become unconscious not only because of those forces of socialization invoked to tame the intensity of taboo sexual wishes, but also because the burgeoning complexity of affective interchange with meaningful intimates makes these early representation inadequate to the task. If erotic desires and their symbolizations toward the analyst in the analysis are "sublimated" into "higher forms," that is, if passion is replaced by "reason," the passions have been both overvalued and undervalued. They are over-valued, really overfeared, as though the desire was actually endangering and undervalued as a potential crucible for the reordering of the inner experience of self and others that occurs in productive analyses.

In the transference, the emergence of intense erotic wishes toward the analyst opens the possibility for reworking bodily metaphors in so far as they have remained a source of pathologic self-organizing assumptions, transcending whatever early fixed associations between gender and function, object and aim, may be constricting current experience. In such reworking, the difficult task of the analyst is to light the passage from old flame to new, but not to carry a torch.

The function of the analysand's free affective imagination with her analyst is not just to tolerate her fantasies in lieu of action (that is, "I wish to make love with my analyst even though I know we will never do that"), but also to broaden the range of a generative affective and ideational interchange that is possible in a strong and flexibly bound-aried emotional closeness. "That extra piece of mental freedom," so rightly prized by Freud, may spring from the richness of emotional interplay that is not yet possible for the child when the genitals first become such important and conflicted symbols of man and woman. This may require the analyst to also involve "that extra piece of mental freedom" to create and protect the kind of analytic space in which sexual desire may continue to fuel as unfettered an exploration of humanness in the analytic experience as possible (Tessman, 1999).

To exemplify some of these themes, I cite three short excerpts and then three longer narratives from women Participants with male analysts:

Dr. Celia Laub (deeply satisfying analysis) describes how indelibly the analysis was interiorized in the midst of erotic love for the analyst. Her awareness that he is a person with a love life of his own, which she must accept, is part of her feeling for him. **Dr. Laub's** father had died when she was only four years old. She told me that her father's life was suddenly "snuffed out" at a time when she had found him her excitingly favorite person. Her imagination reverses the "snuffing out" trauma in preserving her love for her analyst.

CL: It felt so special and intimate during those times when I began to trust myself to guess what might be going on in my analyst's mind. More and more sexual feelings toward him became very powerful. During intercourse with my husband I couldn't keep my analyst out of my mind. I tried. There were overwhelming waves of feeling in just thinking about him, loving his phrases, the way he thought about things, the nuances in his mood, seeing the slight slouch as he walked to the door. But I was always prepared for his rejection of me when I had such feelings, and was very uncomfortable about telling him, unlike about other feelings. Once, at an ocean beach, I remember going farther out than usual so that I could let the waves crash me to the shore while closing my eyes and thinking of him. But it didn't still the feelings. He was my first thought in the morning, my last thought before I went to sleep. It went on like that for God knows how long. I don't think he was comfortable with any of that either. But I learned to live with the feelings and knew that everything that happened in the analysis when I felt that way toward him registered more powerfully; it changed me and is with me still. What was harder, more painful to live with was the sort of secret feeling that he was the love of my life, all the time knowing that that was wrong of me in some way, that his love belonged between him and his wife. But getting to know, and sometimes sensing what he is like, while he also knew me so intuitively, was the best consolation. He did stubbornly confront me with very entrenched ways of relating to him, a stubborn refusal on his part to dominate or lord it over me in any way. The feeling of love for him continually grew. It had a life of its own. I couldn't imagine how that could be snuffed out.

Dr. Rose Lionheart (moderately satisfying analysis) believed that her analyst found her attractive and responded to her desires with some erotic fantasies of his own, which he managed prudently. Her awareness of his feelings eventuated in her sense of an "oedipal victory . . . not happy but triumphant." She continued to have positive feelings about the analysis, although she found her second analysis, with a senior woman, more deeply satisfying.

RL: To begin with, I really wasn't interested in him, just in my boyfriends, and then something came up and I became very intense, which I can do, and I got off the couch and I said, "okay I'm in love with you, that's it, now you know so what do we do?" And he just sat there and said, "we'll talk about it." I marched back and forth for a little while. I was really upset and I didn't like the feeling.
LT: You didn't like the feeling, or was there something about how it was received that was painful?
RL: No. The painful part was that I knew it was a hopeless sort of thing and it was useful in the analysis. His response to it was very

good, and then I got back down on the couch and said, "I knew this was going to happen, blah, blah, blah" and we went on with that.

A lot had happened to me at an oedipal age. Most of that analysis was about these things that had happened, the involvement with my father and, I'm very close to my mother and always have been, but had enormous guilt with my mother. I discovered that in the analysis, which was good. There was a lot of good, but it was not complete and I knew that, and then I think that things were too hot to deal with him.

LT: Do you mean the love and sexual things?
RL: The love things and the sexual feelings and stuff like that was not dealt with him, not well, and then I had another boyfriend. I thought we might even get married, which was kind of nutty because he was crazy, and it was a weird relationship and we went off to a meeting and—
LT: Crazy doesn't mean not intensely appealing.
RL: That's right, he was intensely appealing, he was a brilliant, brilliant man. But my analyst was critical of my going off to that meeting with him, he was critical of every boyfriend I had.

After termination, the analyst once suggested to a married colleague of his that the colleague invite **Rose** to be his date at a dinner dance at the Psychoanalytic Meetings. Being exceptionally good looking, she surmised that the analyst still found her attractive.

RL: He still had feelings for me and was identified with this man.
LT: What were your feelings about his feelings?
RL: Why not? Didn't bother me very much.
LT: Was it the opposite? Was it lovely in some way or not?
RL: It was a little triumphant. Oedipal victories are always triumphant, not happy but triumphant. And it was an oedipal victory. At least that was my impression. and I suspect this guy must have had some clue—he was pretty smart even about himself. I think he had some clue.

Dr. Elizabeth Light is the Participant whose analyst, subsequent to the analysis, lost his license because of sexual boundary violations with other analysands. She refers to her erotic feeling, which "certainly melts all our defenses" as having stayed safely within the bounds of language, although, as it turned out, the analyst was unable to rely on having such boundaries within his own psychic reality.

EL: The analysis assumed these very not so much intense as deep reaching and important proportions in my life, so that I let down all my guards in terms of believing. Even though I challenged him on a lot of issues, I was there ready to believe in something else. So I think I went through pretty much stagewise everything. I went through a lot of preoedipal stuff; he was my mother. I went through a lot of oedipal stuff; he was my father, he was my mother. I had a lot of dreams, in which I was in love with him as a very conscious feeling. That feeling certainly melts all our defenses, that makes us very pliable or vulnerable or whatever word is appropriate. I remember I talked about getting involved literally, physically in an act of love of some kind, and the tremendous price that you would pay thereafter. I talked about my own feelings, my own fantasies, and my own wishes. I felt that they were there to be talked about and they were there to be dealt with through language.

LT: So in some way you drew your own boundaries.

EL: That's correct.

LT: You have a capacity for tolerating intense feelings. It puts me in mind of the book, which is now a movie called the *The Postman*. The title of the book was *Burning Patience*. The poet [Pablo] Neruda mentors the young postman about putting his burning desire into words and metaphors. I can imagine you having "burning patience" in relation to your feelings about him during the analysis as you were dealing with all that. What happens when it turns out that he was incapable . . . ?

EL: It's not a bad kind of patience, for me more light and lively and energized. The being in love is very different from loving and I remember for a period of a month or two, just riding over to his office with the music on. I was aware of all these feelings, and knew this was part of my analysis, I had the right to have them.

Sustained Erotic Transference: Dr. Veronica Clark

Dr. Veronica Clark's narrative illustrates the difference in self-experience and affecto-libidinal constellation that could be engaged in relation to two different analysts. The degree of satisfaction as well as the emotional power of the analyses varied accordingly. A profound and sustained erotically loving transference gathered momentum in her second analysis and eventuated in a painful period of mourning around termination. Postanalytic contact resulted in shifts in her perception of both analysts. Given the mutative depth of her involvement, a particularly poignant venture in self-analysis was jolted into motion by disappointing encounters with the beloved and excellent second analyst, posttermination. Resourcefully she is able to extract in the interview the positive component in her disappointment, namely, that it furthers the constructive de-idealization that she associates with confident autonomy.

The First Analyst (Moderately Satisfying Analysis)

VC: I was given a name for my first analyst by someone I was in training with, and I never questioned it. I should have questioned it because we frequently had a very, very rough time. I think he suffered from being fresh out of training. He was a very traditional classical analyst. It wasn't so much abstinence from intervention. He certainly talked a lot, but it was a classical, theoretical, formal analysis, which I didn't like. The interpretations were very classical. I remember I almost walked out over his penis envy interpretations.

LT: You say you almost walked out. I'm interested in the almost but not quite. Does that mean there was some leeway to disagree and how was disagreement?

VC: There was some leeway to disagree. We certainly disagreed over the penis envy issue. He was willing to give at that point in terms of jealousy over the way men are in their family and society as opposed to their actual penises. That issue was certainly very much there in my father and the way my brother was treated in the family. But it wasn't as though there weren't good papers on penis envy as a metaphor around, so he could have learned. Hopefully, he did learn from his experience with me. His interpretations were classical psychosexual and ego conflict, and they mainly focused on oedipal conflict. But there was always a lot of anger and tension around that very classical approach because I didn't agree with it often.

LT: Are you also saying it felt like he pushed his views on you?

VC: Yes, and a lot of things I said just never got analyzed as I later saw in my second analysis. So we were at loggerheads.

LT: Sounds like you have some awareness of what was done and what wasn't.

VC: What was done that was important was about my relationship with my father, which is partly why I think the transference was also so rocky, it wasn't totally his stance. I had a negative transference that he was dealing with. My father had a terminal disease so there was a clock ticking, and he must have felt that pressure, so there was a lot of focus on that. Whole aspects of my relationship with my father that had been repressed became de-repressed. It was truly shocking. The first five years of my life I had very different, intensely positive feelings for my father and I had no memory of any of that. While it was an unpleasant experience for the most part being in the analysis, I'm very grateful for what got worked out, so that I could have a positive relationship a sufficient amount of time with my father before he died.

LT: I don't even know how to ask this question, but I'm impressed by the fact that you were able to work out, to recover the positive with your father and work that out in the context of a transference with an analyst whose interpretations you felt as dominating you while you were busy not giving in. How did that work?

VC: That's an interesting question I haven't really thought about. What came to mind as I was listening to you is that there were certain times when real things happened that he had to respond to in a very real way, and in those very small real times he was very caring. I don't know whether that helped or I had some subliminal sense of that. But I was always fighting with my analyst about the things I didn't like, approve of, agree with. I never had an erotic transference with him and I can't say I loved the guy. We had calm periods, it wasn't totally horrible, but . . .

LT: But you found him not that lovable?

VC: No he wasn't. I was very intellectually interested in the analysis, and he was extraordinarily smart. He was one of the best dream analysts I have ever come across, and I really learned to analyze dreams with him. A lot of his intellectual power was persuasive because it was right and I could see it in myself, in associations, and as bad as he was in terms of us arguing, we at least argued about it, which was already different from my father. So it was a very high-level intellectual argument that went on and was very charged I think for both of us.

LT: Did that also feel exciting or secretly fun?

VC: No, it was not fun. I didn't even think of it as exciting; now I probably would. At the time, I was just angry. But he made sense a lot of times. Maybe that's how it worked—it was better than my father. He was constant and predictable and very intelligent. I think he got caught up in countertransference. There were enactments going on, looking at it through a modern perspective, that were very similar to what went on with my father. A lot of who's better, who's smarter? Competition!

LT: Was that acknowledged or acknowledgeable?

VC: No. I was aware of it at the time, but didn't say anything about it. That didn't get analyzed, it just kind of happened. The relational aspects went on in enactments. What was workable were the negative feelings. What was unworkable were any positive feelings.

LT: Because? Why couldn't positive feelings? . . .

VC: I didn't trust him. There was a sense of being hit over the head with these interpretations. He was aware of the fact that I felt that way even in my body posture. A lot of the time, I lay down with my hands over my head.

LT: Protecting yourself from being hit over the head?

VC: Right, which was my self-experience very frequently in that analysis, and therefore I could not trust him with the softer side of me, not just the sexual. I couldn't trust him with the softer positive feelings. I wouldn't let that vulnerable side be there. I don't think he could see that, and in some ways that was unworkable because it was all put on me; there was no relational stance. In fact when I went back to see him, after some years, I really went back for a take on who he was, and my experience with him, and to see if, in fact, it had been as bad as I experienced it. What he said at that point was that he wasn't aware of how much my issues had to do with adolescence and that now that he had had adolescents, he had a better sense of the combative quality. But it was still put on me. It was still very much my issue rather than what his contribution to my issue was, the concern about being vulnerable with very positive feelings. So I really got a sense, going back, that reconfirmed what I felt and experienced in the analysis. The other thing that confirmed it: Whenever I spoke to him in a kind of nonanalytic setting, if I've have had to call him about a professional question, I still have exactly the same problem, and it's an interesting transference. When I spoke to him in a nonanalytic situation, I couldn't be clear in my thinking. There was such a level of anxiety that still existed that I couldn't always get my point across, and would get very tongue tied with him because it didn't feel comfortable and safe. Feeling so comfortable and safe in my second analysis, it was very clear to me what the differences were. But there have been other times more recently when I've encountered my first analyst, times that were also work oriented, where it is clear he is very caring, and likes me, and I think is in some ways proud of me in a fatherly way. If I hadn't had those positive postanalytic contacts, I probably would have said that he thought I was very difficult, very neurotic, in some ways unworkable. I left that analysis not feeling great. I don't think it was a good match; I think there was a difference in style. But this is colored because I know him now more as a person than I did then, and as a person he's much nicer and better than he was as an analyst.

LT: It's very interesting, your picturing him both "as a person" and "as an analyst."

VC: It's not clear to me at this point if he's just come more into his own, or if that was his analytic stance and this is his personality. But he hardly ever comes to mind. When I left I didn't have the same kind of sadness that I had with my second analyst. I was glad it was over. It was all intellectual; it wasn't a fully felt experience. The only felt experience I had in that analysis was either around anger or around my experience with my father. So he didn't stay with me that much except in a highly negative way. It was only later when I saw how much had gotten done that I was able to have more gratitude for what had happened in that analysis.

The Second Analyst (Deeply Satisfying Analysis)

Veronica Clark chose her second analyst with certain qualities in mind:

VC: I was looking for somebody very flexible, my first requirement. I was not going to have one more inflexible, theoretical analyst. I also needed someone who was going to be very bright. I hoped there wouldn't be the kind of competition I had felt with my first analyst. I wanted someone who was very theoretically broad and who recognized how bright I was, though I don't think I would have said that then. When I went into analysis I didn't think I was very bright at all. I wanted someone who was also very flexible in the way one worked with individual people, more of a sense of a tailored analysis, to fit me. I wanted someone who would have the flexibility to do that for each person, not just the flexibility in theoretical thinking but in how an analyst works. The other thing I was looking for was someone who would be much more attuned and would work better with feelings. Because I felt my first analysis was more intellectual, I wanted someone I could just connect with, and I don't feel I can connect with lots of people. Those are the qualities that were most important to me and I really did find them.

The analysis begins:

VC: At the beginning of the analysis, I began to wonder about my choice. He didn't say much for a very long time, to the point where I wondered if he was listening. Looking back, while it was anxiety provoking in some ways, it was very different than my first analysis. When he finally did speak some months down the road, he had really been listening. He had gotten it, and had an understanding of me that I was impressed by. Not only did he really get to know me, but also he was extremely kind, and very gentle. I had made it clear that I did not want to be hammered over the head with interpretations. So I think what allowed me to really work on a lot of issues, was that I felt that I could really trust that he would be with me. At times, later in the analysis I did not trust that because he was not always able to understand where I was emotionally. But it was a slow process, slow enough that I could gain trust over time to go into very difficult areas.

Veronica depicts the interplay at times when she did feel misunderstood:

VC: Sometimes there would be a countertransference error, and he would say something hurtful. I would tell him immediately what the problem was, what I thought was happening, and that it was an error. At first he wouldn't admit to any of it. About six months to a year later he would finally understand it, and he would apologize. It took him a while to get some of these countertransference elements. It was hard being my analyst because I was always not only analyzing myself but also analyzing him. I don't think it was easy to hear some of my analyses of his behavior at times. But once I learned that it would take him a while to metabolize what I was telling him, I knew it was okay.
LT: Was it important to you—to have a sense of his inner life?
VC: It was very important to me. I needed to know that in order to really trust him. I needed to really be sure of who I was dealing with in order to really proceed at the depths I wanted to go to. I had an extremely deep analysis. I had some sense of his conflicts. I had a good sense of where he would go with his anger, the degree to which he would take out his anger and the form which it would take. Same with his impulsivity. I don't think I thought so much about his conflicts, as I needed to just have a sense of who he was as a person. The idea of personhood as opposed to doctorhood. I had encountered many narcissistic, incompetent, unrelated doctors. It's not that it all

had to be good, I just needed to know him as a person, and he recognized that and was able to adjust his technique to be more of a person with me.

LT: How would he show his personhood in the analysis?

VC: Part of it was giving me the time and space to analyze, but part
of it was—a real relationship. There was, perhaps, more of an emphasis on the real relationship than [in] most analyses.

Her feelings for him deepened:

VC: I really loved him toward the end. I had complete trust in him,
and I loved him like a family member. That's how much I loved him.
I had a very strong sexual, oedipal transference. A real oedipal transference as opposed to it all being intellectually understood in my first
analysis.

LT: In that oedipal transference, was it also inevitably painful?

VC: When it got painful, it was incredibly painful, and when I got
angry, he was the only person who has seen me be that angry, outside
of my family. I had dampened some of my affect in the course of my
life. What he would do, which I think is also part of his character, when
my feelings would come up, he'd intensify them. I would say, "oh you're
being melodramatic"—as he would talk about rage. At the time, it felt
melodramatic, but he encouraged an intensification of feeling.

LT: Also of loving feeling?

VC: All feelings. He was really feeling oriented, much more feeling
oriented than intellectual understanding of things. He really encouraged it so that the analysis was filled with intense positive and negative feelings. Once it really heated up and got started, it stayed that
way straight through till the day it stopped.

LT: Did you have longings or fantasies about either becoming friends
or working closely together after terminating or . . . ?

VC: I had those feelings in the analysis. I had them postanalysis. But
my postanalytic contacts have been such that I don't really want to
anymore. I think he's a better analyst than he is a person, whereas
with my first analyst I felt exactly the opposite. I haven't been thrilled
with the way he is capable and incapable of relating outside of analysis. I had the experience in analysis of being very well understood,
remembered, and cared about. I had totally different experiences postanalysis, in which I felt that he did not remember, he did not care.
There were several interactions, in professional kinds of settings,
where, for instance, the only thing he could think of to talk to me

about was the restaurants in town. I got a sense from such incidents that he would never be able to think and care about me in a nonanalytic setting the way I think and care about people I care about. In that way, we were very different. I understand it as something in his nature, and it's also something between the two of us. I expected that imbalance. I never expected him to care about me the way I cared about him, and that was always very clear, but the lack of thinking about and remembering has been at times very obvious. I think that the part of his character that accounts for that makes him an excellent, in many ways, analyst, but not someone I would care to have as a friend. It took a while to get to that place, but I can tolerate it now and—I still love him.

LT: Are some of the old longings, after all, affected by whom it is you're longing for as a person, how you now see him?

VC: Absolutely. There is a de-idealization that's gone on. Some of that I think is very organic, and some of that I think is also very necessary for a separation and for the process of becoming your own person. It was stark, but maybe it was stark because the whole thing was so intense. Everything was pumped up to such an emotional intensity, which was necessary to do what needed to be done on some level and was also characterological. Thus, the de-idealization felt stark and wasn't very modulated in me. Being at the same Institute certainly helped the de-idealization process (Both laugh). When I left analysis, I had the fantasy that he'd always be kind of looking after me at the Institute, in a very beneficent way. I now know that's not the case, and that's good because now I've done it on my own, and that's been very helpful. What was a shaky self esteem when I started in that analysis, got a lot better. So knowing that he's not looking after me with a beneficent eye has been helpful.

LT: What do you believe about how he would view all that?

VC: I think he would say I had a wonderful analysis, that it was very successful, that he tremendously cares about me. He might even say he loves me. I think the problems that we've had in the relating afterward are characterological, problems that are separate from how he views me in the analysis. I know he felt that I had the tools and I knew everything I needed to know about what we worked on to continue working on it. I think he would say that, and so would I. And about the ending? I think he would have said that I would mourn him and be done with it. But that he would have an importance to that and me I would have an importance to him. On some level, I think he

really did separate the real relationship and the analytic relationship
and that he thought that somehow or other the transference would
be resolved and done with. I don't think that exists. So where would
he be ideally located? Somewhere in my heart, which is where he is,
and I think that he would say that I am in his heart. I know that's
what he would say as my analyst. It doesn't quite jibe with my actual
experience, but it jibes with him as my analyst. And I definitely feel
like one of his favorites. Not that I don't think he might have similar
feelings for other people or that there might be other intense analyses, or that there might be other people he truly loves more, that's all
possible. But it felt very, very personal, very individualized (very long
pause). He gave me whatever he had to give me. Like me with my
patients. I do feel, still feel, that he was totally committed and that's
one of the ways we fit. It doesn't have to be all roses, and I've learned
a lot from what wasn't good, too. That's important to keep straight—
that he is who he is, and that's a part of the de-idealization. I don't
think I could go back to him as analyst. It's complicated. I think what
has happened afterward put a closure on it. It feels like a closed experience and I really don't feel that there's more to give that I didn't get.

Dr. Clark's process of painful mourning, before and after termination, is described in the chapter, "Mourning."

Maternal Transferences, Male Analysts: Drs. Francesca Emon and Jill Tulane

Several women chose male analysts after a prior treatment with
another male analyst with whom they described having experienced
an intensely erotic "father transference." Their hope and intention
was to be able to use the analyst also as a maternal figure, to engage
the powerful issues that were unresolved with mothers. I will exemplify with two Participants, **Drs. Jill Tulane** and **Francesca Emon,** both
deeply satisfied with their analyses. Both of their analysts seemed to
evoke the kind of trust which allowed for the emergence of the affective constellations that were fertile soil for those issues. Since the early
mother–daughter issues evoked more dread than those in relationship
to men did, this period of the analysis was more fraught with umbrage
than steeped in pleasure. As **Dr. Emon** makes particularly clear, the
analyst's actively attentive and warm attitudes early in the analysis
were not an obstacle to the development of negative and aversive
affects linked to mother.

Dr. Francesca Emon recalls that her first impression of her analyst was based on his interested seriousness at everything she was saying, his compassion, and his apparent lack of either self-absorption or sadism, a contrast to her father.

FE: If you encroached too much on my father's territory or his narcissism, if he felt insulted in some way, he could get very sadistic. I knew [analysts] who were sadistic and others who could be paternal or loving and maternal. Apart from the transference, I sensed him to be a decent, loving, and kind person, and that just got elaborated. I didn't see him differently at the end, but I saw him as more of that, fleshed out more, with an enormous capacity for listening and, actually, nonnarcissistic. Almost unambitious. I still see him this way—there's a way that he has such a quiet touch about his need to assert himself and his self-promotion. He doesn't put his needs ahead of the need of the group. But he's very facilitative, and his style is to be in the background. He's like the soil, as opposed to another plant vying for the sunlight. He likes to help things grow. He's really good at it. What was most sustaining was his attitude. I perceived this to be his character, my experience of his kindness. He was just so attentive and warm. He never said anything that made me think he wasn't interested in hearing more about the intensity of it or that he was disgusted by what I was talking about. I felt that, throughout, except for the periods where I felt he was doing nothing or imagined he was sleeping (laugh).

Dr. Emon traces the course of the analysis:

FE: There was a beginning honeymoon period when I dreamt about him constantly.
LT: Do you remember any of those early dreams?
FE: I do remember one. My husband and I were walking—holding hands, but I was carrying a baby, and I think there was another child. We were at a beach club that my parents took our whole family to growing up. We were walking out of the ocean, and I was naked, not erotically naked, it was more revealing myself to him. You know what I just remember now? There was another part to it. I hadn't thought of this in a really long time but this was true. I couldn't always feel the ground. And I was sort of testing to see where the ground was. So it was something about going deep. And I was smiling. It was a happy dream. Looking forward to the analysis. This may sound naive,

but I've always seen psychoanalysis as the empathic mother. The analyst who will listen, who has patience, who is interested. And also who understands, and that doesn't mean agrees or doesn't confront.

My analyst had a preference for saying less, always. And that kind of ushered in the next phase, which was, "I want you to say more." And this was the meat of my analysis, actually a very negative transference, where I just felt he was doing nothing. I imagined him—Ugh!—sitting back there. If he wasn't asleep, he was reading his mail. Actually, I just changed that. Really, my preoccupation was that he was playing with his mail.

LT: With his male?

FE: That's the way I said it, "Playing with your mail?" And once he said, "Mail? Male?" (Laughs.) Basically that was a negative paternal transference, that he was sitting back there masturbating or something, like my dad would, I mean mental masturbation or whatever, always talking about himself. But I think in large part it was a negative maternal transference. The thing about just not being interested, not listening, sleeping, saying nothing. He is a very silent, no, actually that's not true, I think he sort of swings back and forth from being really quite silent, to being really much more present and even real and letting me see . . . he's not, averse to disclosing something about himself, about his background, and over the years I gathered this stuff. But the negative maternal transference was actually the most important thing.

LT: And how did that feel?

FE: It was terrible. There were years when I really felt like analysis was this huge burden. I had to go, I had to talk into this vacuum, there was no one there, he wasn't gonna tell me anything, how he felt, what to do, advice, or even what he thought about me. I didn't feel I got enough of his analytic thinking about me.

LT: And did that seem like he had formulations which he chose not to convey, or that he didn't think that way, or that he didn't formulate, or what?

FE: I thought all of the above. There definitely were times I thought he wasn't saying what he was thinking and could have. I complained about that bitterly with him. Once I had said, "You're always one or two steps behind me—not only physically behind me, but mentally too, like I have to teach you. I have to say everything. You don't say anything. But I want you to be one or two steps ahead of me." And he said, in his very pithy way, "I know. But I've never been convinced that that's been good for you." And that was very important. Because he was talking about my dad, I think, who always had to be ahead of me, and I would follow. And it deprived me of confidence in my own ideas. There were many men who I had been involved with, who were happy to take the lead and have me be in a one-down position in relation to them. So it was very important. There were lots of moments where he did not interpret or say anything, which, I now believe, and even then somewhat, was extremely helpful because it required me to say what I thought with authority. So I believe that was my analyst's formulation, actually. I think his idea of my analysis was that he had to stay out of my way and let me do it so that I would have no one to thank but myself. And so that I could own it. And I did gain enormous confidence in myself. There were ways that I used to be anxious and that I used to doubt myself that have just gone. It was very autonomy-promoting, but that's not all it was either. I felt very loved. I really did. There's one more thing. Whenever he disclosed something about himself, or about his family, it would come up in a relevant context, and I always remembered it. Always. It was like a jewel.

LT: So that was precious. Because it was something of him?

FE: Yeah. To know something about him. And I don't think it interfered with my having a transference to him. But I also appreciated how he was stepping outside of routine and conventional analytic technique, so it made it more precious to me. Not that I thought he didn't do this with all of his patients, but it would be, maybe, frowned upon by some people. And I appreciated it, that he was not rigid in that way, a feeling that your analyst can step outside the rules momentarily and would for you. I've always had the fantasy that he was a wonderful parent. To be his child would be fabulous, because he's so nurturant. Also in that way the first year of analysis was very positive.

But during that negative time when I wanted more feedback from him and had this idea that he was sleeping, that's what the transference was, that he was bored with me, or I was killing him, or something. And the fact is I had to accept it as transference because I had no concrete indications otherwise. Then I definitely didn't enjoy it, and I was late to appointments more. Probably I would cancel appointments if I had a conflict. I wanted to wake him up. I wanted to stimulate him in some way. And it didn't feel hostile. It felt more like I wanted to enliven him. So it was a dead mother transference. I said that to him. It had that transferential component, but it also was about him.

LT: Do you mean that it was also about his silence which you had experienced, which was actually there?
FE: Yes. And it was enormously healing. It changed how I felt, to be able to say directly to him that significant complaint. I've thought about it a lot. It bears on anonymity, on the role of silence, and how much do you have to do to be the old object? What do you have to do to get at that? I believe more in silence than I do in anonymity. I don't think there is such a thing as anonymity. But I think silence is a very real experience that pulls for neglect. Some people like to think and write about it as pulling for idealization. I think it pulls for neglect and for the negative transference, more often than not. But it's important. And also the whole thing about being outside the visual sphere, as opposed to vis-à-vis, has to be extremely important. It's so ambiguous, because it's plastic, in the sense of the analyst being able to take on a wider range of persona. So, I also remember how intensely negative I was feeling at that time toward him, and I started to experience him as indifferent and not caring, or just not sympathetic enough. Finally, when something hurtful happened to me at work I was talking with him about it, of course, and I was very, very, hurt, and he wasn't saying anything. For a long period of time. So finally I turned to him, not physically, but I said, "How could you? How could you say nothing to me when you saw me suffering like that? How could you?" And there was something about that phrase, "How could you?" It was something I think I've always wanted to say to my mother. "How could you?" I still think that was the most important moment in the analysis because it was a repetition of my experience with my mother. She would stand by doing nothing as me and my siblings or me and my father would be arguing or something.
LT: Do you think that what might also have gotten linked is that at that moment you were able to value yourself enough so that you didn't say, "well, I'm unworthy of your attention," but rather "how could you, given that this is me, and I should have a response."
FE: Yes. That's right. I felt entitled to a response. And I saw it as his problem. Now I think—and even then there was a part of me that knew—this was his restraint, he was trying to give me room to react in whatever way I needed to, and I did. And, yes, I think that it had to do with some certainty by then, some confidence in myself, that I

could demand what I wanted and be puzzled as to why he wasn't giving it to me. And of course it was terribly painful. But, it definitely stands out in my mind as one of the most important moments in the analysis. There was a turning point after that, and it had to do with how I felt. Soon after that was when I knew I was done. I think it had something to do with my anxiety that I was describing to you. It was like a fight I had never fought and I had to fight it. And I did.

LT: So, are you also saying it was possible to have the needed fight with him, that was impossible with your mother?

FE: Yeah. Right. And the change in how I felt after that was palpable. There was a feeling of a resolution. That anxiety that I had, another piece of it lifted. Maybe it was the last piece.

The period just prior to termination began with some denial of how important the analyst had become to **Francesca,** then followed by grief.

FE: I think I kind of bounced into a reality orientation. I remember that I was in denial about who he was to me. Now, in retrospect, it was funny. I was like, "I'm done, and I am looking forward to it. I can't wait to have these hours free. I'm sorry, but I don't think I'm gonna miss this. I think I'm gonna miss you, but I'm not gonna miss this." I was totally in denial of who he was. And I kept saying, "I'm *not* grieving." (Laughs.) He said something like, "Well, what are we to do with the fact that we both know there are no no's in the unconscious?" I don't know what it was about that, but it just broke right through, and I laughed and started crying and, telling him how much I really wanted him to be my mother.

LT: Was that the first time you told him that?

FE: No. No. But it came back in a more sad way, because now he wasn't going to be. So there was just a sadness, a feeling of loss, of this person who was so kind and so interested, and also the loss of this unconscious fantasy that he was gonna be my mother But I wanted him to be in my life. I talked to him a lot about that. I wanted very much to have this patient listener who every now and then would throw out a pearl of wisdom. So from then on it was more like a real termination because I was more aware of my sadness.

Francesca describes his intrapsychic presence since termination:

FE: He was, and is, internalized as a calm, interested other. That actually captures both sides. The interested is more like a representation,

like a related presence that is not dead but that is interested in how
I'm doing and an accompaniment to my internal questioning or monitoring of how I feel. And the other side of it is he's calm, and I feel
calmer. In fact, I grew up, as far back as I can remember, with a kind
of diffuse anxiety at all times. And that went away through my analysis. So I have a feeling of calm that's very nice. And it's partly me, but
with his inner presence.

LT: Are there other ways in which you feel you've changed?

FE: He definitely saw me as a very loving person. And I became more
loving through the analysis, because I was neurotically bound up in
some ways. Neurosis, Agh! It's such a waste! And, I was too concerned
with getting enough for myself and not able to give enough, and now
I'm able to give a lot more. I think he would agree with me in the way
that I see it, and what I needed to do. Especially in the way of coming into my own. And resolving that chronic feeling of being unloved,
which was terrible. And I think he knows that I did that, and how we
did it together.

Dr. Jill Tulane

JT: At the time of choosing an analyst, I thought I ought to see a
woman, because I had had two men [analysts] and I had always been
drawn to having erotic transferences with men, and I thought I had a
lot of stuff with my mother. I expected it would be much more difficult and unpleasant from the get-go.

LT: Like I'll grit my teeth and do it?

JT: Grit my teeth and do it. So I went to see a number of women,
and I didn't feel very drawn to anybody. When I said, "I really am not
sure whether I want to take this year off or start now," they said to
me, "You need an analysis to answer the question," which annoyed
me no end, irritated me, and sort of reminded me of all of the things
I hated most about analysis. I thought it wasn't that they didn't understand the situation, but I thought they weren't wanting to step out of
role and give an opinion. That's how I felt. That didn't help. And none
of them felt right.

So then, I spoke with a friend of mine, and told him about my
dilemma, and he said, "What about Dr. X? He's very good. He's got
time. He's Jewish, like your mother. He's about the same height as
your mother. Maybe between those two things, you can make him

woman enough to suit the bill." So I went to see him. And I posed the dilemma I was in. And he said, "You sound like you're leaning towards taking the year off, and I think you probably should, and it makes a lot of sense to me." That pleased me, and I liked him, and thought he reminded me enough of my mother in a variety of ways that he would probably do. So that's how I ended up with him.

What I remember about my analysis was that I hated it for the most part. Through and through. And when I say that, my actual conscious experience of it was one of feeling rebellious, and wanting to resist the experience of submitting to the process.

LT: You mentioned a minute ago that you leaned toward erotic transferences.

JT: That was not the case with him. It was a perfectly suited maternal (laughs) transference from the get-go. I sort of planned it that way. I would have preferred something else. But I thought this would not be such a good thing for me, having had already two treatments like this, and I really ought to deal with this other half of my existence. Anyway, I was late to my hour. All the time. I don't think I was ever there early. And I think I could probably count on my hands the number of times I was there right on time. I remember I disliked waiting. I didn't want to have to wait in the waiting room. I wanted to walk in. I didn't want to be summoned. I didn't want to have to come too close and pass him and have him look at me from behind. We talked about that endlessly. But I also wore my coat, all the time, in analysis. My rationales about that was that he had a scratchy couch, and I'm very sensitive to that, but it also was a metaphor for my being sort of wrapped up and insulated from some aspect of analysis. At the end, I tried to make a point to take off my coat more and complained about the scratchy couch. It really did remind me a lot of my relationship with my mother. The difference was that my rebellion with my mother was much more silent.

She had been through so much loss and horror in her life, that a lot of my attempts to become independent would be met with my father saying, "You know, your mother is anxious, and you know she has reason to be, and soon enough you'll be grown up and you can do what you want." She was very overprotective. I was everything to her. My mother did and does dote on me, tremendously. It was confining and constricting.

LT: So she was more hurtable than your analyst?

JT: She was very vulnerable, yes. So, I felt more liberated to put it more into action. Literally. I mean, being late, and being irritable.

LT: I am not yours to make up for past hurts?

JT: Right. And, that, in and of itself, looking back, was very helpful, because I felt I really had a force I could beat up against. I remember that a couple of things happened that made me much more aware of what I was doing. I began to act out in a couple of ways that had an effect on him. I got in a conversation with one of my classmates who was in analysis with him too, and we talked about the difference in fees, and it turned out he was paying more. He had a lot more money. And I was paying less. And this got back to and irritated him. He made use of the countertransference to highlight some of what I was doing; it actually made me pause a little bit. Brought it a little closer to home, in terms of my ability to injure somebody, and also the way in which he held forth about it's all being part of the work, yet he was getting annoyed, and that was very helpful to me in terms of feeling like this really was gonna be a place where I could do what I wanted.

I never had the experience that many of my friends had, of this kind of wowing experience of analysis. Never. It always felt kind of a slow, grinding, not thrilling, not pleasant, difficult, arduous task. When, my friends went, "Wow, this was really the most incredible interpretation. . . ." I never had that. Not that I didn't appreciate him or value him or applaud his skill, because I thought he was very good. I didn't feel demeaning of him.

The times that I remember as most striking, powerful, and emotionally potent were always related to when there was a little more disclosure on his part. He rarely said anything about himself, he was quite anonymous to me in many ways, but sometimes, when he would use some aspect of himself or his life and incorporated it, along with interpretation, that made it much more potent. At first I wasn't curious about him at all, didn't think I really want to know. But I became more aware of my curiosity when I began to realize how many distortions in my mind I had about what sort of life he in fact had.

I had imagined, for example, that he was younger, with little children, and I always thought that he had a kind of boring marriage, to a dull, passive Jewish woman, and that he was a suffering fellow, and that analysis was a way out of his boring existence. That was a fully developed fantasy, and I say that because I remember there was a lot of attention about, did I think that I was there to yank him out of that boredom?

LT: So that if you pictured that, then you might have felt that being with you was a very different experience for him than being—

JT: Well, that's what he thought all the time, if there was an erotic transference. It's funny 'cause it really was so much more of a maternal transference, that my relationship to that was that this boring existence was boring because of some sort of inner traps that were not allowing him to capitalize on what was around him, and that this sort of boring wife really could be more interesting and fun if only he could . . . it had a lot to do with my mother's relationship with her past and being trapped in all kinds of traumatic things and so it was a question of how much was he prisoner of his own inhibitions.

Eventually I discovered that he had a very spunky, lively wife. I'm sure this was a true example of repression 'cause I must have known of her, seen her do some things at the Institute, because he actually said, "Well, you must have. . . ." Still, I never felt swept up in the analysis the way a number of my friends did. Ultimately, it ended up being very helpful in my relationship with my mother because I had the opportunity to examine it more thoroughly, particularly [the] sadistic edge of wanting to affect her. It was important to come to realize that I wasn't gonna do anybody in, although I always felt with my mother I was.

Dr. Tulane talks about what changed during the analysis in her feelings toward her parents:

JT: My relationship with my father was always very idealized, and my relationship with my mother was always difficult, although loving. Now that's eased a lot. I think the analysis made it much easier, and I enjoy her a lot more. I also now don't idealize my father nearly as much as I used to. He's come down to size. As, as I'm saying this, I'm remembering probably the most salient dream I had in my analysis near the end. It was about my being reduced to an extremely diminutive size. I came in for my session and was aware of this gigantic expanse I had to traverse in order to get to the couch, which was looming as a huge thing in front of me, and I was walking fast and aware that I was gonna be really late by the time I'd get there because I was so little and the distance was so far. And then I got to the couch, a towering couch, and I am screaming at the top of my lungs to get some help to get onto this couch and I'm thinking he's not gonna be able to hear me. But he does, and he brings over a little tiny ladder that goes up against the leg of the couch, and I then climb up and go running along down the couch, and climb up into the pillow, and there's a nice little sort of dent where my head usually is, and I hop in and feel very comfortable and cozy. Anyway, that was the manifest dream, and I remember the sense of being changed in size, in terms of the people in my life. My mother had changed size and my analyst, had gotten a whole lot bigger all of a sudden in relationship with me, and my father had gotten a little bit smaller, and it was sort of a wonderful dream, that ended up being about how the shifting identifications and the relationship to people were viewed in my mind in terms of how large they loomed in my life, or small, had gone through a metamorphosis. It was right near the end.

LT: It's pictured beautifully, and sounds like he could meet whatever size you were at the moment and hold you with the ladder to where you wanted to go.

JT: Right. I never felt diminished by him. When I terminated, I remember his saying to me, which I've now incorporated myself, something about how much I had taught him, which surprised me, and how much he'd enjoyed working with me. I find I say something similar to patients who terminate with me now. After the analysis, I wrote him a letter, and I reviewed the analysis and said something about how difficult I've been and that how, with it now being over, how valuable had it seemed to me, and I wanted to send him a gift to express that. He wrote me back, thanking me and inviting me to come back any time, both to chat or to check on what I had sent him, and that was very pleasing to me.

Some time after I had terminated I was at a restaurant, and he came in with his wife, and he looked right at me and didn't recognize me, didn't take me in. And I remember being aware of a twinge of "Oh my God, how can you forget me so quickly?"—as well as being totally understanding, thinking, "well, it's a packed room, he's not expecting to see me here, it's dark." But the reason I bring it up is that I was very much aware of a change in my response. At some earlier times, this would have so angered me, that he wouldn't recognize me, and that this experience reminded me of some aspect in my relationship with my mother. It was comforting to me, to see myself able to take in the oversight in a way that did not make me feel angered.

LT: It sounds like, and correct me if I'm wrong, that instead of being just angered, you were empathic with him in vertical life and could have a track of that in addition to the firm grasp of what had been in the analysis.

JT: Yeah. Yeah. That kind of empathy occurred as a result of the analysis. I was much more aware. We've had some contact since then, we're on a committee together now and I'm quite comfortable with that. I feel I can manage that. We can have a good time together, whether it be at a committee meeting or social gathering. I like that. Even if I were to be in analysis with him again, I can handle that. He handles it quite well; he can wear both hats and shines through in being unflappable in that regard.

Dr. Jill Tulane describes the positive sense of having internalized the analyst as dialogic partner:

JT: My experience of my analysis, I have to say, has become infinitely more potent since it's been over, than during. I've not been back, although I've thought of going back, now and then, to just touch base. I think I end up not doing it because I really do feel like I incorporated the process of analytic work. It's with me all the time. That's the biggest difference of all. Before analysis I was observant, but I didn't feel as though I kept up a psychological narrative, with access to myself. I really incorporated that. I feel like I have a dialogue going with him because of this process in my head.

MEN WITH MALE ANALYSTS

He is mad about being small when you were big, but no, that's not it, he is mad about being helpless when you were powerful, but no, not that either, he is mad about being contingent when you were necessary, not quite it, he is insane because when he loved you, you didn't notice.

—Donald Barthelme, *The Dead Father*

The largest proportion of Participants in the study were men with male analysts. They were also the subgroup whose analyses showed the greatest upheavals in degree of retrospective satisfaction according to the decade in which it took place. In particular, during the decade 1965–1975, a tough and belittling stance on the part of the analyst, combined with hardly ambiguous proscriptions about what it took to be manly, was dominant. Wishes for loving closeness with the analyst, erotic or otherwise, were generally regarded as a defensive part of the negative Oedipus complex, to be interpreted away rather than protected or made safe. Frequently such wishes were either crushed or became one more arena in a struggle for power and dominance. In the words of **Dr. Jay Glenn,** "What happened is that his requirement to submit to his intensive assaults got sexualized, and that's where the power issue had to be fought out."

Because of the negative reception of erotic longings toward the analyst, it is not possible to estimate how such desires might have been sustained within a different affective context. In later decades, however, a significant shift in emotional ambience was notable in men with male analysts. Male Participants were then able to benefit profoundly from a respected sense of emotional closeness to the analyst. Within the sample, homosexual wishes and fantasies were most often described as an aspect of yearnings for a father rather than lover. Two Participants recalled the not-uncommon fantasy of being penetrated by their analyst's hard penis from behind in order to strengthen their own penis enough to be able to deal with difficult women. Other homosexual fantasies were described as a medium for desired emotional closeness to the analyst.

How aggression was metabolized within the dyad was another crux. Some encouragement for aggressive sparring, sometimes reciprocal, but not retaliatory, tended to be experienced as liberating, as invigorating the analyses. But forceful domination or hostile aggression from the analyst had the opposite effect. Interestingly, several men who felt they suffered from internalizing what they experienced as the analyst's expectations, identified this in retrospect as a mother rather than a father transference, unrecognized as such during the analysis.

Men analyzed by men in recent decades were more likely to find their analyses satisfying, ultimately feeling valued for themselves in ways that nurtured the kind autonomy that is not based on counter-dependent models of maleness, but cohabits with a sense of choice about individuality in connection.

In no other gender combination were the contrasts in approach between earlier and later decades so stark, although there were some exceptions. In trying to understand these shifts, it is difficult to assess the relative weights of turmoil within the Institute, effects of the women's movement on increasing the flexibility of identifications in men, with some relenting of homophobia, and the progressive trend toward replacing authoritarian with more egalitarian structures in training.

The opportunity lost when the candidate's analyst is not experienced as enabling is major. Ross (1998) pictures the fate of young analysts who are "entrenched in a posture that we might deem 'aim-inhibited negative Oedipal submission,' reinforced in the training analysis, and destined to continue in reality for years beyond termination." At a meeting of the American Psychoanalytic Association, Peter Blos Sr. spoke, on the cuff, of accepting his own analyst's interpretation of his negative Oedipus complex, with its passive homosexual longings to be mastered by being renounced. He wondered wistfully how his life might have been affected if there had been analysis of the progressive (rather than regressive) dyadic isogender relationship, of which he had been deprived. Blos revised his own theorizing (1985), convinced that "The early experience of being protected by a strong father and caringly loved by him becomes internalized as a lifelong sense of safety in a Boschian world of horrors and dangers," and establishes "a libidinal bond of a profound and lasting kind." In adolescence the boy needs a "blessing" conferred by the father. Blos asserted the value of reaching such layers of longings at their affective source in analysis, as well as affirmation of being "grown," now one's own man. Herzog (2001), too, writes movingly about the deep reach of father hunger, as it emerges in the transference and becomes transformed in his patients' experience of him.

Freud's love of his father, often underrated, has been recently reemphasized by Kerr (2002). He also struggled with disappointment in his father, disappointment memorialized in episodes recorded in the dreambook. However he dealt with his feelings about his father, it was not easy for Freud to accept some of his patient's desires. He blamed Ferenczi's "homosexual libido" toward him for much of their eventually tragic alienation. Ferenczi for a time advocated healing through the enactment of affection and was not able to work through either his love or his hate for his analyst. But, as Hoffer (1991) noted, he "had a specific notion of what had to happen before termination could occur." Just before his final meeting with Freud, Ferenczi writes in his diary: "Finally it is also possible to view and remember the trauma with feelings of forgiveness and consequently understanding. The analyst who is forgiven enjoys in the analysis what was denied him in life and hardened his heart. Mutual forgiveness!!" In this way Ferenczi opines that the analyst also seeks restitution for having had to harden his heart.

An ongoing but developmentally changing tension exists between a man's yearnings to be influenced, empowered, infused, and inspired by a man and the need to develop his individuality, to cast off dominating influences, to be "one's own man" (Levinson et al, 1978). Do the pleasures of opening oneself to being inspired inevitably clash with self-respecting autonomy—or not? Ross (1998) notes the problems inherent in the transmission of sadomasochism in authoritarian Institutes and pinpoints the costs of "surrender of power" and "independence of mind and the unconscious sadomasochistic homo-incestuous fantasies that lurk beneath it all." He suggests "moral sadism" rationalized as rigor "was one solution" for Institutes: "The course of least resistance was to enact disavowed identifications with the aggressor and to make the next generation suffer as the previous one had done." Within the research sample, however, those Participants who had suffered in authoritarian (rather than authoritative) analyses, did not seem to transmit these relational templates to their own analysands.

So how were sadomasochistic identifications with authoritarian analysts transformed? In a spectrum of ways. I believe these include, when painful attempts at forgiveness or understanding (à la Ferenczi with Freud) wore thin, the forceful annulment of empathy for the analyst who has wounded by withholding his own. Banishing empathy is preparation for eventually evicting a noxious introject. For the male training analyst, perhaps the wish to immortalize the self through theory or like-minded candidates may be especially piquant in lieu of more direct opportunity for birthing. A Pygmalion countertransference can be intensely magnetic for both members of the dyad. I believe it important, however, that we not invent a new ideal of casting out "influence" in our commitment to egalitarianism, becoming allergic to the longing for inspiration. That could lead to sterile scotoma about opening oneself to the emotional power of what the analyst offers.

I now turn to some examples of the kinds of desires expressed by male Participants toward their male analysts. These will be followed by more detailed narratives of two Participants, exemplifying the two patterns between men I have described.

Dr. Stuart Laraphil clarifies some functions of sexual fantasies about the first male analyst (**dissatisfying analysis**) and the wish for strengthening love from the second (**deeply satisfying analysis**). He elaborates the fantasy that "the primary incorporative act" of taking in knowledge from a man involves taking on his power, and comments, "but, that particular take on it is a boy's concern about the power of the phallus."

LT: In sexual fantasies about the analyst, is there also a matter of taking on his power?

SL: All the time. Yes. That was clearly what went on with me and my first analyst in my fantasies of taking on some power of his that I imagined he had, and part of my ambivalence about what seemed like his sternness, because it seemed like power, too.

LT: Power and withholding it?

SL: Yeah, ironically the withholding itself becomes a signifier of power. He was younger, more virile, more competitive seeming [than the second analyst]. There were more competitive wishes and homosexual feelings and images that had a sexual cast that spoke to that issue of power.

LT: How did he treat those wishes?

SL: I don't have a separate sense of those from what I felt of his overall attitude, which was not one of respectfully welcoming and valuing what was positive in whatever you discover in me, but more finding it out and exposing it to me. And, so the—the sexual longings that are part of tenderness end up getting channeled instead, in part for this reason, through aggressiveness. We're denied.

In contrast, with the second analyst:

SL: The libidinal issues that I'm aware of had to do with wishing to be loved rather than more sexualized versions. And some jealousy about whom he preferred. When I got angry he didn't retaliate, didn't hit back. It's judo. He's not there. Instead, he finds a question to turn back to me.
LT: That sounds like a loving boomerang; he turned it around to come back to you.
SL: Right. It was a loving boomerang. Just that. I sort of enjoyed it. I didn't find out whether he loved me or Jeff [analytic sibling] better, either. The subsidiary motives in the whole thing weren't satisfied, which was satisfying, because I didn't really want him to tell me. I wanted him to be strong enough not to. 'Cause it meant that he would be firm enough to be a good father. It's what boys want. I think they want a father who they see as strong and not able to be manipulated by the kids, so the kid feels safe, but on the other hand not punitive— to address the problem of what do you do when you're a young man and your father's castrated? How do you grow up to be a man if you've got a castrated father?

Dr. David Lawrence (moderately satisfying analysis) also alludes to the wish to be loved like a son by the analyst.

DL: I really wished that somehow we could have eventually been pals in some intergenerational way. I really would have liked that. During the analysis, I really longed for him to love me.
LT: Why were you ashamed, like you said, making it so hard to tell him about the wishes for love?
DL: Because I remember all those wonderings, whether they really meant anything to him. Never really talked about or acknowledged from his end, but when I was talking about a first control and a second control, I let him know I had a lot of feelings for my patients. They were very important in my life.
LT: You were also saying, "Do you have a lot of feelings for me"?
DL: Yeah. And in the oblique he said, "Well, it's not surprising that

your analytic patients would have a lot of importance in your life. You spend a lot of time with them." And that was about the closest. So I took that somehow he would have feelings.

LT: When you wanted him to love you, did you have physical wishes to be intimate with him, or . . . ?

DL: No. I wished I were his son. And I guess he coulda hugged me as my dad.

Dr. Steven Zeller (deeply satisfying analysis) felt that his analyst recognized his readiness to appreciate him as father figure.

SZ: I felt that this was the genuine article. I can't imagine he would-n't pick up at some level that I was primed to appreciate and idealize a father figure that I needed and wanted to be just like that, to tell me how the world works, to let me tell you about me and tell me if it's okay. It was all there, right from the start. Sort of father–son stuff.

Dr. Cecco Angiolieri (moderately satisfying analysis) alludes to a brief homosexual panic which occurred at the very beginning of his first analysis. The analyst's intervention was experienced as helpful without derailing analytic process, and the panic did not recur.

CA: One incident was, the first time I lay down on the couch, I had a panic attack. I didn't know what the hell hit me, because this was nothing I had ever experienced before or after. Then he had me sit up for some minutes until I got some sense of what this was about, to put it bluntly, at the back of it was the fear of a homosexual attack. And, I don't know, various things having to do with my relationship with powerful men in my childhood and so on, came on to work and finally I said okay, I'm ready. So I'd see him four or five times a week sitting up, and then I lay down and continued without anything like that.

LT: During that early period, did you experience him as helpful in how he responded to your being in that panic?

CA: Yeah, he said, "sit up," and that's all. I don't remember what his phrase was, but the idea was, if you can't hack it this way, sit up and we'll talk. It wasn't a question of feeling safe with him because I needed to be safe with myself. The issue didn't have to do with him; it was all my own stuff. And we continued this way in perfectly analytical fash-ion even when we were face to face. He wasn't providing a reassurance or pretense at support or the like, he just said this is the way we'll do it, and we did, and when I was settling, I said it was okay. And we con-tinued with the analysis. My initial reaction to him was, he seemed to know his business and he is not going to do me any harm, so what the hell? I told a friend of mine who asked me what I got out of my first analysis, "I learned to open my mouth and talk."

The second analysis (**deeply satisfying analysis**) was, however, more emotionally powerful. **Dr. Angiolieri** viewed the analyst as having more status in the Institute. He mentioned, "I made a point of not going to someone who was a training analyst with the first, and with the wisdom of hindsight, it was quite clear that I thought I wasn't ready to deal with somebody who was "the big man." **Cecco** discovered that the "big man," unlike what had been dared with his father, could take an attack in sparring stride and without retaliation.

CA: Just being able to make that remark took me four years, because I was very polite, but then I said to him, "You're a dirty old Jew," and his answer was, "I might be an old Jew, but I'm not dirty." (Laughs heartily.) It seemed like he never missed a beat, stood up for himself but didn't attack me. Another time he told me I must be disappointed in him "because I don't have breasts like Dr. X [female analyst]," in that he wasn't going to suckle me the way I fantasized she would, and that was perfectly correct. Apropos my father, I admired my analyst's sense of humor, he had a way of making comments or interpretations which weren't funny, that wasn't the point, but they were expressed in the way that had a certain intrinsic wit, not to make fun of me, but to put things in a perspective, so you looked at yourself sort of differently and the consequences in which you put it, in a way in which was warming—that was some times. Apropos funny remarks, when I was talking about transference, he made the remark "Ve vill see if you vill start to imitate my accent" (laughter from both). I never found myself doing that. But I did find myself phrasing things in ways that he might—that I became aware of. I didn't feel that it was something I was stealing or imposing on myself or pretending.
LT: You could sort of freely take what you wanted and what fit, and you could leave the accent to him?
CA: Yeah. (Laughter.) I never felt toward him literally as though he were my good father versus my bad father, it wasn't any of that kind of stuff, at least as I remember, and as I gave up my worshipful attitude toward these people who were seen as prestigious in authority and the like, I guess I went from sort of a deferential fear to not being either deferential or fearful.

Dr. Seymour Sonenshein (deeply satisfying analysis), as most of the men with male analysts, preferred direct, affectively pungent input by the analyst compared with "neutral silence," which tended to be experienced as emotional absence. The latter frequently echoed childhood adaptations of needing to value competence over emotional life or need. By use of "jokes," his first analyst makes a direct, palatable interpretation about surmised aggression that underlay doubt:

SS: I seem to remember most of the interpretations being in the form of jokes in one sort or the other. I remember one joke, for example, that followed after I mentioned that a casual friend approached me for a loan for some money and my dilemma about whether to give it, my inclination being to give the money but having all kinds of doubts about it. The analyst said, "there's a story about this prominent actor who comes out after the performance and there's a beggar there and he wants some money. He says, 'Please can you give me a loan.' And the actor says, 'Look, let's be enemies right from the beginning!'" (Laughing.) But it was that kind of directness, that kind of sharing that you remember. It's interesting the things you remember. I tend to think that it's the personal qualities of the analyst which are the most meaningful and memorable when it's all said and done.

He contrasts this approach with that of the second, the training analyst (**moderately satisfying analysis**).

SS: He might not make an interpretation or even an intervention for a month, maybe even two months of sessions. Really. It's not that I wasn't going on. I was doing all kinds of work and making connections and making interpretations myself. So you could say he didn't have to, that I can work that way. It has given me the ability to be silent and to feel that it's all right as one of the ways of being with a patient. He would do a lot with just breathing or saying "aha" or just being there.

LT: You also said earlier that you could rely on yourself to cope with some traumatic things that had happened in your life and you managed well. But that wasn't your first choice. You had to do that. And I wonder whether it put you in the same spot, abandoned again.

SS: Right. And I think that was something of the feeling as though, okay, I suffered for my competence, that because I could do that it's as though he didn't have to say more. So, in a sense, I feel I missed out on something, a certain way in which it would have been helpful to get a little more than his sparseness.

Dr. Bob White (moderately satisfying analysis) expands his understanding of his first, too silent, analyst, by reflecting on the usual analytic approach to his generation of candidates in the 1960s and early 1970s.

BW: The way that my first analyst changed for me over the years was that I became very clear about what I didn't get and how deprived I felt, so that when it came time to think about a training analysis for quite a while I was not about to sign up for another analysis, where I would be so alone. And the way I think about it now, less critically, is that I think about that whole time, that whole generation of analysts who were taught that procrustean method in analysis, that if you could, you tried to squeeze everybody possible into the process of doing as much as they could themselves.

Dr. Gary Thomas, (first analysis moderately satisfying, second analysis deeply satisfying) emphasizes the importance of the analyst's combining directness in presence with holding the analysand in mind.

GT: My first analysis went decently. It seemed clear that this was a competent guy. But as a person, I didn't have any feeling of connection with him. And that would have made a difference. My second analyst was totally different. He was a very warm, very generous, outgoing guy. He's a boy from a tough town, smart, no bullshitter, really an iconoclast; he could fight with the Institute when he needed to. But there was a certain directness with that toughness. You call a spade a spade and you don't mess around and you go for it. And his kids were known to be nice kids. He was very much a family person. He was at odds with the establishment of the Institute. And in that respect I think I would have been at odds with the Institute, too, at that time. But I wasn't in a position to be at odds. I didn't know enough to be at odds.
LT: Is there an example of his calling a spade a spade?
GT: Several. At one of the Institute parties, he met my wife and shook hands and exchanged some words and stuff. And the next time I saw him, he said "I've been listening to your descriptions of your wife as borderline, and the woman I met had no resemblance." (Laughs.) I'm sure at some level I felt relieved. He was quite sure of himself. That's another attribute of his. But I think he was right, actually. That was, in effect, saying, "There's something going on. Let's really pay some attention."

Another thing I remember is at some later part of the analysis, probably when he was getting impatient with my not moving on in some direction, he said "There are times in life when we all have to do the equivalent of taking our balls in our hands, close our eyes, and just jump." (Laughs.) And that really stayed with me. I'm not sure it's empowered me, but it was facilitating in some way. It captured something that was very important to me. And it's amazing that these kinds of comments are still resonating. It was both encouraging, we both recognized that there was a change, but he was saying, "You could do more," which recognizes some potential. What was powerful for me had more to do with looking at—it isn't as though I was not thinking about transference, or that he would not comment or raise questions about it—but it seemed to me that what was much more vital and meaningful had to do with making sense of what I was doing with important people in my life. And that was extraordinarily helpful. And not just in how to deal with a person, but that he was very, very good at making connections, at pointing out themes, in ways that did not seem remote, did not seem intellectual, but seemed very present. 'Cause that was his style. He wasn't just talking theory, he was talking about, "You said this at this time and you did this, and that reminds me of that, and what other thoughts do you have about that?" And certainly he would say, "And, that reminds me of this with us," and it seemed to be part of the package, but not the keystone.

Like a number of the men, in childhood **Dr. Gary Thomas** had felt more responsibility for his mother's care than care from her. He does not recall being held by his mother, but felt held in the mind of the analyst.

GT: I don't have a recollection of my being cared for. I've thought about it a lot, of course. I had to in some way be caretaking of my mother, even as a little kid, or I got the message about "Don't make demands on me. My hands are full," which they were. "All of you gotta help me out." Which everyone did, including my dad. So I don't remember her being depressed, but neither do I remember, well, being held by her, actually.

I think what felt most sustaining with my second analyst was that I really felt that he cared about me. He was good for me because he was attentive, he put things together, and he was certainly smart, but not in an elegant sort of way. There are lots of smart people. But I got the feeling that he was really there each time. And remembered. I don't mean perfect memory.

LT: But held you in mind?

GT: Held me in mind. Clearly.

LT: Were there longings for him after termination, longings to see him or . . . ?

GT: Yeah, I did certainly, want to, but it didn't seem feasible or possible or kosher or . . . I think it would have been no problem for him if I called.

LT: If you could have chosen, who would you have wanted to be to him, his kid, his wife, his . . . ?

GT: Who would I want to be? His younger brother!

Dr. Harold Koestner (deeply satisfying analysis) describes his own constraints in curiosity, assuming his familiar position as "outsider," almost as though he did not feel entitled to wanting "more."

HK: I wonder how much my not inquiring about certain things or even being more curious was my almost being overly comfortable in that position. I get something out of it, but I pay a cost, too. Did I miss something? I remember someone saying to me that she thought she had missed something in her analysis if she didn't talk dirty sufficiently. But I wondered whether I might have missed something by not being more actively curious. It came up. I was asked whether I was curious. I tried to deal with it at the time but didn't get very far with it, but that has something to do, perhaps, with how deeply settled into an outsider position I became. Erik Erikson once talked about meeting his analyst, Anna Freud, at the beach, both in bathing suits. But the language remained absolutely formal, and they would still say Herr Doctor, Frau Doctor and so on at the beach (both laugh), everything short of a salute, and so it's probably a matter of balance. Certain things have to be contained and the container has to be there and I think a big significant part of my wish for more has to do with the probably renewed, renewable sadness of accepting that that's the way it was about my own past, and while it's much more laid to rest than it used to be, it's not entirely so, and I'm sure every time I wanted more or even a more expressive face, partly what I was trying to do was to recoup the past, instead of to come to terms with it.

I was very unthoughtful about some of these things, or unmindful of them. Something of that carried over into the relationship with my analyst. Why spoil a good thing? I didn't know what was going on in those rooms [the rooms in his analyst's house]—well, that's okay. Had I actually seen through the window, what would I have learned? Should I? Did I have some curiosity? Yes. Did I give it much play? No.

I hoped that he had warm and fatherly feelings toward me. But I didn't spin the fantasy. I think I can restrict a lot of that. But I know there's a sense of ongoing connection. [He gives an example in which the analyst stated that **Harold** was not a narcissist, and another in which the analyst conveyed that **Harold's** girlfriend had reason to appreciate him.] I know those incidents felt good when they occurred. They wouldn't have unless I had already had in me a yearning for them.

During the time between the late 1970s and mid-1990s, analysts were much more apt to be experienced as emotionally present, receptive to affect and impulse in nonpunitive ways than analysts had been in the decades before. By this time, more theories of analysis, couched in two-person terms (Balint, 1968; Gill, 1984; Modell, 1984), assumed that both members of the analytic dyad contribute to the affective context within which a deepening of analytic work could be part of the yield. There were no indications that these analyses were "watered down" nor that "relationship" replaced interpretive work, nor that negative transference was held at bay by the analyst's communications about the positive potential in the analysand.

Dr. John Deere (Deeply Satisfying Analysis) exemplifies the emotional ambiance in which a collaborative spirit of discovery could emerge. Having grown up in a family deserted by his father, he had little support for metabolizing his own and his mother's resentment or for recognizing the deprivations inevitable with his father not "being there." When in adulthood he finally sought out the absent father, there was further reason for disappointment. His narrative highlights the emotional power of his analyst's ways of "being there with me" and the importance of how he felt he was viewed in the mind's eye of the analyst.

JD: His style was not so much to be active, but to intervene in appropriate ways at appropriate times. And so, my sense of the whole analysis was that he was there with me. I felt he was with me and very helpful in my learning something about myself and about life, for me. Like when I thought I had no choice in that decision about the Institute, and he said, "Whose analysis is this? Whose training is this?" Those kinds of things began a process for me that was immensely valuable.
LT: Did something you experienced with him make that possible?
JD: Letting me be there. That creating a space in which I felt safe.

And felt understood. And felt that I learned something about being an analyst, which doesn't always work with patients—but when it works, it works well—that really is a mutual exploration for a lot of speculation and a lot of tentative approaches. He could say something to me, and I could hear and disagree, or hear it and take it in and say I don't know, and then see where it went. What it stirred in me, where my associations went, and whether in the long run it turned out to be accurate or not. Wasn't a pissing contest, it was really a collaboration.

My recurrent experience with him was that there was a warmth and a sharing around a lot of things that kept coming up in small ways. He was always part of the process between us. That made me feel comfortable. Whether he sensed that I needed that or that's just how he was with everyone, I have no idea. But for me it worked. The ways in which he was present, where sharing my life was the vehicle by which the process took place. As well as being the result of the process. It was reciprocal in an intertwined and complicated way. The telling my story was a way of allowing me into the space and allowing me to make use of the thing in the ways in which he could communicate, which then allowed me to look at my story integrated from a different perspective.

And he was not averse to saying something about his own reactions; it was a way of his sharing something, which appropriately and constructively was helpful about himself and his experience. His view of what would be helpful, what was appropriate, was rather liberating to me, in terms of my education as an analyst, as well as being useful technically in finding myself and getting to know myself. He could allow himself to be there and to share some of his experience with me. The experience of me with me, how I was affecting him, in very useful ways. I think that there were a lot of ways, and this was surprising to me, in which he approved of me. I mean he thought I was okay. And, he thought that my view of myself was not accurate and would challenge it. And why I felt certain ways . . .

LT: So the challenging was something that was on your side?
JD: Yeah, confronting me in a way completely friendly [way]. Why did I hold on to this view of myself? Why did I hold on to this interpretation of events? He wasn't shy about saying that I really behaved horribly in a situation. Or challenge it, especially relationships within my family, my mother. What was going on for me, why I was doing what I was doing? So, I felt an alliance. I felt he was on my side. I felt

validated by him. I really did feel that he thought that I was a competent, decent person. That helped me get more in touch with being able.

John recalls the burgeoning sense of being effective in pursuing what he wanted:

JD: I came in one day, and he said, "My schedule is changing. I don't think I'm going to be able to do five days a week." And I felt angry, and I told him I was angry. I said, "That's not what I signed on for. I signed up for five days a week. This feels right to me. And I really want this. And I'm really pissed." I had never said that to him as directly, and ultimately we worked out a schedule. I said I was willing to move my schedule around in whatever way was necessary to continue that. And so that was the first time. I felt very pleased; it was exciting.
LT: Not only you let him know you were pissed, but you also had an effect.
JD: Yes. That I could be effective. I could speak up for what I wanted.

Dr. Deere described how inadequate and vulnerable to the analyst's disapproval he had felt at the beginning of the analysis. He feared that either the analyst or analysand "would see who I was and would not be able to stand it." He felt the sense of inadequacy changing during the course of the analysis, as he progressively experienced the analyst as accepting, validating, and also challenging. Increasingly, he experienced himself as "a valued and valuable person."

JD: Seeing him at the Institute, hearing him talk, hearing him involved in various things, I saw another side of him. I think he enjoyed being competitive and aggressive and winning. (Laughs.) I think I appreciated that. And he could be challenging in the analysis, with an edge to it, but, mostly wasn't and, I could talk about how that made me feel. Mostly he was not aggressive. I never felt he was hostile in any way. I don't know if he got aggressive in a hostile way. I don't know what he was like in a real fight. I never saw that.
LT: You talked about having had some homosexual dreams. I don't know whether, in talking about those, you felt them as homosexual or wishes to have something from him or whether you felt it as a part of loving him in some way?
JD: It had to do with being close. It had to do with doing something for him, having him do something for me. And being mutually excited. About having a close, intimate relationship with him. It also had to

do with power. I had a wish to be close. Be reciprocal. Not so much to be his analyst. But to be his friend. And to be caring. To be on intimate terms in that way of sharing. To want that with someone, very much so. I think that's something I inflict on my kids! Wanting to know what they're thinking, what they're doing, why they're deciding what they're deciding. My son has gotten much better at confronting me on it (laughter) and also not feeling so intruded upon. When he wants to, he'll tell me to pack off. I'm very mindful of that. Wanting that kind of closeness and connection with them. Yes, I felt it about my analyst.

And there was a kind of honesty; there was no bullshit in the room. I never felt we were in a power struggle. I felt that it was a genuine collaboration, that he was curious about me. I was curious about him. That he saw me in ways that I couldn't see me. That was helpful. That was a primary ingredient of my analytic experience, and I think that I try to do that with my own patients.

For the reader who would like to follow **Dr. Deere** through termination, further excerpts appear in the chapters, "In the Mind's Eye," "Mourning," and "The Analyst Imagined."

The following narrative illuminates some of the features that characterized the small but troubling proportion of unsatisfying analyses of male Participants with male analysts during the 1960s and early 1970s. The analyst was assumed to have power to expose the truth according to theory and to use it (within the reporting Institute) with real consequences for the career progression of the candidate. Too often, these candidates felt shamed for not being how the analyst wanted them to be. The wish for attachment tended to be pathologized. Five different training analysts are reported in this sample as berating the candidate for his "narcissism," four as chiding him about emotionality (e.g., with sarcasm about "crocodile tears"). The aura of disapproval was more confusing in those cases in which the candidate was aware of the analyst's intensity of involvement in the analysis. In one case, the candidate's longings toward the analyst were simultaneously hidden and amplified as part of a sadomasochistic pattern in which the analysand become increasingly compliant and idealizing and did not rock the boat but at high psychic cost. In other cases, the frustrated longings spurred individuation from the analyst, while leaving the analysand to accrue selfhood within. Insightful about what they had experienced, these analysts report subsequently relying more on empathy than exhortation in their approach with their own analysands.

I exemplify with excerpts from the narrative of **Dr. Jay Glenn.**

Dr. Jay Glenn became aware of forging his own identity as analyst to contrast with his analyst's. He had experienced his analyst as not only wielding actual power over the pace of progression of his training, but also in assaulting **Jay**'s self-esteem with a barrage of interpretations about ways in which he "fell short," was "overemotional" for a man, and was only possibly qualified to become an analyst. "He didn't think much of me and convinced me I was somewhere on the lower rungs of capacity and character, compared to other candidates."

JG: What happened is that his requirement to submit to his intensive assaults got sexualized. That's where the power issue had to be fought out. To make a point, he would pound his chair so hard that I had this intensive physical transference feeling that he was going to hit me on the head with an elongated object. If I told him, he would then accuse me of just devaluing him or projecting. He advised me, "You will find that I am a good figure for identification," but I know that my response inside was, "Not on your life!"

Still, **Dr. Glenn** felt grateful for learning about "oedipal conflict, defense and dream interpretation" and the productive self-analysis "that never ends." He was more grateful, however, for a friendship with an analytic sibling, Mark, with whom "giving each other our views" of the analyses over many years helped in untangling how the training analyst's conflicts had impinged on their own. "It turned out that he had had the identical fantasy—about being hit!"

JG: The years I was working it through with Mark, I had intense inner dialogues with my analyst in which I was really going over the ground repeatedly. *He* wasn't saying anything different. But I think I was expressing myself increasingly clearly. I realize *working through* was not the right term. It had to be living through and resolving. Thrashing over that inner presence—which wasn't all transference— a lot of it was relationship. In fact, that's what it *was*. Then Mark and my sharing our experience postanalytically was very important, working out the negative aspects of the dyad really did require . . . I don't think I could have done it by myself . . . it was too intense. But it hasn't occurred for a long time. I easily bring him back to mind with a certain vividness, but I don't feel him as a presence or what *he* might say doesn't come up, so it's a very clear and vivid memory but not an active presence. I guess that's interesting. In defining an introject as an inner presence that has its own behavior toward you, seemingly, that's at least how it's experienced, I would say he faded from being an introject to a memory. . . . You see, I couldn't keep my analyst as introject and have my full self, because I couldn't develop a level of confidence and self-liking that I think is appropriate to me, and have him active in my inner world. There is still a modicum of residual sadness that it couldn't be otherwise. But with that came my determination never to do that to anybody myself—what I care about is people developing into themselves, to work with what is negative and blocks, absolutely, but also with what there is to grow. I wish he could have known me. But he couldn't. That is, he could've known a lot. That's another thing that contributes to my own work. It's is so extremely important for any patient to know that you know them. And that you know them in the ways they are already developed, in the ways they potentially can develop, in the ways they are in trouble. The whole thing, known, because . . . we're an investment in their life. So I think that's a residual sadness. But like my mother, he is now more a memory and less a power.

During **Dr. Glenn's** interviews (30 some years after the analysis), the insight emerged that it had been his mother transference of being inadequate to fulfill the size of her ambitions that had been constantly reinforced through his analyst's communications, unacknowledged and unanalyzed. Meanwhile, the analyst had forcefully enacted (and verbalized) his theory that, as father figure, his cutting **Dr. Glenn** down to size in oedipal competition would do the analysand good. I said I was astounded and asked how he'd done it—preserved the good stuff and made the rest be "history."

JG: You gain what you can, while *not* getting into . . . my analyst often spoke of confrontation as *the* technique to deal with narcissism, which justified, in his mind, a very intense kind of hostile way he went about things. It left me to take the content that is meaningful but not identify with, or really succumb to, that very hostile confrontation. I think if I had not had my father, it would have been very different. One of my friends did not have a very good father and had to identify with my analyst markedly. That was part of what saved me. I had a better relationship with my father. So, I could give up on my analyst and keep my dad.

Several features of **Dr. Glenn's** narrative underline his resources in withstanding the analyst's influence on his own analytic functioning. He had stressed having entered analysis with a strong positive identification (although not conflict free) with his own father, which continued to sustain him through the analysis. Second, he was able to draw on the connection with the analytic sibling to work out the kind of individuation from his analyst that the analytic process did not bear. Third, his own nature stood him in good stead.

MEN WITH FEMALE ANALYSTS

She is a friend of my mind. She gather me, man. The pieces I am, she gather them and give them back to me in all the right order. It's good, when you got a woman who is a friend of your mind.

—Toni Morrison, *Beloved*

Beware! Beware!

His flashing eyes, his floating hair!

Weave a circle round him thrice,

And close your eyes with holy dread,

For he on honey-dew hath fed,

And drunk the milk of Paradise.

—Samuel Taylor Coleridge, "Kubla Kahn: A Dream Poem"

Male Participants were less apt to be analyzed by a woman than by a man. The proportion of women analysts at The Boston Psychoanalytic Institute was relatively small, as it was in the rest of the country. With the increasing number of women trained in recent decades as psychoanalysts, these proportions have already begun to shift and, judging by the proportion of women in the current population of analytic candidates, will shift further in the future. With one exception, the female analysts described in the sample were at least 25 years older than their analysands, some in their 70s when the analysis began. Insofar as age may affect the transference constellation, this subgroup differed notably from women with male analysts, some of whom were much closer in age.

The men's analyses with women analysts were most often good experiences. Four of six of the men with women training analysts were deeply satisfied, two moderately satisfied, none dissatisfied. Including nontraining analyses, five of nine were deeply satisfied, two were moderately satisfied, and two dissatisfied. Because the total sample is only six training analyses and nine analyses total, the numbers are only suggestive.

None of the men reported a sustained passionate erotic transference, either sexually or in the form of feeling "in love," although flickering romantic fantasies, like waltzing with the analyst, did occur. When asked after directly in the interview (in the absence of spontaneous mention), recalled erotic fantasies might be described by Participants as "slight" or indirectly "inferred." Interestingly, such references were apt to include a quick association to, or fantasy about, the husband or another man in the analyst's life. This was unlike those women with male analysts who dwelt at length on their immersion in feeling overwhelming love and desire for their analysts. Nor did any man describe painful waves of longing for the analyst in the years after termination. Several men explicitly identified age as a factor that shaped transference: "She was too old, and somewhat crippled. I never saw her as sexual being." In some instances, there were also references to not engaging in battle with the analyst.

None of the men spoke of experiencing a period of "paternal transference" toward their female analysts, although one Participant referred to attributing "super-ego" functions to her. In this way, there was also asymmetry with women Participants, several of whom initiated discussions of their "maternal transference" to their male analysts.

The men did, however, allude freely to a variety of "maternal" transferences infusing the analysis. The analysts (like their male counterparts) were viewed as powerful in their potentially critical judgment, as well as in various facets of their competence and "wisdom." They were portrayed with very active rather than passive "maternal" functions, operative in the service of the analysand's interest and supporting rather than controlling his autonomy. Simultaneously, they were viewed as empathetically receptive. Several men had in common the following perceptions: The analyst was experienced, in contrast to the mother of their childhood in important ways. Becoming aware of what the inner presence of the analyst meant occurred over a long span of time. For example, **Mozes Nounous** comments that increasingly, 30 years after the analysis, now that he is closer in age to what she was, he is aware of how identified he is with some of her traits; **Saul Green** gained a permanent sense, active 50 years posttermination, of having had a loving mother. **Harold Miller**, 40 years after the analysis, felt a new wave of appreciation for his analyst's undogmatic interest in his point of view, in contrast to a more recent encounter with a "dogmatic" analyst. Finally, several men spontaneously described, as a yield of their analysis, the "transfer" of their positive feelings about the analyst to an improved relationship with another important woman in their lives; the transference template was enacted in a positive way outside the analysis, as the analysand "moved on" from his attachment to the analyst.

A question remains about whether the transference constellations, as experienced, remained protective of more risky, deeper layers of vulnerability associated with sustained erotic desire toward a female analyst. If so, a further question remains about whether the pursuit of such levels, if reachable, would have been of further benefit or not. Because a number of the analyses were experienced as profoundly transformative (although each person identified some limit or omission, as did all Participants who were deeply satisfied), there can be no preemptive assumption.

The range of desires experienced by men with female analysts has been debated for some time. Lester (1985) reported that in her practice, she found "only mild, transient, muted, and unstable erotic transferences from male patients." Person (1985, p. 284) posited that the erotic transference utilized as resistance is more common in women in analysis, whereas resistance to the awareness of the erotic transference is more common among male patients. Kulish (1989) interviewed 17 senior female analysts. A few "described experiences with male patients who had strongly erotic transferences toward them" (p. 67), but most said they had not seen such cases.

Goldberger and Evans challenged the assumption that male patients do not develop strong erotic transferences to female analysts and provided an "update" on their own earlier findings (Goldberger and Holmes, 1993): "With regard to the erotic transference in the male patient–female analyst dyad, we believe that the findings reported previously—that is, that male patients display an entire spectrum of erotic transference phenomena with their female analysts, ranging from the very constricted to the intense and florid—have been amply supported by data from other analysts" (p. 186). Since that time, there have been numerous published reports of erotic transference in men (Gornick, 1986; Meyers, 1986; Davies, 1994, 1998; Tessman, 2001).

It is not surprising that a man's erotic feelings toward a female analyst might have a different form and function than a woman's for a male analyst. For both, cross-gender transferences distill a foray into dealing with otherness. Nonetheless, because usually the first caretaker for both boys and girls is still a woman, the male analysand with a female analyst is confronted with the regressive templates of his first relationship, whereas a female analysand with a male analyst can experience her separateness from mother in her feelings toward the man. A wish for emotional merging with mother may derail the gender identity he has set into motion. Incest between mother and son may be abhorred more vehemently than that between father and daughter. These differences are reflected in the kinds of formulations about the dynamics of male desires with female analysts that have been put forth.

It has been noted that female patients in treatment with male analysts tend to work backward developmentally from oedipal to preoedipal issues (Liebert, 1986), whereas male patients in treatment with female analysts tend to recapitulate the developmental process, plunging directly into the preoedipal maternal transference with erotically based oedipal and paternal transferences emerging relatively late in the treatment and then in attenuated form. Diamond (1993) suggests that erotic oedipal transference requires the differentiating force of paternal transference. The Participants seemed to provide such a force themselves (in the absence of feeling "paternal transference") when inquiry into erotic feelings toward their analysts produced rapid associations to a man in her life.

Karme (1993) suggests that

> the oedipal erotic transferences, and the defenses against them, may pose particularly difficult problems for the female analyst. The male patient's feelings of shame and humiliation often mobilize in the female analyst, as in a good mother, the need to protect his masculine ego. She may therefore readily support his need to suppress his sexual feelings, especially if she feels directly responsible for them. Guilt over perceiving herself as provocative, a seducer, is another common countertransference problem. This guilt may be compounded with erotic countertransference feelings, which can lead to embarrassment and confusion, mobilize images of the incestuous mother, and evoke in her feelings of repulsion, disgust, and anger. On the other hand, to counter their fear of vulnerability

and passive dependency, male patients may become hostile or
subtly threatening. . . . Desexualizing the analyst or debasing
her as a sexual object is another defense male patients employ
to gain control and power [p. 192].

To assess therapists' awareness and flexibility in responding to gendered transferences, Kulish and Mayman (1993) studied the transference experience in 47 supervised long-term therapies. They observe
that "male therapists apparently are more likely to be drawn into
paternal transferences, but they are also more able to see themselves
as maternal objects than are female therapists able to see themselves
as paternal objects. Female therapists are less prone to accept male
role transference than male therapists are to accept a female role transference" (p. 301).

Undoubtedly, both the female analysts and their male analysands,
who were Participants in the study, were prone to be self-protective
about erotic transference and countertransference stirrings in the
diverse ways suggested by these theorists. I must note, however, that
the Participants felt satisfied, and deeply, respectfully engaged by the
analyst around the issues they brought to the analysis. There were no
descriptions of the analysand experiencing rebuff or aversion to the
emergence of erotic fantasies. The implication may be that these analysts tended not to be immobilized by countertransference inhibitions,
while maintaining their own erotic inner life in modest reserve.

Here are several excerpts, followed by more extended narratives
of two analyses.

Dr. Jack Robinson (Deeply Satisfying Analysis)

JR: There was a certain awe that I felt for her—an extra special measure of putting on a pedestal, very much associated with her famous
background—which would make me feel some pride but it didn't feel
quite real. I don't think I really ever expressed all that. It was something that went through the whole course of my analysis and maybe
manifested itself in the fact that I didn't battle her.

To begin with, the first time she said anything after I had talked
for x number of minutes, she said something that was so empathic
and which reflected such care for me and clearly an ability to know
what I was feeling or even to help me identify what I was feeling about
what I was saying. That was a memorable event. No one had ever

reached me the way she had at that time. I will remember that experience until my dying day. Of course, that was just the first of many such times where I experienced that from her. That was very special. And I felt that for the most part continued. She would greet you at the door with sort of a nice welcoming smile but rarely anything but that. Not "Come in, good morning," anything like that . . . no words. Sat down, lie down. She played it by the book, and she did that very well. There was a kind of very solidified professionalism in the way she knew about being an analyst in her style. And yet, within that structure, she could be extremely empathic and warm and make that kind of contact that makes you feel that there was a caring human being behind you who was listening and thinking. So when it really mattered, looking back, what the hell difference did it make if she didn't understand why I was late in a blinding blizzard or why if I got sick I couldn't come in? I felt that there were times when she could meet me half way. She had a very good sense of humor, and that was very good for me. I'm sure it was good for all of her patients, but that was one of the ways in which I felt she was meeting me part of the way. She was hardly sphinx like if I was relating something humorous, which she appreciated with a chuckle, and sometimes there was a smile in her voice. When I could see her at the end of an hour with that kind of exchange, you could see a warm twinkle in her eye, so this was not somebody who didn't smile. She always smiled. Even if she didn't talk, she smiled. But there were also certain times when I just said "Well, she's just not going to understand this—let's go on to something else."

LT: Like?

JR: With her background and how she grew up, I never felt that I could fully explain the kind of street culture, the games and what the other kids were like and what some aspects of home were like. I did the best I could. I felt she did the best she could to understand, but there were certain times that her responses suggested to me that there was some basic elements in our respective backgrounds which were very disparate and perhaps hard to bridge. Or, she would project from what she would hear. Something that she might have thought was clarifying to interpret, and I would hear it as sort of off. So I would try to go back to explain it again or fill it in or put a little more tonality and color into it the best I could. Sometimes I just didn't succeed or she didn't succeed. But it never became really a major issue nor diminish her in my eyes. I felt that there were enough times when she evinced a compassionate nature, and then I was satisfied. I didn't think it was because of an empathic dissonance. So I'd move on and maybe we would get back to it. I rarely got angry with her. I used to have dreams about baseball when I was on the couch. And that might be interpreted by her as a resistance. And I think occasionally she did that because she didn't understand baseball. That was a big impediment in a way.

Clearly the transference was elsewhere with her. Her being as old as she was relative to me had created a certain flavor to the maternal transference, to the extent that the erotic was almost absent. And I think that maybe the analysis suffered from that, just thinking retrospectively. But, I felt that I had a good opportunity to work things out between myself and my mother. What happened postanalytically over the years, my relationship with my mother deepened and improved. And she was a difficult woman to have an improving and deepening relationship with. But I found a way.

Dr. Mozes Nounous (Deeply Satisfying Analysis)

MN: After termination I had quite a positive feeling about her. But the issue of critical superego was still pretty thick. I still had a lot of difficulty with that strict superego notion of transference. Maybe I didn't let her off the hook in that sense. While growing up, I became the strong one. Too early. And not only that, but I had this sort of alliance with my mother, this closeness, which was wonderful because she always made me feel good, but very, very strict. We got punished. I expected my analyst to do the same thing of making me feel good. But if she had, I would have been very suspicious. (Chuckles.) She did say about my mother that some of that sounded to her awfully strange. Then she actively helped me with my wife. She, for instance, would say such a thing as, "Why don't you take some flowers home for your wife? You're having a rough time, and maybe that shows a little at home too, so why don't you take some flowers?"

LT: How did you experience that?

MN: Partly, as "mind your own business." And partly very, very sensitive in a way that was sort of nice, helpful.

LT: During the analysis and then afterwards, when you visited her, person-to-person, did you ever feel like you loved her, or not that strong and direct?

MN: No. Nothing that strong. How I would describe it: I had an alliance with her. By that time, I had learned to appreciate what she had, what a model she had been for me. Because, by that time, I was more aware of how I emulated her. But it was never erotic. It was not only her age, but she had very little attractiveness as a woman in that sense.

LT: Where in the imagination do those feelings go if the analyst doesn't appear suitable? (Laughter.)

MN: Of course, there was my wife. A very attractive, sensual woman. I think I can say it was not a very prominent part of the analysis because—what I'm saying is, I assume, because there was so much else to deal with.

LT: One of the things you said last time was that it has taken many years to feel free about your aggression and claim it as yours.

MN: Yes. And that was not in the analysis. It was not until much later that I could begin to feel free, to express some things. I have much more a feeling about the analysis having to deal with all the agony there had been in my life, and that had to come first. That sort of feeling together with her, joking, and meeting of the minds and stuff like that was a help in doing that. There was a lot of struggle, internal, in me. With so many issues, my own background before the war, the strictness of my mother, the whole thing about my Jewish identity, and also about being a man. That I had the right to be a man, not needing permission. And in a way I was able to do that with her.

It was a very positive thing in many ways. She had a sense of humor. And I loved it. And we had a good laugh together. We also, of course, had struggles. But that laugh, and the maverick quality came upon me like it sort of sprouted from somewhere. And, she was so unorthodox in so many ways, like having the dog in the office.

She once had a rip-roaring, yelling, screaming argument with her daughter. I was in the waiting room. It stopped because then she would come in, get me, and we'd go in the office and she would say something funny, sort of detached, about mother and daughter arguments. It has a lot of meaning for my analysis because my analyst was not like my mother at all. She was sort of hanging loose in many ways. She was a maverick, and that's a very important thing. I only realized much later, more than 30 years later, that I had become a maverick. Somebody called me a maverick. Me, a maverick?

LT: And did that feel good?

MN: Terrific. But that was also an identification with her. A very obvious one. But the whole maverick thing—it took many many years until she came up in that way in me.

Dr. Saul Green (Deeply Satisfying Analysis), of all Participants in the study, was most avid about experiencing his analyst in the role of an actual substitute mother. He felt that the death of his own mother while he was a child remained core trauma throughout his life.

SG: I felt her very much as a mother figure who really cared about me, and this was before we had become "friends" after the analysis. She had been of tremendous help in my life and also in experiencing my previous time on earth in terms of its painful episodes, especially around my mother's death and various other insecurities. But as time progressed, my attitude toward her changed to more on an equal level, because one of my problems during the analysis was with the inequality in the relationship and then, afterwards, I felt her as a very dear person who was very important to me. And that was real, it wasn't transference. I convinced her to see some of the shortcomings of the analysis, that I had to do a lot of work on my own which I suppose is part of it anyway. Much of my growth happened after the analysis. The analysis was like the seeding of that possibility, that I had to keep watering and fertilizing and so on, and of course it keeps going on forever. There's a great feeling of gratitude and warmth toward her, and a sense that she was really a mensch. When I can look at her objectively, she looked quite masculine, but then when she smiled, or in another perspective she looked quite motherly. Her masculine looking physical qualities did in no way interfere with that maternal female giving part. I think that was the most powerful aspect of her personality. Sometimes during analysis I felt her to be quite stern looking, but I think that was my projection and my fears. Of course, I wanted to be her favorite and wanted to know did she really like the others better or she really liked me better—all that silly stuff that goes through one's head. But later on I was proven right because after the analysis she was a real dear friend and a motherly mother figure who was really still interested in my welfare.
LT: During analysis did you want to know her private thoughts?
SG: Absolutely!

Dr. Horatio Encarta (Moderately Satisfying Analysis) makes a very brief reference to erotic transference when asked.

HE: No, I don't remember much about any erotic transference, but I guess there might have been, slightly.

LT: What was that like?

HE: Some feelings for her, and then I would sort of tease her, telling her that she gave her husband a hard time, which I think is probably right. I don't think she liked my saying that too much. But besides that, why have an erotic transference to an old bag? I think men are more inhibited about having sex with an old woman, than women would be with a man.

Drs. **Raphe Lieberman** and **Phil Langer** shared a woman analyst, with whom both felt deeply satisfied, during approximately the same time span. Each had had a previous harsh and "disastrous" analysis with a man. The core qualities and communications of the female analyst sounded very similar in the narratives of the two Participants; variations seemed fitted to the different issues brought by the analysands. A sense of intimacy within firm boundaries was conveyed to both analysands. Whereas **Dr. Lieberman** described the analyst's capacity for great warmth beneath apparent reserve and formality, **Dr. Langer** appreciated her "caring without impingement." Each of them had experienced their prior analyst as adding to, and thereby ossifying, their overwhelming sense of guilt. The shared analyst analyzed the sources and functions of the guilt, while actively questioning the kind of self-criticism that had inhibited life choices and self-regard. Each of their previous analysts had been scornful or dismissive of the analysand's potential attachment, as well as highly authoritarian, whereas the shared analyst framed the analyses within a reliably sustaining bond. To make the comparisons meaningful, some references to the prior analyst are excerpted as well.

Dr. Raphe Lieberman (Deeply Satisfying Analysis)

Dr. Lieberman and his three analyses have been previously mentioned in the illustration for categorizing levels of satisfaction with the analysis. His first analysis took place in medical school. The second was begun as training analysis but resulted in his being transferred to a third analyst to complete his training.

Dr. Lieberman found his original training analysis "a disastrous experience" during which he felt labeled as being intractably "narcissistic." Emblematic for Raphe of the analyst's disapproval of his wish for attachment was his response to Raphe's dream about "walking down a green glade . . . following him, clearly looking for a father and idealizing the father." The analyst had said, "You can't follow me, this is no garden path." When this training analyst suggested he transfer to someone else because "this analysis isn't working," **Dr. Lieberman** sought a consultation about his choices. The consultant conveyed what he felt was problematic in Raphe, in the face of the analyst's harsh judgments: "What is your difficulty in believing in yourself?"

LT: You mean how come you believed him about you?
RL: Yeah, in essence.

    Raphe chose his next analyst because she seemed particularly respectful.

RL: During that analysis, I felt just very accepted, very safe, very cared for, cared about, in a wise presence, someone who saw behind the formulas. Although her language at that time was fairly classical, it was never used as a club.
LT: You are describing a lot of things but one of them pops out: "But it was never used as a club." It sounds like there also wasn't an issue of her controlling by what she—quote—knew about you or what she thought she knew. That that wasn't her bent, whereas with him, it comes through as a huge issue, sort of rammed at you.
RL: Right, absolutely. My next analyst temperamentally was very different. She's very dignified in boundaries in some ways. Once I brought her her newspaper lying in her driveway, and that had to be analyzed. Some people find her removed and formal. I think that's a facade. I think that there is a tremendous warmth. She can also be in your face at times, putting reality in your face, making me question my reactions. And it's been hard for me to reconstruct this, but my first training analyst essentially, somehow, drove me further into my bad first marriage with guilt.
LT: This might be all off the mark, and probably is. But being that he wasn't someone one could get attached to openly, did it make it harder to break up the marriage, to lose everything while there was no other refuge? In that way the marriage may have seemed better than the analysis. Of course, I don't know what all the issues were in that.
RL: I think that's right and that following that dream with his saying, this isn't a garden path, you know it is symbolic of just that. Any

wish that I had to attach to him—and I did, compared to the first guy in medical school—I then felt guilty or ashamed of that because of the way he dealt with it.

LT: This may be in the category of impossible questions but is there a way to portray what came through to you in the analysis, or about how you were viewed by your third analyst that made it feel essential to move out of that marriage in order for you to get the most out of life or be the most yourself? And that made it okay to go ahead and unmarry?

RL: This is, in part, reconstruction, but she certainly helped me to feel good about myself or accepting of myself and who I am. She's got a way of putting reality in your face. If someone was not treating me well, she would say, "Do you really think that such actions are justifiable?" or "Do you really think you did such and such" when I felt overly guilty. And also, "Are you going to pay attention to what such and such felt like?" Among other things, she's clearly very good at presenting one with reality and the implication of raising questions, so I did much more of that. In that analysis, too, I went a long way toward understanding what my first wife was supposed to solve for me. She was this brilliant Phi Beta Kappa and had a more prestigious medical school than mine. If someone this special could love me and marry me, I must be all right. So what if she is borderline and I have to save her life and all that. That's what didn't get touched at all in the earlier analysis. But my third analyst helped me to see what my wife was meant to do for me and helped me to feel and do otherwise for myself. She helped me recognize and deal with the guilt in initiating this break.

LT: Are you also saying something else, which is that, at the time of that marriage, who your wife was somehow gave shape to who you could value yourself to be and that you kept your eyes closed to your own value, as your consultant had picked up?

RL: One of the things I talked about was how perfect my original training analyst was in terms of an object to beat up on me. I know about myself that there are still issues. I'm not comfortable with anger; I'd like someone else to carry my anger for me, and I don't like conflict all that well. The questions behind that were whether I'd chosen someone who's a punisher, but I don't feel that's so.

LT: That comes back to one of the things you said last time, that off and on she will say, "Dr. Lieberman!" in a particular tone of voice and then you know she's gonna fight for you.

RL: Right.

LT: And not against you. But can you also recall conflicts between you—you said you had scuffles.

RL: Yeah. We inferred sexual dreams, some sexual feelings about her I wasn't aware of. There was a dream about killing off her husband or her husband dying and having her to myself. And in fact during a conflict late in analysis with her, it was when I was acting out something sexually that followed that investigation of sexual feelings toward her, she took a very firm stand against acting out and I said, "You're giving me orders again like my second analyst" and she took a very hard stand on it, fought it, and then saw my point. I felt that I would have come through it on my own to the same "right" decision. It was a bit of avoiding looking at various feelings, but I felt and still feel technically that she should have shut up and let it develop in the analysis. But I did say that, and she chuckled, and that was all right. But she said it actually in other words than acting out, more like, "for heaven's sake open your eyes, what do you see?" I had said, "You were in favor of my getting involved; you didn't think I needed to feel guilty about my past marriage," and it took me a while to realize that there were these other issues involved. So, she wasn't telling me what to do, but she said, who are you choosing? The words were very different, but that's in a sense modeling the kind of candor and directness that I wanted to attain more of for myself.

We talk about termination:

RL: My fundamental feeling, an absolutely essential feeling, was that this was someone who cared about me and who affirmed me and that I had gotten what I wanted from her. That I could be in a better relationship and feel better about myself. Then the whole interest in work, what I focus on in my work and writings—the ideas I developed— started sometime after termination of that analysis. I'm not sure how much it came up in the analysis, but just intuitively she was not humiliating and is someone who pays great attention to self-esteem issues, while her view of the analytic process was very much an interpretive one. She may not have articulated that, so then I think both my own writings and the theoretical positions I've come to were ways of finding a language to stay in touch with her and that work.

I don't remember very clearly the last hour but I remember the feelings of just tremendous gratitude and I remember hugging her and being hugged by her and the gratitude was for helping me to get out of a bad marriage relationship and to be open to a new one.

LT: Comparing her with your second analyst, what do you think his stance about termination would be?

RL: This is all fantasy, but I think he would say, "It's over, put it aside, get on with your life, don't think about me. I'm not going to have you follow me down a grassy path." So, I don't think there was much room for fantasies, or play with him. Giving up attachment, it's almost like separation is the name of the game. But of course what came to me is more in sync with the notion that one goes through the matrix of selfobjects through life. I think my third analyst would stand for the comfort, the expectation of cherishment that continues.

Dr. Raphe Lieberman returned to see his third analyst when he suffered the death of a family member and intermittently afterward. When she retired at a very advanced age, because of an illness about which she had openly apprised her patients, he continued to feel very warmly toward her and sad about her infirmity. She accepted his gift of a warm, luxurious throw. She died within months.

Dr. Phil Langer (Deeply Satisfying Analysis)

Remarkably, **Dr. Langer,** having suffered through extremes of trauma, emerged with a rich and imaginative emotional life, incisive humor, and a determination to wed intimacy to autonomy. Born to Jewish parents in Europe during World War II, survival depended on escape. While fleeing from the Nazis, 3-year-old **Phil** was carried in a sack to a neighboring region, where he and his mother stayed in hiding with a farmer who had been paid by the absent father to hide them. Because **Phil** could only speak Yiddish, he was required during this time to remain totally silent, with the exception of the noon hour when he and his mother went into a field where he was allowed to speak. Mother was lovingly devoted. One can only fathom how such necessary compliance with staying silent could have been impressed on such a little boy if one takes into account not punishment but life-threatening risk. Reunion with his father, postwar, was brief because his father became ill and died. A longing for this father, once experienced as close to him, lingers. His stepfather-to-be also escaped from the Nazis, but not before his wife and two young children had been killed. When the new family came to the United States, they lived a more ordinary life, tempered with the philosophy that they must now move on and avoid thinking about the loss and terror of the past: "'Don't think about it.' That was my mother's line."

Sadly, **Dr. Langer's** first analyst was experienced as a comfortless, moralistic, authoritarian figure who exacted compliance without seeming awareness about what might be reenacted within the dyad. The analyst espoused the belief that one must adapt to painful realities without attempting to change them, that the analytic task was just to enlarge the capacity to bear pain. Resigned compliance, rather than mastery through the resourceful escape designed by his father, would have, of course, been catastrophic for **Phil** in his early life during the war. But such an attitude toward change also limits any individual's hopes and intentions of pursuing life goals effectively. Not until the second analysis do issues around the constraints of automatic compliance rather than the potential of autonomous choice become tenable leitmotifs. Here are some excerpts from memories of the first analysis. **Dr. Langer** begins by underlining two features of the analyst that undermined the possibility of being emotionally involved: He slept a lot and eventually was physically ill without admitting it.

PL: He slept in, say, 85 percent of the sessions. And when he fell asleep, his pipe would fall onto the clipboard. Now this may have been his own alarm clock, but it was also something that I became aware of.

LT: Did you tell him?

PL: Yes. That I did. At the time I had my own difficulties about authority and rebellion. I told him, but it never occurred to me to do more than tell him.

LT: Was that a silent piece of the authority issue you mentioned, that you thought you had to take it?

PL: That's the point I'm making. Yes. That at the time, it never would've occurred to me that I could get out. In retrospect, I was horrified when I really let myself look at this, it's as though I'd dissociated that. It never occurred to me: I could leave. That this was nuts! Sometimes Brian [analytic sibling] and I joked about his sleeping during sessions. He had even more trouble with him, but it never occurred to him either to get out. Because he was in the midst of a marriage, and he would tell the analyst he wanted a divorce and was told, "No, you can't." I'm bringing up that, in some odd way, he did things that really were not analytic. There are different areas: moral judgments, interfering in life decisions, sleeping, whatever. But the point is that none of us ever said, "That's it. I'm leaving." It's ironic, vis-à-vis knowing when to get out, that I think one of the major gains I've made with the second analyst is being able to pay attention to my perceptions and act on them, essentially believing my own perceptions. Professional things, it's not a problem, usually. But personal things, it's as though I don't believe what I see. And with my first analyst, it was one long sleep.

LT: The "I don't believe what I see," where do you see that as coming from? Such unbelievable things had happened in your life.

PL: Yeah. And I think that's where it comes from. I don't have many things to thank him for. I'm not bitter any more—it's been a long time—but one of the things I really did learn from him was . . . the trouble is that he couldn't, nor could I link the two together. I learned that really I had lived most of my life in this way. Not believing what I saw. When it was something that was in any way threatening. Internally threatening or externally threatening. And so it was almost like living two lives. And that I actually did gather from my work from him. The only trouble is that we never linked that with the transference, to what was going on in the here and now. I don't even know if you want to call it the transference. That we never connected the two.

LT: I wouldn't call it just transference, because it sounds like he was doing something actually that contributed to ongoing threat.

PL: That's right. I mean it wasn't transference. It was real. And so I had really lived much of my life until then in that way. That I simply had not paid attention to what I saw that was in some way threatening. And so I had, in retrospect, been rather asleep. So psychoanalysis was also something I slept through for a long, long time.

Dr. Langer comments on his memories of the traumatic past:

PL: I've heard the stories. My memories are mostly affective. I used to be terrified of the dark. I used to be very afraid to be alone. I had pieces of feeling—but it's extrapolated. I have some memories, vague memories of, so this guy took me in a sack. And we were gonna go to this lawyer's office, in a building whereas the SS had their headquarters. So apparently the story is, me in the sack, my mother, we marched up to this lawyer's office, past the SS guard, and in the lawyer's office, they opened the sack, there I was, the lawyer was amazed, and in the back of the building was waiting a farmer. A Gentile. And my mother changed her clothes and became a peasant. Looked like a peasant. And I was put back in the bag. And the Gentile drove us out of the ghetto. Because apparently they delivered food and stuff in and out, they traveled in and out of the ghetto. And then we lived on this farm.

LT: Your mother had been able not to show fear. Is that right or not?
PL: Yeah. Yeah. My mother she was quite intrepid. She was very brave. So we lived on this farm, my mother and I. My second analyst has said that the one thing that probably saved me was [that] we never were separated, my mother and I.
LT: So growing up was always in her orbit?
PL: Yeah. My mother doesn't, didn't believe at that time in any kind of separation. It wasn't just in her orbit; it was a lot more like in her skin. She had many times risked her life for me so that I understand it. She really was very caught up with me, and she had done a lot to save me. And so she was terrified of losing me in any fashion. And when we came to the United States and the dangers were considerably different, then it became losing me in some emotional or psychological fashion. And that's a trap. It's the way I began my first analysis. It's the way I began my second analysis. When my mother came up, I said, I recall, "I owe my life to my mother." Without actually ever hearing the multiple meanings. And it was only with my second analyst, years later, that I heard the various meanings of that. Not just I'm alive because of her, but, in the old biblical tradition that, my life is hers.

After the war, father, who had been paying the farmer, returned. He came and got us. And I do remember that when he came, I didn't know who he was. I have a lot of feeling about him, but until very recently didn't remember him at all. And yet it seemed clear that, in one fashion or another, he was really extraordinarily important for me. I see from what I began to remember he and I were quite close at times. But I can remember, kind of, feel periods of closeness. Before he died, he was in the hospital. He told my mother, "Don't worry, as soon as I'm okay we'll get the money together and we'll go to America." But it was clear he was going to die. I remember just being there with him. And talking to him. And then I had this one very vivid memory, wandering around this apartment and coming upon a figure on the floor. In sheets. With canvas around it. And not knowing what it was. And walking up to the face. It was my father. I think I moved the sheet. He was in the apartment overnight, but he was dead.

Phil's story of the brief reunion with the dying father was wrenching to hear. We talk about his disappointment that the first analyst, throughout the analysis, was more like an absent and dead father than the earlier father with whom he could be close.

PL: That's a good point. I think that I desperately wanted him to be my father. Maybe that's part of the bitterness, but he really couldn't be, wouldn't be. He was too caught up in matters of his own. And I have yet to see a person he treated who thought very highly of him, and who's not bitter and angry in some way, while people whom he supervised or whom he taught adored him. He was always late. One time, he left the tape recorder on from the teaching session he had just before me. During the session, he said to me, "Oh! I guess I left the tape recorder on." I said, "I'm not so happy about that." But no response from him. He would always be slightly contemptuous. I once had a dream; he said, "Now you've had your oedipal dream." He was not good with dreams. He was interested in the idea of bearing affect. That was his shtick, his only shtick.

LT: What did he do that either made it easier or harder to bear affect? And what was your sense, if there was a sense, of what he wanted you to be like or be like with him?

PL: Certainly "be like" wasn't very hard. Because he was quite didactic about that. I was having trouble with my first wife and he said, "You don't divorce. You tolerate affect."

LT: Did he say why you don't divorce?

PL: No matter if you change it, after you've changed it, it will be the same again. So he was very clear about how I should be. The notion was that you tolerate pain, you have pain. And that's life. And a certain part of me felt that made sense. And I think another part of me just felt I was not having any of that. I'll tell you a story that captures a lot of it. One day he said to me, "I'm raising my fees." "What do you mean you're raising your fees? You haven't even talked about raising your fees." And while I was lying there, a piece of paper suddenly appeared in front of me. It was a memo from the Institute, saying that training analysts were allowed to raise their fees from $35 to $45. I looked at it. He said, "See." So I said,"You're allowed. That doesn't mean that you have to." . . . I don't really think he liked me. I never really thought about it before now. I think he tolerated me. I don't know what the truth is, but that's my fantasy.

LT: In view of your having said you wanted him to be your father, what would you have liked from him, or, were you aware of wanting him to say or do or feel . . . ?

PL: I wanted him to do what I was reading about in training. I wanted him to explain things to me, about what I was talking about. I wanted him to put things together in a way that made sense to me.

Yes, I could tolerate more affect, maybe, toward the end of the analysis than I could at the beginning. I cried a lot. But I didn't know what I was crying about. I cried because I missed my father? Or I cried because of things with my mother?

LT: If you cried about missing your father, would he ever have said, "Here it is again. I am not being who you want me to be, because I have disappeared on you too. I'm asleep."

PL: No, I don't think I ever heard him say he's not something the way we all do when the patient's disappointed and we say, "You're disappointed because I'm not. . . ." What he said was always about defense and affect.

Dr. Langer further described the analyst's stance as caustic and deprecatory, a caricature of the "neutral" analyst who stayed uninvolved with "your mishegas" and assumed he had none of his own.

PL: So that was one piece of it. The other piece of it that occurred to me in retrospect that really wasn't good for me is he was, in this somewhat crazy way, selfless, or looked as though he was selfless. Whatever you needed. You need an extra session; he'd see you at 6 o'clock in the morning. Selfless has to be put in quotes. He would do it and one had the sense that nothing was beyond him in terms of putting himself out. But I never felt it as being particularly generous. I felt it as selfless, which has a very different quality to it.

LT: Which is not a good model for feeling entitled to live a life for oneself?

PL: Exactly. And there's a kind of ascetic, cold, and somewhat superior quality to selflessness, the way I'm using it. It's not a generous or generative quality. It's a picture of oneself. It doesn't give you a sense of the other person. One tries to maintain one's own image with oneself and to the other person so it's got nothing to do about the other person. So that there isn't the interchange. I knew that his wife was often screaming at him, that I could hear. I must have thought to myself, "This man has to be a little angry about being screamed at." And that kind of gnomic, avuncular Delphic and essentially absent attitude of his had to express something. A lot of what it expressed was absence. That's the point about the oracle of Delphi, you never knew who the hell that was. He didn't give much room for one to think, for me, at any rate, about oneself. Nor to think about him. Instead, what one had was really a caricature. The more I think about it, a sterile kind of field. At the same time there was this notion that one doesn't alter one's external reality at all. One learns to adapt.

The issue of divorce, which I was thinking about at the time, or the issue of being angry with somebody, or the issue of taking something personally. Almost anything was to be understood. But reality was not to be altered. He had this notion that you can't ever alter reality in a way that fits you better. And he used to harp a lot on my intolerance of helplessness, which was fair enough. That was one of the useful things he did say. I have a very hard time with passivity and helplessness. It's quite true. Or of a certain kind, at any rate. But that became kind of a mantra for not doing anything in the outside world. And for me that's not very helpful. I'm not sure it's helpful for anybody. I think he required idealization. Idolization. I think it was very important for him to be met with open-mouthed awe.

Phil Langer emphasized the barriers to communication. While the analyst became more and more obscure, the other person in the relationship was "required to be more and more awestruck by that kind of obscurity that masqueraded as profundity."

PL: He was sometimes utterly unintelligible. One couldn't make out what he said that had anything to do with what one had just said. And he wouldn't explain it. And because of this compliance stuff, I could weave all kinds of connections. So, that was him. He was certainly locked into an unhappy marriage. Because one can't change anything. One is stuck and one has to make the best out of where one is. He didn't think you could have a better life. Except insofar as you could make one inside yourself. If you change it, you'll just do it again. You know, kind of the repetition compulsion writ large. But without much room for anything else, for creativity, or for some other more autonomous way, more independent of conflict.

LT: How did termination incubate, in you or in him?

PL: Me. I didn't know when to terminate. Most of my friends were beginning to terminate. It had been about four and a half years. In retrospect, I wonder if I terminated because I knew he was going to die, unconsciously or subconsciously, and I wanted to get out of there before he did. 'Cause he died. Can't remember, it's either six months or a year and six months after I terminated. It was somebody I knew who had walked in, for his appointment, and he was dead. I once walked in, and I had to wake him up. He was in his chair asleep, and I had to touch him, which was just horrendous. I couldn't imagine touching my analyst, you know? Shake him. Ask him if he was okay. And then he insisted on having the session. I said to him, "What are we doing here? This is crazy!" He said, "I'm okay." I remembered that I imagined, after my termination, I would feel great and I would be ecstatic because it was over. I didn't feel great, and I wasn't that ecstatic. I walked out. It was nice not to have to schlep down there. And that's about the size of it. I'm out. I'm done. And I don't want to come back. And I thought I should feel sad.

LT: What was the last good-bye like, just before you left that session?

PL: It's interesting. I haven't thought about that. The last good-bye was my feeling sad and telling him that he'd been quite helpful; I was grateful. It was, in retrospect, me at my almost compliant best. Almost compliant best because there was some authenticity to it. I really was sad.

LT: Was there sadness in giving up the wished for part? You talked about how much you wished he had been like a father.

PL: Yeah. That's what I was getting to. I felt authentically sad, that it was the last time. And he was about (laughs) to leave.

LT: Did it hurt that . . . I don't know whether you felt you mattered to him, that you would mean something to him afterwards.

PL: Zero, zilch. I hadn't realized it until I told you last time that I didn't think he liked me. And I think that's right. I don't think he disliked me, I think he was indifferent.

Dr. Langer describes how he experienced his second analyst.

PL: Very, very different. Intellectually and emotionally. She feels, to me, extremely engaged with me, in a way that is very important to me. Others would use the word respectful, which is true for her because she's very respectful and she listens. But, for me it's the feeling of really being engaged with somebody, where, you know, it literally is engaged like the clutch of the motor. In that sense of connection. She is someone whom I feel warmly about and who I know feels warmly about me. Someone who does what it seems to me is analysis and someone who is interested in thinking something through with you and in being free to alter her viewpoint with new information, where there isn't kind of a sense that you're up against somebody who you push so far and then they say, "But this is analysis." Where the script has been written without you. In one fashion or another. Either as a deep script—this far, no further. Or right at the top, saying, "No." That, rather, vis-à-vis the negotiation, that it's a negotiation with her, it's trying to understand something. Two people trying hard to understand something.

So that she's a kind of more tolerant, mother of ambivalence. That things have meaning rather than things have value. That thought has meaning, but isn't something that makes one bad, to really make it simple-minded. So that she, is a kind of constant presence for me about that. And I like her. She likes me. I mean, I would hope so. It would be difficult if she didn't. But still, she doesn't impinge. One can care and impinge. For me, with my history with my mother, what's been so important is somebody who cares but doesn't impinge. That would be, for me, the crucial matter. Because I have such a horror of the caring that becomes impinging. She felt that I could make my own decisions. And she would try to help me figure out why I was making them. But that my decisions were my business. She wanted to hear about them, but I could make my own.

For example, she was also going to raise her fee at some point, and I objected. And she has never changed that fee, actually. Where I just decide. Where, for my own kind of autonomy I needed to say "no" and have the "no" count. It really doesn't matter what the fee is. It's that it has to be a negotiation, and it means something to the analyst and something to the patient. And it reminded me yet again of how little negotiation there was with my first analyst. If I got angry at him, he would see it as my problem. There wasn't any kind of sense that something had happened between us that might be affecting things. If I talked about other women, it was a way of not bearing affect. If I talked about things at the Institute, it was that I was impatient or that I wasn't able to adapt. That was the notion.

Whether it's as an analyst or as a person, I now feel much freer to have a position and to hold to that position without feeling conflicted about the matter of holding to it. When you have a position, there's the thing where you listen to the other person and take their point of view in mind. That's one aspect of it. But the other aspect of it is, can you hold a position without feeling ambivalent about just having a position itself? And that second one is the one that I used to have trouble with and that she has helped me a great deal with. I'm perfectly willing to hear another position, but at least I know I have one. And that it's not in some way selfish to have a position. And that's been very important to me. The deeper issues about compliance didn't come up till later.

I saw her for a number of years, and then I stopped and then went back to her twice a week. I first terminated when I got very involved in another love relationship and felt I couldn't do both, and I left her, terminated, which years later, we figured out as, I never forgave her for saying, "Well, if you have to go you have to go." And it was really quite casual. And I said to her, "I was thinking of quitting." And I quit. And always thereafter I thought she wanted to get rid of me. (Laughs.) It felt to me like I overstayed my welcome. That that's what she was saying to me. Only years later I saw . . .

LT: Could it be that she was trying not to make you feel you *should* be coming, owed it to her to stay? Like with your mother?

PL: Oh yeah. I think probably, if anything was on her mind, it was that. But I took it a certain way, that had to do with feeling I'd overstayed my welcome. Which was a theme that I could remember being extremely important to me when we first came to the United States. I always felt like I had overstayed my welcome. And only later did I realize that that theme had to do with my mother and I in those fields. At noon. You know, in the middle of the day. The talking hour would end. I would have to be sensitive to my mother's anxiety that maybe we had been there too long. I would have to break off. And so I would have to be careful about overstaying my welcome, upsetting her. It never even occurred to me. It was just this thing that over the years burbled and burbled and burbled and then suddenly it just opened up the analysis with her. It had to do with that time as a child, my whole fear of staying too long somewhere. And it also took me all that time to realize how compliant I had been. How almost false-self-ish I had been in much of my life and much of my analysis. I used to tease with her, and it was really true. No matter what she said, I could have 10 associations that would prove her right. I could always find a way of agreeing with her. Because I could be facile without being very genuine. And it took me a long time to really recognize that.

LT: So we better watch for that slippery slope here! (Both laugh.) What made it possible to shift from that?

PL: I began to notice it and talk about it. This is probably not what she would say, but this is my memory of it. That there was a period of about six weeks where she didn't say anything. And so it was hard for me to prove her right. (Laughter.) And, the thing that was so striking about that time was I didn't feel at all uncomfortable. I gradually felt more and more and more comfortable. With talking. And, in terms of the space that we're talking about, the kind of transitional space where I began to really open up with her. I began to think there was this space where I could be genuine and where she was accepting. So at times I've asked her not to talk. Because I find it distracting. Not because I've gotta be it and it's gotta be my space and I'm king of the world. But because I still have a propensity to slide back into being compliant.

LT: You talked about how in relationship, how with your mother, it felt like she owned your psyche in some way, and that coming into your own, to allow yourself to claim a separate world inside yourself would mean to cut her off.

PL: Exactly. Exactly. But my second analyst showed me that there is room for that. My first analyst was demeaning. Dismissive. You could say that he dismissed even my compliance. And if even that's dismissed . . . (Laughter.) And meanwhile I didn't get on with my life. Her whole attitude is different. She laughs at my jokes. But there's this kind of constantly reasonable, "Now, **Dr. Langer**, we both know . . ." she'll say to me, or "Do you really believe that?" And there's a kind of slightly humorous quality.

LT: When you describe that, I hear the, "Now, **Dr. Langer**" already saying something playfully with, even calling you **Dr. Langer** at that moment, as though pointing to a gap of something you both know and something you don't know—in the irony of intimate distance or something like that.

PL: Yeah. And, actually, it's something I like. Because then, when it's intimate, it's really intimate. During the first period of analysis with her, I never remembered or mourned my father's death. But I had this period where I remembered the affection. Later, when I went back, there was a period of time where I had to sit on the couch. I didn't look at her. But I had to sit because I could capture the feeling . . . I know this is so . . . it was kind of muscular memory. That I had to sit to remember. We were sitting shiva for my father. Before that, it was unbearable. Because my problem had always been that. I truly didn't remember. When we came to the United States, my mother said, "Okay, we all have to learn English, and you're gonna teach us so we can't speak Yiddish anymore." Then we actually don't speak Yiddish. So sitting again in the same position very low. I remembered my father's death and sitting shiva for him.

LT: So, actually you're saying, ironically, "in her presence, I could bear it. With the man who was preaching to me about bearing pain, it was unbearable."

PL: Exactly. So the time with her was extremely powerful in terms of being able to grieve my father's death.

LT: Do you ever find yourself wanting to think about, or [being] curious about, or taking pleasure in perhaps knowing more about her inner life?

PL: Not really. I saw that question on the list and knew what my answer was, but I am just thinking about why. I hadn't thought of this before, but I think I knew too much.

LT: Too much, to know of mothers, all the time, and to have had the responsibility of that?

PL: I knew too much about her. I don't want to know. What I know about my second analyst is who was in her family. But my sense of her from what she conveys is of someone who lives the way I think I would like to, who had very intimate relationships, who has this dignity, has that quality.

Phil describes an occasion of seeing the analyst in a restaurant and being struck by "how seductive, playful, and tender" she was with the dinner companion, conveying a "very nice, warm, close quality."

LT: There's a new word you've just come out with. Tender.

PL: Right. That is a new word. It's not a word I use very much, actually. Though I value it a great deal. And I just was struck by how she was with him. I thought, "Now there's a woman I could fall in love with." My hunch is they were old friends, but there was just something very genuine and very nice about it. And that's my picture of her. And what I saw was not at all inconsistent with what I had seen. There wasn't anything underhanded about it. It was just out in the open tenderness and friendship.

LT: And did that stir up a longing to someday be her friend like that?

PL: No. No. I wouldn't want the relationship to be any different. That's not the nature of it. And running into each other socially would be too superficial. If I talk to her, I want to talk to her. Do I want her to talk to me? I think we'd find that extremely awkward. That may be my projection. And again, because of, what we were both saying about my mother, I like the distance. I value that. And I value her. And I value what she has done with me enormously. But I don't want to change it to be something else. I don't think that would make it any better, any richer.

There's a feeling I have about her. But I know it's a feeling. There was a time a while ago when I was just beside myself with pleasure about my life and my work with her and everything. And I had this fantasy, which I told her about, that we would just dance around the office. I said to her, "Look, we should go dancing. We'll turn on the music here and we'll dance. We'll just do the waltz in your office." I was quite serious about the fantasy. To me dancing is kind of utter abandon and pleasure. The notion of it, just the fantasy. That's what it was with her. But ending is also important. She was very clear about that. I think she was capturing this fantasy of mine, which is, "Hey, it's eternal. We'll go on forever." Sometimes I live my life as though I were 20. In other words, that eventually one day, when I'm older, I'll get serious. Well, I'm older. I have to be serious now. And I agree with her completely. You gotta stand up, pull up your pants, and be on your way. And those are the pants you gotta wear. I didn't want to be in treatment forever. I wanted to be on my own, to live my own life. But I'm kind of the New World generation in terms of good-bye. I don't think good-byes are forever. As long as we both live, if I have trouble, of course I would call her. No question about it. And where is she located inside? I think, as a kind of ego ideal, a kind of loving superego, somebody who would help me monitor some of the really harsh aspects of my own relationship to myself. She stays as a kind of constant presence for me in terms of that. Meanwhile, I think that she would want me to do as well as I possibly could and that she has my best interests in mind about that. It would give her pleasure. It's not that she needs it. But it would give her pleasure and it would give me pleasure for her to know that I was doing well.

9

WOMEN WITH FEMALE ANALYSTS

I don't remember when it was that my mother's feminine sensuousness, the reality of her body, began to give way for me to the charisma of my father's assertive mind and temperament; perhaps when my sister was just born, and he began teaching me to read. There was, is, in most of us, a girl-child still longing for a woman's nurture, tenderness, and approval, a woman's power exerted in our defense, a woman's smell and touch and voice, a woman's strong arms around us in moments of fear and pain.

—Adrienne Rich, *Of Woman Born*

Is the one unpardonable sin

Our fear of not being wanted?

For this, will mother go on cleaning house

For eternity, and making it unlivable?

—Robert Lowell, "Unwanted"

There were six instances of women with female analysts, all of them training analyses. Comparison of the numbers of women with male and female analysts for "total analyses," and "training analyses" shows about three times as many (19) women with male analysts generally, whereas for training analyses, there was approximately an equal number (7) with male analysts. It raises a question of whether, given the goal of becoming a woman analyst, women felt more drawn to choosing a female analyst with whom to identify than when the analysis was entered for solely personal reasons. Judging from my own clinical experience with female analysands, however, I am aware that personal issues bring women to female analysts as well, perhaps more in recent times.

The Participant's analyses were judged to be deeply satisfying for two (33%); moderately satisfying for three (50%), and highly dissatisfying for one (17%). The numbers are, of course, too small for reliable inferences. It is of interest to note, however, that the proportion of deeply satisfying analyses is much less than for men with women or women with men. It is comparable to the experience for men with men, but without the cluster of disastrous analyses within a particular decade. None of the analyses of women with women in the sample were initiated during the last decade studied (1985–1995), so most recent shifts in analytic approaches are not reflected. In particular, erotic components of loving transferences might (and do) appear more directly in current analyses.

All but one woman made some reference to her wish for a strong and accomplished woman analyst with whom she could identify. In particular, some stressed their admiration for a woman who had navigated successfully around the obstacles of subtle and not so subtle discrimination against women in medicine. In several cases, the Participant had vacillated between wanting to pursue surgery, pediatrics, or psychiatry prior to analytic training. One Participant commented that psychiatrists "as teachers" had been generous to her in offering supervision and encouragement and that these women teachers were easier to identify with than the male surgeons. The women analysts seen by Participants seemed to share that vision. Although all were described as "classical" in approach, some seemed unusually active in fostering the Participant's career advancement, with aspects of mentoring added to analyzing. In two instances, the analyst initiated arranging a meeting between her analysand and another senior analyst who could facilitate career development. Active opinions about career choices were offered (in retrospect, not always wise ones). One analyst, some time after termination, reviewed the writings of the Participant, offering helpful suggestions about the content and how to get it published. In contrast, however, the very area of professional competition or envy was found to be unresolvable with the analyst for two other Participants. **Dr. Heather Rodine** told me she could not have published her own work until after her analyst died, 15 years after the analysis, believing the analyst would view her writings as invading the analyst's territory. **Dr. Zelda Fisher** similarly felt that the analyst protected her "turf" in her chosen area of professional focus.

Thus, in both positive or negative directions, the realm of professional development seemed to operate outside of "neutrality" in the analyst.

Although wanting the analyst to be "strong," some of the women simultaneously expressed a yearning for closeness to the analyst in signs emblematic of femininity. One Participant decided to buy her lingerie at the boutique her analyst frequented; another most appreciated the analyst's teaching her where to buy her clothes to dress attractively. There seemed to be a wish to feel themselves into the analyst's femininity while identifying with her professional role.

Three of the women whose mothers had been disappointing came to analysis with a strong positive grandmother transference, a sense that grandmother had believed in them and encouraged their individuality. Others who chose a woman analyst had had some prior treatment with a man and wanted to resolve those issues that they felt as obstacles to their feeling close to a woman.

Perhaps surprisingly, some analysts seemed to give mothering a subtly lower priority than energy devoted to profession. **Dr. Eleanor Brown's** analyst had said (some time after termination), "What do you want all those children for?" **Dr. Emma McClinton's** childless analyst was especially unsupportive during Emma's pregnancies and could not seem to relate to issues concerning her children in terms other than blaming Emma.

None of the women reported experiencing erotic love for, or expressed erotic fantasies about, their female analysts. This differs from my own experience with female analysands. Additionally, women sometimes express the wish to be inside the vagina or body of the woman analyst, not in a regressed or erotic sense, but rather to feel the femininity of the analyst directly either as "practice" or permission for their own. In turn, the woman analyst can feel a deep affective connection with the enriched interiority of her analysand's sexual sensations and their contribution to her inner psychic life.

Although the Participants' feelings were not experienced as erotic, **Dr. Baranger** did describe enduring love and a tender wish to cradle the analyst when she became terminally ill. **Dr. Rodine** experienced a period of loving feelings that ended. **Dr. Lionheart** felt affection that continued in the posttermination relationship. If the early oedipal period, during which active libidinal wishes are directed to the mother's body (Edgecumbe and Burgner, 1975), were represented in the analyses, they took more oblique forms, such as pursuing, outside the analysis, a very vigorous involvement with the external world, or reacting intensely to the jealous, possessive, and exclusionary components of friendships with women. To put this phenomenon into its time perspective, **Dr. Brown's** comments (**moderately satisfying analysis**) were enlightening:

EB: Later my sense was that she was so uncomfortable with pre-oedipal transferences, I think that's what she was hearing. At the time, all I picked up was discomfort. Once I picked up that regressive things and fantasies were looked on with criticism, I censored—although not consciously. So, what got inhibited would have been there had it seemed like a more legitimate thing for a young analyst to be experiencing. Now our candidates, as you know, will talk about all kinds of things like homosexual transferences that would have been totally out of line then, just never openly discussed. It felt like it wasn't permitted. That was the biggest failing in the analysis, she just couldn't really . . . she and her theory, about how you were supposed to be . . . so that just never opened up in the transference.

The impact of sociocultural context was felt in the female–female analytic dyads—differently than for the men, but as equally relevant. Women's expectations about their roles were changing. The models of femininity that were presented to them during their childhood no longer fit their adult lives. Bernstein (1993) notes that women no longer wanted to live lives like their mothers, and that this produces specific conflicts:

> Autonomy, independence and assertiveness, the qualities most valued in our society are considered unfeminine. Women face a dilemma: In order to be feminine, they must relinquish the very character traits that they later need to develop their own potential. . . . The girl, during the oedipal and adolescent stages, is struggling simultaneously to attain or retain individuation (be different) at the same time that she is forming identifications with her mother to consolidate her femininity. She is caught in tremendous conflict, trying simultaneously to be unlike (retain autonomy) and to be like her mother (retain femininity) [p. 34].

My own clinical experience suggests that dilemmas over identification with mother are compounded for women if mother has not been able to be self-respecting or happy about the choices she felt were available to her. If mother conveys a devalued view of herself, with undercurrents of self-hatred, not only does the daughter miss a viably positive identification, but a fear of mother's fragility or envy complicates her attempts to individuate. In that context, mothers may be described as unable to make a robustly tender affective connection with the daughter, while emphasizing external appearance as a measure of value. As Robert Lowell's poem implies, the "fear of not being wanted" is read into the mother's "cleaning house for eternity and making it unlivable." The house of the mother's body may then be experienced as unreceptive to the girl's inner life in its sensual expression and is aborted in the process of her attempts to suppress or to "clean out" her own.

Recent, revised formulations about female sexuality contend that intimacy, rather than genital sensation, may be the organizer of women's psychic development and is associated with greater fluidity of object choice, including moving from heterosexual to lesbian object choice in search of emotional intimacy (Elise, 2002b; Fisher, 2002; Notman, 2002; Kirkpatrick, 2002; Reed, 2002). Kirkpatrick (2002) concludes that "girls' sexuality seems more driven by object seeking, boys by pleasure seeking. This seems true of adult sexuality as well" (pp. 196–197). She relates this to an organizing effect of testosterone on the brain. Because the mother (or caretaker) is the first love object for both boys and girls, women have experienced a homoerotic relationship, a template that continues to have its effect. Elise (2002a,b) highlights the importance of maternal response to the daughter's early desires for her. If mother cannot cathect her daughter erotically, (like she does her son) but views her only as a nonsexual object, a wounding sense of failure may prevail. She believes "a daughter's erotic desire in relation to her mother would eventually integrate early sensual elements into an oedipal romance. Invalidated desire for mother can lead to a general deflation of female desire" (p. 169) and that denied desire for the analyst may parallel other foreclosed desires in the patient's life (p. 170). Elise makes the point that women want to be able to want. I agree with Elise that women's active assertion of desire is an aspect of freeing sexuality and is not adequately accounted for by its relation to inhibited aggression. Women analysts may have a particular opportunity with their female analysands to apperceive the interiority of women's sexuality in psychic life (in the transference or as experienced in relationships outside the analysis) and to analyze the obstacles to its articulation and vitality.

How the early women psychoanalysts regarded maternal functions in and out of analysis is highly complex. Anna Freud, dedicated to working with very young children separated from their parents in war, was struck by, and responded to, their separation anxiety as much more distressing from mother than father and only healed by sustained maternal input. Yet she cautioned the analyst to strictly avoid maternal gratification for the patient, expressing the viewpoint that only neurotic, oedipally conflicted issues can be helped in psychoanalysis, in contrast to deficiencies in the maternal environment. She feared the kind of regression that would intensify longings for mother and distract the patient from the work at hand. Helene Deutsch stressed the girl's identification with mother as primary in her development, but felt that career interests were inevitably part of a "masculinity complex," from which she herself admitted suffering. She said her own mother "was a mean woman and I didn't want to be like her. She beat me, not to punish, but just to vent her anger about my not having been born a boy." Deutsch theorized about women's need to flee from femininity because of its masochism. But she also believed that femininity is not fully developed until one is a mother, nursing a baby. Why? Because the intense longings for a blissful union with mother can that way be fulfilled with the baby. Karen Horney, adoring her own mother early in life, applauded femininity and mothering. She too wrote about the "flight from womanhood," but for social rather than intrapsychic reasons—namely, that men were more valued and empowered. She described men's envy of the mother and defensive denigration. But eventually she attributed character disorders, such as compulsive strivings for love or power, to the mother's narcissism, that is, having used the child for her own subjective needs. Melanie Klein, who was convinced of the child's envious and rageful wishes toward the mother, perhaps had the most difficulty being a mother herself and was never able to reconcile with her sadly embittered analyst daughter (Sayers, 1991).

As contemporary female analysts, our beliefs about how we are, or should be, involved in our patients' development emerge as guiding, as well as conflicted, parts of our self-image. But grappling with whether we are too "gratifying" or "withholding," are able to sustain a full-blown erotic or negative transference, give in to the wish to comfort for our own sake, and so on occurs in the heat of what the individual analysand has brought to the analytic dyad at that moment in time, in collision with our own particular nature. What strikes me about the narratives of those women Participants who were deeply satisfied with their analysis is that although directly erotic desires toward the analyst did not seem to emerge, a gratifying sense of emotional intimacy became comfortable for both members of the dyad, and ambivalence was recognized without retribution or disruption of the bond. In contrast, the more problematic analyses were characterized by more or less disruptive alienation when competitive issues were enacted in the countertransference, or, in the case of **Dr. McClinton's** analyst, all wishes for intimacy were rejected.

Three brief vignettes precede the two more extended narratives:

Dr. Rose Lionheart (Deeply Satisfying Analysis)

Dr. Lionheart experienced her second analysis as very satisfying and portrayed the feeling of a progressive identification with her analyst.

RL: It was a very nice relationship—I had great respect for her and liked her very much. Was it different from how it was with my first analyst? It felt different to be with her, and with a woman, and I was much more in awe of her than I was with him. She was older and very well known.

I remember everything with an intensity because I'm like that, but there was nothing that was really painful as I look back. But I had a dream in which the Queen backed up against a fireplace and burned her behind [both laugh], and I told her the dream and we both laughed because it was so obvious—this was in the middle or toward the end of the analysis—and we both recognized that I was also embarrassing the Queen. I thought of her as the Queen.

LT: Are you saying you both laughed and understood the ambivalence that wasn't remote?
RL: That's right, and there were many things like that. And I recall that I got interested in what she wore. So then I used to buy my lingerie at this lovely little lingerie place where she bought hers, and I switched from the kind of silk cape my father would have picked for me. I went to the tailor who made her capes in beautiful wool, and I had mine made there, too. I could never look like her, because she was taller and with white hair, but nevertheless, there were some reasons to feel I was very much identified with her. I don't think we ever analyzed the identification.

LT: Did you feel that not analyzing it was as an obstacle in any way, or that it stayed as a silent, good bond?

RL: No, I thought this was kind of a good thing, that it was nice. She was a nice person to identify with and the little sort of eccentricities that I adopted were very harmless and disappeared after a while of themselves. I still like nice lingerie and love capes, but I rarely wear them anymore, though I had loved them even before I saw them on her.

LT: You mentioned that issues about aggression were easier to approach with your first analyst than love and sex. How was that with her?

RL: She seemed like such a straightlaced woman, so I don't remember talking too much about sex. I remember mentioning homosexuality, and she wasn't particularly interested, because I thought why wasn't I in love with her?

LT: And you weren't?

RL: I wasn't—no, and I thought there's got to be something, but that never really got anywhere, so if there is some, it's way down deep someplace. I haven't found it.

Later in the conversation:

LT: With both of your analysts you describe a sureness that they liked you.

RL: Oh yes, absolutely and admired me, too. I had very good feelings about my analysts. I don't remember any really bad things, that we didn't work out. I can feel angers, but some people are bitter about their analysts and their analyses, and I never felt that way. I think I was helped an enormous amount by these people. With my first analyst, I always felt sort of sorry that we couldn't completely finish, but it was okay because then I went to her and I think I got more.

Dr. Heather Rodine (Moderately Satisfying Analysis). Having struggled to establish a profoundly affecting, helpful communication with her analyst, it was excruciating for Heather to feel she had lost access to the analyst within as resource. She attributed this loss to the analyst's intermittant "schizoid walls of withdrawal" posttermination and felt some of the gains of analysis were permanently "ruined." Chapter 2, "Conversations and Process," illustrates her way of using the interviews to disengage from the analyst.

HR: I sensed that she also functioned on nonverbal and visual levels, like me. There was an intuitive sense of what I was talking about and a willingness to accept whatever meager conceptualizations I could make and to allow for the open space for me to fumble in until I found the language that was going to get us there. But it was difficult, and, because words could only skim what I was feeling, massively frustrating for a long time. One thing that sustained me during those times was a positive transference that didn't get elaborated until later, but there was something about my analyst that I was able to connect with my grandmother, a belief in "live and let live," as opposed to the intrusions and distortions of my parents. My grandmother was the only one who understood and was on my side when I was a child. I really protected myself from my analyst's intrusions for a long time. She used to say afterward, "You always corrected any interpretation I made." If she came close, it wasn't that close, and I would alter it.

LT: Did you have to make it your own?

HR: Yes, so that they were my words. If she was close to comprehending, that was probably all I could tolerate, but I think it was an absolutely necessary isolation within a relationship, being in the presence of somebody else who didn't have an ulterior motive or agenda. But I also felt she was also very uptight. My image of her was of the uptight lady in the black dress, buttoned to the top. She didn't have any dresses like that.

LT: Does black dress, buttoned up, stand for not easy to enter?

HR: Yes, and for not being at ease about showing warmth, any mutuality. (Laughs.) Eventually, her costume changed. Probably half way through the analysis when some of the storms had subsided. One day I was able to say, "I realize that all of this negativity and anger that I've been saying that you feel toward me, I don't feel that you feel that. I think it's me." And she was very relieved about this turning point in this terrible period of my treatment, the recognition of, taking back the projection, of understanding and working through something. Since then, there has been very strong identification professionally. I think some of the strength that I feel in myself is rooted in the analysis, rooted in her strength, professionally. I had wanted an analyst with that kind of strength.

LT: Was any part of that rooting ever a feeling of "I love this person" or more like I am close to and like her, or a quite different mix of feelings that are not as unadulterated as that?

HR: Through the latter part of the analysis, through many years it was very powerful loving feelings. (Pause.) I don't know if any of that is still somewhere in the background, but I can't feel it. I don't think

it's there after all that happened later. There were things she just couldn't help me with during the analysis, nor later when we became friends.
LT: Which you mentioned you thought had to do with her nature?
HR: Yes, and with the limitations of her analysis. There were two pieces and they may be related. One was this issue of not having been able to work toward a real position of mutuality with her own analyst, and so she couldn't do it with me on a deeper level. The other was about her need to minimize the father, which made me feel that if I turned from feelings about her to him, I was just being defensive. But after the analysis, if we had a wonderful discussion about psychoanalysis or life, she would suddenly pull back in a scary kind of schizoid withdrawal—chilling—something I had never encountered in my life before.

Later in the conversation:

LT: You've said you were both drawn to a friendship because your vision, your interests, were shared. What's your notion about termination with you? Do you believe she went through something in relinquishing you as her analysand?
HR: My sense is that she could not easily make the transition because the person who could function so openly in analysis was not able to do so in reality, and there was some carryover. But I think the abruptness of enviousness or shifts in the relationship were tied in with that. During the terrible couple of years when she wouldn't speak to me or answer my calls—I think because she knew she was ill and was hiding it—the schizoid fence was there, there were no openings. I know I suffered, assuming it must be my fault, but I lost what I had had, lost out in some way permanently and in a way for a period of time. I guess she was in two places, as an analyst and in the residual transference, whatever one wants to call it. I very much felt the loss of her, in a sense betrayed by her, not having her help with that. Then there was the relationship with her in the outside world which eventually had to do with her illness and our working through together the transition from analysis to friendship. I could deal with her illness, to help care for her, to feel sad at her death, but that didn't affect what I had lost internally. I think that fantasy is far more important, and we really have no way of knowing, probably even by the end of an analysis, the place we find in our patient's internal world, and the freedom to be able to fantasize really belongs to a very sacred part of the patient that has to do with wishes. And once one moves out into the world, I think

it is so destructive to patients and I think I'm talking about my own analysis and my fight to hold onto the internal analyst and to allow that process to go on when issues between us had to get resolved in reality. It was an intrusion I can look at in two ways, that her problems in the real relationship with me, and her illness took away something that was in effect an analytic birthright, which was the harboring of this transference object within as a resource for myself. One could also look at it as an experience in reality that forced me to work through to another place where I don't have that, and therefore I rely on myself and I live more in reality.

Dr. Zelda Fisher (Moderately Satisfying Analysis). Dr. Fisher, analyzed by the same analyst as **Dr. Rodine,** felt profoundly helped in a number of domains. But some of her eventual feelings toward the analyst were marred by the troubling sense that certain countertransference rivalries had remained unresolved. Not only did the analyst seem ambivalent about the value of **Dr. Fisher's publications** during the analyses, but she also, some time after termination, made use, without consent, of a particular issue discussed in the analysis that the analysand later wanted to elaborate in her own writings. This raises the question, To whom does the analytic content belong?

ZF: I asked around and said I was looking for a strong female who was married, who had child, a role model. Because I had lots of good fathers, and really felt it important that I had a strong female. So they recommended her. And, wow! She was, incredibly articulate, so well put together. I had always felt a bit like a slob. My mother just didn't, I didn't have the girl thing from my mother. She didn't teach me how to put on makeup, how to get dressed with slips. I just didn't know about those things. I don't know whether she didn't know how to do it, or I didn't take it from her. I was supposed to be the son in the family. So an important thing my analyst did was to tell me about places "that's where you should buy your clothes."
LT: So, you wanted strong but also female.
ZF: Yeah. Without knowing that at the time. I did know it superficially but I didn't know the depths of it. So the kinds of things I remember from my treatment was the day she told me about wearing slips so that wool skirts wouldn't itch or stick to your tights. So I think about kind of a developmentally deprived person. And she didn't make those kinds of overreaching interpretations that my first, inexperi-

enced analyst did, about penis envy, when I needed some very direct confirmation—not advice, but more a parenting I had missed, reality help, in areas that were just deficits for me.

LT: To be an actual helpful person?

ZF: Yeah, to be an actual person. That's really right. I could then face the pain of having grown up in a household with incredible mourning going on. She helped me articulate that. And I changed a lot. I was very depressed. It wasn't really depression. It was mourning. I was guilt-ridden, and she helped liberate my playfulness a lot. But what was precious about her role as an actual other, was about clothing, and also, when I was pregnant with my first child I felt her presence very much in a way that my mother couldn't manage. By the time I terminated, I felt she was like this wonderful safe environment that was both inside and outside at the same time. She was a lot of resources. And now it's not so much her; it feels very much like me now. Not her. But the real piece of her, that I'm struggling with, is around her competition. And I think she would say "Yes, you should struggle with this part of it, and I'm sorry I couldn't help you better at the time, but I hope I gave you the tools to do so yourself." But, I can't deal with the content. I just can't. And I have been trying. So that stays painful. I talked about it in analysis when I found out that the Journal was taking my article. She asked me how I felt about the fact that I had published and she hadn't. Before she had. I said, "Oh, no big deal. Yours is much better than mine is. Yours'll come out soon." I remember my voice. I could hear it. "Oh, that's ridiculous. Yours was great, good. Mine was garbage." And then I had a dream which I talked about, where I was walking by the public library, and a lion, with a mane sort of like her hair, jumped on top of me. I realized, here it was, she was gonna pounce on me for retribution. For writings, for the Public Library. What a great dream! At that time I was so excited, I said, "The unconscious is the best, isn't it? What a wonderful gift."

But I couldn't ever figure out whether it was okay for me to write, or why it was that when I described how easily a colleague could write because she had no conflict about it, that my analyst said, "She's writing prematurely. She doesn't have enough clinical experience." I figured she must mean me, too.

Then, some years after I terminated, someone had heard her give a paper I hadn't heard that later came out in an article. She had talked about a piece of my treatment without asking me permission. To fit into her theory, she described me as "a woman envious of her male colleagues," which is not something she had ever interpreted to me. And she also includes something that I was actually publishing myself, without citing me either. I was really upset and wrote her a letter about it. It took months to get the courage to write this letter. This was so hard, to ask for recognition by her. It was very painful. But I did it. And then, not so long after that, she got sick. And I never heard from her. When I wrote this letter and didn't hear back, that was the closest to my saying, "I want to be seen by you as a colleague."

LT: Had there been a longing also to become friends with her eventually—you mentioned knowing of another analysand of hers who did, after termination.

ZF: More as a colleague. I think by then I realized how we were just not the same. She dresses too formal. I don't think we would have enjoyed each other, to go play. But I wanted to talk to her about the work that we were doing,

LT: During the analysis, did you ever feel like you loved her? Or hated her, and . . . ? Where did that go?

ZF: I never felt love and hate like that. I felt affection, admiration. I felt incredible gratitude a lot of times, and appreciation for what she had given me or how well she had listened to me, my experience of really being heard. But loving? Not, like, erotic loving. I wasn't erotically drawn to her. I was at the time erotically drawn to Peter Wright [male supervisor] (laughs). I keep him as a good inner object always. More so than my analyst. She's not there in terms of my writing. I don't know how she would feel about my writing, because she couldn't respond at the time. I really needed her to respond. I never will know whether she felt like I was in her turf. So I never felt recognized, only in this pathological way. I never felt that she did get something out of working with me and that she respected me as a colleague. And this is the reality hook that makes it hard. Maybe I really was hurting her by publishing a paper before she did, when she was so many years older.

LT: What's your notion of how she would describe you if she were asked, "What's **Zelda Fisher** like?"

ZF: What would she say? A grieving woman who was also playful, very curious, high energy, too rebellious, a little too rebellious for her own good. Scared. And maybe too haughty about writing, not really ready to be a grown-up.

I now turn to two more extended narratives, one of a deeply satisfying analysis and the other of a highly dissatisfying analysis:

Dr. Julia Baranger (Deeply Satisfying Analysis). Dr. Baranger illustrates that experiencing the analyst as being reserved may have advantages when it resonates in positive ways for the analysand. Similarly, particular areas of inhibition, which are surmised as existing in the analyst, can be accepted as such, as long as the sense of warm connection to the analysand is present. Unlike **Dr. Brown,** who had seen the same analyst about a decade earlier, **Dr. Baranger** did not view her analyst's nature as creating a constraint in the reach of the analysis.

JB: She had strong beliefs about women in medicine and started out being very generous, offering to supervise me during my psychiatric residency and to talk about what it meant to be a woman in medicine in those days. And, of course, I was very excited about that and I took her up on it.

LT: That's an interesting situation at the start of analysis. You had some sense of her beforehand and some sense of how she viewed patients and dynamics. And she, in turn, started with the sense that you knew something about her point of view.

JB: And ambitions and a woman's ambitions. She was clearly masterful in what she did. Very well respected in the community. She was a major figure in the psychoanalytic community as a woman. That made me feel very appreciative of her and want to be like her.

LT: You bring up already an interesting theme about women with ambition and that that facilitated identifying with them.

JB: Right. And she introduced me to Dr. Hochstein [a well-known woman analyst]. She took me to see her, to talk about the same issue. She asked me whether I would like to meet with this analyst and discuss with her the issues that she and I were discussing in relation to women in medicine and in psychiatry, and I was very eager to do so because, of course, I knew about her. We had a meeting in which I was convinced that my analyst was much more simpatico with me than the other woman analyst.

The analysis began and proceeded on a very positive note:

JB: It quickly got to be very important and very valuable to me. I was very much in awe of her. I idealized her a lot. I think that I had another powerful positive transference that it took me a while to appreciate, but my second mother, so to speak, was my paternal grandmother, who was the matriarch of the family, and she had the same first name as my analyst. And in many ways physically resembled her. She also had a kind of sense of propriety and reserve that was similar. And my grandmother loved me very much and was extremely supportive of me all through my childhood, even when I got into difficulties with my own mother. She would champion me. She was on my side, and regarded me as very important in the family. So there were a lot of things that came together. But I idealized her a great deal, for a lot of the analysis, for the first part especially.

LT: During the beginning, a quality that you mention about her is that there was reserve in the sense that it sounds like you didn't feel intruded upon. I don't know if that's right.

JB: I think that was very important. Also because that was one of the negative experiences I had with my own mother and because part of my persona is a similar kind of reserve. So that I felt more comfortable with that.

LT: At the same time you describe a readiness on her part to actually intervene in going to bat for you.

JB: Yes. Like my grandmother did.

LT: Yes. And you said you idealized her a lot. In what way . . . in the sense of being drawn to her, that the most wonderful thing was to be with her, or in what you felt about what she was like or . . . ?

JB: Both. I loved the time that I spent with her a lot of the time. And I thought she was very wise and very esteemed by other people, too.

LT: And you said "at the beginning." Did that change?

JB: Well, there were plenty of periods in the analysis when I would be furious at her and when I was angry and challenging. There was one particular time that was hard for both of us, pretty far along in the analysis, that certainly did challenge the idealization. As you know, one constantly hears stories about everyone in the Institute. That included stories about her being described, in a particular instance, as very critical. That was very challenging because it demonstrated a kind of judgmental, hypercritical quality that I had been afraid of, but never perceived in her toward me. I was really concerned about her capacity to be judgmental because one of my biggest struggles was my own self-criticism and my own tendency to judge myself and, since it always goes both ways, I, in addition to my altruism and commitment to doing good things, I was always struggling with my tendency to criticize and to judge people for not living up to my high standards.

LT: So, are you saying, "I looked to this person to be a more benign

superego to identify with, and then I worried about whether she would
be able to help me with that"?

JB: Periodically I would worry.

LT: Were there issues in you that were not easy to bring up with her,
but that you felt no obstacle to engaging directly from her? And were
there other issues that you feared would really rock the boat between
you, or that you felt afterwards were untapped during the analysis?

JB: I don't think that I thought anything that was worthwhile was particularly easy. Even my love for her was difficult at times to express.

LT: Difficult to express—how did you feel it was received?

JB: I thought she received that warmly and graciously. But the other
things that are typically more challenging to deal with were certainly
true in my case. Aggression and anger and sexuality were very challenging. She did better or worse in different ways dealing with those
subjects with me, in retrospect.

LT: Sexuality, including sexual feelings toward her, or more sexuality in . . . ?

JB: During the times that I was aware of having sexual feelings toward
her, she was quite responsive and supportive. But in general terms . . .

LT: Do you mean being a sexual woman, outside in the world?

JB: Yeah. I do think that she was warmly connected with me, and
that that's what allowed her to engage in an intimate relationship, but
I think that there were times when her sense of herself outside of the
exclusiveness of our relationship did intrude. And they were, unfortunately, ways in which I was quite naive and rather prudish when I
started my analysis. Now that I think about it, I was very young, I
was only 25. So I was anxious and inhibited about sex, though I had
had boyfriends all along and I had the feeling from her that she was
also prudish in some ways. So that, although she talked a good line,
there were moments when I felt she was less than comfortable with
some of the things I was talking about, not necessarily with me. And
in retrospect I became more aware of that. I wasn't aware of that at
all at the time. What I perceived was permission to exclude certain
areas of sensuality and aggression in sexuality from my repertoire. My
perception was, well, she doesn't like it either, so it's all right for me
to avoid it. One of the things about her that I appreciated the most
was how she grew during the course of my analytic experience with
her! In the beginning, she was much more focused on oedipal matters
and theoretical formulations, although she was not an overinterpreter

at all. She was very silent, but never in an abandoning way, although I experienced it that way. She was not rigid. She certainly had rigid parts of her personality, but I think she was much less rigid as an analyst than in other parts of her life. I mean, I have a sense of her being reserved to an extreme in some situations and critical. And, some people were afraid of her, some of my colleagues. I think she really did bring the best of herself to her analytic work.

Julia reflects on her feelings about termination:

JB: It was very sad, but I was very happy in my life then. And I felt I had accomplished a great deal. And just about everything in my life at that point was going pretty well. So I was prepared to start out on my own. The sadness was really about missing her. Missing the time with her, missing her as a person.

LT: And did it feel like a good-bye forever, or did you have . . . ?

JB: No, I visited her a couple of times later. And she had let me know that she did have contact with patients afterward. And I had the sense that she would be warm and giving to me in that case, but that she would maintain an amount of reserve, which would make it comfortable for the two of us. And that was indeed the case. Some time later when I developed migraines, I made an appointment with her, because though I had them before, they went away early in the analysis. And she made an interpretation, which I think was incorrect, but she made it very nicely. And they went away and didn't return. I think it was the connection with her.

LT: You're saying something very piquant about the gift of a wrong interpretation that can nevertheless work.

JB: She cared enough about me to want to give me something, to want to help me. She was not judgmental toward me.

LT: Were those the issues in the relationship to her during the analysis, that you think of as making the biggest difference, or more specific interpretations, or the cumulative interpretations?

JB: Never specific interpretations. Not cumulative interpretations, either. It was the relationship, really. It was the abiding sense of tolerance and positive regard that I felt. I really felt that she loved me. In spite of all I revealed to her, which I had never revealed to anyone else in my life.

LT: Or, possibly, also *because* of all you revealed to her?

JB: Well, the positive regard only had its power in that context.

LT: And did you feel you loved her?

JB: Oh, absolutely! Always! I mean there were moments when I hated her. But the general tenor of the whole business was that I loved her and afterward I loved her.

LT: And where does she sit now in your inner life?

JB: She remains a very positive part of my inner experience. I think most sustaining was the degree to which we accomplished an amelioration of my self-criticism through my belief in her acceptance and approval of me at a deep level, which was sustaining and continues. The experience as a whole was a very positive one, and partly because it had been so rigorous. And it did play a major role in my falling in love with my husband. I have been extraordinarily lucky in my choice of a husband and in the relationship we've been able to make together. In a funny way, I credit that partly to my analyst, because I had the fantasy when I met him during the analysis that he would be her choice for me. And also, of course, in my work I consciously and unconsciously modeled myself after her in various ways during that early part of my experience as a clinician and later I came more into my own.

LT: Do you think she was with others like with you, or . . . ?

JB: I have the fantasy that my relationship with her was unique. How much she changed in her way of being with patients according to the people that they were I don't know. I expect she must've some. I know that what was most painful of all was her death. She died, and things were happening in my life I would have wanted to talk about with her. So, I used to visit her grave. It was a sense of just a presence. Her enduring presence. I don't go there anymore. But I feel that from her.

After the tape was turned off and we were walking to the door, **Julia Baranger** was tearful as she said that the time of the analyst's dying was very hard because the analyst, due to her reserve and sense of privacy, didn't want any visiting, whereas **Julia** "wanted so much to see her, to hold her and cradle her. I wanted to sing her the lullaby my grandmother used to sing to me. I, in fact, did go around singing it in my head when I knew she was dying. Interestingly, it was a child's lullaby about Jesus. I had found out she was at least brought up Christian, and my grandmother, who sang to me, was a devout Christian."

   Dr. Emma McClinton (Dissatisfying Analysis). Dr. McClinton's
first analyst exemplifies a number of the qualities that I have previously described as associated with unsatisfying or damaging analyses,
including envious and blameful attitudes, unacknowledged "enactments" under the guise of "neutrality," and the kind of attachment
barrier that would have made revealing ones needs ill advised. This
particular analyst's tendency to blame others was legion. For example, it was said of her that whenever she farted during an analytic hour
she would insist the patient had done it. **Dr. McClinton** had wanted
to see a woman analyst "to gain a closeness with a woman that I perhaps never had," because her mother had seemed inaccessibly
depressed during her babyhood—"I think I was left alone"—and to
deal with her sense that mother had taken more pleasure in her son
than her daughters. When she entered analysis, **Emma McClinton** was
happily married, pregnant with her first child, and looking forward
to becoming an analyst.

EM: I think I have two ways of relating. One is open, more trusting
and caring and giving. I feel deeply connected. And another one is
quite a fortress. I *can not* choose which one will be there for me. This
fortress doesn't occur with my patients, but it did with my analyst. It
was a terrible disappointment that I felt, to have such a fortress for
at least six years with her, that she was unable to allow me to trust
her. I wasn't aware of it at the time, except that I felt that I couldn't
talk with her. And when I did some things to avoid it, she took it very
personally. And didn't understand it. She just thought I was against
her or resisting her. Or that there was something inherently the matter with me. I had thought of myself as a very happy person before I
began my analysis.

   During the initial phase of the analysis, the analyst emphasized a
"neutrality, which meant no response. And getting no response was
too familiar from my mother." When **Emma** criticized her analyst to
friends outside the analytic hour, she felt the analyst responding with,
"Why are you talking about me outside the hour and spoiling my reputation?" I felt it as such a slap on the hand, such a discouragement
from talking about her or transference feelings. I did not feel she analyzed what that was about. But that she didn't want me to do it."

LT: That sounds far from the neutrality she emphasized.
EM: I did feel like she was a killjoy. The worst part of that was that
at no time did I feel that she at all could feel what I was feeling when

I was pregnant. Why didn't I stop and change to somebody else? I wanted to be an analyst, and I didn't know that this was even possible! The analysts had a lot more power than they do now.

LT: So in any case it was your feeling that you were trapped, if you were going to be an analyst, or also that there would be retribution if you . . . ?

EM: Definitely.

In a number of actions, affecting the life of the analysand "outside the hour," the analyst was "fairly punitive." She withheld recommending that the analysand begin seminars after the first year of analysis. She referred patients to **Emma's** analytic sibling, but not to her. When a motherly neighbor with whom **Emma** talked about the analyst said, "'Oh, your analyst is jealous of you. This woman has no children, no marriage," **Dr. McClinton** recalls, "I didn't believe that."

LT: You didn't believe that. What was your hunch about her?

EM: I thought she thought her parents didn't love her because she wasn't a boy, and she couldn't help me with that. She denied that. Mostly, I thought it was me. It was how I failed to engage her. It didn't feel like she'd like me better if I were a boy. But it did feel like I wasn't elegant enough or smart enough or [pause] insightful. It's not just that she didn't see what was there, it's that I also didn't show it. And she did not relate to important things in my life. Pregnancies. I would complain later on about how hard it was for me to take care of the children. And she would say, "Why do you need to take care of the children!"

Dr. McClinton recalls wanting to take a break from analysis to focus her involvement on her new baby and its siblings. "She said, 'You can't. You have to come right in here, if you're going to do this.' And I thought that she was concerned about getting paid."

LT: You wanted her to support a close bond between mother and baby—with the time needed for repose with each other, for that deepening of connection. During your own childhood with whom could you feel most intimate?

EM: Oh, my father. Very much so. So he would be the person, where I feel good about myself. But I would be more imitating him than . . . that would be when I'm feeling good, that would be being like him. He was pretty terrific. He can be very focused with why don't you try this, try that. Incredibly involved. My analyst would say, "Why do you idealize your father so much?" So I felt like another support was kicked out. And if you didn't agree, then what's wrong with you. So there was no sense of working together. And about the transference with my mother—there was very little self-reflection on her part about her role. As I try so hard, with my own patients right now, and my own children, to say, "Now what is this with me?" My patients say to me what they find helpful is that you acknowledge your values and then we can talk about it. "Do you feel such and such?" "Yes, I did." Whatever. But with her there was no acknowledgment ever.

Emma observed signs of cancer in her analyst after "she had had her first surgery. She denied there was anything wrong with her. But I knew her hand was swollen."

LT: So, she actively disputed correct perceptions on your part?
EM: Yeah, it was very odd. I saw her as very authoritarian. Now, I was looking for a strong woman . . .
LT: So was that part of the "you must be right and something is wrong with me" conclusion you came to so sadly?
EM: It's like I come and go, I can be in the shadow, and I come out of the shadow. And in this analysis, I was in the shadow and stayed there.

Emma told me, at the beginning of our second meeting, that the "horrible old feelings" about the first analyst "did come back" after talking about them in a way that "felt regressive." We returned to the incident of her having complained to others about the analyst "outside" the relationship to her.

LT: What I wondered was whether that wasn't an essence of things, that you *needed* to tell someone outside of the relationship to her, that you weren't getting what you needed.
EM: This feels right.
LT: And that it was like when your mother was depressed. Then it turned out to be good for you that there were other people outside.
EM: Good point. Feels quite right.
LT: And that both the need and resourcefulness on your part, to look to others in relation to your mother, was part of what that event was about. It didn't seem recognized as such.
EM: It just got closed off, that's right. When I wanted the pain of that analysis to go away, the way I handled it was always to say I didn't have an analysis. It doesn't count.

LT: I think I hear what you're saying. If you nullify it, it can't hurt you?
EM: No, it's not that it didn't exist, but this was not an analysis. This was something else. It was an exposing, in every way, an exposing of what I didn't know about. The struggle of whether my view of her is projection or not is very difficult. I struggle with it still, because I don't want to necessarily not acknowledge my part in it and not change. I mean, not change in characterological ways, so that these kinds of things don't happen again. It still affects me in several ways. One is that whatever isn't worked out, isn't worked out still, and secondly, the ramifications of my inability to be with her, in a way that I could show her who I am, still has ramifications for my present and my career. So, yes, I am sad about that.

About a decade after termination, **Dr. McClinton** sought out a second analyst for treatment:
EM: It took me a very, very long time to trust him for a sense of really paying attention and caring in a way that, although professional, did attempt to integrate, you could say, both parts of me. And I was able to bring in the sense of the father transference. I have a very strong masculine identification that has been part of this, the defenses of valuing of independence, autonomy. Though I had wanted a woman, a strong woman, I didn't know how strong the rejection feeling would be, which I was never able to overcome.

He was just so different. He was very much willing to give me control of the process. Quite literally. Come when you want. Pay when you want. Pay what you want. He saw that as something he needed to do for me to be trusting. He also tried in a very realistic way to continually point out to me what I do that I do, how I am. Which was very different from the—quote—neutrality. It would be much more about things in my life that go well. Something honest but that reinforces morale, helps my self-esteem. And from her, there was a neutrality and lack of response, no matter what, that was so deadening and did remind me of my mother, who had a philosophy, initially with me, of being humble, praise will be spoiling. It felt like the same response. So the transference with him was much more similar to that with my father, which was helpful.

Dr. McClinton contrasts her sense of how each analyst would view her. Whereas the first analyst "would say that I was shallow, defended, superficial. Unable to be intimate," the second analyst would describe her as "resourceful, very helpful to my patients and family . . . that I help people with their potential."

EM: One of the first things he said to me was, and it really helped a lot, there was a lady and she had seen 10 potential analysts, everybody in town, and she chose me, and he said, "Why do you think this person would choose you? She saw 10 people. She's a knowledgeable woman!" And when I ran that group, no one ever missed a session, and he pointed to that and said, "What's that about?" And that was helpful to me, because there is a way I have of denying that piece.

LT: So, in some way, he saw that you were a compelling person who brought people there. It sounded like last time, as you were describing your first analyst as well as your mother, that you concluded there was something missing in your compellingness to engage them. And that that question was an undercurrent.

EM: That's right.

LT: While it sounds like your second analyst said, "Look. Pay attention to the effect you have!"

EM: Yes, I'd say exactly that. I didn't engage my first analyst. I mean, I don't think so. I know so. (Sigh.)

The second analyst's ways of engaging with her included the following:

I felt he was very observant and very supportive in an ego way. If I were going to give a talk and I would leave the briefcase. (Laughter.) "You're disorganized. What's it about? Don't forget your briefcase." And, helpful in helping with the children. I can't tell you if I learned this from him, or if I knew how to do it, but I'm very good at getting people from one place you want to be emotionally to another, whether they're my patients or my children .

LT: A minute ago you were saying that he would say, "You're disorganized, what's that about?" Is there something either disorganizing or uncohesive about trying to relate to mother or your first analyst, in that the center of you can't meet the center of them in a focal or a vibrant way?

EM: Yes. Yes.

LT: That's different with him?

EM: Yes. Although I think that there is plenty about the transference there, it's certainly so much more in form. I always saw myself as attachment avoidant, but I think I'm much probably closer to attachment dis-organized in regard to women. Yes, I think you're quite right. Now it's much less. Almost gone.

LT: So he could see things about you very easily.

EM: And what could I see about him? He's very intelligent, much smarter than she was. Although when she might have been bright, I never saw it. He thinks about people, about his patients, after they're gone. Now that was very important.

LT: After they're gone?

EM: When they're not in his office.

LT: So you inhabit a space in him.

EM: Very important to me because I do think this is a difference between my mother and father, too. Dad doesn't forget. Mother, you remind her you're there, but she clearly hasn't kept it in mind, and I really felt this with the first analyst. But there's a sense of occupying a place in him. And his desire to be helpful. And by the way, I'm also very good at this, at keeping my patients well in mind.

Termination, in the sense of saying a permanent good-bye, does not feel like an essential part of the therapeutic or analytic process to her, but of importance is that "you can terminate in the sense of being a more equal person." Ideally, then, "you can still be connected as colleagues and as caring people." At termination with her first analyst, **Dr. McClinton** felt an "incredible sense of relief" and "not a bit" of longing or mourning for the relationship, which she would now describe as "terribly destructive." In contrast, she expects that the second analyst will matter to her as long as he lives. She feels that she loves her second analyst in some way and also that he has affection and some kind of love for her: "I think both were important, to be able to be loving, to being loved."

EM: I found him steady and believing in me, but I did not really feel a connection with him until more recently. And that was due to his ability to maintain his sense of himself in the face of my being criti-cal or distant. Whatever. So he hung in there, and he was willing to make all kinds of—it wouldn't be real accommodations, but sort of fit my style in a way that I needed. But there was a real belief in me and a sense of me, even if I couldn't always show it. And important was his allowing a very profound depression and regression that took place in our work together.

Emma clarifies that by his "allowing regression," she means, "He understands the feeling of needing a mother. And so I felt the safety, which I couldn't feel with my first analyst with that, at all."

While the first analyst "seemed to demean" any area of interest and expertise **Dr. McClinton** developed, the second analyst showed a great deal of "respect" for the quality of her work. She notes that her own analytic style "may be more modern" than his, but their styles are similar in their empathic presence with patients.

EM: When I do therapy and analysis, he definitely is there. I am a little more modern in the sense that I am more likely to share my thoughts or on occasion my experience, than he is. But, I would say, what is like him really, is a continual sense of empathy, and when I don't have the empathy I always ask where it is: "What's getting in the way?" I think he really did struggle to maintain empathy with me, despite whatever I might have put in the way and tried hard to figure it out if he couldn't. He trots to sort of be in step with me.

Emma describes how the sense of his presence supports her confidence as analyst: "I didn't think of it like a father, I thought it more like a mother. Someone sitting by your side. That would have been very absent in my life. And my mother didn't struggle to see where I was coming from."

Dr. McClinton's confidence also involves being able to claim her own positive qualities. She likens her analyst's task in this to the "Wizard of Oz, who didn't give anyone anything that they didn't already have."

THEORIES OF THOUGHT

Flout 'em and scout 'em; And scout 'em and flout 'em

Thought is free.

—William Shakespeare, *Twelfth Night*

The focus, so far, has been on those perceived qualities in the analyst that are associated with the analysand's judgment of satisfaction with the analysis and with those variations that have to do with the gender combination of analyst and analysand. In a shift of focus, this chapter explores one aspect of the analysand's frame of mind, namely, those theories about the generation of his or her mental processes that are brought to the analytic encounter. I have chosen this dimension for illustration because it colors the experience of oneness and twoness within analytic process, as well as the experienced reversion of twoness to oneness induced by termination.

I have suggested that transmutative processes are fostered by oscillations in the analysand's experience of the analyst as attuned to his or her inner life and then as infusing otherness. These modes correspond to the phenomenologic sense of being inside oneself, generating one's own intrapsychic world, and the sense of being engaged in the intersubjective, dyadic creation of meanings—what Tronick (1998) calls "the dyadic expansion of consciousness." Oscillations in "being distinct from" and "being together with" in the process of "loose coupling" are regarded by Sander (1997) as optimal in early development. Within analytic process they seem to augur well for the projective–introjective flow that accompanies change. There are, however, major individual differences in the propensity toward organizing inner experience in a more self-contained versus interactive way. To be sure, when inner life is pictured as self-generated, the role of the other is, of course, no less essential—to recognize, accept, and thereby to verify the individuality of the person. The range of such propensities can be glimpsed in individuals' theories of thought. As well, convictions about the locus of change within the psychoanalytic process exist as undercurrents to one's theoretical allegiances. There are those who view intrapsychic life—its conflicts and internalized others—as primarily subjectively created (albeit with the essential recognition and reaction from others). Others believe that selected aspects of actuality in object interactions, as experienced in developmentally changing ways, constitute the nucleus of internalizations. The optimal role of the analyst tends to be pictured accordingly. I believe that the analytic situation simultaneously always evokes one-person and two-person aspects of the analysand's psychic life, but that one or the other will be in the foreground for different individuals, as well as at different periods of the same analysis.

The research Participants varied in how they conceptualized the nature of their own thinking, and, naturally, at times they held more than one theory simultaneously. Any particular formulation, like other choices in theory, tended to be profoundly personal (D. Jacobs, 1992). At a deeper level, it expressed those quotidian ways invoked to metabolize the entry of another person's influence, affects, and ideas into inner psychic life, as well as the particular blend of pleasures, anxieties, and defenses evoked by that process. Such individual variation in accustomed and preferred ways of generating ideas were highlighted by the transition, at termination, from analytic process to a self-analytic mode. It affected how termination was experienced and colored the lingering quality of interest in the analyst.

Of course, all thought is ultimately intrapsychically generated, even when there is a sense of intersubjective resonance as generating an idea. As Bion (1977) has said about the analytic situation, "We're both in this alone" (p. 37). But engaging in dyadically evoked ideation involves a different kind of affective stimulation, with different effects, than what is evoked by the autocreated. For illustration, I choose excerpts from the narratives of two analysts who shared the feeling of being ready for termination, looking forward to being "on my own." There are contrasts in their views about the nature of their thinking, however: **Dr. Encarta** is high on the spectrum of experiencing himself as self-created in the area of ideas, whereas **Dr. Stuart Laraphil** is high on the spectrum of enjoying dialogic stimulation to evoke his ideas. Ironically, **Dr. Laraphil's** example of how he solved a scientific problem demonstrates not his dependence on the ideation of the other but the opposite: The solution had incubated within, but its emergence in consciousness was postponed until the reunion of the collaborative dyad. I begin the excerpts from each with their comments about termination and then look backward to associated themes.

Dr. Horatio Encarta (Moderately Satisfying Analysis). What **Dr. Horatio Encarta** most freely prizes about himself is being an original thinker. He is known as a significant contributor to psychoanalytic theory. He speaks of himself as an "auto-didact" and comments, "I've never collaborated with anyone" professionally. He reads voraciously, however, and notes that he relies on his reading for needed intellectual stimulation. Valuing the self-created, he crystallizes the autonomy of his thinking by protecting his freedom to resist unwelcome impingements. He mentions his belief that "to preserve ones creativity, one has to block out the Other." He has had only one analyst.

Dr. Encarta recalls both having been satisfied with his analysis and having been glad to end it. He states, "I have no complaints about my analysis, nothing. I had positive feelings about it." Nonetheless, he was anxious to terminate and did not experience ending the process or relationship as a loss. When I asked if his readiness to terminate his own analysis affected what he deems important about termination with his own analysands, he responded:

HE: I can't think so. I think that too much is made of the termination business. I think it becomes kind of a precious issue, and it isn't precious. I don't see any problems with it. You do what you have to do to terminate.

Nevertheless, several years after ending his analysis, **Horatio** created symbolic reminders of his analyst in a number of ways, suggesting that she remained a presence in his psyche. For instance, he named his dog after her, a dog he recalled as developing "a difficult nature" and apt to bite little children. Thirty years after the analysis, he had the recurrent thought that his wife would die at the same age at which his analyst had died (which she didn't do).

Dr. Encarta had seemingly always had the capacity for excitement over self-generated ideas, learning, and achievement. Early in the analysis, when he happened to discover chess, the gratification was in learning it, not playing with others. He recalls the analyst's interpretation:

HE: I remember exactly, at the very beginning of analysis I developed an interest in chess, which I never had before or since, and the interpretation had something to do with being placed in some kind of competitive situation or conflict but, interestingly, I bought some chess books, I started to learn chess, and then I just dropped it completely.
LT: Before playing with other people?
HE: Yeah, I didn't play with anybody, that wasn't the point.

Analogously, he arrived at the goal of becoming a psychoanalyst by systematic reading—first Pavlov, then Freud—and not through particular experiences with relationships.

LT: During that time, or in medical school, or between medical school and BIPSI, were there some people in the field who were inspiring or personally important as mentors or teachers?
HE: Didn't have any. No. Didn't meet anybody.

He mentioned later in the interview, however, that as a resident he was exposed to a psychoanalytically oriented department with inspiring teachers. By then, he had made up his mind about becoming a psychoanalyst. He comments about his choice of analyst: "I think I wanted a woman," but didn't "shop around." He liked the first person with whom he interviewed who had time to see him. Asked about how he experienced her early in the analysis, he said, "She was very active in making interpretations, and I felt she was kind of a nervous woman." He recalls some examples of their interchange, including his teasing her about his belief that she gave her husband a hard time.

LT: How did she react to that sort of teasing or generally to criticism, or . . . ?
HE: Probably not too well. I don't think I criticized her very much. Now she claimed, at one point, that I was aggressive toward her. That I was more aggressive than I recognized. That probably is right. But I never even really recognized that. In my memory, I never really got very angry at her. But she felt as if I gave her a hard time. When I think about it in retrospect, I don't think she did much interpretation about my competition with her. And, obviously, I've always been in competition with her. I don't think that was ever really dealt with in the transference. There was not a great deal of direct transference interpretation. In my memory of it, it largely had to do with other people outside the analysis and so forth.

Horatio remembers being quite involved in the analysis, feeling nourished by a sense of deep understanding and acceptance of his individuality that was at odds with how he had experienced the family of his childhood. As an only child, he had been made much of by both parents and grandparents, "treated rather like a crown prince." But he felt even as a child that his family lacked the kind of intelligence he had and recalls that he would often not talk to them in spite of their prodding. With his analyst it was different:

HE: She was somebody I could talk to. So I think that must have contributed to the involvement.
LT: You say your experience in this was very different from the way you engaged with your family when you refused to talk. Was there also a sense that for the first time someone understood you in the way that she did and that you could express yourself as more fully yourself?
HE: Yeah. I think that's right. Which was good. Because I know myself to be a very dependent person. I need the presence of the other person while being in myself. And I felt very much accepted by her in some full way.
LT: So you're also saying you didn't feel her as judgmental?
HE: No. I was judgmental toward her. I don't think she was judgmental toward me.

We discuss some other features of the analysis:

LT: If you think of what kinds of things about it were the most sustaining, or what kinds of things about it were the most painful, where does that land you?
HE: I tend not to remember pain, so [long pause] I can't remember those things. I tend to put painful things behind me as fast as I can. I don't deny things. But I try to just close the door on them.

When the analysis had proceeded productively for five and a half years **Dr. Encarta** was restive to end it.

HE: I was anxious to terminate. I was getting tired of the process. I wanted to be on my own. It was an achievement. I'm achievement oriented, so it was something to get through the analysis. I wanted that achievement.
LT: And did it feel like she supported that?
HE: Yeah, I don't feel she hung on to me beyond a reasonable point.
LT: During the analysis, did your notions of what she was like as a person shift, and in what way?

HE: I don't know if it shifted. I always thought that she was more neurotic than I was. My feeling about her is that she functioned best in life as an analyst. She was much better behind the couch than she was as an ordinary human being. She was a very difficult person. But I had none of that with her. The only thing she had with me after the analysis was when she invited me to teach with her and I declined. I think she was angry about that.

LT: You say you declined, and also that you had a picture of how difficult she was. Did you figure you would then move from what sounds like a special, protected place on the couch, where she was at her best, to being in the line of fire?

HE: Yeah. I thought she was too difficult to get along with.

LT: If you were aware of her being a difficult person, did that affect how it felt lying there, in her hands, so to speak?

HE: No. I think I trusted her and felt intuitively—and I think I was right—that she was a very good analyst. And that she functioned best in that fashion, so I trusted her as her patient. I think she was caring. And she showed that when I went back to see her several times because of some unexpected trouble in my family.

LT: That's kind of a piquant description I'm not sure I've heard before in quite that way, of somebody who, as a human being, you wouldn't want to get intimate with, but in the analysis, was very caring. And how, in your mind, did those two fit together?

HE: Well, it would involve my speculating about her character. I think there was a sadistic element to her character and that, when she functioned in a very caring, giving way, this is very reassuring to her . . . her being relatively decent.

Dr. Encarta described the analyst as both "active" and "meddlesome." This was generally accepted as "analysts intervened in all kinds of active ways that people don't do today." The one time **Horatio Encarta** felt distinctly unsupported by the analyst was when his wife needed to be seen for a referral and the analyst offered to do the evaluation but then subsequently made comments about seeing better functioning in the wife than **Horatio** had depicted.

HE: I felt that she was not taking my side in the matter, but actually I think that she did see I was putting up with a lot of shit, and I felt her sympathy for that.

LT: As you think back to the analysis, what were the issues that you felt, in her working with you, were helped greatly, and what were things that you were left to do on your own afterward or wish had gotten taken up in some other way?

HE: The area I remember being helped a lot, which was important, was the areas of my grandiosity and feeling omnipotently destructive. That got pretty well analyzed. I think what I liked about my analysis with her, was that, despite her being viewed as a classical analyst, she knew a great deal about early development. And she was quite in tune with that, so I think there was a great discrepancy between what she wrote and what she did. Therapeutically, I think there was some benefit, in that I had a psychosomatic symptom. I had heartburn, or I was involved in my stomach, or I don't what the hell it was. But, for some mysterious reason that disappeared during the course of the analysis. I mean it wasn't specifically analyzed. And I think the analysis helped me sexually. I think the anxieties I had about female genitals, the cloacal fantasies were analyzed, and resolved, so I'm not inhibited sexually. Analysis purified my view of the cunt.

LT: You have told me that separations are terribly upsetting and anxiety provoking for you, and darkness, and other kinds of things connected to that. Did those issues get approached in analysis?

HE: No. No. None of that. Also I don't think she handled direct transference affects all that well.

LT: Do you mean both anger and desire for her?

HE: Maybe anger, more than desire. She didn't like it, well; I don't like it much, either.

LT: Well, it's not to like, but it's still to do . . .

HE: Yeah, I don't think she was as comfortable with it.

LT: Do you ever think, "If she could only see me now"?

HE: Yeah, I think she was competitive with me, come to think about it, because she was around when my writings first came out, and I don't think she liked it very much, she never said anything very positive about it. Very peremptory about it, dismissive of it.

I ask about his reactions some years after the analysis:

LT: When you heard about her having a rough time as she was getting older, from others who visited her, did you feel any pull toward or push away from connecting yourself in some way to her then, or visiting her?

HE: No. I didn't visit her. I didn't see her particularly. But I felt badly when she died, that she didn't enjoy the fruits of her professional labors, that she didn't have a period to become a kind of senior citizen of analysis. That didn't happen for her.

LT: What are your notions about how she experienced you during your analysis and around termination and then afterward? If she had to describe, if somebody else said, "What's this **Dr. Encarta** like, as a person?"

HE: I think she liked me, which was important. I think she thought I was bright, and she valued that.

LT: Then as you came to terminate, any memory of what issues got taken up toward the end or even what the last day was like?

HE: I have absolutely no memory of that, interestingly enough. The only memory I have is not termination, but coming to see her occasionally after termination. She sort of maintained an interest in my life, as it were. But I don't know what she believed about termination. The classical idea was that you would develop a transference neurosis, and you resolved it. Period. Then it's over. That you would feel like anybody else, toward your analyst. Those were the teachings. But looking at her behavior, asking me to teach with her, I think in some ways she felt more need to keep attached to her patients and to me than I felt. I suppose I think sometimes in terms of my competitive feelings, what she would think of me if she were alive.

LT: And what would she, now . . . ?

HE: I think she'd be proud of my achievements. But also competitive. I think she may have been competitive to the extent of being angry that I didn't give her sufficient recognition or pay sufficient attention to her contributions or simply being influenced by her ideas. I haven't had this thought before. Maybe she didn't really want her patients to be truly independent of her, that is, to really stand on their own feet completely, independent of what she believed in. I don't think she quite achieved that position.

LT: That's interesting. In terms of supporting your autonomy, which is very important, period, plus important to you. And the whole issue—I wonder if this was a silent one between you—of your experience of her wish to influence you and shape something of your thinking, while you strongly had your own ideas.

HE: That's true.

LT: Did you have a yen, during the analysis to know the flux of her inner emotional life? Or did you rather want to be free from the sense of being influenced by the feelings you might then have had about her?

HE: I don't think I was that interested in her, in knowing more.
LT: And now?
HE: No.
LT: If you imagine running into each other now and could talk freely, what would you picture that each of you would say, and what would you think and not say? If she came bopping down the street?
HE: I don't know, because my thought was somewhat intellectual. That I would not like getting involved personally, but I think I'd want to know what she thought about what's happening to psychoanalysis and what her reaction is to it. She'd probably be disgusted by what's happening to psychoanalysis: The whole fragmentation, the lack of discipline, the lack of clear thinking, the erosion of standards, the whole business. Sort of the loss of, the loss of what I'll call quality.

Dr. Stuart Laraphil: Stuart Laraphil has a reputation for helping the collaborative generation of ideas within a dyad or in a group. He is apt to spontaneously articulate linkages between the thoughts or meanings expressed by others and to mingle them, appreciatively, with his own. He was deeply disappointed with his first analyst but felt altogether different about his second. The shift from dialogue back to soliloquy infused his experience of termination of the second analysis:

SL: I have one very clear memory about that shift. And it was shortly after we actually terminated and I woke up with an interesting dream. For the moment, I had forgotten that I wasn't going to see my analyst, and I was excited. I didn't realize there was excitement until the disappointment that was about to follow, you know? Because the feeling was of excitement that I would get to go share this with him. And then, when I realized that I wasn't going, the feeling was like, what's the point of having a dream? It was the wind kicked out of me. Why bother to dream? If I can't share it with him. What meaning, what value does it have? And it took a while till once again I could recover the value of dreams for myself, but for a little while there was this sense of loss and loss of the meaning of things that were connected with my relationship to him, and dreaming being the clearest one. But I think there were other sorts of phenomena like that, things that I observed and then had a sense of loss . . . like catching myself at a slip or something, along the same lines as the dream, evidence of the unconscious life.
LT: You touch something else very interesting. People posit the self-analytic function as heir to the analysis. Yet, actually, analysis is a

two-person interchange, while self-analysis is not. So it makes sense that the one doesn't translate automatically into the other, though it may be part of its yield.

SL: I agree. That's right. It goes even a little deeper. It goes into the nature of thinking. There's probably a considerable divergence between different people in regard to what I'm about to say. But, in general, I think in the context of talking to someone—and I think I'm on one end of the spectrum in that regard—it's the context of inter-action with somebody where I discover often what I think. I may have potential thoughts, the incipient versions of thoughts that don't form until I'm in the process of articulating them to somebody else. That also picks up a two-person part of getting the juice flowing, this qual-ity of thinking and talking being coterminous. Did I tell you how I solved my thesis problem when I was getting a doctorate before med-ical school?

I worked on a problem that was a fairly famous old problem in my field that resisted solution for a long time, and I had a wonderful thesis advisor, a sweet, generous, and brilliant man, and we developed a close relationship. We wrote a book together and in connection with that he had tried to solve this problem, and had done a fundamental piece of the work, but had not been able to solve the general prob-lem, because there were certain tools that were needed that hadn't become available but had now been developed. So there was a chance of solving the problem now. And we met together, a couple of days a week, just the two of us, for a year, his giving me essentially, a two-person seminar on this problem, sweet and generous of him. We'd get together and talk. It started off with his just teaching me and eventu-ally became more collaborative. There still was a major creative step that had to be taken. I finally understood at least where the nature of the problem was, and was struggling with it for weeks, months, largely on my own. And then he went away on vacation, so I hadn't seen him some weeks, and we then ran into each other by chance when he returned. As we greeted each other warmly, he said, "How's the prob-lem going?" And I said, "Oh, well the way you solve it is . . ." and out of my mouth came the solution to the problem. It took essentially another year to make that solution actually work because there were glitches and things that had to be done, but it was the essential idea. It was in that moment that I solved this hundred-year-old problem.

Without the context of this conversation stimulating it, I don't think I ever would have known. And I wonder to what extent people whose thinking is more autonomous from the need for direct interaction are doing the same thing I do, but they are able to continue, to have the conversation with an internalized other, and that thinking always requires an other. My favorite experience—I love it when it happens— is when I can't tell where the idea came from. When two people are talking, or a group of people sometimes, and the idea emerges from the interaction, and it's not one person's creation, and that no one would have done it without the interaction happening—I love it. It's making babies together. I actually think that analysis had a somewhat inhibitory effect on this nature of thinking for me. Because it's too one-sided. I might actually do better work on my own analytic tasks, in a freer interactive conversation. Because of this quality of eliciting my own recognitions about myself in the context of a back-and-forth, and the ideas emerging somehow in the space between that's created by the two people.

I asked **Dr. Laraphil** what thinking about his second analyst is like for him now. He replied:

SL: When I think about him, I mostly recover a sense of pleasure. I don't think about him very often, but when I do, it's almost always with a sense of pleasure, though the emotional intensity about the whole thing seems to have diminished quite a bit over the years.

I asked how the idea of termination had evolved and if he thought whatever was the analyst's theory about "resolution of transference" played a role:

SL: I think the theory has changed drastically, too. When I was in training, there was still the idea of the resolution of the transference neurosis, although the studies of Pfeffer and others had cast some doubt on that. But it was still the reigning concept. And now it already seems anachronistic.

At the time, I wanted to get on with my life. I'd been in analysis for many years, counting both analyses, and the first, bad analysis had been much longer than the second, good one. I was moving along in the Institute. It seemed like the right time: I didn't see any impediments amenable to analytic work that argued for my remaining in analysis.

These were the criteria I had in mind when I raised the issue with him. And he answered open-mindedly, "If there isn't anything else you'd like to work on, maybe it makes sense to think about ending analysis."

Prior to termination, **Stuart** discovered that the analyst could see him as a person, separate from his patienthood. During the analysis, the analyst required eye surgery and had to be out of the office for a while:

SL: I decided to drop off at his house a record, Jeff [analytic sibling] and I had bought for him, since he wouldn't be able to read and the record was something he could enjoy without using his eyes. He saw me dropping it off and opened the door and invited me in, so we talked for a few minutes. He told me he'd been denied [temporarily, owing to the surgery] his major tool . . . he may not have used the word tool...or major activity as an analyst: he'd been told that, during recovery from the surgery, he was not to nod his head. He said, "That's 50 percent of what we do." Terribly funny. And I had had the feeling that I was doing something naughty; that even though I was doing a nice thing [taking him a gift], I was violating the rules. First session back, I talked about how surprised I had been, and he asked, "What do you do when a guest shows up at your house?" I knew at that moment that he'd said something profound to me, and it has stayed with me. He reminded us that we are a reality at the same time that we are also in the roles we assume while we're doing analysis. These other roles in life are important and real, too.

After termination, **Dr. Laraphil** enjoyed several conversations with the analyst when they ran into each other at the Institute. In addition, when he and his analytic sibling "crashed" the analyst's 75th birthday party, given for him by colleagues at the hospital where he taught, they were again, with humorous interplay, made to feel welcome.

SL: There was a sense of welcome and friendliness and being glad to see me. If there was something I wanted to talk to him about, I would, without any delusional beliefs in my being super-special to him. I don't think my first analyst would feel that way. It would be hard to reach out to somebody when you have the feeling you aren't wanted.

Dr. Laraphil elaborates his experience of the differences between his first and second analysts. He recalls an incident during the second analysis in which he had blurted out to a colleague his awareness of the colleague's daughter's problems, a comment he then felt had been hurtful:

SL: I was really so disappointed and angry at myself for my insensitivity, and I said, "I must have had a hostile reason to do such a cruel thing to this man I barely know." And I was trying to figure out what when my [second] analyst came out with, "'Must have' means maybe not." One of my favorite phrases ever since. So in contrast to my first analyst not allowing us to realize we didn't know what was going on, the second asked me just to reflect on what it felt like, and what I was feeling, and I began to articulate what those subjective states were.

LT: One of the things I start musing about, as I'm listening to you with your first analyst, is that some people who have a rotten experience in a first analysis then turn deeply against analysis. And others don't. And I don't know what the difference is. For instance, what made it possible for you . . . you talk about being aware of what you suffered and how important it is to you not to repeat that with either your patients or your children. From what you said about your patient, you are quick to be compassionate, accurately so, with what her feeling states were, without glossing over the troubles. That sounds very unlike what you experienced with your first analyst. I wonder what made it possible for you to continue the commitment to analysis in view of how it could hurt?

SL: That's a good question. I don't know the answer. I think I experienced what went wrong with him as a reflection of his character. And also with me. What was wrong with me, too, but not wrong with the idea of analysis. In other words, I still felt that learning about myself in the context of a conversation with someone that's invited to deepen itself continuously, which is one way of thinking about what analysis is, is humane and potentially helpful to many people.

Stuart Laraphil's first analysis took place while he was in medical school. He describes some of what attracted him:

SL: My interest in the inner world. And some of it was narcissism, the overvaluation of my inner world as so worthwhile that it would be worth mine and anybody else's spending endless hours in attention, on the fascinating subject of me! So that bit of narcissism had mixed with something that was, basically, of interest. And I liked the idea of the intellectual breadth of analysis, of a way of thinking that would incorporate vast areas of human interest and inquiry, from art to science, with ordinary human life in the middle. So that attracted me, too. And I saw psychotherapy as a more degraded and inferior kind of watered down version. I don't anymore. But that was my rough impression—and too common at the time. It was more elitist, that's why I went into analysis. So the pretentiousness and the response to that is evident from the reasons I gave for going into analysis. If I remember right, I went into analysis with my first analyst because Socrates said that the unexamined life was not worth living. One should examine oneself. It was some kind of highly defended, mostly defended against shame, to sort of brag and present myself, to kind of show off, which are parts of me. I would think that he'd sense right away that, most clinicians would feel that underneath that is a person who is pretty afraid of feeling ashamed. But I remember that one day, near the end of my time with him, I was anxious about something in some very specific way and he said to me, "Congratulations. I think you've just felt anxiety for the first time in your life." It was a very snotty thing to say. I think it was also inaccurate. It showed how little he could sense that I was actually very anxious most of the time. Although I handled my anxiety with a kind of narcissistic defense. So it felt a mean thing to say and it was wrong. I didn't think of it as shame at the time. But I think much of the anxiety I had was related to the possibility that he would subject me again to the kind of humiliation and shame that was more or less constantly a part of my inner life and certainly throughout my childhood and adolescence. But basically I wanted him to be a dad, a good big brother. I wanted him to like me. And I always felt his kind of coldness and distance as criticism, as nonacceptance. If I had been able to stop and take it seriously, it would have hurt. But I sort of rushed through without thinking, and he only made occasional, sort of disembodied comments, some of which were rather obscure to me. When I'd ask simple questions, often he wouldn't answer. So there was that backdrop of so-called neutrality, but actual neutrality requires at least raising questions about people's self-criticism. I don't know how much he actively did it and how much he did it by simply not questioning the assumptions I had about my inner badness. I wish I had been strong enough, or even aware enough to realize there was a possibility of asking myself, "Was this particular analyst right for me? Was this process right for me? Should I consider changing or leaving?" I never did. It wasn't till much later that I looked back and realized I could have done that.

I think one of the good things I took from that analysis, although not healthy in the long run, was that I could identify with what I thought was strength and aloofness on his part, to support those defenses of mine. What happened is that as the years went on, my own maturation and diminished need for these defenses, and what I learned from patients and my basic pleasure in more interconnection with people, led to a shift of my style where I became increasingly myself. And my second analyst played a big role in this, modeling this for me. I saw what was wrong in that first analysis, so I could be an analyst who's less hidden behind a wall and more direct and empathically involved with my patients.

THE TRAINING CONTEXT

Polyani suspected that science's system of masters and apprentices protected it from rigidity. The apprentice learned high standards of judgment from his master. At the same time he learned to trust his own judgment; he learned the possibility and the necessity of dissent. Books and lectures might teach rules; masters taught controlled rebellion, if only by the example of their own original—and in that sense rebellious—work.

—Richard Rhodes, *The Making of the Atomic Bomb*

Complications intrinsic to training, compared with "ordinary" therapeutic analysis, have long been debated. Preeminent among these complications was the impact of the "real" power that the training analyst had over the career of the candidate, compared with emotional authority stemming from transference. The controversy over this issue eventuated in a groundswell of policy change from "reporting" to "nonreporting" Institutes. The intent was both to preserve the confidential relationship with the analyst and to diminish the actual power of the analyst over the career progression of the candidate. By 1982, seventeen U.S. Institutes stated that their training analysts do not report, whereas seven made reporting "optional" (Orgel, 1982). At the Boston Psychoanalytic Institute, the vote to abolish the "reporting analyst" system did not occur until November 14, 1990. In practice, however, most training analysts did not report evaluatively on their candidates during the previous decade. Some saw it as unprincipled to do so. Prior to the vote, there was considerable controversy about what the advantages and disadvantages would be: "What was left in the eighties was the potential for such intervention, which didn't get used" (A. Kris, personal communication, 2002).

Issues of reporting were not the only focus of debate. Between the 1950s and the 1970s, a series of panels and symposiums were devoted to problems stemming from candidates' characters (e.g., too "normal," with ego-syntonic defenses), from the training analysts (too aggrandized), and from the context of the training setting (which mixed actual authority over the candidate's career with transference authority). There was much less attention to what happened when things went well until Shapiro demonstrated, in an empirical study in the 1970s, that a majority of candidates felt satisfied with the therapeutic gains in their training analysis and did not find the training setting a major obstacle. A very significant minority of candidates, however, did have major dissatisfactions, which the group attributed to unchangeable countertransference reactions in their training analysts. Shapiro pointed to the importance of characterologic match between candidate and training analyst (Shapiro, 1974).

With the exception of Shapiro's alert about mismatches, the troublesome characteristics attributed to candidates and training analysts were viewed more as givens rather than in terms of the dynamics of mutual influence of analyst and analysand in transference–countertransference impasses. Such an omission would have been natural, because the infusion of the analyst's personal subjectivity was thought of as an interference with abstinence and neutrality, whereas the character of the analysand tended to be portrayed as a more-or-less penetrable wall of resistance to insight. Although there was a high degree of awareness and insight about the dangers of the training analyst's unconscious need to be in the role of powerful model to the candidate, this did not necessarily translate into practice.

In the mind-set of the times, the Oedipus complex stood as a primary organizing principle, which not only had the privileged position as interpretive content but also colored assumptions about the meanings of dissent within the training setting. Criticisms by candidates of the training analyst were frequently considered to be signs of oedipal "acting out" that called for analysis and cure. One research Participant told me, for example, that his analyst divulged to him what was expected from an analytic sibling (a message the candidate interpreted as "fair warning" to him). A seminar leader had complained to the candidate's training analyst that when his candidate had criticized her, it signified that he was acting out an "oedipal attack," for which she expected the candidate to apologize before there could be hope of advancement. This was not acknowledged as a lapse of confidentiality between seminar leader and training analyst about the errant candidate, nor between the training analyst and his analysand, whom he discussed with his analytic sibling.

The context of training can skew the analytic interaction toward a more intellectualized, rather than a freely regressive or affectively compelling, engagement. Balint (1954) held that training analysts tended to pounce interpretively on the earliest signs of negative transference in ways that led to intellectualization of the issues rather than risking the full brunt of whatever feeling experience was to emerge. A. Cooper (1985) reported after a conference of training analysts that "In discussing differences between the training analysis and other therapeutic analyses, some of the Participants had the impression that deeply regressive processes . . . were often prevented or inhibited in the training analysis, with both analyst and analysand lacking the courage to include this as part of the work with a future colleague" (p. 57). In contrast, "A great emphasis was placed on the achievement of the capacity for self analysis on the part of the training analyst in the training situation" (p. 57).

Concern that a candidate's eventual autonomous functioning might be compromised by a regressive phase in the analysis that could leave him vulnerable to the potential misuse of emotional power of the analyst may have also had a role in how suspect the tendency to idealize the analyst became. Idealization was viewed with mistrust and explained as either indicating dependent wishes to partake of magic powers or as a defense against unconscious aggression. It certainly may serve these functions, or it may constitute an adaptation to the analysand's perception of the analyst's need for admiration. I believe it important to differentiate defensive idealization from idealizing affects that have a different function and are hurtful when rejected, however. An affective thrall may allow for the emergence of transformative processes in the safety of yielding self-protectiveness to the intimate influence of the analyst's communications.

Already in 1933, Ferenczi anticipated current concerns about unrecognized influences of the analyst on the analysand:

> Gradually, then, I came to the conclusion that the patients have an exceedingly refined sensitivity for the wishes, tendencies, whims, sympathies and antipathies of their analyst, even if the analyst is completely unaware of this sensitivity. . . . Normally they do not allow themselves to criticize us, such a criticism

does not even become conscious in them unless we give them special permission or even encouragement to be so bold [p. 225].

Bernfeld (1962) resigned from his position as training analyst and argued against the training system:

> It is inevitable that the analysand—in certain phases of his transference—has exaggerated thoughts about the eminence and professional capacity of his analyst. Frequently remnants of this transference attitude persist long after the analysis. . . . If the training analyst combines the transference authority of a father with the power and authority of office, his job as analyst becomes very difficult indeed. In our training system we elevate every training analyst to a power and prestige position. We thereby disturb perceptibly the transference in the personal analysis whereas in fact or maybe only in my opinion, under less artificially complicated circumstances, the personal analysis is just as difficult or as easy as every other psychoanalysis. All that one needs to conduct the personal analysis of a colleague is the colleague's cooperation, some experience, and a lot of tact [p. 480].

Anna Freud (1950, cited by Kairys, 1964) also graphically described problems in the training analysis:

> It would be viewed as a gross technical error if an analyst accepted as his patients persons from his close social environment, if he were to share his interests or opinions with them, if he were to discuss them in their presence; if he were to criticize and judge their behavior and discuss it with others and would permit himself to draw realistic consequences from his judgment; if he were to intervene actively in his patients' lives and offer himself as an example to them, and permit them at the end of the analysis the identification with himself, and his professional activity. The training analyst commits every one of these gross technical errors in the framework of the analytic training situation. It remains an as yet unanswered question how much the transference situation of the training analysand is complicated and obscured by this technically deviating

procedure. One hears again and again among analysts the complaint that the analysis of the future analyst fails to succeed
therapeutically as well as the analyses of most neurotic patients.
Many analysts suffer from unresolved infantile attitudes which
disturb them in their affective relationship to their environment,
or from unresolved transference fixations to their training analysts, which influence their scientific attitudes. They remain in
a state of dependence on their training analyst; or else they separate from him in a violent revolt against the unresolved positive relationship. This is often accompanied by clamorous,
hostile, though theoretically rationalized declarations.

Unlike Bernfeld and A. Freud, Heimann (1954) and others took
the position that there are indeed special risks to carrying through a
training analysis successfully, but these are not counterindications to
the practices then current in "reporting" Institutes. Holding that
responsibility to the profession has priority over commitment to benefit for the analysand, Heimann (1954) discussed the analyst's predica-
ments as problems that the analyst should be able to transcend:

> The analyst's personal problems that may be considered as spe-
> cific to a training analysis derive from several sources. Personal
> conflicts with colleagues, friendships and animosities, may rouse
> anxieties about his reputation. The training analyst may be
> ambitious and want his candidate to be brilliant in order to
> prove the quality of his work, and more so perhaps in a Society
> which comprises controversial groups. He may have formulated
> some new points of view and may wish that his candidates
> should become convincing representatives of his theories. And
> let me add a more serious point: that there may be discontents
> with his own analytic experience, and doubts in the truth and
> effects of analysis which would affect him particularly in the
> analysis of a future analyst [pp. 162–163].

Alongside these reservations, Heimann saw opportunities, provided
the analytic pair was up to the task: "If the extra-analytic factors of
a training analysis are not allowed to become sanctuaries for resistance, they prove fertile for the analytic work." She supported this idea
with the following reason: "When the analyst acts as the representative of the training committee, the analytic situation essentially

assumes the character of a triangular relationship with the analyst in the role of both parents, and often specifically of the 'combined parental figure'" (p. 164).

During the time when opinions were polarized about the evaluative role of the training analyst, there was consensus about a number of observations, such as the narcissistic temptations for the training analyst, but these concerns led to opposite conclusions. Within one set of beliefs was the assumption that the analyst would, through his or her self-knowledge, be able to resist these temptations; further, in this model, the analyst assumed that he or she knew what was best for the candidate, had the responsibility for instilling suitable character traits, and assumed a position of parental authority in the sense that criticisms or disagreements with the training analyst were treated as disrespectful oedipal challenges to that authority. A common aspect of analytic ideology deemed the candidate in need of rebuke or being put into his or her place by pointing out failings. This often included the notion of breaking down "resistance" to admitting "illness." Holding this outlook together was a commitment to the analyst's self-analytic function as the best—and final—hedge against the acknowledged pitfalls within the role. Although self-analytic capacity is indeed a most necessary and valuable resource for the analyst, reviewing this literature, one cannot but be struck by the degree of idealization being accorded to the prophylactic powers of insight in the service of honest self-appraisal; at times, it seems almost as if surviving the ordeals of being a training analyst equip one to occupy that role. Here is how, for example, Bibring (1954), an advocate of reporting, describes the additional challenges that must be met and overcome:

> Only he who has experienced an analytic working day following a public discussion at the Institute, or the like, in which he has had to encounter himself all the next day seen through the eyes of his many candidates, discussed by them from all angles, as to appearance, age, intellectual performance, personality traits (true and projected)—all this tinged with boundless adoration or bitter sarcasm—this analyst will understand the additional task and commitment of the training analysts. The narcissistic solution of accepting the adoration as reality tribute which we deserve and to ward off the criticism as neurotic by the minute analysis of all its details is perhaps very tempting but equally fatal; so, too, would be any inclination to overlook

one's own problems of counter-transference which are heightened by this general situation and may lead to participation in
the acting out process of competing, taking sides, or expecting
special loyalty from one's candidates, etc. [p. 169].

Lampl-de Groot (1954) agrees with Bibring that "the training analyst has to live up to the demands of self-knowledge by self-analysis
as far as is possible to accomplish this." Alluding to Freud's words
"Analyzing spoils the analyst's character," she cautioned:

The analytic situation, in which the analyst is the leader, the
patient's confidant, the object of the patient's love, admiration,
and infantile adoration, is a real temptation to the analyst to
mobilize his own feelings of grandeur and to overrate himself.
Therefore it seems to be of extreme importance for the analyst
to know his own personality in its actual proportions, his
capacities as well as his limitations and his faults.

However, she also acknowledged that "the drawback of self-analysis is really the countertransference; this means that self-love easily
prevents us from seeing our own shortcomings. Each of us has his
own particular blind spots" (p. 187).

In parallel fashion to her emphasis on the self-analytic challenges
in the training analyst's role, Bibring stressed the crucial relation of
the development of the self-analytic capacity in the analysand to termination of the training analysis:

As our last point we must now consider the termination of the
training analysis. I would like also to consider here its beneficial effect on the deepening and stabilization of the analyst's
self-awareness—in contrast to the more limited gains of the
patient for whom contact with analysis ends when his personal
analysis is terminated. If constant concentration on the unconscious conflicts of other human beings is to become an advantage instead of a danger, the candidate must have acquired in
the course of his didactic analysis the ability and readiness for
self-analysis. . . . The candidate's feelings of responsibility
towards his self-awareness and insight, ought to show unequiv-
ocal evidence of having shifted from the childlike condition of
needing the presence of the analyst in order to be concerned

with one's psychological processes towards the independent and tenacious interest of the truly mature analyst to promote this knowledge at any price. Only if this change has been clearly initiated do I feel free to consider termination [p. 172].

That the "real power" of the training analyst in Bernfeld's terms might prove a complication in the termination process did not go unnoticed. Weigert (1954) commented:

There is sometimes more insecurity about the termination of a training analysis in which the transference emotions are shielded from full expression, in which the atmosphere remains more intellectual and the revelation of the unconscious is retarded by the typical defenses of compliance and submission. Acceptance by the analyst and secondarily by the institute becomes a goal more important than the process of self-revelation. Free associations are unfree in so far as they are directed by the unconscious wish to bribe the analyst, to conform to his expectations. The analysand is driven unconsciously to manipulate the analyst into the role of the gratifying, protective parent, the magic helper. A trainee not only emulates the analyst in his style of work, he incorporates his philosophy, he intuitively reads the analyst's mind, listening to his interpretations as if they were compelling orders of an auxiliary superego. He follows the automatic pattern of earlier adjustment to authority. The analysand assumes that the analyst wants him to be more aggressive or less conventional, more ambitious or more affectionate, and he adjusts to these assumed superego commands by unconsciously pretending the desired behavior. The subtle unconscious hypocrisy of such adaptation, the "as if" performances of the analysand, interfere with the autonomy of the superego and the growth of ego strength. Therefore, the defensive compliance may sooner or later turn into scornful rebellion, if the analyst does not succeed in time in seeing through the analysand's unconscious maneuvers. . . . Termination is indicated when the analysand dares to relinquish a dependent identification for a mutually respectful differentiation, when the anxieties about loss, about incorporation or being incorporated, anxieties reflected in an unrealistic concern about success and failure, can be transcended [pp. 635–637].

Like Bibring in the 1950s, Fleming argued during the 1960s and 1970s for standards of what the training analysis and the candidate should be accomplishing. In 1978, Fleming and Weiss proposed a "procedure for correlating the experiential learning of a training analysis with the next phase of training" (p. 33). A long list of expected achievements required before matriculation contained a number of familiar qualities considered ideal. For instance, "The training analysis will have provided a firsthand and very personal experience in learning about unconscious conflict, anxiety, resistance, defence, symptomatic behaviour (such as learning blocks), genetic determinants, dreams, regression and transference." Other items on the list are much more selective in prioritizing the value given to specific content in the analysis. For example, "The training analysis will have developed some insight into the Oedipus conflict in particular and how the candidate solved it for himself" (p. 36).

Fleming and Weiss propose guidelines for evaluating the candidate's progress and readiness to analyze a patient. Following is just one of the six lines of questions recommended:

> What is the stage of transference development? Is the transference neurosis still being resisted? If so, this form of regression can be interfered with by matriculation. The responsibilities and conflicts associated with courses and cases can very easily be used to avoid the transference neurosis by mobilizing a flight into health and/or success. Is the transference itself so entrenched as an erotized resistance in defence against narcissistic injury that the analysis appears stalemated or in danger if matriculation occurs? If so, it may be that the candidate is not analysable or not analysable by his present analyst. Has the candidate experienced negative transference? Has triadic transference material appeared or is it still dyadic? This bears on the strength of the narcissistic core, the level of object relatability achieved, and the solution a given candidate found for his oedipal conflict [p. 38].

During the same decade, Shapiro (1974, 1976) studied the response of 123 analysts to an anonymous, self-reporting questionnaire about the correlates of therapeutic outcome of training analyses and the impact of the analyst's evaluative role. Problems in the training analysis were grouped into three main categories: personal problems of the candidate, problems felt by the candidate to stem from the training analyst, and problems related to undertaking psychoanalysis in the context of the Institute training program. Among those who had been highly satisfied,

> many reported confidence in the analyst's skill and in his ability to understand them. A number noted that, since the analyst was "outside the inner analytic group," the training situation "did not put additional pressure upon them to perform" . . .
> Two-fifths reported difficulties . . . felt to arise from problems posed by the evaluative and reporting role of the analyst, from countertransference reactions on the training analyst's part, or by difficulties reflecting excessive (global) identification or overestimation of the training analyst" [1976, p. 15]. Of the fifteen who felt "somewhat dissatisfied" with their therapeutic results, thirteen "claimed that severe or major countertransference reactions or inimical personal qualities of the training analyst burdened their analysis heavily. Interferences arising from the dual role were less frequently reported" [1976, p. 16].

Shapiro (1976) stresses that

> this heavily burdened group deserves special emphasis. Of the 35 analysts who reported severe personal problems (characterological or symptomatic), over half also reported additional severe complications which they attributed to either the training analyst and/or the training context [p. 18].

He comments that

> The extent to which difficulties were attributed to the training analyst was both unexpected and distressing to me. As Sadow (1973) pointed out, "While the claim of countertransference problems does not necessarily mean that this was in fact the case, at the very least, such a belief implies an unfinished analysis and ineffective communication between analyst and former patient about the incomplete aspects of their work." One-fourth of the respondents, 32 analysts, ascribed one or more severe or major difficulties to their training analyst. . . . The candidate's

own personality patterns undoubtedly played a role in shaping the transference-countertransference interplay reflected in these judgments about the training analyst. The study suggests, however, that true countertransference problems and other difficulties felt to be derived from the limitations of the training analyst may be more common in training analysis than are generally acknowledged. . . . In this study these problems were particularly heavy burdens for those who reported dissatisfactions with their therapeutic results. Seventeen of eighteen such graduates viewed their severe or major problems as stemming at least in part from their training analysts; in three-fifths, these were designated as serious and insurmountable during training analysis [Shapiro, 1976, pp. 21–23].

Problems stemming from the training setting were less conspicuous a source of difficulty than those arising either from the personal pathology of the analyst-in-training or the complications felt to derive from the training analyst. Shapiro (1976) points out that

many analyses during training benefited from the input from the training setting. Shifting between being a patient and being the analyst, empathizing with analytic patients without overidentifying, analyzing errors, blind spots, countertransference reactions to patients, and defensive reactions to supervisors often enriched personal analysis and facilitated the uncovering and resolution of conflicts. Thus, in summary, the much maligned training setting in analysis appears to have hidden inherent value, reinforcing the analytic process and creating additional stimulus toward personal and professional growth in a majority of analysts-in-training [p. 36].

Shapiro (1976) also stressed, however, that a favorable match between candidate and training analyst "loomed very large."

Shapiro's (1974) finding that the training context of the candidate's analysis was not in itself the chief source of dissatisfaction is compatible with my research data. Although the training context, especially during the days of the "reporting analyst," was experienced as emblematic of such exigencies as the legitimization of the analyst's monopoly of power and knowledge, the particularity of each analytic couple remained pivotal to the likelihood of satisfaction with the analysis.

The research Participants' narratives suggest many an echo at BPSI of the conundrums that animated the controversies discussed here. Almost all Participants alluded to their initial awe, a mixture of anxiety and pleasurably felt inspiration. Idealization of Psychoanalysis, the Institute and the analyst can have multisided and individual meanings. Clearly it is crucial that candidates in training have some assurance that allowing themselves to feel inspired and excited is respected as salient feeling which fuels the affective learning and will not result in actual vulnerability to having advantage taken. Bion (1992) contended that:

> There is a great difference between idealization of a parent because the child is in despair, and idealization because the child is in search of an outlet for feelings of reverence and awe. In the latter instance the problem centers on frustration and the inability to tolerate frustration of a fundamental part of a particular patient's make-up. This is likely to happen if the patient is capable of love and admiration to an outstanding degree; in the former instance the patient may have no particular capacity for affection but a great greed to be its recipient. The answer to the question—which is it?—will not be found in any textbook but only in the process of psycho-analysis itself [p. 292].

One Participant described his experience of the Institute as follows:
Whenever I would be in the Institute auditorium, I would sit in the second or third row on the left, which is where I always sat with my father in synagogue, every Saturday. And so I would love it at the Institute. I had no idea what a match it would be, analytic thinking. I had some image of what I wanted to be, the kind of psychiatrist I wanted to be, but I had no idea how it would be more than I ever dreamed of. Medical school was very different than analysis. And for me, this was Talmudic. One lecturer who came to the Institute was going on about Freud the Conquistador, and there was a reverence, and I felt in that the orthodox rabbi, you should and you shouldn't, but there was also the idealization and you must obey, and Freud was the Conquistador, and you're gathered to pay respect. The whole thing fit, and I bought it lock, stock, and barrel, and loved it. I mean, you could say identification with the aggressor. With the lecturers, the older they were, and the more sure they were, and the more orthodox they were, the more comfortable I was, and the better the love affair.

12

EVOLVING IDENTITY AS ANALYST

Let each man exercise the art he knows.

—Aristophanes, "The Clouds"

While controversies (described in the previous chapter) flourished about almost every aspect of the training analyst's optimal relationship to the candidate, there was still consensus that the personal training analysis remains the heart of psychoanalytic training. Silber (1996) puts it this way: "For the analyst to work effectively, to enjoy and believe in his work, his own analytic experience has to have been fulfilling and convincing in both a personal and professional sense." Is this empirically borne out? I believe the jury is still out.

The jury is not only out, the jury is baffled. Our theories have long held that identification with the analyst and his or her analytic function is the cornerstone for building one's own analytic capacities, just as we have long believed that a good identification with parents is needed for healthy development. Repeatedly, and most often, there are vivid and demonstrable examples of this process. The assumption that it is invariably so, however, ignores those resilient analysts who emerge from disappointing or damaging relationships to their training analysts to become excellent analysts themselves. We need to question what makes that possible. And, regardless of whether his own analysis was satisfying or not, the practicing analyst needs to shape (and accept) progressively the identity of the particular analyst he or she becomes by also individuating from the initial identification or active disidentification with his own analyst to becoming the natural inhabitant of his or her own approach. The way in which such individuation evolves seems different for those who felt their analysis to be deeply satisfying or beneficial from for those analysts whose analysis was experienced as unsatisfactory or damaging. Satisfying analyses often yielded deep identifications with central aspects of the analyst's ways of being with the analysand, such as that essence—almost signature—of his affective presence that had been most transmutative. In contrast stood those who experienced the analysis as more hurtful than not. They tended not to pass on this wounding legacy, but instead, through intuiting the specifics of how they had been failed, in disidentification with the analyst, forged an impressive commitment to fostering analytic process. At the same time, almost all Participants described distinctive features of their own approach which, for good reasons, differed from their analysts, going beyond either identification or its opposite.

Participants were articulate about various aspects of their own analytic approach. They were apt to portray their analysts as either enabling them to become themselves or as encouraging identification with the analyst's own approach (that is, "I'm teaching you to be like me"—a part of the Pygmalian countertransference reported by some Participants). Some recent graduates had as well-developed points of view and reasons for these as their older peers. I noticed that those who, postanalysis, continued to love and admire their analysts most were not apt to minimize their differences. As Loewald (1962, 1973) observed, what results at the end of analysis is emancipation, not identification, if the feelings of mutual abandonment can be analyzed, and the relationship rather than the object is internalized. The rich array of personally arrived at theories and practices, an aspect of identity as the particular analyst one is, will not be fully elaborated here because it might make the Participants more identifiable, but it underlines the vitality of diversity in contemporary practice.

To access how the Participants experienced the manner, the matter, and the mind-set of the training analyst in relation to their own approach, they were asked to consider the following questions:

Where is your analyst in your inner life as you practice analysis? Do you experience your own ways of being with patients as close to or very different from your analyst's, and in what ways? Do you want to pass on the "legacy," radically alter it, or have you felt it pale in relation to your own distinctive style as analyst? How did you metabolize converging influences from supervisors and from him (her) when you were doing control analyses?

Dr. Stuart Laraphil's views trace the evolution of analytic identity when things go well:

SL: In the early years, I had an abstract idea of what I was supposed to be like as an analyst, therapist, and psychiatrist. It was composed of several parts. One, my perception of various mentors, teachers. Another, my perception of my own analysts. Both of those, of course, partly determined by my own preconceptions. I think it's a common developmental experience that in the early years, there is an often conscious, and always preconscious, image of what one is striving to be like as an analyst, and there's a fair discrepancy between that and one's natural personality and behavior, with a consequent strain. And my experience of what happens is that gradually you become yourself. The two come together, and you learn that you can use who you are, your own dispositions and spontaneity, interests and knowledge in the service of analytic work. And so the work becomes much more natural. And a lot more fun, a wonderful experience of freedom that's enlivening. Because there's a deadening quality to having to disavow and control and limit aspects of yourself in order to become some overvalued image that you think you should be. That affects a great deal of how I feel about being an analyst these days, as opposed to earlier. Part of that diminishing belonged to the sense of the overvalued role of the Institute. My analysts and supervisors now have a continuing role, but it's in how they've helped shape what *I've grown to be* rather than what I'm trying to be. In earlier years, at times I would hear myself imitating him [second analyst], or even [first analyst], too. Often, those were times of doubt and anxiety about what I'm supposed to be doing. Those moments evoked from unconscious memory something that he would say, or just a gesture of his. So, at times of need, I might pull them out. Now it's much more blended into who I am, so I'm seldom conscious that I am thinking of or acting like either my supervisors or analyst.

As **Dr. Laraphil** emphasized the "liberating" effect when "you gradually become yourself," others also spoke of the increasingly good fit between their own nature and its expression in their analytic manner and mind-set. This included awareness of how they differed from their training analyst and, at times, the bonus of picturing their analyst's support and acceptance of the difference.

The feeling of having internalized analytic modes that had been experienced with the analyst in deeply satisfying analyses was most apt to reflect remembered basic attitudes toward the analysand, helpful ways of communicating, and the quality of the analyst's affective presence. Differences in theory or technique more often lay in the specifics of content and communication: when and what to interpret, how freely to confront or to self-disclose, and so forth. Some Participants mentioned that their own approach was informed by the sea change in psychoanalytic theorizing that has taken place since they were candidates. Refreshingly, several recent women candidates with male analysts stressed that their style or nature was more aggressive or confrontative than their analyst's and that they had felt supported by their analyst in that development.

In analyses judged as moderately satisfying, the quality of affective interchange described was sometimes differentiated from the content. Some of these analyses had been described as staying at an intellectual level of insight, without great affective power; as reaching stalemates over particular interpretations (such as penis envy); or as limited by self-censorship, for example, based on clues that preoedipal longings would reap the analyst's disapproval. In others, the basically good feeling between the members of the dyad infused the analysand's subsequent analytic work. Several moderately satisfied, and even dissatisfied Participants noted that they did learn particular, useful analytic skills, such as dream interpretation or defense analysis. Because unsatisfactory analyses might be superceded by a more satisfying analysis, it is difficult to ferret out the influence of each in later analytic identity.

For those analysts who had wounding experiences with their training analyst, a special sensitivity around how they had been failed tended to develop into empathic care in respecting the patient. Most often, a second analysis, when sought, was especially valuable. But in its absence, access to peers, older colleagues and particular supervisors became major anchors in troubled waters. Much as resilient children are often found to have the capacity to make the most of relationships offered by others than the primary caretakers, these analysts evinced such capacities, too. Within the array of supervisors, faculty, and peers, there was often enough choice so that a meaningfully constructive person was found. But not always.

Excerpts follow from Participants at each level of satisfaction with their analysis.

Analysis Deeply Satisfying

Dr. Katharine Maxwell: When I think about myself as an analyst, I think I do a lot more interpreting than he did, of transference particularly. I think he really allowed me to run the show. When I was dealing with transference issues, it would be brought in. But he rarely would make a transference interpretation if that's not what I was talking about. He stayed very close to where I was. Which is wonderful, on the one hand, but I feel, and I see in myself that I'm more likely to point that out, if I see it happening, even if my patient hasn't brought it up yet. Not if I feel like I'm on a completely different track, but if I feel like that's what's going on and they're not quite seeing it. He didn't do that. He was very respectful of exactly where I was. I have mixed feelings about that now. But the other thing I think is that I lived in the transference much of the time with him, and my patients may not to the same extent, so that it may not have needed to be said by him, because we were already there much of the time.

Katharine then mentioned a supervisor whom she liked but who suggested she interpret a lot of things that she felt would constitute an empathic failure on her part, and "my analysis with that patient has actually gone much better since I stopped supervision, because I'm not saying those things. I mean, now I say them when I feel like I want to say them, not because my supervisor thinks she needs to hear it, and it just feels freer now." She then returned to the topic of her own approach and an awareness of difference from her analyst:

KM: The one problem I often have around this issue of the inner presence of my analyst is that, as an analyst myself, I'm not him. And I can't be him. And my patients, in general, I think experience me very differently than I experienced him. And I often have to struggle with that. I'm much more confrontational. I'm much more direct. I'm much more blunt, critical. An analytic patient who I just saw today is very angry about something I said to her yesterday. And I was thinking it was rare for me to be angry at something my analyst said to me, because what he said was—not always, but most of the time—just so empathically attuned, and in the end that was wonderful for me. I'm not sure it's the only way to be a good analyst. But I often feel his inner presence in terms of thinking I'm not being like my analyst now. I'm not completely 100 percent letting this person know that I so believe in them and I'm so on their side. When I feel like they're doing something that's really screwed up, I'm much more forthright about that. And that's just who I am. I think I use aggression a lot more than he does. I think I have more aggression than he has, even as a person, forget as an analyst. And then I hear my analyst say to me, "But that's who you are, and that's fine." I sort of then hear his voice saying that's okay. But it's something I'm always aware of. I know how much it meant for me to have someone like him as an analyst, and I'm just different. I don't even know that it's better or worse, but I'm different.

Dr. Francesca Emon also resonates with her analyst's affective way of being with her, while feeling free to experiment in evolving her own approach:

FE: I love this question because my analyst was obviously so much a part of my training and thinking about how to be an analyst That was always very active in my mind during my analysis. And I would say that his way of being an analyst has been very influential in the way that I am. His ease with his technique, it just seemed to be a natural flowing from who he is. Even the restraint, I think, comes very natural to him. And the joking and the periodic disclosure and his comfort with that influenced me a great deal. And also the fact that he didn't do that kind of defense analysis which I was being taught in other contexts. For a period of time that was very confusing. I was very identified with the way my analyst was and I was kind of trying that on for myself with my first control with types of interventions that I thought my analyst would have done. Later on, I felt him as tremendously supportive of my own style and adding to it, by delving deeper or sharing a particular formulation. I think that your way of being an analyst should be a reflection of what you believe in and what you believe works. It's not separate. Technique is not separate from your character, even when you're holding yourself back. All of those postures or ways of intervening are genuine if you have a way of conceptualizing technique that fits with your values and you feel like you're doing a good thing. The whole question of anonymity and trying to be a blank screen, you would have to really believe in that. I think that what promotes transference is ambiguity, not anonymity. Patients selectively attend to what they're sensitive to. And not just what they distort, but what's important to them. So, that's why I think having a seamless relationship between your personal style and your technique is very important in terms of your patient's experience of you.

LT: And as you do analysis now, does it sometimes feel like your analyst is sitting by your side, or any of the supervisors, or does that happen less, or do you tell any of them the especially good lines or how is it . . . ?

FE: Yes, my analyst is one of many now, as opposed to the only one. And I'm in there, too. Probably that's the main experience—of myself.

And I feel like I'm experimenting, too. How am I different? I probably formulate more to the patient, out loud, than my analyst did. I tell the patient what I'm thinking they're doing or struggling with more. Not in an authoritative way. In an offering it as a possibility way. Which, of course, my analyst did in the very same way. But I do it more. And now I experiment, like with defense analysis. (Laughs.) As much as I think it can get in the way, there's a time and a place for it, where I experiment and then it can actually be helpful.

Dr. Jack Robinson: conveys the fruits of feeling "compatible" with his analyst, despite great differences in their backgrounds.

JR: She did not visit much of anything of her own concerns or Institute feuds and politics on me. I mean to her great credit. I learned at her feet that you keep your life out of the analysis, you keep the prejudices out of the analysis to the best that you can. But we haven't gotten to the parts that I feel absolutely tremendous about, which is that we had a real compatibility there. I felt she and I were in some ways alike in spite of her European background, which made her oblivious to certain things, and 45 years' difference in our ages. We were alike. For example, if you feel that there is a place for an analyst with a good sense of humor working with a patient, you have to become exquisitely sensitive to how to manifest that without making a patient feel that you are laughing at him or her. I never felt that with her or me. And I can count on fingers of less than one hand any patient who ever thought that I was laughing at them. I think I subconsciously took in a lot of the way she was with me and incorporated it in noticing and being respectful. In some ways I have her to thank for that. Now, looking back on a long career, I'm more aware than before that my analyst showed the way. She had a very good style, was very serious about it. And she was very good at dream analysis. Some dreams you wish you could go through the floor, right? And not have to listen to what you had dreamt or what it had meant. But they were mostly very positive analytic experiences, and I learned 99-point-something percent of what I ultimately learned about dreams from the way she did it. So, if there was anything that I incorporated directly into my technique, it was her active interest in dreams. And her manner of getting me to associate to the affects and the details. If anybody ever talks about me as an analyst, they might say, "He was very active, very interested, and worked very hard with me on my dreams." And that would be a great compliment to me.

One of things that turned me off during training was very much linked to—I just cannot deal with people who don't ask themselves, "How do I know? How can I be sure?" I really did enter with a tremendous excitement about exploring intrapsychic connections. I really thought that was fun. But I felt that as I got into this actual institution, the style of my teachers and the people I was supposed to learn from, like my supervisor Dr. X, he could be brilliant, but he never questioned whether he was right or wrong. He never labeled a hypothesis as a hypothesis. It was an absolute fact. And the narcissism that went into that! And that got institutionalized. You either had to take it or leave. Not take it or leave it but take it or leave. My analyst acted like there was nothing more important than the analysis, but without the self-importance, without narcissism. And that taught me the most.

Dr. Julia Baranger comments on changes in her theoretical model over time in relation to her ongoing identification with her analyst's ways:

JB: I think that my rhythm of doing analytic work was very similar to hers to begin with. I was a very silent analyst. I was sparing in my words when I did speak. I was generally very positive and accepting and warm toward my patients, the way I experienced her being toward me. And I recognized a lot of the themes from my analysis in my patients' material. Of course, there aren't too many themes, when you look at it. How much one, when one's beginning, does that more than necessary, I don't know. And I felt that I had something to offer them because of the experience I had from her. I had a sense of how positive an experience an analytic treatment can be, and how I was doing for them what I wanted to be doing for people.

My theoretical model has changed a great deal since those days. I'm much less silent now, although I am probably still on the relative end of silence with my patients. And I have a kind of charge to myself to keep learning this stuff, which I also had when I was in treatment with her, but I was so heavily influenced by her that I didn't do it as much, didn't have the confidence either. Another thing is that I notice myself being more different with different patients than I used to be in the beginning.

Dr. Mozes Nounous gives a different twist to the time span involved in an unconscious identification with the analyst's ways:

MN: I did connect my way of analyzing with her. But not any more. I mean, now it's mine. I'm doing it now. And we may agree and, if I met her, we would have fun together talking about it, but it would be mine. What I'm doing, I've been doing in my own way for the last 20 years, particularly as I got freer in myself. It's mine. And I absolutely accept the fact that it had to do with my experience with her, my affection, and the ego ideal quality. As I told you, she was known as a maverick, which had a lot of meaning for my analysis because my analyst was not at all like my mother, who was very strict, My analyst was sort of hanging loose in many ways that I wouldn't have been able to do at the time, but now I'm much more comfortable about being like that, too. I'd been so unsure of myself when I started out, but when somebody called me a maverick too I realized it's a belated identification with her, but it couldn't happen for a long time, because I had to get freer in myself before I could use it—personally and in my work.

Dr. Celia Laub speaks of not identifying with her analyst's style even as she feels her approach resonates with how she experienced her analyst's affective presence:

CL: I would never *want* to imagine myself in his style because he was such an original, and that was precious to me, so I wouldn't want to see a clone. But what is imprinted in me permanently is some sense of what made the analysis work: his extraordinary capacity to intuit what was going on, seemingly out of nowhere, the way he could play with the unconscious and find unexpected ways of communicating about it, the way my struggle with difficult, impossible things involved his struggle with the temptation to take refuge, too. All those features of him are lively presences; they are touchstones when I'm analyzing and make me soul search when they go awry. Though he and I have such different characters, at times comically so, that I believe we'd, willy-nilly, have feelers out for different issues, use different barometers for deciding to make an intervention, and so on. I sort of like the experience of difference between us, when, at a deeper level of feeling and attitude, I believe that there was so much in sync, so much shared.

Moderately Satisfying Analysis

Dr. Eleanor Brown highlights the changed assumptions, such as the increased tolerance for ambiguity, and the two-person field, that now underlie analytic practice, including her own. But she had experienced her analyst as liking, respecting, and having her interest at heart and finds that she still identifies with aspects of her analyst's emotional stance:

EB: I think of my style as analyst in some ways like hers though it's changed over the years. I mean, I don't mind somebody screaming at me, but I don't know whether I would scream in an analytic conversation because it's just not part of my style, really deeply. Sometimes it would be useful to be able to have that emotional range, but I think I have identified with this style of hers in a lot of ways. There are people who have a more direct affective style. I think I could use that and my analyst didn't have it. But I think the big issue retrospectively is the difference in the oedipal focus. And the other artifact was operating on a reporting system so that it wasn't just a theory where censorship—it was one's real concern, whether you said it consciously or not—but if you said or did the wrong thing that you wouldn't progress [in your candidacy]. I think the whole practice has changed. The whole two-person field, the idea that the analyst is not a blank screen, is enormously different, and the awareness of the analyst contribution. The other thing that's really changed is that at worst, the analyst looked for data to confirm a theoretical preconception. You looked for oedipal material, or you looked for aggression; you looked for primal scene, or you looked for whatever you looked for; it was this has got to be that, it wasn't how can you understand this in a variety of ways, and that is a shift. It's become more open. A lot more shifting views as to what's pathology and what's developmental, not so precut. There were the believers and the heretics, and now some of the heretics are the new believers. Certain things were acting out, and certain things were neurosis and so on—we're a little more unclear about that than we were [in the past]!

Dr. Horatio Encarta stresses the transmission, from his analyst to his patients, of feeling deeply accepted:

HE: I think I'm much less active than my analyst was. I pay less attention to interpretation. I don't take it as seriously. But I think where I share some good things is that I think I share a sense of acceptance. I think I am deeply accepting of my patients. Nonjudgmental. They may irritate me. But I'm tolerant a lot of the time.

Dr. Bob White didn't realize until the second analysis what had been missing in the first, namely, the active communication of the analyst's emotional engagement. Here are excerpts about the effects on his own way of analyzing:

BW: In my first analysis, it would've been helpful if he would've said more about how he experienced me. How he experienced what I was saying. I could've used a little bit more close process monitoring to bring out the things that I think sort of slipped away from me. My own style, I think, was affected in two ways. The kindness part stuck, with the, sort of the feeling and desire, that I wasn't gonna run out . . . of strength or kindness or heart in treating in analysis a sick and challenging patient. I trusted that part of me which I had always felt was a part of him and was very good, that caring, kind part. I think I've carried that with me. But it's only in retrospect that I realize—even then as I was doing my work, with depressed and difficult patients and supervising, I could never be as standoffish as he was. It just wasn't in my nature. Didn't think it was right. That I think was the most important instruction. . . .

My second analyst is much more with me than the first. Thank God for that second analysis. And it's had much more to do with the way I am as an analyst. And in analyzing, my memories of him get reevoked as I'm listening to everybody else. It's a pleasure to have him in my mind. He's with me every day! I don't think I'm as buttinsky as he was. Nor do I need to be in charge the way that he did. But I certainly need to be involved.

Dissatisfying Analysis

Dr. Irving Mazur traces the evolution of his approach to progressive freedom not to enact the exact opposite of his experience with his analyst:

IM: In my own work with patients? For the first years after the analysis, I think I stayed much more identified with patients than analysts. I bent over backward to keep from inflicting on them that know-it-all superior attitude that had landed on me from my analyst and had felt so awful. Eventually, it came to me that in that mode I was too gingerly about confronting negative feelings directly. I had too much need to be the good guy, like some people who have had a cruel father and vow to protect their kids from that. And in some secret part of myself I still wanted to measure up in my analyst's eyes or please him by copying his approach—demeaning interpretations and all—he acted so proud of it, and I knew he had an eye out for people's loyalties. I was ashamed of even feeling tempted to fall into that because I couldn't approve of how he did things, but I no longer have to be the total opposite of him, either. Because being the opposite, I think, involved some denial of my own aggression, when it came up with patients and sort of constricted things. What I've learned in my peer supervision group, with people I very much like and respect, is to comfortably do both, to show to the patient the valuable stuff you can see, or see as a potential, and at the same time confront aggressively, but not be needlessly cruel.

I'm also convinced now that the real crux of the work comes when the patient tests to see if you can survive and hold and reflect back what some of those dreaded inner states are about once their guardedness—and my own guardedness too—has let down. What guides me now is trying to stay aware of what is in me and in the patient that will let the analysis deepen.

Analysis Experienced as Changed from Deeply Satisfying to Dissatisfying

The analysis of **Dr. Elizabeth Light** was the only one in the study felt to be highly satisfactory at the time of termination and damaging by the time of the interviews. She had discovered within two years of her termination that her training analyst was losing his license because of multiple sexual transgressions with patients about which he had lied to her and to others as well. A silence was felt to descend around her because her peers did not seem to register the catastrophe at her level. She did not seek another analysis or analytic therapy. Still she preserved the positive elements of her analysis in her work with patients:

EL: His style, and I happen to have identified with it, is that the best interpretation is one the patient makes. His created an ambience in which you were willing to explore yourself in whatever direction you wished to go. I think that's what he provided for me. He became mother, father, family, everything to me. Someone else might put it in words, but he never had to put my feelings into words. He birddogs the affect. He was right there affectively with you and if you, like right now I'm feeling sad, tears well up, he'd be right there. He would not only encourage the expression of the tears, he would give you the feeling that he was there to receive them with you without being intrusive about it; that they were good tears, that they would lead to something; that the act of crying would be a healing experience for you. Now, he never said any of those things to me. I say these things to my patients sometimes, to patients who seem to need that initially. Maybe this is my own stuff, and I'm just relating my part of the dialogue of things as they went along. But his empathic kindness is something I respect, and I think that he helped me to become a much better listener and to be less judgmental toward myself and toward others.

13

ANALYSIS ENDING AND UNENDING

In real life, only death and hostility bring a libidinal relationship to an end. The kind of termination psychoanalysis demands is without precedent.

—Martin Bergmann, *Termination: The Achilles Heel of Psychoanalytic Technique*

The moon burns in the mind on lost remembrances.

—Wallace Stevens, "The Men That Are Falling"

The analysis, the carrier of extraordinary intimacy, ends. The wings of desire must be folded. The dialogue to which they lifted becomes soliloquy, ushering in those transformations that are still to come in postanalytic psychic life. Completing analysis is meant to highlight the autonomous personhood of the analysand with freedom to "think ones own thoughts" (Symington, 1990) and to dare authentic engagement with others. The sense of personhood has many facets. In Loewald's (1988) wording, at termination "being more individuated means experiencing the loneliness and vulnerability, and the richness and freedom of individual existence" (p. 160). How do these self-developments cohabit with the inner connection to the analyst, and how does the actuality of the analyst infuse the after experience, in accordance with Symington's (1990, p. 95) notion that "analysis gives us evidence that the way one person acts affects the capacity for choice in another"?

Pondering these issues involves considering what the termination process asks of the analyst and analysand and how it might be affected by the contribution of each. I believe that how analyst and analysand envision the tasks of termination is joined to their preferred understanding of the very nature of internalization and the role of transference in analytic process. This involves beliefs about the relevance or irrelevance of the relational context of intrapsychic life. The analysand will glean and react to the analyst's attitude toward the meaning of their connection.

Historically, a fulcrum of psychoanalytic theory was that transference feelings comprised a distorted view of the analyst, to be corrected and resolved during the analysis, after which the analyst would no longer be needed as transference figure but instead would be internalized in identification. Analysts' beliefs about the optimal connection or detachment from the analysand during and after termination have been clearly declared as a corollary. In praise of detachment, for example, Etchegoyen (1991) is succinct: "The destiny of a good analyst (in the patient's mind) is nostalgia, absence, and in the long run oblivion" (p. 637). Lacan contended that the analyst must be knocked off the pedestal of "the one who is supposed to know" and argued that "the psychoanalytic experience consists precisely in evacuating it" (Etchegoyen, 1991, p. 129). Lacan stated that the analyst's significance should drop away "like a piece of shit" when the patient can do for himself what he had wanted the analyst to do for him (Lacan, 1959, cited by S. Cooper, 2000, p. 274).

If one understands transference wishes to be, first and foremost, a displacement of the old onto the new, consisting of a transfer of wishes experienced in childhood toward a parent, then the resolution of that transference is naturally equated with the resolution of the connection to the analyst as psychically important. But if one understands transference wishes as emerging into the analytic space in a form already altered by the particular affective presence of the analyst, then the analyst, in his or her reality, is positioned differently in the transference and necessarily also at the time of termination. If what has been internalized is based on representations of a dialogue of affects experienced with the analyst during the emergence of changing desires, then something about the nature of the analyst, as experienced, becomes an essential component of what is internalized and what becomes memorable in consequential ways. Termination then confronts the analysand with synergizing the ways he knows, and has been known, through that interaffectivity experienced with the analyst, as well as with the necessity of taking leave of the analytic intimacy. Optimally, the analysand feels the option to experience the connection to the analyst in whatever way is most generative to his or her further self-development. That is, the analysand might accentuate finding zest in feeling separately complete, while viewing self-analysis as self-generated. Alternately, he or she might value access to a dialogue with the analyst within, while treasuring a meaningful sense of connection. Or both these perspectives may come into play. My own view is that, within individual variation, the analytic process involves simultaneous and oscillating strands of such subjectively intrapsychic and intersubjective experiences, each with dynamic impact on what follows next. The rhythm of engagement and disengagement, of feeling together with and distinct from the analyst, varies according to the propensities of the individuals within the dyad. A kind of deep, affective interplay that may be riveting (and risky) for someone who yearned for reciprocity in emotional engagement with a parent in vain may feel burdensome to another who has had to disengage from impingement by a parent and now values the liberation for individuation more.

For many decades, and despite some dissenting voices, the development of the "self-analytic function" and the "resolution of the transference" were deemed to be central criteria in judging readiness for termination. Neither of these criteria has turned out to be good measures of a generative analysis, however. Follow-up studies indicate that the subsequent use of self-analysis is not correlated with resolution of transference, and that transference is not resolved in any case, even though it is transformed in various ways. Kantrowitz, Katz, and Paolitto (1990 a, b, c), in comprehensive follow-up studies, report that "the successful resolution of the transference neurosis, a traditional measure of analytic success, does not seem to be correlated with the development of a self-analytic function, improved reality testing or later growth" (1990a, p. 491). In regard to patients' knowledge of their analysts, the authors note the following:

> Given that analysts strive to maintain a certain anonymity with their patients and that patients' perceptions of their analysts are greatly shaped by the complexity and depth of transference reactions, it is especially striking that patients' perceptions of their analysts as real people often have considerable reliability when compared with more "objective" evaluations [1990c, p. 674].

Kantrowitz et al. found that "7 out of 17 patients studied retrospectively felt analysis reinforced earlier painful experiences, rather than enabling them to understand and come to some resolution in relation to the past" (1990c, p. 683). The proportion of dissatisfied analysands in their study is larger than for the Participants in the current study, but the finding that patients' perceptions of their analysts as real people have considerable reliability seems in accord with the Participants' portrayals of their analysts. These perceptions, needless to say, inform how the analysand takes leave.

Meanwhile, the criterion of "resolution of the transference" as a sign for termination has changed over time in psychoanalytic thinking. The clearest progression, as Bergmann (1988) points out, can be seen in the writings of Loewald. In 1962, Loewald stated, "Analysis is in itself a prime example of seeking a substitute for the lost love object, and the analyst in the transference promotes such substitution. The goal, however, is to resolve the transference neurosis, a revival of the infantile neurosis" (p. 261). By 1971, Loewald had come to regard transference "as denoting the retransformation of psychic illness which originated in pathogenic interactions" in childhood "into an interactional process with a new person, the analyst," with the potential for "the emergence of novel interactional possibilities" (p. 309). Resolution of transference thus redefined was no longer viewed as the goal. In 1988, Loewald further commented on the patient's contradictory urges during the termination phase between emancipation and "the wish to hold onto the satisfactions of a libidinal object relation with the therapist." He added, "That internalization does not preclude object relations, even though termination stops contact with the therapist as therapist, that indeed internalization rather expands object relations and raises them to new levels—of that patients are not fully aware at the point of termination" (p. 164). He pointed

to another dimension of internalization. Internalization is not solely a matter of internally reconstituting a renounced object relationship (as in mourning and in superego formation); it has a component of another kind. As in early development in particular, there is an element of smooth transition and passage between partners, something seamless, without a sense of loss and grief. What is taken in is more of the nature of a gift, or is becoming a trait or an attitude and stance now held in common. . . . The internalization phase of mourning is leavened with such nonseparative elements. . . . The therapist's presence and interpretive participation in the mourning process not only help to make mourning a conscious experience. As tangible manifestation of communality in mourning it tends to put in relief, more toward the end, those nonmourning elements of internalization [pp. 165–166].

Stolorow and Lachmann (1984–1985, p. 34) also question the renunciation of object cathexis: "The requirement that the analytic relationship should end without residual transference feelings seems to us to be unwarranted." Bergmann (1988) suggests that the notion of "resolution of the transference" was modeled on the concept of "dissolution of the Oedipus complex" and points out that the Oedipus complex is rarely, if ever, dissolved, and that the same holds true for the resolution of the transference. "What we need to aim at is not to resolve the transference neurosis but to make sure that it forms a productive inner structure in the life of the former analysand" (p. 151).

The notion of being able to renounce an object tie through identification has had far reaching influence as a pillar of psychoanalytic thinking. Both the resolution of the Oedipus complex and the capacity to detach libido from a lost object have relied conceptually on identification as a fulcrum. My own clinical experience with children in treatment who have lost a parent through death or divorce has taught me (Tessman, 1978) that the libidinal investment in the object tie persists, that identifications cohabit with an inner mental representation of the lost object, albeit often unconscious, which continues to fuel a quest symbolic of reengagement with the wanted absent person in the external world. It seems to me that if one assumes that the desired fate of transference love, when renounced, is for it to be consigned to identification, one ignores the generative possibilities of the ever-changing feelings for the analyst in the after life of the analysis.

Analysts' individual preferences in stressing either the self-generated or the relational sources of mutative internalizations lie on a continuum. A solid body of theory, however, beginning with Ferenczi, rests on the premise that the quality of the relationship with the analyst is intrapsychically active in influential ways. Strachey (1934) introduced the analyst as a new and kinder superego figure. Balint (1968) elaborated the idea of a two-person psychology (first introduced by Rickmann) and held that the analyst's attitude toward offering a particular kind of object relationship is essential to the analysand's development. He contended that "it may have a crucial influence on the treatment whether the analyst interprets any particular phenomenon as a demand for gratification or as a need for a particular form of object relationship" (p. 162). Balint (1950, 1952) was the first to speak of termination as "a new beginning" that appears regularly at the end of analysis and constitutes an essential mechanism in the process of cure. He argued that the analysand's partial satisfaction in "primary love" that appears in relation to the analyst near the time of termination, must be understood and respected as preparing him for "mature love," the capacity for which "depends largely on the patient's gradual allowing of more and more rights to his objects" while also able to attend to his own demands (1950, p. 196).

Ferraro (1995) views termination

> not as the gradual epilogue to a process that is effectively complete and merely needs to be rounded off, but rather as a highly intense mental experience which calls for the mobilization of the combined energies of analyst and patient alike if it is to be confronted. . . . The sense of the whole analytic experience, in my opinion, may well be forfeited unless this phase is managed satisfactorily [p. 62].

Ferraro and Garella (1997) write:

> The termination process can be regarded as the psychic work performed by the analytic couple in order to arrive at its own dissolution. While [it] seems to be directed towards the accomplishment of a separation, that is actually the ultimate and extreme moment of working together. . . . The event of termination lies at the point at which the trajectory of the analytic couple diverges into the separate trajectories of the individuals composing it. The divergence is at least potentially a catastrophic situation, because it establishes two different domains, a before and an after; moreover, it is irreversible. . . . From this point of view, the terminating couple is faced with the communication "this message is not (or is no longer) a message," which is a paradoxical and irreducible situation. The heirs to the paradox will be the individual members of the couple, and they will resolve it individually in the form of their own experiences and psychic contents [p. 30].

Others have located signs of approaching termination by considering changes in the affective ambience within the process. Ferenczi (1927) had asserted that whenever the analysand is able to be completely candid and spontaneous, the resolution of the transference and the termination of analysis are approaching. Weigert (1952) carried this further, judging the terminal phase of analysis by shifts in the transference–countertransference configuration. She stated, "We know that the resistances of transference disappear toward the end of a successful analysis and that a greater spontaneity between analyst and analysand is established. The spontaneity of the analysand is only possible if he no longer feels compelled to please, to placate, to test, or to provoke the analyst" (pp. 466–467). Weigart observed that what is noticed by the analyst in himself or herself is a greater feeling of freedom and relaxation with the patient, insofar as the previously unresolved transference-proneness of the patient had resulted in a subtle tonic vigilance on the part of the analyst.

Orgel (2000) notes that "experiences of bittersweet transience are particularly penetrating and profound in the termination of a psychoanalysis" (p. 720). In addition to the patient's "hypercathexis of the memories of the lost object," Orgel observes an increase in his own use of his analysands' words and gestures, in what seems a nonconflicted counteridentification with his analysands' ways of being, communicating, and working in the analysis:

> Their personal language, bodily attitudes and rhythms, and so on affect my own more strongly during sessions, or at other times my thoughts turn to them, probably reflecting my parallel wishes to hold on through my identifying with them. These interlocking identifications, partial and transient, contribute essentially to my attunement to my analysand, and they are intensified, in both of us, in the painful hours when loss is anticipated, especially during the termination period. . . . As my analysand prepares to renounce the ongoing analytic situation, I sense a meaningful change in the relationship. Individual sessions feel crucial, thick with overt emotion; the analytic experience as a whole seems more real and valuable, even as the analysand questions its lasting value more skeptically. . . . What ensues is like ordinary mourning but also unlike it. For one thing it is entered into more actively and knowingly and is rather less imposed from the outside—at least this should be so. . . . It is tempting for either (analyst or analysand) to mute

this often painful experience. . . . To help the analysand confront these affects and to confront them in oneself means freshly
accepting ones sense of hurt, perhaps outrage, at being seen as
flawed or weakened, to be discarded. No longer needed and
useful—an acceptance in which one has no recourse to defensive compensatory fantasies about being a wonderful analyst.
One tries one's best to surrender to being killed unconsciously
and replaced, without falling into depression, needing to retaliate or becoming seductive [pp. 731–733].

Hurn (1971) underscored the "separation phase for the analyst"
and defines some of the satisfactions gained by the analyst during the
analysis. At termination, both members of the dyad face loss, because
it is "a separation between two adults whose relationship has been in
the nature of collaborative work on a momentous enterprise" (p. 345).
Schmideberg (1938) emphasizes the importance of the analyst's accepting the analysand at termination as an individuated other:

It is certainly gratifying to the analyst if the patient as a result
of the analysis not only gets rid of his symptoms but advances
in his whole development. One should not be too ambitious for
him and above all not judge him by one's own standards. He
should live his own life and conform to his own ideals and not
to those of the analyst. A possessive attitude in the analyst is
even worse than a possessive attitude in the parent. I consider
it satisfactory that a number of patients whom I analyzed successfully differed as fundamentally from me after the analysis
as before it in their political, religious, social and artistic convictions [p. 141].

Freud (1940), too, in his final communication, specifically warned
against the analyst's temptation "to create man in his own image—
indeed . . . he will be disloyal to his task if he allows himself to be led
on by his inclinations" (p. 175). Similarly, Rangell (1982) cautions
that termination may newly revive old temptations for the analyst:

In the terminal stages of psychoanalysis, when anxiety as a
motive has been diminished and the time for decisions and
action is correspondingly closer, it is especially important that
analysts not impose, unconsciously or consciously, their own
preferences on their patients. Tempting as it sometimes is, a

deliberate effort must be made not to succumb to patients' ambivalent urgings for the analyst to make their decisions in life. Life goals are the patient's to choose and execute [p. 386].

It seems to me that there is a fallacy in the traditional reasoning that literal separation from the analyst, with de-idealization, is a linchpin to individuation. De-idealization of the analyst is frequently viewed as important to the individuation of the analysand. This goal may be communicated to the analysand as one more achievement expected after termination. It is easily misunderstood as a pressure to renounce lingering feelings of love. De-idealization can occur in a variety of ways, including through intimate knowledge rather than distance. When observation of those actualities of the analyst that have significant meanings to the analysand are experienced as permissible, the analysand's recollections, idealized but also perspicacious, generate rich clues to what has transpired and not transpired between the members of the dyad.

I believe that a hallmark of a successful analysis moving toward termination, may be something beyond gratitude between the analyst and analysand, namely, the analyst's sense of being able to trust the analysand to perceive increasingly his actuality, despite all the reasons the analyst may have had for mistrust of his original objects. This state may signify that the principles the analysand has used unconsciously to organize the experience of traumatic affect have changed. Awareness of being trustworthy to the analyst furthers the analysand's leeway in the necessary period of transformation, postanalysis, for creative reflection on the bittersweet irony that just when the dyad had learned how to be together, the time has come to be apart.

The research Participants conveyed differences, according to their level of satisfaction, in regard to how the decision to terminate occurred. In dissatisfying analyses, the decision was either made by the analyst or planned according to the Institute rules about when termination was permissible. In contrast, the timing of termination was either consensual or first broached by the analysand in all instances of deeply or moderately satisfying analysis. Satisfied Participants conveyed that they did not feel pressured either to remain in analysis when they felt ready to terminate nor to relinquish the inner attachment to the analyst after termination. The sense of choice was stressed.

The following questions in the interview were intended to tap what Participants surmised about their analyst's attitudes toward their posttermination meaning to the analysand: What do you think are your analyst's beliefs about what aspects of the "transference," what aspects of the relationship to him or her, what aspects of his or her meaning to you should be resolved by the time of termination? What do you believe might have been his or her aim as to where the analyst would be "ideally" located in your inner life from then on? How does that fit with your actual experience? With the teachings in your Institute at the time? And now?

Some examples of responses follow:

Deeply Satisfying Analysis

Dr. Eva Jason: We never talked about termination in terms of what I needed to resolve in my feelings for him in the analysis, and I can't remember a lot of discussions about it in seminars either. I do remember feeling that the time had come, that it made sense to end, that so much had come up and been worked on in surprising ways—that I hadn't known was possible—and I felt sort of ready to be on my own, that I more and more analyzed what came up on my own anyway. I knew he would keep me company in my mind about that. But the sadness of actually losing him hit me very hard. I think he was able to really make the difference, that the analysis might be finished, but my feelings for him weren't. So he didn't put any pressure on me to have him mean less to me—in fact, in some ways it was the opposite because I got to know him better and better toward the end. We joked a lot more easily, he meant more to me and he seemed okay with that.

Dr. Francesca Emon: I remember him saying that he would always be my analyst. So I had the impression that this was an open door. It was gonna end this, this frequency and this period of time in this way with the structure, but that, I could go back when I needed. I don't know where I got that, because I don't think there's any formal teaching.

Dr. Stuart Laraphil: I think the theory has changed drastically. You were alluding a little while ago to the glasnost, the change in the theory of our field, as well as the practice. So when I was in training, there was still the idea of the resolution of the transference neurosis, although the studies of Pfeffer and others had cast some doubt on that. But it was still the reigning concept. And now it already seems anachronistic.

I had never thought about that as an institutional reflection, 'cause very often, in the clinical sense, the analysis can replace—become its own justification—and replace life. Instead of keeping in mind that it's in the service of something. I think my terminating my analysis was based on those kind of criteria. And my analyst's asking me, when I raised it, was largely in keeping with that, like, "Is there anything that you feel you need to get accomplished here before you leave?" rather than some abstract criterion. And I wanted to get on with my life. I was moving along in the Institute. I didn't want to remain an analysand. It seemed like the right time to end analysis: there was nothing impeding me that looked like it was amenable to analytic work. When I raised these issues with him, he'd answered open-mind-edly that if there wasn't anything else I'd like to work on, maybe it made sense to think about ending analysis.

Dr. Veronica Clark: I'm not quite sure what he would feel needed to be resolved at the time of termination. I know he felt that one needs to resolve as much as one can—if there has been trauma, there is no res-olution. But I think there is understanding, a certain acceptance, and a living with. I know that his sense is you are always working on it, and I know he felt that I had the tools and knew what I needed to know about what we worked on, to continue working on it. I think he would have said that I would mourn him and be done with it. But I would have an importance to him and that he would have an importance to me.

Moderately Satisfying Analysis

Dr. Horatio Encarta: I don't know what she believed. The classical idea was that you would develop a transference neurosis, and you resolved it. Period. Then it's over. That you would feel like you would feel toward anybody else, toward your analyst. Those were the teach-ings. Now whether she believed it, I don't know. I think through her behavior, in some ways she felt more need to keep attached to her patients and to me than I felt.

Dr. Seymour Sonenshein: I don't know that it was ever, during my training so formulated as that. It just wasn't paid attention to. But nevertheless, one thing that is relevant in my experience would be the feeling that the patient is not so much in the thrall of the transference, that they don't have any sense of themselves as a separate person or you as a separate person. Part of the achievement would be for them to get to a point where there is a sense of both. At least there is enough of a sense that the analyst is someone out there living their life with their person, and you are a separate person, and you have your life and your ideas and ways of thinking about things. And some sense of that to my mind is an important part of feeling that someone is ready to terminate. But we can see from what we know about termination that it is never really complete, either in the analysis of what might be covered or that the transference ends—as it were—it lives on.

Dissatisfying Analysis

Dr. Irving Mazur: When he announced suddenly that we would terminate that summer, he made it pretty clear that he expected me to be grateful that he now was declaring me fit enough to graduate. It was like having survived fraternity hazing as lowly neophite, but it had been so much worse. It didn't occur to me until long afterward that my feelings were hurt about his sounding eager to have me end. It wouldn't have helped to have hurt feelings during that analysis because he would take it as one more weakness on my part, or fear of competing with father figures, with superiors like him. I think he thought I should be completely independent of him now if I'd resolved that enough to terminate, but at the same time to be grateful to him for that. I was in that paradoxical limbo.

Dr. Emma McClinton: What aspects of the relationship she would think should be resolved by the time of termination? Well, since I didn't have an attachment—a relationship—I don't know if she didn't allow it to happen. But it didn't happen.

14

MOURNING

I know you—solitary griefs,

Desolate passions, aching hours

—Lionel Johnson, "The Precept of Silence"

Some griefs are med'cinable.

—William Shakespeare, "Cymbeline"

Toward the end of analysis, the ways that analyst and anlysand each elect to greet the question of mourning will affect how the termination is felt, at first with the analyst and then in solitude. A unique opportunity springs from the fact that the very person whose loss is being mourned—that is, the analyst—is initially still present to receive and to respond to the emergent affects. Although it has been said that it is not possible to mourn alone (E. Furman, 1974; Hagman, 1996), that may be more true of the young child for whom the caretaker's participation in his or her grief is prerequisite (R. Furman, 1964; Tessman, 1978) than for the adult who ends analysis and then continues to experience the loss of the analyst in solitude. Nevertheless, I believe that if the analyst's tolerance for grieving is low, this will be communicated in ways that may short-circuit the analysand's possibilities in experiencing rather than disavowing grief. Or, if the analyst has unconscious difficulty relinquishing the analysand, while yet needing to protect a sense of self-sufficiency, there is apt to be pressure for the analysand to unconsciously maintain attachment and loyalty without the release of acknowledged grief within the dyad.

The content of what the analysand mourns is as individual as the affective and psychosexual interplay with the analyst has been, a personal reflection of what has been experienced or forsaken as impossible to experience within the dyad. Although the notion that mourning the analysis is part of its completion has gained acceptance by most psychoanalytic theorists, it is important to observe that mourning is not a universal response to loss, and it should not be prescribed as an expectation for the analysand. Nor should the analyst feel devalued, as if nothing of consequence had happened, if mourning is not highly visible. It has been shown that the bereaved, for example, show great diversity in mourning or its absence, both culturally and individually (Hagman, 1995, Nussbaum, 2001). For some analysands, the predominant meaning of ending analysis may be authentically linked more with affects belonging to mastery, zest, or fulfillment rather than sorrow.

There are several controversies about the role of mourning at the end of analysis. Is mourning essential to complete analysis, and if so, why? Is it the analyst as "transference object" or the actual person who is mourned? Is the task of mourning a renunciation of the analyst or of one's own infantile, omnipotent, or oedipal wishes? What factors in the analysand's development, the analyst's actuality, the genders of the dyad, and the cultural context of values are facilitating?

I first want to engage the question of how mourning affects the relationship to the person mourned. Beginning with Freud and continuing in psychoanalytic theory thereafter (especially in the literature on termination) has been an association of mourning with a decathexis of the lost person, as part of a renunciation needed for the "acceptance of reality." As Freud (1917) originally put the argument for decathexis, "Reality testing has shown that the loved object no longer exists, and it proceeds to demand that all libido shall be withdrawn from its attachments to that object" (p. 244). I disagree with this premise and regard grief as an opportunity for as yet unknown revisions of the relationship within, rather than as simply a renunciation. During the 1970s while treating children who had lost a parent through death or divorce, I observed (Tessman, 1978) that decathexis did not follow loss, even when the child acted as though he or she were indifferent. Rather, a quest for the wanted absent person continued in unconscious and often ingeniously disguised ways (such as in symptoms) together with an amplification of aspects of identification. A. Kris (1990) also stresses the "freedom to remember the lost object" and speaks expressly of the need to "challenge Freud's view of mourning." Kris states:

> This [Freud's] view describes accurately the fears of the person
> who cannot complete mourning. Reality, in fact, demands only

the acknowledgement of loss, which is very different than withdrawing all libido. Mourning does not create loss, it permits mourners to regain those portions of themselves that are tied to the lost object and to reacquire the freedom to remember the lost object and to form identifications [p. 624].

In a similar vein, Hagman (1995) notes a vitalizing reengagement with the lost person during productive grief, rather than either depression or decathexis, which he sees as features of inhibited states of grief. Explicating the distinction, he vividly describes cases of delayed mourning seen in treatment where the patient is able to surmount the inhibition and resume the process:

The patient, after years of inhibited grief, frequently revels in his or her emotionality, and there is an intense engagement with others (especially the analyst) at the point of greatest sorrow. Life becomes more vivid and accessible to these patients, far from the colorless and empty world that Freud describes as the experience of reality for the bereaved. Ultimately these patients do not disengage from the deceased; rather, there is a revitalized engagement with the object internally, and also externally with transference figures, to such an extent that one can observe not decathexis but a heightened re-engagement with the dead person and eventually a transformation of memory into a permanent part of the patient's internal world [Hagman, 1995, p. 913].

Our theories carry with them some degree of expectation vis-à-vis the analysand in so far as capacity to tolerate grief and mourning has long been proposed as a developmental achievement. Deutsch (1937) first described the absence of grief in patients who later in life suffered from what she termed "unmotivated depression." She saw the incapacity for mourning as a residue of childhood insufficiency: "My hypothesis is that the ego of the child is not sufficiently developed to bear the strain of the work of mourning and that it therefore utilizes mechanisms of narcissistic self-protection to circumvent the process" (p. 12). R. Furman (1964), however, demonstrated that even very young children can tolerate grieving when they discern a caretaker's permission and affective support. Zetzel (1970) included a tolerance for both anxiety and depression as an essential component of the "capacity for emotional growth." In its development, she pointed to the importance of the child's early establishment of more than one successful dyadic relationship. Jacobson (1957) addressed the difference between the experience of sadness and depression:

> Even though sadness develops from loss and deprivation, which tend to provoke aggression, its qualities hint at the involvement of predominantly libidinal cathexes. Angry and sad moods, for example, commonly exclude each other, although frequently aggression is used as a defense against a painful experience of sadness. In other words, unlike depression, sadness as such does not involve an aggressive conflict, either with external reality or endopsychically. . . . Clinical observations suggest that sadness predominates in depression only as long as the libidinal investment in the object world can be maintained [p. 87].

The timing of such sadness is another matter. My own observations in working with the bereft have been that: "The libidinal longing for the absent person is frequently not re-experienced until some rage (and protest)—which was also withheld from the absent person or his image—has been expressed" (Tessman, 1978, p. 146).

Klein (1950), who viewed mourning as part of the development from the schizoid to the depressive position, first argued the idea that mourning is an important part of analytic process, although her depiction of mourning did not focus on the actual loss of the relationship to the analyst.

> Even if satisfactory results have been achieved, the termination of an analysis is bound to stir up painful feelings and revive early anxieties; it amounts to a state of mourning. When the loss represented by the end of the analysis has occurred, the patient still has to carry out by himself part of the work of mourning. This, I think, explains the fact that often after the termination of an analysis further progress is achieved; how far this is likely to happen can be foreseen more easily if we apply the criterion suggested by me. For only if persecutory and depressive anxieties have been largely modified, can the patient carry out by himself the final part of the work of mourning, which again implies a testing of reality [pp. 78–80].

Johnson (cited by Weigert, 1952), working from different theoretical premises, attributed the analysand's grief to the loss of his or her oedipal fantasies. She described the terminal conflict of analysis as fully reliving the Oedipus conflict in which the quest for the genitally gratifying parent is poignantly expressed, and the intense grief, anxiety, and wrath at its definitive loss are fully reactivated. A lack of mourning, by these lights, spoke to a refusal to relinquish the oedipal wishes:

> Unless the patient dares to be exposed to such an ultimate frustration he may cling to the tacit permission that his relation to the analyst will remain his refuge from the hardships of a reality that is too competitive or too frustrating for him. By attuning his libidinal cravings to an aim-inhibited, tender attachment to the analyst as an idealized parent, he can circumvent the conflicts of genital temptation and frustration [pp. 467–468].

Weigert similarly believed avoidance underlies the lack of mourning:

> The termination of analysis is an experience of loss which mobilizes all the resistances in the transference (and in the countertransference too), for a final struggle. Termination of analysis can be compared to a difficult landing maneuver in which a whole crew of libidinal and destructive forces are on deck and in action. Every step forward in the patient's real life—as well as in his analysis in which he catches up with his incomplete development implies a painful loss: the desires and gratifications of yesterday have to die that today can be fully lived. . . . Graduation from analysis is a seriously painful loss which calls forth the labor of mourning. In all neurotic patterns, the patient has habitually avoided this labor [1952, p. 467].

Speaking to the controversy over whether the analyst is lost as "real" or "transference" object, DeBell (Robbins [Panel], 1975) has emphasized "the mourning work of giving up the analyst as real object, which the analyst has become during the course of the analysis." In DeBell's opinion, giving up the analyst as a real object cannot be solved by analysis; this loss cannot be analyzed, it can only be borne. He feels mourning is not necessarily prominent or overt but asserts his expectation that the patient manage it successfully:

> Objects may be given up by expressing negative feelings toward them or by denial, neither of which is analytically appropriate. The former would be destructive and the latter pathological.

Mourning at termination is a task which an adequately functioning ego would be expected to manage successfully [p. 169].

There are, sadly, experiments in nature that cast light on the assertion of DeBell and others that the mourning may be for the real person of the analyst. A wrenching disruption of the "real relationship" with the analyst is the focus of Rendely's (1999) account of the grief she suffered when her analyst died in the midst of her analysis. Lord, Ritvo, and Solnit (1978) also studied analysands whose analyst died while they were in treatment and found that mourning ranged from intractable (36%) to nondiscernible (22%) to so-called normal mourning reactions in the middle range (42%) that lasted for about a year. Pathologic mourning was correlated with a personal history of early loss and deprivation. The authors also consider the inability to mourn:

> Our impression is that the nature of the analysand—analyst relationship, that is, the transference–non-transference balance, which promotes psychoanalytic treatment, also plays a role in determining the quality, intensity, or absence of mourning when the analyst dies. In this study, certain analysands with a definite sense of their analyst as a real person also gave the clearest evidence of a full-blown transference relationship and the most intensely felt mourning. When a transference–real person balance did not exist, however, mourning evidently could not occur. This was true where the analyst was experienced to an exaggerated extent as a transference object. That is, the transference reactions dominated the analytic situation. At the other end of the spectrum, no mourning was reported in several instances in which the analyst's behavior discouraged or masked transference reactions. . . . Our findings affirm the concept that the analysand's mourning process does not derive solely from the broken and unresolved transference relations to the psychoanalyst. It is also significantly based on the loss of the analyst experienced as a human being in his own right [p. 195].

Orgel (2000) not only regards mourning at termination as essential, but also traces its lineaments back into the analysis at earlier stages. He states that "analysis activates mourning throughout its course and therefore progresses painfully" (p. 722). He notes that "every analysand eventually comes to know what every analyst lives with: how much one cannot be, cannot have, and that one will eventually have to decide to walk away from analysis in order to choose a path that opens into the future." He believes (like Loewald) that "the ability imaginatively to experience the loss of the object—essentially a mourning—allows its gradual replacement through its internalization. Permitting this accession of loss and mourning alters the analysand's self-representation, and enables an internalization of the analytic process to occur." S. Cooper (2000) similarly sees the end in the beginning, or at least in the middle: "the ability to observe and work with the analyst's limitations may be usefully regarded as a necessary part of grieving and mourning about the nature of limitations in relation to analysis, the analyst, and self-experience" (p. 101).

The analyst's own contribution to the possibilities will reflect those aspects of his makeup which he is able to actualize in his analytic role, combined with his feelings about ending with this particular analysand. Needless to say, where the analyst makes regular recourse toward a vigorous "psychic retreat" (Steiner, 1993, 1996) or participating in "defensive shielding" (Freedman and Lavender, 1999) in the face of depressive affects, this will have an impact. The particular kind of loss experienced by the analyst at termination has been described in a number of ways, most often with an emphasis on the analyst's reluctance to give up his or her role as needed, and influential object. Buxbaum (1950) called it the "very flattering role of 'the wise, foreseeing, almighty analyst'" (p. 186). Keiser points out that "the analyst must be sufficiently attuned to his own unconscious to be able to decide whether he has a reluctance to give up the personal enjoyment of the analytic relationship" (Robbins [Panel], 1975, pp. 166–167). Weigert (1952) notes that "in the countertransference the analyst may vicariously enjoy a protective permissiveness that he could never experience in relation to his own parents" (pp. 471–472). This empathic identification with the protected part of the patient may pose a problem with loss at termination. Eissler (1975) cautions that if the elderly analyst keeps on aging,

he gradually loses all those contemporaries to whom he had become attached in the course of his life. . . . The impoverishment of love objects will often lead to a greater cathexis of his professional life, . . . indeed, in rare cases his patients may be the sole love objects left him. . . . Under such conditions, optimal distance between the analyst and the patient may be lost [pp. 147–148].

Viorst (1982) studied the sense of loss described by 20 analysts she interviewed about their responses to termination. She reports:

Only one analyst interviewed claims no problems with loss at termination. "Professionalism," he remarks, "defends against loss." At the opposite end of the spectrum was the analyst who maintained that "partings are always traumatic" and ought to be eased whenever possible. Eased for the analyst—not just the patient. . . . He eases his sense of loss through the fantasy that he'll marry each woman patient and become the intimate friend of each man. And finally, he notes, when he finds himself focusing on the monetary loss, he knows he's defending against the pain of parting. . . . Dr. E. [another analyst] tells how, gradually, over a long span of years, he learned to fully let himself feel and mourn his own losses. Now, during termination, he says, "I sit in my office, my eyes full of tears half the time. And it's nothing that I fight—I let it happen." Dr. F., though conceding that certain obsessives may be easier to part from, notes some sense of loss at all terminations. One indication that it is time for termination, she observes, is the ease and comfort and smoothness of the work together. "And this is the dilemma," she adds, "that just when the patient becomes a great pleasure to work with, you have to let go." . . . Dr. G. said she finds it hard to part from those patients she calls "lively," patients who have a sense of humor, "who don't show the usual deference," and "who give me a view of life I might never otherwise have gained" [pp. 402–405].

How analytic candidates mourn their analyses was recently studied by Craige (2002). She surveyed 121 candidates who had completed their training analysis about their posttermination experience, then followed up a smaller sample with telephone interviews. Time elapsed since termination ranged from 1 month to 21 years, with a median of 2 years. The majority of candidates, 76%, reported experiencing a sense of loss that lasted more than a few days after termination. It was judged to be highly painful by 23% and accompanied by a low to moderate degree of pain for 52%. On average, respondents who experienced a sense of loss reported that their experience of loss lasted between 6 months and a year.

Interestingly, candidates experienced the "loss of the unique analytic relationship" even more strongly than a "general sense of loss after termination." Of the entire group of candidates, 94% reported a sense of loss of the unique analytic relationship, with a mean score of 4 on a scale of 1 to 5 in response to the question, "After termination, how strongly did you experience the loss of the unique analytic relationship?" The finding that almost all candidates experienced a strong sense of loss of the unique analytic relationship is particularly noteworthy because 97% of her sample expected to see their analysts after termination during the course of their professional activities. The prospect of contact after termination did not eliminate the experience of loss of the unique analytic relationship. This contradicts the prevailing theory that mourning is circumvented in training analyses because the candidate expects future contact with the analyst.

A second important finding by Craige was that the more satisfactory the analysis, the greater was the sense of loss of the unique analytic relationship after termination. It correlated positively with

> the candidates' overall experience during the analysis as measured by such questionnaire items as: positive experience, successful experience, strong working alliance, intensely experienced transference, and warm relationship. It was also positively correlated with a sense of having achieved something valuable and of taking a step forward in adult development after termination. In other words, a strong sense of loss of a successful analytic relationship was associated with an overall positive experience during analysis and with a strong sense of achievement and positive progression during the post-termination phase [p. 517].

> Surprisingly, neither the sense of painful loss nor the loss of the unique analytic relationship was significantly correlated with significant emotional loss in childhood or adulthood or with the emergence of loss, trauma, or separation/individuation, as important issues during the training analysis [p. 518].

This is also at odds with prevailing theory about painful terminations.

Craige (2002) reports that 34 candidates (28%) were disappointed with the results of their analysis. It appeared that "while the majority of candidates had a satisfactory analytic experience that they missed after termination, there is a subset of candidates who had a disappointing experience in analysis and experienced pain after termination because of their disappointment" (p. 518). Candidates in the high-disappointment group were 10 times more likely than candidates in the low-disappointment group to report that their analyses came to termination primarily because of stalemate or a sense that no further gains would occur. Only 32% of candidates in the high-disappointment group reported a reasonable resolution of personal concerns as the primary reason for termination, whereas 88% of the candidates in the low-disappointment group listed a reasonable resolution of personal concerns as the primary reason for termination. The high-disappointment group had significantly lower scores than the low-disappointment group on posttermination experience in the following areas: consolidation of identity as an analyst, sense of having achieved something valuable, taking a step forward in adult development, and loss of the unique analytic relationship. Females had higher mean scores than male candidates on pain experienced during the termination phase and on intensely experienced transference during analysis (pp. 519–520).

Craige interviewed 20 of her respondents by telephone to elaborate her findings. She found that often with a sense of struggle and doubt, the analysands who had had low-disappointment analyses invoked the internal image of the analyst and began actively employing the analyst's attitudes and methods to understand their own reactions to losing him. Craige (2002) comments:

This study demonstrates that the loss of the analyst may be anticipated but cannot be fully felt, mourned, or analyzed during treatment. Those difficult tasks fall squarely on the analysand standing alone during the post-termination phase. The study also suggests that the loss of the unique analytic relationship may be a more important component of post-termination mourning than has been appreciated [p. 535].

Many of Craige's findings are in accord with, and relevant to, my experience in listening to the narratives of the research Participants. Although most Participants reporting a deeply satisfying analysis described a painful time of missing their analysts, this was not true for all. Among those whose training took place in earlier decades, when termination of the analysis signified graduation to membership in the Institute, there were some Participants whose sense of accomplishment overrode potential affects about the loss. Those with unsatisfactory or damaging analyses suffered painful endings, but without resolution in mourning. Some had felt stymied, by what was experienced by them as rejection, in making an attachment which could lead to the internalization of the relationship in ways that could be mourned (for instance, **Dr. McClinton** with her first analyst, **Dr. Lewis** and **Dr. Lieberman** with his second analyst), or if they had become attached to the analyst, they never felt sure of their welcome. Others were unsure of their analyst's capacity to receive and process mourning (for instance, **Dr. Levy**), or they felt left with the task of extruding what they now experienced as a noxious introject (for instance, **Dr. Glenn**). None of these situations invited affects belonging to mourning, although pain, disappointment, and inability to feel valued were present.

At the other end of the continuum were those who felt profound love for their analysts (for instance, **Drs. Maxwell, Laub, Jason, Clark**). The analysis had been deeply satisfying for each of these Participants and a consensually agreed on termination, felt appropriate. They reported that at the time of termination they were feeling happy with their lives (although aware that some issues would remain) but mourned painfully for the ending of the intimacy with the analyst for whom they felt love.

The following are illustrative excerpts from one man and one woman about their passages from termination to the after life. Both analyses took place in the 1980s. They happen to exemplify some of the gender differences in styles of mourning within the group who found their analysis deeply satisfying. Each Participant pictures both a sense of loss of the distinctive relationship to the analyst and some zest for autonomous self-discovery. Each grappled with how to connect or disconnect self-analysis to their feelings about the analyst.

Dr. Veronica Clark (with her second analyst): The clues to termination were, you go around issues over and over again. Those were issues I will have the rest of my life, without total resolution but a lot was resolved sufficiently. There was certainly connection of affect to memory and the ability to do that, though I know now there is still more to understand in my self analysis. So I felt ready to stop. It was my choice and timing, and I felt very good about it. But the last few months were horrendous. By then I had this intense amount of feeling which *I* was very comfortable with and I think actually scared *him*. [Both laugh.] He said something like, "Do you think you're going to need to see me maybe on a regular basis when you stop?" I said, "No, I can deal with this." I was heartbroken that I was going to miss him, not have him as such an intense part of my life, not have him to talk to.

The missing was horrible, really, it was very painful. Another candidate told me it took two years before she really felt she was over her termination. And I went to analysis horrified at the time, telling him if it was going to take two years I was going to kill him! I couldn't tolerate those feelings for two years, but there was a very long post-termination time when I missed him and that was very painful. I thought about him every day after I left. It was like a real mourning for a very, very long time until one day I noticed that I had gone through the day without thinking about him the way one does in mourning. It was more than a year, and it was less than two that I thought about him that much. But it was a very difficult time.

Dr. John Deere: I had been doing five days a week for six years, and it was really a part of my life—the first time I had had an experience like that where I could really find myself with another person. I found it immensely helpful. After termination, I thought a lot about that. I remember that last session. It was very teary. Very sad. That something was coming to an end. I remember thinking I was going to keep track of where things went for me in terms of this process and come back and talk about it.

LT: So you figured it wasn't good-bye forever.

JD: No, I wasn't feeling that for a lot of reasons. I was going to run into him in BPSI, I was gonna run into him in the street, and I could come back. So, it didn't feel like "Good-bye. I'll never see you again." But afterward I wondered, why did he push termination once he thought my associations meant I had it in mind? But I also thought he was right in some ways. And discovered that serendipitously within the next couple of weeks. The day I finished my analysis, we went off to a big vacation. I had been looking forward to it. I finished analysis in the morning, we left that evening, and for several weeks, instead of enjoying it, I was just grumpy. I was hard work for everyone concerned. It was not an easy trip. And then we had planned to go to hike, and I suddenly said, "I really want to go to a different city" to see what I could see. So we went there, and I was still in a dreadful mood, not fun to be around.

LT: During that time, was there any sense of search for him, of looking around and knowing he wouldn't be there?

JD: No. I had no sense at the time that it had anything to do with having just terminated, no connection to those weeks just being grouchy, angry, difficult. When we got to the hotel after an exhausting trip, I immediately wanted to go out again and see the city. Went out and started walking. At night. It was awful. We left on a night train and my wife, and the kids went to sleep, and I couldn't sleep. I'm lying there and suddenly it dawned on me that it was my sister's birthday. I had a flood of associations to how difficult vacations have been since the kids were born, and I became suddenly aware of how important a feeling loss was. Loss of being displaced by someone else, and sibling rivalry. I had talked about these things in analysis at various times.

LT: But then that loss hadn't happened yet. It was before you were without him.

JD: Right. And a lot of things fell into place. That was the first piece of work I had done on my own, after the analysis, and I was very excited about it. I lay there on the train laughing. I thought it was very amusing, this sort of "aha! I see it now." And the rest of the trip was much better. Through the course of that year, a lot of things like that kept happening, so the next year, I made an appointment to see him, wanting to tell him how much I had done, and how excited I was about the process that continued for me, and, he was mildly interested. I think in some way I was saying, "Aren't you pleased with me?" And I don't think it registered with the same impact on him that it did with me. I was so excited about it and about myself. I was full of beans, wanting to share it. I don't think he was indifferent about it, but it didn't have that valence for him. He hadn't actually been part of it. And that was, in a way, a disappointing experience. I realized that going back for a one-shot deal did not make a lot of sense, because it wasn't satisfying. I enjoyed seeing him, each time I ran into him on the street, 'cause I like him a lot. But, while I never had the feeling that I couldn't go back and do more work together, if I wanted or needed to, I felt on my own. And that wasn't a bad thing. It was sort of a bittersweet realization.

15

LEAVE-TAKING

Parting is such sweet sorrow

—William Shakespeare, *Romeo and Juliet*

Walking on the sands

I decided to leave you.

I was treading a dark clay

That trembled

And I, sinking and coming out,

Decided that you should come out

Of me, that you were weighing me down

Like a cutting stone,

And I worked out your loss

Step by step:

To cut off your roots,

To release you alone into the wind

—Pablo Neruda, "The Dream"

The period of leave-taking when analyst and analysand adjourn to their separate futures has caught the attention of a number of analytic writers. Loewald (1962) contends that reinternalization of the analyst determines "whether separation from a love object is experienced as deprivation and loss or as emancipation and mastery" (p. 263). It has been noted that future-oriented fantasies appear and become significant features. Shapiro (Firestein [Panel], 1969) noted an upsurge of fantasies about a postanalytic relationship with the analyst. Fleming (Firestein, 1969) made a distinction between termination and other separations in the course of the analysis. At termination, the patient is leaving the analyst and not being left. She stresses that the patient needs to recognize that the analyst can allow him to leave.

Leave-taking plunges the analysand into the affective states associated with old losses and separations. At the same time, in the mode of being an active rather than passive Participant, there may be a heady urge to celebrate what has taken place, to welcome as permanent the analyst within, or to actively grant oneself nostalgia for what will not be. For analytic candidates, in the past, when being able to terminate analysis was linked to graduation, there was also the halo effect of success and looking forward to membership in the Institute. For those who had dissatisfying analyses, decisive leaving (as in Neruda's poem) can become in itself an achievement.

The actual leave-taking often has a bittersweet quality in its particular mix of sorrow and zest. Balint (1950) posited a shift in self–other experience that led to a sense of new beginning toward the end of a successful analysis:

> This development goes parallel to, and depends largely on, the patient's gradual allowing of more and more rights to his objects, i.e. by developing his capacity for testing the reality with regard to his objects and in this way endeavouring to arrive at an acceptable compromise between his and his objects' demands. If this process can develop in an undisturbed way a surprisingly uniform experience dominates the very last period of the treatment. The patient feels that he is going through a kind of rebirth into a new life, that he has arrived at the end of a dark tunnel, that he sees light again after a long journey, he experiences a sense of great freedom as if a heavy burden had dropped from him, etc. It is a deeply moving experience; the general atmosphere is of taking leave for ever of something very dear, very precious—with all the corresponding grief and mourning—but this sincere and deeply felt grief is mitigated by the feeling of security, originating from the newly won possibilities for real happiness. Usually the patient leaves after the last session happy but with tears in his eyes and—I think I may admit—the analyst is in a very similar mood [p. 197].

Balint adds that this satisfactory ending occurs only in about two out of ten cases.

Blum (1989) observes that "the bittersweet last hour, so meaningful, often patently concerns plans involving replacement of or reunion with the analyst" (p. 291). He notes that patients become aware of time. Anticipation is intensified and often disguised and displaced onto other issues. There are specific references to the past, present, and future; to future plans; to permanence and transience; to time lapses and limits. Time may be freedom or tyranny—manipulated, saved, lost, killed—all referring to time as a transference object and to the analytic process and separation. The time limit itself has its own influence and unconscious meaning. Patients may be mobilized (or occasionally immobilized) by deadlines, reminiscent of Samuel Johnson's observation, "When a man knows he is to be hanged in a fortnight, it concentrates his mind wonderfully."

Lipton (1961), writing about "The Last Hour" emphasizes that "patients frequently look to some form of transference gratification at the conclusion and tend to use this period as an important enclave for fantasies. One of my patients said 'I have hoped that during the last week you would answer all my questions'" (p. 324). While Lipton makes his case for stringent neutrality on the part of the analyst to the last hour, Ekstein (1965) stresses the positive functions of the spirit of "afterplay" in linking satisfaction to memory (p. 42). This "afterplay" asserts through the play that the source of gratification did come and will come again. Out of the act of gratification, he develops a kind of play that recollects the past, the successful task that leads him to the development of adaptive capacity to prepare for the future. Much of what looks like the compulsion to repeat is but a new spontaneous trying out of wings (p. 65).

Calef and Weinshell (1983) describe a puzzling termination phenomenon:

> An occasional analytic patient in the midst of the struggle over termination, expresses in one way or another the wish to return to analysis at some indefinite time in the future. Simultaneously, he expresses satisfaction with the results (at least in part). Though termination was agreed upon and there is no apparent reason to continue (the analysis appears to be at an end), there persists for the patient the sensation that something has been left undone, that there remains 'unfinished business.' The hope

is that the ineffable will perhaps be capable of verbalization and dealt with at a later date [p. 642].

The authors contend that "consummation is the issue which, apparently, is equivalent to being finished and to completing the analysis." The sensation of "unfinished business" is an affect (not simply a judgment) that arises from the "absence of the consummation of the oedipal wishes" (p. 643). By contrast, they argue, should the analysand make a rational judgment that the analysis needs to be continued because analytic work remains to be done, this knowing carries greater conviction and is not accompanied by an inexplicable sense that something is not finished but needs to be some time in the future.

In general, the psychoanalytic literature, with rare and recent exceptions (Davies, 1998; S. Cooper, 2000), does not deal with meanings of the analyst that go beyond oedipal conflict. It seems to me, however, that for those who have come to love the separate subjectivity of their analyst, leave-taking is inevitably painful, a piquant recognition that an intimate erotic relationship with the analyst is taboo not because of required oedipal renunciation, but because consideration for his or her separate libidinal subjectivity precludes it.

Craige (2001), in an empirical study of how analytic candidates mourn analysis, finds: "Typically, upon leaving their analysts' offices for the last time, candidates reported feelings of accomplishment, pride, success, relief, liberation, and progress mixed with feelings of loss and anxiety about how they will manage on their own" (p. 13). One candidate, for example, "felt a mixture of actual happiness and excitement . . . as well as some trepidation" about whether he was prepared to be on his own "and some sense of loss." Over time, he "felt more the sense of excitement about moving on into another phase of my life."

Surprisingly, among the research Participants described in this volume whose memories of the analyst were vivid and whose analyses ranged from deeply satisfying to highly unsatisfactory, a number could not recall the last hour or leave-taking. Others made reference to the combination of zest and sorrow, remembering the last hour as tearful but also energizing, with a heady sense of having arrived at a place of confidence about wrestling with life's complications on their own. While the men made more references to relishing the sense of autonomy and inner choice, women were apt to emphasize that zest was connected to newly being able to risk being themselves, because the analyst had seen them for who they were and preferred the vitality of their personhood to their previously needed modes of excessive adaptation to the wishes of others. For the majority of those who had felt their analysis to be highly satisfying and who did remember the leave-taking, the good-bye brimmed with a mixture of feelings—tender and painful—with prospective nostalgia and pride in what had been accomplished with the analyst. A sense of gratitude was frequently mentioned but interestingly had not always been expressed. For some, it emerged in an imagined after conversation with the analyst (described in the chapter "The Analyst Imagined").

For many Participants, there was clarity about what was still wished for, although for others such awareness only developed in years after termination. Three Participants, deeply satisfied with their analyst, exercised their choice to delay the leave-taking, with insight about what they still needed and hope for its accomplishment.

The urge to be done with the analysis was strongest in those for whom the analysis had felt wounding. It was also, however, the dominant feeling tone for some others at each level of satisfaction with the analysis. Brief excerpts from Participants' comments about the very end of the analysis are followed by two examples of delayed leave-taking.

Deeply Satisfying Analysis

Dr. Eva Jason: The last moments were so full of feeling I could hardly speak—which was totally unlike that especially free flow of expressing myself the weeks before. I could hear things he had said to me over the years all at the same time. The last goodbye at the door, I didn't even try to touch or embrace him goodbye—though both my heart and body wanted to—because that would have felt almost like a trivialized form of what the longing for him had meant to me. But we did look into each other's eyes, and that was enough. Driving home, it was hard to see because my tears kept coming.

Dr. Julia Baranger: It was very sad, but I was very happy in my life then. And I felt I had accomplished a great deal. And, just about everything in my life at that point was going pretty well. So I was prepared to start out on my own. The sadness was really about missing her. Missing the time with her, missing her as a person. That was so clear at the very end.

Dr. Cecco Angiolieri: The ending was liberating. I had a strong conviction that I had done what I needed to do and I didn't feel that I needed this guy, you know, it must have been good analysis.

Moderately Satisfying Analysis

Dr. Seymour Sonenshein

LT: Do you remember the last day?
SS: No, but I can allude to the fact that there was a lot of crying. I remember feeling that a lot came out at the end that related back to some of the loss that I felt in relation to my mother, and I think that was part of the termination, at the very end.

Dr. Horatio Encarta: I couldn't wait to get out of there. I wanted to tell her "stamp me kosher and let me go." I wanted to be done and on my own, and graduating was my accomplishment.

Dissatisfying Analysis

Dr. Jay Glenn

JG: After four and a half years, he said, "Doctor, I think in a month and a half we can stop." [Laugh.] "Now, Doctor, this is a trial termination. And, come back and see me."
LT: Termination was his decision, he first brought up when you . . . ?
JG: Oh, he determined the whole thing.
LT: What did that feel like, that month and a half . . . ?
JG: I thought, "Fine. I want to get the hell out of here." I've had enough of this fellow. Only postanalytically two of my analytic siblings were telling me what they really thought: that he couldn't stand it that I had once specialized in the area he did. That hadn't occurred to me, but I think that they probably were right. One of the last things that happened in my analysis was he was telling me, out of the blue, that he'd been going through some old papers and found a paper that he had written on that syndrome. Naturally, I say, "I'd like to see it." So the next time he brought it in, got up from his chair, had rolled it up, threw it at me on the couch, and said, "There it is, Doctor, now what are you gonna do with it?" (Laughs.) So I read it. It was a good

report. Before I returned it to him, I was sitting on the toilet and quite unbiddenly had the fantasy of using it for toilet paper. (Laughs.) A fitting, fitting finale.

Dr. Phil Langer

PL: My friends were terminating, so when I proposed termination, he said, "Okay." But, we didn't do anything like it says in the books, like "we'll go over everything." And you don't have to do like it says in the books but a little bit, it would help to go over things. But if I ever asked for something, or got angry at him, he would always see it as only my problem. There wasn't any kind of sense that something had happened between us.
LT: Being that you had had a father, whom you loved, die when you were little, did he take that up in terms of what it might mean about termination?
PL: No, never.
LT: Or what the good-bye evoked, or how he felt you would think of him afterward? Or how he might think of you?
PL: I can't imagine! God forbid! No. Absolutely none of that.

Leave-Taking Postponed

The unconscious nature of the analysand's remnant fantasies of fulfillment has been stressed in the literature, along with the implication that the analyst must stand firm about the necessity of renunciation. Yet I was struck by a number of instances in which the Participant was well able to formulate what was still needed, and the analyst responded with a flexible variation on leave-taking, namely, to postpone it, even though the analytic work in other areas seemed complete enough. In the following two instances (of **deeply satisfying analyses**) the reasons for not yet taking leave did not stem from forbidden erotic wishes toward the analyst, but, instead, involved the benefits of solidifying internalizations for **Dr. Harold Koestner** and an aspect of self-experience in the presence of the analyst for **Dr. Emma McClinton**. **Dr. Koestner** ended the analysis, but availed himself of continuing with his analyst in therapy. **Dr. McClinton** could not foresee ending at the time of the interviews because she had hopes of feeling more equal in her interchanges with the analyst.

Dr. Harold Koestner

HK: About three quarters of the way through the analysis, I summoned up enough courage to tell him the impact on me of his inexpressive face as I went in the door each time and I did notice that there was a bit of expression in it. It wasn't clear what it was, which is probably appropriate, because it was consistent with remaining neutral, but the uncertainty of it evoked two major anxieties—how much might there be a danger, one of aggression, and how much might there be a danger, a risk of someone not being there. It was enough for me to feel it almost every time despite what had to be a steadily accumulating evidence over several years that that kind of trouble wasn't there. The composition of what I was anxious about changed with time, but I think I wanted more of a presence of him inside me, more of a reassuring introject to be able to deal with that, than I could quite muster. I eventually did express it, and then there was a very small change. The face was not immobile, it moved when I came in, there was always a hello and a good-bye after that, which there wasn't before. But still, if there was a day when it didn't happen, I could slip back into anxiety fairly easily. I needed something internally and externally of course at the same time, and I think something did develop with time internally and I was better able to be conscious of, and live, feel, and sit with those feelings, but I wished they weren't there to that extent. So, while terminating, I arranged with him to move from analysis to therapy, and then there were very explicit greetings and smiles. It became clear to me the inexpressive face had been part of his analytic technique. What did feel most painful and different was around termination of the therapeutic relationship, not of the analysis, with him. I did not feel that kind of anxiety any more. I just felt loss—missing, someone was missing, a different feeling. That's what felt like the real termination. Whereas moving from analysis to therapy felt different in many ways, and it was a termination of the analysis as the work had been carried out, but the relationship was certainly not terminated. In many ways, it was enriched.

Dr. Emma McClinton, deeply satisfied with her second analyst, in contrast to the first, has seen him for an extended period of treatment. Tears rose quickly when I asked if she could envision ever wanting to end.

LT: You were telling me last week that you have come up with what seems like the nicest solution to the pain of termination, which is to say, "I'm not going to do it." Is there a feeling that his input will always be crucial, or is there a feeling that maybe this work will be accomplished, but to say good-bye would be unbearable?

EM: I think that's right. (Tearful pause.) I can understand that.

LT: It must feel like—if someone comes to mean a great deal to you, it doesn't quite make sense to have it built in—that this valuable person—that no matter what, one says good-bye. Or that at least at some moments, something doesn't make sense about that while it does make sense at other moments.

EM: Hmm. Yes. I see it when you do that piece of . . . I'm seeing two postanalytic patients now, and I feel like you can terminate in the sense of being a more equal person.

LT: How do you mean?

EM: You can terminate with their neediness, and that can be recognized, or at least in my work, I usually have a formal termination in that regard. And then later they might come back. On a completely different footing. But then the question is, what is in the relationship that lets you make that shift? And I haven't made it yet.

LT: When you say, "What's in the relationship," and you've also said you're oriented toward the future, what can you picture that might be different?

EM: (Long pause.) Uhmmmm—Could be equality, an equality in discussing ideas. But I think that for women in general, this is a hard place. This is one of the reasons we don't get through the glass ceiling. In general, I would say it's very hard to do that. But particularly for me, it's very hard to do that.

LT: You conveyed a sense of your analyst's ability to see you for who you are, and to respect . . .

EM: Yeah, I don't think it's his problem. Again, that's clarifying, because it would be my father's problem, as it was my patients' problem.

LT: Well, Prospero, in *The Tempest* was happy to lay down his magic tools and no longer be so powerful for his daughter because he thought it would liberate him, as well as her.

EM: Wow! You know what? I think that's the secret of the end of analysis. I found, when I get to a certain place with my patients, as I did with both of the two women who have come back postanalytically, actually, it was a feeling on my side of I'll put down my magic wand, but we can still be connected as colleagues and discuss their issues and as caring people. But you have to put down, give up, I think, break the magic wand. And one of the questions, for me, is, having a hard time, how to do that shift. That is really the issue. I think that you got it. For me, where I am right now, and also in relation to my father, who is old, and about to have to—lay down his magic tools . . .

LT: And to have his daughter not idealize him . . . in the same way . . .

EM: And that has been the struggle.

LT: Without either disappearing?

EM: That's right. That has been the struggle. And I think my analyst definitely is good with that. I think I'm very good with that in terms of my patients.

LT: So he and you have that in common.

EM: Yes. I think it's not easy, though.

LT: Would there be a pleasure lost in not looking up to him in the same way? That lovely feeling that goes into awe. And also, do you think the analyst has to change, too, and recognize what isn't the same anymore?

EM: Uhmmm. As parents do in letting children go.

LT: One of the things you said you liked about your analyst was that he stayed himself, no matter what you might do. That you don't have to worry about that. You describe him as very empathic, that he sort of trots to keep in step with you, but doesn't get derailed by what you . . .

EM: Exactly. But this piece about the magic tool is so important. Because, again, it goes back to the *Wizard of Oz*. You know it. You know it. (Laughs.)

LT: Is that what the Wizard of Oz said?

EM: Well, the Wizard of Oz didn't give anyone anything that they didn't already have. You only need to be the Wizard of Oz as long as you need to be the Wizard of Oz.

LT: And are you saying it's the analyst's province to help the person recognize what they already have in them?

EM: Yes. Who they already are.

LT: And why it hasn't been communicated in certain situations when it hasn't . . . like in your first analysis.

EM: Yeah, going back to whatever there was with her. I didn't, couldn't communicate to her who I was. With my analyst now, if I were ending with him I think it really would be what we have been saying, "Thanks for putting down the magic tools . . ."

LT: And now we can have fun together . . . ?

EM: Yeah!!

16

SELF-ANALYSIS

To make a prairie it takes a clover and one bee—

One clover, and a bee

And revery.

The revery alone will do

If bees are few.

—Emily Dickinson, "Poem 1755"

Ideas come to us as the successors to griefs, and griefs, at the moment when they change to ideas, lose some part of their power to injure our heart; the transformation itself, even, for an instant, releases suddenly a little joy.

—Marcel Proust, *Remembrance of Things Past*

The distinctive kind of reverie the analytic process aspires to foster is self-analysis, intended to continue the analytic process when the analyst is no longer present. Self-analysis, or the "self-analytic function," has been considered an essential capacity for the analyst and assumed to be a yield of his or her own analysis. Is self-analysis a monologue, a dialogue, or does it, like the analytic process itself, partake of both? Bion (Boris, 1986) assigned a crucial function to the analyst's reverie in analysis, believing that "the capacity of another to intuit and imagine one's state of mind gives life to the mind and restores life to minds gone dead"(p. 167). For him, however, an essential feature resides in the "paradox of a mind deceiving itself and the process of intuition by which a second mind can realize what the first no longer can" (p. 182).

Freud had referred to psychoanalysis as conversations rather than monologues of free association. His belief, in essence that the good talk of the "talking cure" presumes an interchange between two, has been underrated from the time that the notion of analyst as blank screen became dominant. Gill (1994) pointed out that while the ideal of free association (as producing primary process material) would tend to make analysis a monologue rather than a dialogue, "The analyst inevitably influences the patient's flow of associations by what he or she says and does" (p. 91). What influences the free associations in self-analytic reverie? Lewin (1954, 1955) suggested that the distinction between solitary free association and association in the analytic situation is the presence of transference in the latter, although defense is present in both. Freud was aware of problems and limitations of a related sort at the very time of his self-analysis. He wrote to Fliess on November 14, 1897, "I have realized why I can analyze myself only with the help of knowledge obtained objectively (like an outsider). *True self-analysis is impossible;* otherwise there would be no neurotic illness" (Freud, 1900, p. 281).

Among the creators of psychoanalytic theory, one finds striking instances of self-analytic work that did not stem from that positive identification with their analyst that was later assumed to be the route to the self-analytic function. Freud (1900) linked the self-analysis he presented in the *Interpretation of Dreams* to the loss of his father: "This book has a further subjective significance for me personally— a significance which I only grasped after I had completed it. It was, I found, a portion of my own self-analysis, my reaction to my father's death—that is to say, to the most important event, the most poignant loss, of a man's life" (p. xxvi).

Ferenczi, who has been described as "the founder of all relationship based psychoanalysis, and explorer of countertransference" (Haynal, 2002), saw his postanalytic self-analysis as rooted in his disappointment in his analyst, Freud, rather than in positive identification with him. He wrote Freud and confided to his diary (Dupont, 1994):

> I needed a very painful self-analysis, carried out afterwards and quite methodically [January, 1930, p. 312]. My own analysis could not be pursued deeply enough because my analyst (by his own admission of a narcissistic nature), with his strong determination to be healthy, and his antipathy towards any weaknesses or abnormalities, could not follow me down into those depths and introduced the "educational" stage too soon [March, 1930, p. 314].

His need to communicate with Freud did not abate, however, and he continued to share much of his self-analysis (with selective omissions) with Freud during the years of correspondence and friendship between them.

Kohut exemplified a different evolution of productive self-analysis. He proposed a new theory of self to deal with his dissatisfactions with classical psychoanalytic technique. Kohut's widow and son asserted in the introduction to Kohut's correspondence (Kohut, 1994) that "it was almost certain that Mr. Z. was in fact none other than Kohut himself" and that "the case reflected his unsatisfactory first analysis with Dr. Ruth Eissler in Chicago, and his efforts at self analysis in order to overcome remaining difficulties" (Baudry, 1998). If they were correct, of which we cannot be sure, then his more forgiving self-analysis also had its origins in Kohut's disappointment rather than in positive identification with his analyst. I mention these examples because, almost ubiquitously, the origins of postanalytic self-analysis have been presumed to stem from positive identifications with the analytic function of the analyst.

Conway (1999) used an empirical phenomenological research method in a study of three subjects who had completed an analysis or psychoanalytic psychotherapy, with the aim of identifying themes of posttermination experience as they emerge spontaneously in the speech of those interviewed. Conway found that "it is in times of crisis, confusion or loneliness that the therapist or analyst is most missed and mourned for by all subjects (and interestingly, it is also at these times that the capacity for self-analysis is also experienced most consciously)" (p. 570).

Although classical criteria for successful termination laid heavy emphasis on resolution of the transference neurosis and the development of the self-analytic function, empirical follow-up studies some years after termination suggest that the transference neurosis may become altered and adaptive but does not disappear. (e.g., Pfeffer, 1961, 1963, 1993; Oremland, Blacker, and Norman, 1975; Norman et al., 1976). Other studies (Kantrowitz, Katz, and Paolitto, 1990a, b, c) have shown that the development of the self-analytic function is not correlated with the degree of resolution of the transference neurosis, at least as judged by the analyst. The authors suggest, "Some patients are able to acquire what we have traditionally considered an important analytic result, the development of a self-analytic function, without working through the transference neurosis" (1990b, p. 652).

More patients asserted that they do self-analysis than could give any examples of the process. They could, however, talk to themselves in a comforting way at times of stress. Two different uses of self-analytic function were distinguished: one to acquire insight, and the other to achieve greater affective comfort and increased affective regulation.

It is often said that the problem with self-analysis is the countertransference. There is no reason to believe that self-analysis is spared whatever self-protective maneuvers characterize the individual, albeit with the hopeful proviso that analysis has made them more transparent. M. K. Kramer (1959) wrote vividly of the limitations of self-analysis:

> I feel certain that every analyst who has tried to continue analysing himself has had the experience of encountering insurmountable resistances. At such times, dreams are forgotten and associations remain fruitless. Interpretations are tentative; they prove to be wrong or sterile intellectual speculations. Any insight that might occur is apt to be about a minor matter and does not lead to a resolution of the conflict. Superego promptings to continue the analytic efforts lead to further awareness of the frustrating power of the resistances. One often has to admit defeat. There were many instances when I had to abandon such efforts as useless [p. 18].

In contrast to self-analysis, Kramer distinguished another activity, which she termed "auto-analysis," that continues "of its own accord, i.e. not activated by conscious volition."

> The non-volitional nature of the autoanalytic function was demonstrated to me repeatedly by the emergence of analytic insights when I was not actively seeking them. . . . In reviewing the knowledge gained about my unconscious in this spontaneous way, I found a remarkable continuity in the material . . . though the episodes of insight were often separated by considerable periods of time. The spontaneity of the emergence of this material and the continuity of content gives evidence that the analytic process can become an autonomous, non-volitional ego function which automatically deals with whatever is most strongly cathected in the unconscious [pp. 17–18].

Kramer likens this process to E. Kris's (1956) discussion of the "good hour" as one can observe it in patients well advanced in psychoanalytic therapy, in which the material emerges "as if prepared outside awareness" (p. 447). Gardner (1989), meanwhile, holds what he calls "self inquiry" to be central to analytic process in the first place:

> The pursuit of psychoanalysis is the pursuit of two self inquiries. . . . Every patient and every psychoanalyst has struggled and will struggle between aims to advance self inquiry and aims to obstruct it. The aim to obstruct lies not only in the aim to avoid the pains, and pleasures of facing the music to which self inquiry leads, but in the aim to preserve the pains, and the pleasures of playing detached and laudable disseminator or receiver of arrived "truths." The most radical, enduring and worth-conserving contributions . . . have come, I believe, and will come from reciprocities of self inquiry. When things go best, psychoanalyst and patient advance their own inquiries and, in the advancing, each other's. This reciprocity asks and creates a fuller mutuality . . . that expresses and favors the beneficial growth of both the patient and the psychoanalyst [p. 8].

Elsewhere (Smith [Panel], 2002), Gardner is cited for his observation that while the understandings he reaches in his self-analytic work differ in form and content from his experience while analyzing, both are essential for self-understanding.

Craige (2002), interviewing analytic candidates about their post-termination experience, found that in the candidates who felt they had had successful analyses, the capacity for self-analysis seemed to rest, at least initially, on their ability to sense the analyst's presence internally. Candidates frequently mentioned evoking their analyst's image to create an inner conversation with the analyst.

Although we tend to refer to the self-analytic function somewhat glibly, taking for granted what is meant by it, it probably encompasses a variety of mental states, including achieving new insights, preventing new insights, talking with oneself in "comforting ways" (Kantrowitz), and memorializing the analytic relationship by psychically conjuring up the analyst. Like free association, it may flow most productively when it is "auto-analysis" rather than a consciously willed task. Its origins in the affective interplay with the analyst is suggested by theories involving "reciprocal self-inquiry" (Gardner). Nonetheless, we must be open to the possibility that it can flourish either because of this or in spite of it. As Mitchell (2002) puts it, "Knowing oneself is a complicated business, because knowing one version of oneself can be a defense against knowing and being surprised by other versions of oneself. Thus, in contemporary psychoanalytic terms, knowing oneself is much less a goal to be achieved than a process to be immersed in" (p. 110). Caper (2002) posits an object relations view of self-analysis. He challenges the notion that the patient becomes able to carry on the work of analysis through identification with the analyst. He sees identification as an attack on the "link" to the object experienced as separate from the self. He believes that linking, as opposed to identification, "allows the patient to experience his own point of view (unconfused with that of the analyst) and the analyst's point of view (unconfused with his)." According to Caper, "The goal of analysis, is to allow patients to observe and think about their own state of mind, thereby creating a 'link with themselves' and thus to continue the analysis on their own" (Smith [Panel], 2002, p. 223).

I now consider self-analysis as it emerged in the narratives of the research Participants. As in my life I have been spoiled by the luxury of having friends with an affinity for self-analytic associations, I had to remind myself that it is not the most usual state of mind. That being said, I repeatedly found that the interview process, with most Participants, flowed within a self-analytic mode, without it being specifically identified as "self-analysis." I thought of it as a self-reflective frame of mind, which could also (selectively) enter into our communications; it was, as Mitchell put it, "a process to be immersed in." For example, even the request for the Participant to invent a pseudonym was at times met with humorous self-reflection. One Partticiant wrote back, "This was almost too much of a challenge to my fantasies. 'Pee Wee' Reese and 'Duke' Snider were not sufficiently analytic monikers. Winston Churchill reveals a grandiosity I'd rather conceal. I think Jack Robinson is just right. How about you?"

Many Participants spontaneously alluded to self-analytic modes as keeping them steady company in one way or another. It was particularly emphasized as steadying and useful when engaging with patients, a simultaneous track of affectively colored associations about what the patient communicated and one's own response. Regardless of their particular theoretical orientation, most Participants assumed that such "uses of the self" (T. Jacobs, 1991) for a simultaneous perspective on the patients' and their own reactions were an integral feature of their analytic work.

For some, self-analysis had become an automatic channel of experience, without the necessity of conjuring it up. Others spoke of access to it when intentionally invoked. For still others, it was piquantly associated with awareness of holding the analyst in mind. For instance, there were numbers of allusions to pangs of regret during the year after termination, when the former analysand came to a self-analytic insight or dream interpretation, felt the urge to share it with the analyst, and then faced the reality that this wouldn't happen. The disappointment was not in the analysis or analyst, which Ticho (1967) posited as characteristic of the final stages of consolidating a self-analytic function posttermination, but did tap into lingering longings for his presence. So, when a conscious sense of connection does not exist, one of the functions of self-analysis may be that it brings the analysand into unconscious connection with experiencing the absent analyst.

Valuing self-analysis turned out not to be correlated with the level of retrospective satisfaction with the analysis, however, so, unlike most theoretical assumptions about its origins, it did not necessarily signify a positive identification with the analyst or his or her analytic function. I believe that this was because some Participants who had felt damaged by their analysis needed to deal with this trauma, first of all, by a prolonged and painful period of self-analysis. Rising from procrustean couches, they gained some hard-won sense of mastery through self-inquiry (in two cases, shared with a colleague) and became particularly attuned to monitoring their own reactions and associations with patients, intending to foster the kind of "reciprocities of self-inquiry" that had eluded them with their own analysts.

Some Participants, at each level of satisfaction, mentioned that much of their development in self-awareness occurred through self-analysis posttermination. Others noted that conscious evocation of the analyst during self-analysis fades over time. Finally, some analysts are by nature more introspectively inclined than others, both as they enter and as they leave analysis. Yet if the analysis provided the kind of access to inner life that diminished the need for self justification or defense, then the self-analytic net was cast in more affective and imaginative seas—with the risk, of course, of making waves.

Self-protective modes could be subtle in limiting the scope of self-analytic exploration. For example, two people might make a habit of analyzing their dreams and consider this self-analysis, but one person might also welcome awareness of his motivations in how he relates to others, whereas the other person may keep himself resoundingly oblivious to how his motivation contributes to the quality of his relationships. When working with patients, such a difference is consequential, because it affects the willingness to claim one's share in the creation of transference–countertransference turbulances.

As none of the interview questions were specifically directed toward self-analysis, the following excerpts are drawn from spontaneous comments of the Participants. In framing the questions, I was hesitant to invoke the word "self-analysis" because it has been so strongly prescribed as what *should* happen, and I didn't want the direction of response to be skewed toward what might be considered preferred. I did, however, ask the Participants at some point about where their ways of being with the analyst had gone after termination. Some spoke of self-analysis, but more mentioned a changed directness in communication with their spouse, friends, children, or patients. A number of men mentioned that they had, for the first time, established close friendships with another man or several other men, especially analyst peers, which included intimate, self-reflective conversation about personal feelings.

Some excerpts at each level of satisfaction with the analysis follow.

Deeply Satisfying Analysis

Dr. Veronica Clark: What he [second analyst] means to me inwardly? I'll go back in ways that I use and do not use my internal sense of him. I use him less and less as the years go on. It became more of the usual solitary self-analysis each year. I require less of the kinds of thinking that bring him up as part of the self-analysis. Or, an issue might occur—I will consciously go back to my analysis and do another piece in my own working through, realize where we had stopped and where I took it after that. I do a lot of that, due partially to who I am, partially to who he is and what I got, what we did together in the analysis. But my first analyst [**moderately satisfying analysis**] didn't stay with me that much except in a highly negative way, so I never seemed to bring him up in that way.

Dr. Jack Robinson: I don't know how long postanalytically I may have dreamt about her. Of course, like everybody else, my dreams about her were disguised. It would be somebody else or we would quickly understand, even in the telling of it, some disguise and displacement. But she was so good at that, and I tried to keep tabs on my dreams in the postanalytic period and analyze them. And like with all good intentions, there's a fade out period in time. [The analysis happened many year earlier.] Occasionally, I would still make an effort to analyze my own dreams. And I still have dreams that reflect a lot of neurotic stuff from my childhood and [I am] a lot more comfortable, since the analysis, with what they mean, so I can bear to think about it.

Dr. Eva Jason: The first stretch after the analysis I held him in mind so much that all the self-analysis felt like a way to continue talking to him inwardly. But I wanted to continue that process—almost like a tribute to the analysis having been that good—and that meant having the courage to dig into things I don't like about myself, not just the easy stuff because otherwise it wouldn't be like the analysis was. It was most useful when I just let myself sort of daydream, letting my mind wander where it will, rather than actively trying to figure things out. And when I'm with patients I feel wide open to those clues emotionally because I don't not want to miss what's going on in me about what's going on in them. And he is not part of that—it's me and myself—although I admit at times I have the fantasy of telling him about a particular piece of work with a patient, just sharing the patient with him, and being curious about how he would hear it.

Dr. John Deere: But for me, in a way, the end of the analysis was a beginning. An extended journey of getting to know myself.

Dr. Celia Laub: I liked the differences between my analyst and me, and they became a very important part of my experience in the analysis. The times he came up with very different images and metaphors affected me powerfully, sort of shook me loose from a lot of old limits in how I saw things. I notice that now when I'm trying to analyze my feelings or why I'm acting in a particular way, I'm apt to go as far as I can with that, but if I'm stuck I can invoke his rebuttals to my self-critical or denying and defensive conclusions and that takes me further. And anyway (laughs) probably the whole process of self-analysis, which feels so natural to me now, and which I want to keep active for my own sake as well as my patients—probably most of all it still reminds me of being with him.

Dr. Saul Green: I think much of my growth happened after the analysis. The analysis was like the seeding of that possibility, then I had to keep watering and fertilizing and so on, and so of course it keeps going on forever. It was immediately after when I was on the analytic couch, and as years went on, that perspective of looking inside and trying to find out what's going on with my motivations, my feelings, my self, and so on, I can sense that period of awakening because I think I was pretty naive when I went into analysis and that naivete was at least reduced to a considerable degree so that I could become more fully aware of many of the things in myself that I wasn't aware of and hadn't wanted to know.

Moderately Satisfying Analysis

Dr. David Lawrence: Somewhere in the four-and-half, five years of my analysis, I clearly internalized my analyst—in spite of all the negative stuff and troubles I had with him. Afterward I often would have conversations with him in my mind about certain situations, and how to handle this and that. And that was a helpful presence. So I think that he, as advisor-like, was very much with me over the first period of time after termination. So when did I stop that? Really, 19 or 20 years ago. I was surprised by how much analytic work went on long after the termination. I mean especially about what I felt about him, and I guess some of that just has to get worked out on your own. Because one gets a different perspective when one's not feeling the same feelings. In fact, it's similar to working out a relationship with a dead parent; you certainly work through a lot with a dead parent. Your feelings and your understanding of that person, the question of can he bother me now? For instance, I very much wanted to be his special patient, and I gave that up.

Dissatisfying Analysis

Dr. Irving Mazur: I think for me that self-analysis became necessary during rather than after the analysis. The things he was saying to me felt so depressing. He thought that nothing good could happen until I became less narcissistic, and he just lit on all my resistances. I felt less and less like telling him what went on with me, and there was a lot I never told him. But during that time, I had a sort of private track of self-analysis, my thoughts to myself about myself, which, in a private joke to myself, I labeled "defense analysis"—namely, in defense of myself! After that analysis, my self-analytic thinking became much less defensive, but it wasn't till lately, since I've been seeing Dr. X [another analyst] that I've looked forward to what that kind of thinking can tap. Now I think it can be rich, like dreams.

Dr. Jay Glenn sought to rid himself of the analyst within, whom he experienced as a wounding introject. The process is described in chapter 7, "Men with Male Analysts." It had been extremely helpful to him to talk with an analytic sibling over an extended period of time to analyze which aspects of the demeaning analysis derived from the problems of the analyst and which reflected his own issues. He comments about self-analysis:

JG: A very important part of my analysis was postanalysis. After Mark [analytic sibling] and I got that work done, and the self-analysis was quite continuing, there came a point where I made a kind of major internal shift to much more relatedness. It had not happened during the analysis. I never was schizoid or anything like that, but it was much more relatedness, much more investment, outside myself, and it was a very interesting time because, it was a time of real change, and it was quite disorienting. I have thought at the time that it was like somebody who spoke about reading *Catch-22*. He said that he felt like he was two feet off the ground reading it. I thought at the time, I feel all the time like I'm about two feet off the ground. There's something gone that was there. There's something here that wasn't there before. And I can tell you, I don't think there's ever a day that hasn't been self-analytic in my life since then. There's a continued process and I rely on it for myself and with patients. And with that there's been a shift, and it was occurring during that time, in relation to family and to patients and to friends.

Dr. Elizabeth Light had been deeply satisfied with her analysis at termination but was highly dissatisfied by the time of the interview. She suffered from the events surrounding her analyst's censure, about 10 years earlier, after multiple sexual transgressions with patients, about which he had lied to her and to others as well.

EL: I think I left the analysis with the sense that it was a good analysis, not perfect. I knew, sort of, what parts had not been discussed, that some things are undone, but I also knew it was my job to finish things up for myself. The timing of the good-bye to him felt one-hundred-percent right. I spent two years thereafter dealing with his meaning in my life and my awareness of my being, my internal being, with a sense of completion to it. I carried on the analysis in myself—and had a sense of his real presence or being, turning more into an introject of some kind.

LT: It sounds like a generative introject that you are describing.

EL: Very much. If this had never happened, the bad stuff, I would have retained a very good, solid feeling about myself and psychoanalysis. So, when I found out about what had gone on, I knew that my whole life had changed. Then I began to lose my empathy for my analyst and to spend a year or two with what felt like extracting . . . because a good introject had turned toxic, and I had to get that out of me. It was a lot of work on my own.

LT: You may have just landed on one terrible complication. During an ordinary termination, one doesn't lose one's empathy, one's feeling for the person, and having to make oneself do that sounds devastating.

EL: Yes, usually we try through our work to replace bad introjects with good ones. I felt I had developed something very positive inside me during the analysis. The question of what I created, what was me and mine, and what belonged to my analyst was hard. How to get rid of the negative aspects became an issue for about two years after that—so it was several years ago. I think it was through a slow two-year process of a lot of sleepless nights, a lot of thinking, a lot of dreaming, a lot of writing. I was very active with self-analysis. I had to be. It was not a passive thing. It didn't just happen.

17

DILEMMAS OF
POSTTERMINATION CONTACT

The after-play, the epilogue, links the past to the future.

—Rudolph Ekstein, *Working Through and*
Termination of Analysis

Traveler, there is no road; the road comes into being as you go.

—Antonia Machado, cited by Marcelo Perez in
The Termination of the Training Analysis

As analysis ends, the image of the analyst as person acquires new piquancy for the analysand. There are at least two reasons for this. With fresh ways of "being together with" as well as "distinct from" (Sander, 1997) the analyst, earned during analysis, the analyst as subjectively created object loses luster, and his or her actual nature is given more psychic space to come into view. Meanwhile, the sudden absence of the physical analyst vitalizes his or her image in conscious and unconscious fantasy, once more accentuating the question, "Who is this person who has been so important to me?"

Fruitful probing toward termination can bring the dyad's imagination to what the analysand's needs and fantasies are about the future of the relationship. If there is posttermination contact (more likely for candidates in analytic training than for others), the sense of intrapsychic knowing of the analyst may be enriched, confirmed, ruined, or revised by the analysand's conclusions about how the analyst in sight collides with the analyst inside. The actuality of the analyst, as it selectively infused the analysis, is now broadened to include the actuality of the analyst as ordinary person in the external world, as well as his or her relation, posttermination, to the analysand.

Early in psychoanalytic history, attitudes toward posttermination contact between analyst and analysand took into consideration the verity that in addition to the analytic relationship, a relationship between "real" individuals exists. But it was traditionally assumed, that the analysand's individuation from the analyst requires definitive separation, which in turn was then expected to usher in the necessary libidinal renunciation. This assumption may underlie some of the divergence about how patients, who seek out their analyst for further contact, are thought about. Such patients have been characterized as still having particular difficulties, such as deficiencies in the capacity for internalization, a history of severe early losses, unanalyzed separation anxiety or primarily preoedipal problems. (Schlessinger, 1974, 1975; Lord et al., 1978; Blanck and Blanck, 1988; Luborsky, in Schacter and Johan, 1989). The implication has been that if the ex-analysand ever wants to see the analyst again, something did not go right. But a different way of thinking emphasizes the naturalness of some posttermination contact in terms of the shared task of evaluating the analysis as evidenced by posttermination developments and the wish on the part of the analysand to share positive, progressive life developments with the person who knows him or her best. It also provides a way to confirm the analyst's genuine interest. Because a number of empirical investigations suggest that a high proportion of patients considered to have been "successfully analyzed" recontact their analysts in one way or another, pathologizing the wish for posttermination contact seems misguided and may have, in the past, prevented its optimal use.

I believe that the value of postanalytic contact ranges from beneficial to its opposite, in concert with the singular dynamics within each analytic dyad as well as to the uses to which it is put. Although a clinical follow-up appointment or a return to the analyst for a further piece of therapeutic work is, of course, different from a social or professional encounter within the Institute community, both are considered here as bearing on the quality of synthesis of the image of the analyst as analyzing and as existing in the external world. Naturally, the frame of expectations undergoes more alteration in social or professional encounters than in posttermination clinical sessions, in which the sole, explicit goal continues to be a focus on the intrapsychic life of the analysand. Yet subtle differences in expectations appear in clinical posttermination meetings as well. Rangell spoke of patients returning, not for further analysis but for "look-ins into their psychic lives" (Hurn [Panel], 1973, p. 189).

Bases for friendly feelings between former patient and analyst have been discussed throughout psychoanalytic history. Greenson (cited in Gumbel and Heimann [Panel], 1970) noted: "In 1939, Sigmund Freud wrote, "Not every good relation between an analyst and his subject during and after analysis was to be regarded as a transference; there were also friendly relations which were based on reality and which proved to be viable." Anna Freud in 1954 stated: "With due respect for the necessary strictest handling and interpretation of the transference, I feel still that we should leave room somewhere for the realization that analyst and patient are also two real people, of equal adult status, in a real personal relationship to each other" (p. 142). Greenson ventured that "psychoanalysis proper is only possible when a patient has the capacity for both a transference as well as a non-transference relationship to the therapist" (Gumbel and Heimann [Panel], 1970, pp. 144–5). It seems to me that the analysand's opportunity for an affective synthesis about where these dimensions of transference and "non-transference" meet potentially makes the analyst more useable over time as an inner resource with whom to identify and disidentify, to love and to be angry with.

Rangell (1966) had introduced the notion of a "postanalytic period." He believed that the analyst can make two errors with his former patients at this time:

> He can persist with his analytic posture after it is no longer proper to do so, which can lead to a long, unnecessary period of inhibition and dependence on the part of the ex-patient; or he can make the opposite error by rushing into excessive gratification of the former patient, which can be reacted to as seductiveness or threat and lead to bewilderment, acting out, and opposite types of pathology.

Rangell identified the postanalytic phase of analysis as an important sequel to the analytic work itself but believed that big differences exist at this time, depending on whether the analyst is ever going to see the patient again, and if so whether only occasionally or relatively frequently as a colleague in the analytic community. Others have concurred with the opinion that because analytic candidates are able to skip the final good-bye, leaving the final separation from analysis incomplete, they become unable to identify with the kind of mourning and separation reactions that other patients must deal with. For example, Novick (1997) contends that "our choice of profession has allowed us to bypass the mourning that is crucial to the termination phase. Termination without mourning is not termination and if we persist in denying the difference, then termination will remain inconceivable" (p. 151). Annie Reich (1950), on the other hand, pointed to a positive posttermination impetus for candidates to resolve transferences:

> With students who have the occasion to meet their analyst professionally after termination of analysis this process progresses faster. They have the opportunity to see their analysts in the frame of reality, and the magic omnipotent features of the relationship collapse more readily under these conditions and may be replaced by a mature friendship or a working relationship [p. 132].

Reich recognized the value of de-idealization as a component of postanalytic contact, but she did not address the function of postanalytic contact in the process of mourning the loss of the intimate analytic relationship.

Craige (2002) recently questioned whether it was true that analytic candidates' expectation of postanalytic contact averted mourning. Using questionnaires and some follow-up phone interviews, she asked psychoanalytic candidates about the process of mourning analysis during the posttermination phase. She found that 94% of the 121 analytic candidates surveyed experienced a strong sense of loss of the unique analytic relationship after termination of their analysis, even though 97% expected to see their analyst after termination (p. 517). Candidates who experienced the most painful and prolonged mourning for the analyst were also those who felt their analysis as most successful. There was not a correlation between early loss or trauma in the life of the candidate and intensity of painful sadness in the year after termination, although such a correlation had often been hypothesized by others. Craige noted that the propensity for such painful missing of the analyst was strongest in women with male analysts. This was true in my sample as well.

Buxbaum (1950) said, "I cannot conceive of therapeutic results continuing firmly when the analyst rejects the former student-patient after the end of the analysis. . . . Transference may recede, but there will always be a residue of it, which may serve as a stimulus to further emotional health or neurosis" (p. 188). She adopted a procedure of assuring terminating patients that they could return to see her, even without suffering symptoms or distress. She believed "that such a procedure removes the traumatic effects of ending an analysis in an active way . . . it also proves to the patient that the analyst is not afraid of personal contacts, which has been frequently one of the patient's problems" (pp. 188–189).

The effects of posttermination contact were discussed by the panel, Evaluation of Outcome of Psychoanalytic Treatment: Should Follow-Up by the Analyst Be Part of the Post-Termination Phase of Analytic Treatment?" (Schacter and Johan, 1989): Luborsky reviewed several outcome studies conducted by someone other than the treating analyst and reported both positive and negative effects. The patient's expectation of a routine follow-up was apt to have a positive effect in maintaining the gains, particularly in patients with a deficiency in the capacity for internalization. He pointed to a possible negative effect in that it may hinder the completion of the work of separation for some patients. Schlessinger concluded that follow-up interviews by other than the treating analyst consistently facilitated the self-analytic function of the former patient. Although he did not recommend "routine" postanalytic contact, he felt it was generally desirable and that an iatrogenic factor may be introduced by an analyst who regards any return of a former patient—for whatever reason—as a sign of failure. Wallerstein felt that in some cases follow-up by other than the treating analyst speeded up the process of separation, whereas in others it delayed separation. Martin noted that in no instance did follow-up contact with the treating analyst have any damaging effect on the patient.

Hartlaub, Martin, and Rhine (1986) canvassed all graduate members of the Denver Psychoanalytic Society about their experience with patients making contact with them after the analysis. Two thirds of the analysands had made some kind of contact with their former analysts within the average time of 2.6 years since termination. The authors comment: "We had presumed that recontact would occur more frequently by patients with preoedipal or parent-loss pathology than those with primarily oedipal problems, but our survey did not support this hypothesis, nor was there any statistically significant correlation of recontact with age, diagnosis, or length of analysis. Only the correlation of sex and recontact was significant, with 76% of women and only 50% of men making recontact. Brief contacts with the analyst after termination were common across all diagnostic categories and age groups" (pp. 899–900). Although the most frequent reason offered by the treating analyst was "reworking of termination issues," it is clear that the majority of analysts had more progressive motivation. So that what often appears to the analyst to be an unresolved termination issue may well represent some new aspect of adult development requiring recontact. They comment as follows:

> The fact that this finding surprised us led us to recognize that we had all shared the unconscious fantasy that after a successful analysis the patient would not need further contact with the analyst, or, conversely, that recontact somehow cast doubt on the completeness of the analysis. The fantasy existed although none of us could recall ever actually having been taught this [p. 894].

Schachter et al. (1997; Schachter, 1992) have been the most persuasive advocates of posttermination, clinical follow-up contact as propitious for maximizing the benefits of treatment. Based on experience with patients seen for follow-up in a variety of circumstances, the authors suggest that posttermination meetings can stabilize analytic gains, provide a joint assessment of analytic outcome from a useful later perspective, and provide an opportunity for further analytic work. Schacter et al. stress the following:

> It should come as no surprise that even a brief revival of the past analytic encounter may also stir up grief for the lost analytic relationship (which is soon to be lost again). This is evidence of the enduring power of an analytic experience, even years after successful termination. Perhaps an expectation of a painful resurgence of grief on the part of both analyst and patient has played a role in the reluctance we analysts have had to consider such meetings [p. 1185].

In 1994, Schacter and Brauer (2001) updated the earlier study of what analysts reported about posttermination meetings in relation to what the analyst had told the patient about the possibility of such meetings before termination. During the 5-year span between 1989 and 1994, there was an increase in the number of analysts making statements to patients regarding posttermination contact. What the analyst said about it to the patient was associated with the likelihood of posttermination contact. The "hypothesis that women analysts were more likely to have posttermination contact with their analysands than men analysts, was confirmed" (p. 1127). A new, intriguing finding was "a powerful, positive association between the degree to which the analyst reports thinking about his/her most significant analyst and the percentage of his/her analysands contacting them within the previous six months" (p. 1128). Analysts who think more frequently about their former analyst were more likely to feel that they benefited from their analysis, to feel positively about their most significant analyst, and to feel that posttermination contact with their own analyst enhanced the results of their own analysis. In addition, analysts who reported collegial contact with their most significant analyst had more posttermination contacts with their terminated analysands than those who did not. The authors conclude, "Thus, analysts who maintain feelings of attachment to their own analyst are more accessible to their patients' contacts and continued attachment" (p. 1130).

Most recently Schacter (2002) addresses the rarely discussed topic of friendship between analyst and former analysand:

> Posttermination meetings will rarely develop into a friendship, and when this occurs it requires major changes of both patient and analyst. The risk for the former patient is that the friendship may founder and leave the former patient without either friend or analyst, but with unanalyzed negative feelings. The patient must abandon the comfortable investiture of the analyst with benign authority and omniscience, and the analyst must relinquish the gratification of this investiture and become much more self-disclosing. These changes are of such magnitude that even if the taboo about developing such friendship diminishes or disappears, it seems likely that development of such a friendship will be a relatively rare event. Developing such a friendship will probably always mean traversing a rocky path—as do many other journeys that we value [pp. 218–219].

To weigh the rocks on the path described, one would also have to confront the asymmetries of desire within the dyad. Although the risks of the analyst's "exploitation" of the analysand's attachment have been stressed in the literature and are common warnings in Institute lore (and do happen), it is much more usual for the analysand to yearn for friendship, leaving the analyst inundated by former analysands who have this wish. Perhaps some of the taboo on friendship has usefully functioned to protect the analyst's legitimate freedom to not feel pressured by such desires on the part of his analysands, without having to act in personally rejecting ways.

Some of the conflicting motivations for the analyst are noted by Hoffman (1996):

> The very fact that we usually maintain the analytic frame even after termination to the extent that, for example, we do not become friends with or socialize with our patients in the usual sense, indicates that we want to preserve rather than undo the special kind of presence in our patients' lives that the analytic situation fosters. So those of us who are interested in developing more mutual and egalitarian relationships with our patients should not deny the extent to which we are drawing upon the ritualized asymmetry of the analytic situation to give that mutuality its power. The asymmetry makes our participation in the spirit of mutuality matter to our patients in an intensified way, one that helps to build or construct our patients' views of themselves as creative agents and as persons ultimately deserving of love [pp. 120–121].

To explore the wishes and practices about posttermination contact with the research Participants, I asked the following questions: "What kinds of professional and/or social contact have you had with each other since the ending of analysis? Have you hoped for such contacts or wanted to avoid or minimize any encounters? Do you feel he (she) has wanted to avoid such contacts?"

The research Participants wishes for postanalytic contact or its avoidance showed great variation according to the level of satisfaction with the analysis, in concert with the specific dynamics of the dyad's affective dialogue. In addition, opportunity also varied. When it was possible, the chance to synthesize the image of the idealized analyst with the more ordinary being was enriching for the majority of analysands. Others avoided after-contact, however, with the intent being to protect what had been created in the analysis, not to dilute or alter its essence. Problematic after-contact occurred when the need for continued love or loyalty stemmed from the analyst more than the analysand, and problematic avoidance took place when there was a continuation of the analytic stance of abstinence within which the analysand felt diminished as eternal patient, still beholden to the unchanged structure of the prior analytic asymmetry. The presence or absence of postanalytic contact did not in itself correlate with the eventual usefulness of the analysis, but whether the postanalytic relationship or freedom from the relationship fit the analysand's psychological need for metabolizing termination did. Reactions to postanalytic contact never seemed simply neutral, however, and could create new emotional challenges. For example, **Dr. David Lawrence,** who had described his analytic relationship as: "like a marriage—I learned where not to tread," found himself on untrod paths in postanalytic encounters, leading him to deepened self-analysis about his analyst's meaning to him. **Dr. Veronica Clark** was shaken by the unforeseen task of having to blend her strongly positive relationship with her analyst during analysis with the lack of connection she felt later when conversing with him at a conference: "I had the experience in analysis of being very well understood, remembered, and cared about. I had a totally different experience postanalysis where I felt that he did not remember, he did not care. . . . So, though I still love him in a way, I would choose not to work on a committee with him. I don't want to activate transferences or countertransferences. I'm at peace and I would like to stay at peace."

The recognition that the analyst remains a lively force in the analysand's inner world of objects, in both very satisfying and unsatisfying analyses, has consequences. It adds to the complications for the analyst as well as the analysand. For instance, does the analyst have a responsibility to behave in a way that preserves the image of a "sustaining introject"? If one answers in the affirmative, does this continued role freeze the quality of asymmetry in the relationship in such a way that the analysand continues to feel beholden to past but not future developments? If the analyst persists in being "careful" with the analysand, does that inhibit a fuller authenticity that would add knowledge to what the analysand has surmised about the analyst's affectivity? Of course, the asymmetry during the analysis is not just one of asymmetry of need (and hence emotional power) but also asymmetry of knowledge. The actuality of the other member of the dyad outside the analytic hours is much better known by the analyst than the analysand, skewing the vulnerability of exposure. (And it is a known phenomenon that when one has bared all, one may question,

"Will you still respect me in the morning?") Yet particularly when an analysis has been very good, the urge to feel comfortable with the analyst as person may be strong, a natural addendum to the surmising of the analyst's mental processes during the analysis, and, after mourning for the lost intimacy, a liberating consolation and bonus in the process of giving up earlier idealizations. But can it be attained? Numbers of Participants noted that the kind of emotional intimacy they have experienced in the analysis could not be duplicated in a casual interchange or social relationship with the analyst. One Participant put it this way: "It doesn't feel like it's about us not being happy to see each other or talk to each other, because we are. It just feels like the situation doesn't allow it easily." She expressed her sadness about the ending of a most cherished relationship and added, "Even if it doesn't end, even if we become colleagues, since we're on the same committee, or if one day I should be fortunate, bold, and ambitious enough to become a training analyst and sit in lots of meetings with him, still, it would never be the same, can't be the same. In a way that's good; in a way it's such a loss!"

Some Participants noted that a period of time was needed to consolidate the inner presence of the analyst before they wanted more ordinary contact or knowledge about him or her. Then the pleasure at discovering other aspects of the analyst's person was often accompanied by recognition, acceptance, and at times cherishing of the analyst's singular nature, with loved and admired qualities as well as vulnerabilities and quirks. Several people, both men and women, mentioned becoming more comfortable with each other as a postanalytic goal, a confirmation to them of the changes in relational patterns achieved during the analysis.

For some, there were perplexing discrepancies between their sense of the analyst as person during and after analysis. Several people noted either that he or she was "a better analyst than person" or "a better person than analyst." Among those who felt the analyst brought a better self to analytic work than "real" life, posttermination "normalization" of the actual relationship tended not to occur, regardless of whether there was much or little contact, and sometimes analytic gains were experienced as having been spoiled.

When lingering erotic or loving wishes toward the analyst remained strong, casual posttermination contact (such as chatting at a meeting) could evoke paradoxical reactions. On one hand, there was great happiness in whatever interchange with the analyst took place.

On the other, contact with the analyst was apt to evoke a fresh bout of longing and grief. It is, of course, this very state of longing and grief that clarifies once more that although the analyst might be welcoming, the intensity of desire and meaning is not reciprocal.

Such a final confrontation with knowing that the analysand has very limited (although real) meaning in the life of the analyst may be postponed until after the analysis because the analyst's affective presence during the analysis submerges it. When the interchange has been rich in "mutual containment of affect" (S. Cooper, 2000), the analysand is left, ironically, not only with her own longing, but also with an intimate sense of having embraced the analyst's nature, which now, by mutual agreement, is banished to memory. The reasons for this may be understood rationally but feel emotionally bewildering or insoluble. The ironies in these issues, along with other grief work, were inescapable during the analysand's self-reflections after termination.

The postanalytic encounters between analyst and analysand revealed very personal signatures of each member of the dyad. Some analysts, affectively very present in the consulting room, were pictured as uncomfortable with social encounters outside it, and their analysands had the task of integrating this side of the analyst's nature. Others were described as "unflappable" in maintaining several roles (e.g., as colleagues on committees or other joint endeavors), while also continuing to be available as analyst if the need should arise. Still others invited a social relationship right after the ending of analysis (such as to play tennis), seemingly oblivious to the complicated meanings it might have for the analysand. In earlier decades, a number of analysts invited analysands for a visit that had a social format (with tea and cookies) within a year of termination but remained clearly boundaried.

Analysands, in turn, ranged from the majority who yearned for some kind of personal knowledge or connection to others who preferred to feel free of it. The analysands who were relieved to keep their distance from their analyst's intrapsychic lives tended to be people, both men and women, who had felt too drawn into their mother's affective states, privy to more than they had ever wanted to know, or else who were sensitive to impingements. Prone to separation guilt for wanting to live a life for themselves rather than for a self-involved parent who expected to be the center of their child's psychic reality, they were relieved to find a respect for boundaries in their analyst, a sense that the analyst didn't need the analysand for his or her own purposes. As one Participant said, "I thought both of my analysts were happy guys, with very good family lives. That was important to me. With my mother, there was always that sense of something more needed from me, while what I could do was never enough. But with my analysts I never felt I had to complete them or their lives, that they wanted or needed me for that."

A number of analysands did have a role in their analyst's lives, years after termination, when the analyst became infirm or terminally ill. In some cases, this enhanced the use of the analysis; in others, it was ruinous to it for a long period of time.

Participants' portrayals of posttermination contact have been grouped according to the level of satisfaction with the analysis. I summarize some of the features that characterize the dilemmas of posttermination contact at each level of satisfaction and illustrate with excerpts from the interviews.

Deeply Satisfying Analyses

In the most satisfying analyses, anticipations and fantasies about the dyad's relationship in postanalytic life were apt to be discussed. For the analysand, a complex view of the nature of the analyst often infused the anticipations. Such anticipations did not remain static after termination, but shifted and evolved, with room for surprises and some adaptation to what was learned. It tended to be important to the analysand to be welcomed as a respected colleague, with a press for the analyst, in tandem, to change something in the quality of his or her communications. Noting their own increased sense of autonomy (which had led to termination and continued afterward), that is, thinking, shaving, and loving outside the orbit of the analyst, some Participants emphasized the confluence of signs, in the analyst's behavior, that he or she recognized it as well. Such changes involved revisions of the analyst's representation of the analysand. The analysand at times expressed appreciation of the delicate balance involved in the analyst's allowing for pleasures in shared interests, a continued "meeting of minds," but not imposing a value of being identical—in the words of Berenstein (2001), a mandate that "you must be like me."

When love for the analyst had been the deepest mutative strand, the posttermination period was complex. Because that love had a particularity created during the analysis, the person of the analyst could not be replaced in the analysand's feelings, even though new and rewarding ways of relating reshaped other relationships—with spouse, friends, children or patients. For these individuals, it seemed that the analyst might remain vividly loved always, although progressively inhabiting a smaller space in the analysand's psychic life. In their wishes about posttermination contact, these Participants were apt to ponder the analyst's nature as well as their own, with some resultant ironies. For example, one woman expressed the following: "By the end of the analysis, my sense was that his extraordinary intuition, which had been lovely for me, was partly based on his probably having felt a pull, as a boy, to stay ever-attuned to his mother, without enough input from his father, that he had felt too responsible to freely do what he wanted. But I came to love best those times when he slipped out of his usual empathic stance to some really off-beat association of his own making, that vigorously spontaneous side of him that is very rich and unique. So I very much wanted him to feel freed from having to respond to me, not wanting any relationship after termination to be based on that, as much as I also wanted it."

Analysands with a high level of satisfaction did not seem to idealize the analysis or analyst excessively. They were able to identify either some specific area of discord or disappointment, "something more" they might have wished for, or the need to accept whatever they viewed as a quirk. Following are some further excerpts from those with deeply satisfying analyses.

Dr. Francesca Emon: I remember him saying he would always be my analyst. So I had the impression this was an open door. It was going to end, this frequency, this kind of time in the structure of the analysis, but I could go back when I needed.

I asked about her view of the Institute's attitude about posttermination contact.

FE: I don't know where I got this because I don't think there's any formal teaching. I took the termination seminar but I got this more from what I know everybody else does, in informal revelations about what goes on. I have the impression that people periodically go back and also that they have working relationships with their analysts at the Institute, and that all of this is just a mixture, and people vary in how well they tolerate it. My impression is they manage it themselves.
LT: And you were saying you wanted him to be in your life somehow. Is he in your life?
FE: He kind of is. I've recently gone back to see him as my analyst for just a few sessions. At the same time, we are on a committee

together, and the combination seems to work just fine. It's flexible. Sometimes he's my analyst; sometimes he's more real to me. I don't find it a problem. I haven't wanted to be more in his life than I am, but I wouldn't want to be less, either. I like that we can work together. I have a very good feeling whenever we're together, like on a committee or whatever. I feel deeply respected and very supported in his presence. I'm not derailed by his presence.

Dr. Steven Zeller: We have had a little bit of extra-analytic contact—not on any regular basis, but a handful of times. When he approached retirement and began withdrawing from Institute activities, he said to me, "It's time to let other people take a turn." That was toward the end of the analysis, but it reinforced that sense that he was both moving on and making way.

LT: And giving a blessing?

SZ: Exactly. He was giving a blessing. I had a dream in my first analysis that Chairman Mao toward the end decides to step down and give the Gang of Four a chance. This sort of made it real. I went to hear him at a conference. He was urbane, funny, and intellectually vital. He touched on everything from analysis to literary criticism. I was so proud. I thought he's all over the map. I'm all over the map. I could identify. And also, he was funny. That was familiar from the analysis, but the degree of it was new.

By now there is a mix: I have memories that will remind me of something in analysis. Then I have the sort of thing like dreams I analyze where it's a good feeling, of something having come from my analysis because, look, here's the evidence. I liked being able to analyze it, with the sense of it as a result of my analysis. And then there's the real world. Sending something back and forth and just enjoying either hearing about how he's doing or sending something I was proud of, that I thought he'd enjoy.

LT: Do you remember the first time you decided to get in touch or send something?

SZ: We chatted at the end about being colleagues. We were both going to be in the same area for vacation after the end of the analysis, so we had even talked about getting together. That had significance to me, that it would be sort of a symbol of our new way, but the dates didn't turn out right, so we didn't end up doing that. I think that happened first and then I sent him a talk I had given that I had enjoyed doing because I thought that he would appreciate it, including its humor. He sent me his course list for a course in a new area he is thinking about. I certainly appreciate what he does, and I enjoy the idea that he appreciates what I do, too. He once got in touch with me when he saw a write-up of me taking a new position. It was again, a combination of the "blessing" and conveying appreciation.

Dr. Cecco Angiolieri's second analyst also conveyed a sense of blessing by an affirming vision of further developments in the analysand's life:

CA: Years after the analysis was over, I met him at a party after my wife had died and I had remarried, and my second wife was pregnant and I was past 50 and it was a very nice encounter, very warm without being pushy about it. He said he felt confident that I would be able to manage having a second family at the time. He told me then something about his own family, which he had never spoken to me about before. He and his wife were childless, which he regretted, but was very happy about the close relationship he had with his brother's kids. I didn't know it during the analysis, but he would make trips to see them.
LT: What you are describing now sounds like his freely offered pleasure in your marriage with children, when that was something he hadn't had and had wanted.
CA: That's right, he didn't begrudge it, it wasn't an oedipal competition, so that was one of the self-revelatory remarks which he made to me, eight or ten years after the analysis. He died not long after that, but that has stayed with me.

Dr. Harold Koestner: For several posttermination dyads, there was some ambiguity about whether the analyst intended to remain solely an intrapsychic presence or also an occasional actual presence. Such ambiguity was apt to stimulate an awareness of hope, disappointment, and the need to come to terms with lingering longings.

HK: Some years after termination, there was the teasing of myself, with what I might have wanted. I felt it around my wedding, interestingly, because he had said . . . there was a referral he sent me once. I was speaking with him about that and I mentioned that I was going to be married, and he congratulated me and said, "Let me know when" and that left me with a bit of a puzzle. One way of dealing with that was to send an invitation. I was thinking, Would he come or not? and I got a very nice card saying they couldn't join us but he'd be there in spirit, but I remember until I got the card, I couldn't know, and was wondering. I'd assumed until he said, "Let me know," that of course he wouldn't, so that actually stirred something up that otherwise wouldn't have been stirred up. Was it created anew then, was it probable or unlikely? It was a bit of jolt, it gave me a glimpse into something that of course would have to be there, and also I did hope but expected it probably wouldn't happen. It didn't happen. I did feel disappointed, but still it was my hope. They were manageable feelings, but I realized of course when I noticed myself feeling this hope, feeling the disappointment that, yes, there was something more I wouldn't have minded having and there is a certain amount of deprivation that is built into any professional relationship for good reasons, and I felt it and, it must have been resonating of course with how my mother's was. I'm sure my transference to my analyst was a mixture of the paternal and maternal transferences. As the purpose of an analysis, after all, is not to leave one empty, I'll no doubt continue to live with that.

Dr. Mozes Nounous exemplifies those Participants who took an active role, including visits, when their former analyst was infirm or dying. The effect varied greatly according to whether the analysand felt compelled to be more involved than she wanted (like **Dr. Rodine**) or welcomed the chance to express caring for the analyst in this way (like **Dr. Green**). **Dr. Nounous** was at neither extreme.

MN: Do you know what happened when she retired? How we took care of her? Because that's a special story. Years after I was through analysis, I did visit her sometimes, and I took my son and wife with me. So she met the family. And that's the kind of person she was. Then she was ill but was working still, still very active. It meant something to me to be able to say, "Now this is the lady that you always heard about, and this is my son," because she had helped me with both my wife and son from what I said. She was always very likely to do that.
LT: Did she seem the same person as in the analysis, or were there other things about her that affected you?
MN: Whatever I learned later accentuated more of what I already knew, since she was so freely herself during the analysis. But years later, I was called by Irene [an analytic sibling], who told me that my analyst was by that time in a nursing home, that she and Martha [another analytic sibling] are taking care of her, because her daughter

lived far away, and she had nobody here. So they would bring her things. Visit her regularly. They asked if I would be willing to help out. And they called several other former analysands. And we did. I went there several times with cookies or something. And we would talk. She was by this time very frail. But mentally she was pretty good. And we took care of her. For me, it was like getting in touch with the real person more. We still joked together. I told her what I was into, what had happened in my life and career. But it was a little uneasy because, from being an analyst, even though there were many years in between, to be a person with the condition she was in. Was it my mother all over again?

LT: Having to be careful of her?

MN: Yes, and take care of her. There was a feelings of friendship and warmth, and while this was by far the predominant feeling, there was also a nasty feeling in the sense of, a reversal of roles . . . a mixture of doing it with affection, which obviously was there, but also a little bit of the feeling, "Now I'm in charge. Now I am the strong one. Okay?" But, that was good.

LT: Ahh! And was that reversal at all lonely, or as though you had lost her guidance, or more like "now I've come into my own, and you loom a lot littler?"

MN: No, not a loss of guidance, the second of what you said. More like victory.

Mozes elaborated on his sense that his analytic siblings, Irene and Martha, felt their attachment to her more wrenchingly than he did. At the funeral they couldn't stop crying, while he felt tearful and moved "but not to that extent." He stressed several times that Irene and Martha took more responsibility for her than he, visiting much more regularly and so forth, so it may have been important that he felt free to limit his involvement, unlike what he had needed to do with his mother.

Dr. Rose Lionheart also described a combination of social visiting with her second analyst (**deeply satisfying analysis**) with later visits to her in the nursing home. She compares postanalytic contact with her first (male) and second (female) analysts. She speaks initially of her first, male analyst (**moderately satisfying analysis**):

RL: Afterward we were in the same social circle and we would meet at parties lots of times. I was still single and I would go as a single woman to these things, and there was always a little play. He was very careful. We were at the APA meetings one time at one of the dinner dances, and he was very wary. There were just the two of us standing there, and I said, "You could ask me to dance, you know." So we started to dance and he was sort of holding me at arms length and I said, "I'm not made of glass," so he laughed and he said, "Well, you know it's not such an easy thing" or something like that.

LT: Was this shortly after the analysis?

RL: Not right away but it was pretty shortly—not long enough to give me any long period of adjustment. I never had to mourn the loss of him. There was never a real termination because it went right into a social relationship. He was always very cordial, and we met socially many times. He was at my house. He once insisted, many years after the analysis, I was still single and thin and very attractive. I was at this New Year's Eve party and it snowed and it was completely awful and he lived nearby, but he insisted on driving me home way across the city, as I remember it, against his wife's objections, and the host said, "You know you can stay over, we can find a place for you" and he said, "Oh no, I'll drive her home" and in the midst of this slop, must have taken hours to get home and hours for him to get back to where he lived. His wife came with us, but he drove me home. That I felt was strange, too. So that was my first analyst.

My second analyst was a very straightforward, classical-type analyst but when I finished the analysis, I was invited to her house for dinner, and we became friends and I would see her. By the time I wanted to return to an analyst for a short time about problems with my child, I would not have wished to go back to her, given her age, and went to someone else. I don't think she was actually still in practice. Later, I used to go out to see her. She was in a nursing home and I remember driving out with my husband, and she still could recognize me and was happy to see me and she talked about people in the Institute. I still felt we could still get on the same wavelength. When she thought someone was awful, she was very free to say so, as was I!

Moderately Satisfying Analysis

Analysands with a moderate degree of satisfaction conveyed two alternative patterns. In one, the analysand tended to identify some aspect of the analyst's character, with which they continued to struggle and which they felt had impinged on their freedom to engage some important issues during the analysis. One person described her analyst's "schizoid with-drawal," and "difficulty in experiencing mutuality." Another struggled with the sense of competitiveness and areas of "false self" in the analyst. In such instances, postanalytic contact tended to confirm the perceptions and did not necessarily ameliorate the effects of the particular limitations. Nevertheless, in some cases the positive interactions during the analysis continued their momentum in internalized dialogue with the analyst, whereas in others the access to the internalized analyst was experienced as "lost." In a second pattern, the analyst was described as a kind person and the analysis as supportive but stopping short of reaching core issues. As **Dr. Raphe Lieberman** puts it: "I never felt deeply understood or connected to him, although it was pleasant. Afterward I didn't miss him." No person in the "moderately satisfied" group, however, felt that the analyst was personally rejecting or avoided all postanalytic contact.

Dr. David Lawrence found features of postanalytic contact with his analyst problematic. But he continued to feel grateful for the ways the analysis had led to beneficial change, ways that allowed him to enter a happy, well-matched marriage as well as to feel that his own aggression and competitive strivings could be expressed without retribution. His experience of the analyst during the analysis was already marred by some troublesome aspects, which did not, however, preclude the sense that the analyst basically had his interests at heart. The analyst tended to be boastful about his and his relatives' social and financial position. This dimension of his life involved some unacknowledged camouflaging of his ethnic origins. **Dr. Lawrence** was privy to information about these matters through a friend. He viewed his analyst as presenting a "false self," which impinged on **Dr. Lawrence's** grappling with his own conflicts and aspirations in these areas. He also felt that the analyst, with deliberation (or intent) withheld any comforting qualities during the analysis and maintained a competitive stance, within which the expression of aggression was possible but the expression of loving feelings was not. He comments, "and as I told you, my mother had been so competitive with me." Aggressive freedom was an important issue in the analysis because it had not been acceptable to either of his parents. In addition to wanting to be recognized as a potential collegial equal after termination, there are remnant longings to be welcomed into the closer knowledge of the analyst and his "interior" (his house) in ways that had eluded the affective interchange during analysis. He comments about the tone of termination and the content of posttermination conversations:

DL: I had a really weird last session. He told me we would have it sitting up. I wasn't expecting that, and somehow I didn't get to talk about things I would have liked, would have talked about. It became kind of chatty. Kind of like being invited for tea or coffee. Without the tea or coffee. I was about to terminate, so I had things to talk about that I never got to talk about. That would have happened anyway. But he inserted it into my hour. He made it his hour. His termination. That would be fine if he had previously said, the last hour we'll sit up and we'll chat. Then I would have had my last analytic hour the time before.

I went back twice briefly. I remember I was worried about money and my big mortgage and paying for college tuitions, and he said, "You should just buy a summer house because if you need to sell it to put the kids through college, it'll have appreciated," totally missing the fact that I felt like I didn't have two nickels to spare, let alone to buy a summer house.

At the time when I went back, one of the women I was supervising had a crush on me and wanted to go out for lunch. It was very exciting. I was thinking about doing it. And he said, "Don't go out to lunch." And it just seemed so, again, preemptive, and so . . . why not? And why did he have to say anything? Why couldn't he just have seen what my fantasies about it were? So I don't think I would go back to see him again now.

I have bumped into him a fair number of times, and he always asks about how the kids are doing in school, so our conversations are kind of limited to that. And he would talk to me about what his kids have achieved. I don't know if he really asked how I was, but he asked about the kids, where were they in school. I knew that his kids had gone to the school that was a little fancier, but he didn't stress that then, so it was not that condescending. But the stuff about his social position in the organization I was a member of was still certainly a putdown. I guess I experience more and more a sense of disappointment, but not angry disappointment, about his false self, about pretending he wasn't Jewish and stuff like that.

Dr. Lawrence then commented impressively about having learned to accept people's quirks and considering these qualities to be his analyst's quirks.

DL: It was like a marriage; I learned where not to tread. But I still would like to find out what he's really like. (Laugh.) I have thought about going back and saying that, but I don't want to go back as a patient. I just didn't want to be charged for it. I mean, it wasn't the dollars, it was just that it also defines in some way . . . that I'm still viewed as a patient . . . that I'm not accepted in a way.

David Lawrence notes that the analyst maintained the formality of his title long after termination:

DL: Years after termination, I needed someone to see a young adolescent, so I called him up and left a message, and he called me back and said, "Hi, this is Dr. X." And I wasn't calling him to be my doctor. And it wasn't a bad case. It wasn't a borderline! People who were supervised by him told me that they had supervision not in his office but in some room in his house. Supervisees could get to see it. Why couldn't I? It was just a different way of being viewed. So, you know, I just didn't want to be still seen as a little kid, a patient. That kind of feeling. But I can't really say, let's meet but don't charge me. Or, I'd like to get to know you, but don't interpret this as a patient's thing, but as a former patient's thing. He would have to be ready to shift roles. I could've said, "Do you want to have lunch sometime?" or something like that. To sort of catch up. But I would have to believe— to get a sense that he does his work differently. So I would have to have a nontherapeutic interaction with him before I would consider going back into a therapeutic relationship with him—I felt it was unnecessarily harsh and difficult. And I wouldn't want to subject myself to that again. But it was a long time ago, and I'm sure people do things differently. I do. And he probably does things differently. But, I don't know that I would go back to him. I might go to someone else. Someone more understanding. [Laughs.] 'Cause I don't have a real relationship with my ex-analyst.

Dr. Seymour Sonenshein found his training analyst somewhat formal and conservative, both personally and theoretically, compared with an earlier analysis with a very senior analyst, who had been more affectively present, warm, humorous, and spontaneous. He did also like the second analyst, however. He speaks of posttermination connections to the training analyst.

SS: We had this summer house, and he had one in the same area—I knew vaguely he went there. In a way, it felt embarrassing or it felt this is a little too close. It seemed as though it was not proper. I don't know if you've seen that movie about *What About Bob?* [A comedy about a patient who follows his annoyed therapist's footsteps on vacation, moving in on him and his family, but turns out to be less neurotic than the therapist.] (Both Laughing.) I didn't want him to feel that way. We all have our feelings about meeting patients and how to be able to do it in a relaxed way and to feel okay about it. My wife liked the area where we had the house. And I think for me it was an effort to try to feel comfortable with the idea. I thought this would be an achievement to be able to be there and meet him from time to time and to be able to feel comfortable enough about it and to feel like we were two grown-ups.

When I saw him at the Institute, it was very discreet and sort of controlled in that situation, but certainly I thought there was some warmth. He wasn't encouraging a great close relationship, but I think he was genuinely glad to say hello and talk for a few minutes. And then some summers I would see him in town where we had the house, but somewhat at a distance, neither of us being close enough to say hello. On the other hand, sometime we would run across each other and we talked a bit more about what's going on with life. I think he became a lot more comfortable, too. He was still a charged presence, but there was generally a good feeling about meeting him.

Dissatisfying Analysis

Analyses judged as dissatisfying or damaging tended to have a sad (yet often personally resourceful) aftermath for the analysand. Some Participants were haunted by a continuation of inner feeling of being unliked or unwelcome, a degree of rebuff that occurred only in this group. But others encountered "actual" directly rejecting or belittling behavior in postanalytic encounters. Unlike the majority of Participants in the study, fewer of the highly dissatisfied sought a second analysis but tended to stress their dedication to an ongoing self-analytic process. Interestingly, one Participant, who had had a hurtful analysis with his first analyst (followed by a satisfying second analysis), managed to bridge the first analyst's "Olympian distance" at a social occasion many years later and arrived at an empathic sense for the analyst as a traumatized person whose constraints were separate and unrelated to the former analysand.

Dr. Jay Glenn, who also felt that his analyst had subjected him to a series of put-downs, describes his posttermination encounters.

JG: Before termination, he informed me that his practice was to have a follow-up appointment in six months, so I went. I told him I was doing better, and things were going okay. I gave him some kind of example, and he lit up enthusiastically and said, "Now, Doctor, could we ever have gotten at that if we hadn't really taken on the narcissism and entitlement first?" (Both laugh.)

LT: What did you say?

JG: I smiled and said, no. I validated it. Because he was so deeply invested in it and he was in his 70s by then, and it was so clear that he felt the need for validation and this he considered his legacy.

Dr. Glenn portrays the last encounter with his analyst:

JG: My analyst wrote a long paper that really spelled out his contribution. At one of the Institute anniversaries, some of the real old-timers gave little talks. And he said—would be typical of my analyst —he was so glad to see his ideas coming to the fore in theory and glad to be one of the originators. At that dinner, when we were breaking up, I went over to him and was sort of interested in his knowing, and I said, "Dr. X, I just wanted you to know that I'm being considered for training analyst now." He wouldn't look at me. He sort of glanced up, a little bit, sort of very slight. It was just him and me. (Laughs.) And he absolutely did not respond at all. It did not disappoint me, actually. It was a confirmation. I think he had trouble connecting with it. I don't think he knew me as someone who could get there. I told you about how little he thought of me, what he thought I couldn't be like or accomplish. So it was interesting, true to form for him with me. That was the final contact I had with him. [**Dr. Glenn** did not seek a second analysis.]

Dr. Noah Levy had reported remaining haunted by the unanswered question, "Could he ever like me as I am?" This question shadowed potential postanalytic contact as well. The analyst had declared an arbitrary termination date of less than two months after he first raised the issue. **Noah** describes his reaction:

NL: In those days, the idea was that it must be good if you are told you can leave. So I can't be as sick as I thought I might be. So, gratification in that department overrode the doubts that really couldn't surface then. And my inability to go back to him after I terminated was really related to that, to be seen as competent. I never, ever, could imagine how I could tell him what upset me about him. I grant this was neurotic and nuts to some degree, but I just imagined he'd be very hurt to feel that I felt all these things. And that's true to this day. But

I did feel them. And the other thing was, I felt I didn't have his permission exactly. I felt he's very edgy about regression. I don't think this is the guy you call up and say, "Hey, can I come back?" I know one of my dear friends did that, and it was fine. I didn't feel that license. I think I always wanted to know the usual thing, did he like me, or was I the worst pain in the neck, or what? All of us had that feeling with him. I realize that some of that vulnerability was in concert with the things that I could feel if you're worried about that, but some of it was kept alive because of his peculiar way. He would do things in such a preemptory way. Everybody I knew who knew him would say, you'd be having a conversation with him, he'd suddenly say, "Gotta go." In the middle of the sentence. So, everybody got this idea. And I had that experience. I've run into him in social situations and watched him back away all of a sudden. It was a strange social cue. You could feel it all the time in the analysis. He'd just suddenly change the topic, and things were abrupt. He just stopped abruptly, like stopping the analysis, too. So he kept a lot of that same feeling going after the analysis. I think I was desperately trying to find out, as I still am to this day, was I okay? I was trying to find out, "Why did you make this preemptory termination date, didn't you like me? So you didn't like me. Who did you like better?" There was always something contingent, something weird all the time that threw me off, that kept alive the doubts I entered analysis with to this day.

When the aged analyst suffered from disabling illness, a friend who visited him told **Noah Levy** that the analyst had "been very up-front with a number of people that he'd rather not have anything to do with them now. So he just brushes them off." The analyst had said, "That one is just not somebody I want as company now. If they call I just tell them, 'Call me back sometime—later.'" So I have stayed in dread of calling him, and of having to live with the answer the rest of my life." [**Dr. Levy** did not seek a second analysis.]

Dr. Stuart Laraphil, who had had a dissatisfying first analysis, clarifies the ameliorative effect, many years later, of viewing his first analyst from a different perspective. This took place when he found himself seated at the same table as his first analyst, posttermination, at a wedding:

SL: It was a wonderful experience. Because we sat and talked a bit, person to person, in a way we never have before. It wasn't all that I might have liked, but there was some openness back and forth. And I got to see him in ways that I've never seen him before. Like, I didn't know that he was flirtatious until that night. It became quite obvious that he's a very flirtatious man, and I'm a pretty flirtatious guy myself. But I never knew that that was something he and I shared. I actually liked seeing his flirtatiousness, even though it made me feel a bit of competitiveness to see him putting his arm around various women in front of me and sort of owning them.

What I had felt before was this somewhat Olympian, off-putting attitude toward me and toward others. I was always astounded when I saw him at the hospital years later that he was the only person there who called the trainees by their titles. Dr. So-and-So at the lunch table. Always. So there was a formality about him that was out of keeping with the general culture, and I also felt, when pushed a little bit, he has a somewhat paranoid attitude about the world. I've been on committees with him where sometimes he's been usefully accurate but he always goes to the danger that this person is going to screw you somehow, so you gotta protect yourself. So some of what I felt personally in the analysis I've seen in other aspects of his life. But sitting at the same table, hearing something about his terrible, traumatic life story when he was a child—actually more from his girlfriend than from him—gave me empathy for him. And that was helpful to me. Whether it would have been helpful to an analytic task for me to know more about him while I was in analysis is a different question, but it certainly was helpful for me in coming to some terms with unresolved nagging feelings about him and moving on. It's not so much his shift, that he became more open to what he was rejecting in me before that affected me so much. It was his allowing me to see him as a person.

A Postscript on Postanalytic Contact

I have noted that the postanalytic encounters between analyst and analysand reveal very personal signatures of each member of the dyad, and that "There is no road. The road comes into being as you go." In the following instance, there is material from the analyst's as well as the analysand's point of view.

Toward the end of a deeply satisfying analysis, and in the context of both painful leave-taking and serenity with what had been achieved, the nature of the postanalytic relationship between the analyst and analysand was much discussed. A sense of increased comfort and spontaneity with each other, which characterized the end of the analysis, became a hopeful blueprint in the mind of the analysand for the relationship after analysis, while the analyst expressed also that encounters in a "professional–personal" frame seemed both possible and comfortable. During the first year posttermination, her pining for him did not abate. The second year, a number of encounters did occur, somewhat awkwardly, including being together at a small dinner party. The analyst then conveyed that he had not been comfortable during these times after all and would prefer to avoid social mingling. Her distress at his seeming wish to have nothing further to do with her tapped those core issues of rejection that she had felt were laid to rest during the analysis:

> I felt that I needed to get clearer about the meaning of this, even if I was not going to like the message. And emotional directness had been valued, so powerful and liberating, during the analysis. So, with some trepidation, I decided to write to him and I said: I continue to wrestle with what your preference for no more social encounters means and seem to see it differently from day to day. I gather this is a change from the "professional–personal" frame you felt was okay for the past couple of years, since social mediates both. At the level of meaning, I find myself in confusing territory. To me, it felt like the work done together was, among other things, signified by being more comfortable with each other, a measure, a picture of what had significantly changed. Was that simply a sustaining illusion on my part, or was that so and now has reverted back to early times, or is that so but strongly not your cup of tea (which would be 173% legitimate)? Or is your message in the verity that the treasure is the internalized dialogue with you (for which I've been deeply, repeatedly grateful over the last couple of years); that I've been blind as the proverbial bat in daylight by still seeking some kind of connection when I should just "move on." Let me be clear that whatever the meaning, what suits you is a leitmotif which needs no justification—and it is always some pleasure (even when I don't like the message) to me to hear what you think.

The analyst's reply brought not only peace and contentment, but also a renewal of her delight at his habitual fierce fidelity to veracity in himself and in the other person as well. She felt that the power of his message lay not in his understanding of her by itself, but in his willingness to make the emotional connection that made that possible. Also characteristic of him, she noticed he did not resort to being defensive. Here is his response:

> Thanks for writing so forthrightly. I am sorry if I have been confusing by sending forth mixed messages. Let me be as clear as I can. It simply is not wholly comfortable for me to plan meetings, or informal get-togethers, with someone with whom I have worked, played, wrestled, laughed, wept (and the whole gamut of feelings) in an intense analytic situation. (It took me a relatively long time to learn to drive a shift car.) I feel personal affection and deep connection with you, but I cannot easily translate that into a sphere outside the office setting. I am always pleased to see you and to learn about how and what you are doing. It's true that I had signaled and hoped that somehow it would easily and naturally work out that we would have some ongoing contact without having to spell it out in advance. But what has evolved, disappointing to you and in some measure to me too, is that I have not found such a way, other than ordinary events that might bring us together, or professional contacts, such as the programs in which we both took part. I know that practically that is likely to mean very little contact. So, one possible avenue is to leave it open that you return from time to time for talk and review of how you are and any issues you might like to air with me (and that invitation includes airing issues you have with me!). Meanwhile, keep in touch as you wish. With warm wishes.

She experienced the analyst's most surprising statement, that he felt personal affection and deep connection with her, as a lasting gift, affecting her profoundly, and other concerns melted away. This excerpt edifies that misunderstandings occur posttermination, just as they do during analysis. When the door is not barred to whatever kind of communication illuminated the heart of the process, "the after-play, the epilogue, links the past to the future."

From the poet Sue Standing comes the phrase, "As if the last rooms of memory hold only light."

18

THE ANALYST IMAGINED

O, let's go away together, pleads the soul.

—H.D.'s last words about Freud [Norman Holland]

In the wake of a satisfying analysis, the analyst resides within and can be called up as partner in dialogue and fantasy. Or he may reside quietly near the wellspring of consciousness, lending a certain coloration to mood, tempo to motion, form to how feeling is fathomed. This kind of presence can be tapped and is surprisingly vivid. Such experience differs from actual posttermination contact, although it may be affected by it.

Schlessinger and Robbins (1975, 1983) noted that many former patients make use in fantasy of the "benign presence" of the analyst to facilitate the solution of conflicts after analysis. On the basis of research regarding how patients represent their therapists, Rohde, Geller, and Farber (1992) report that self-perceived improvement is positively and significantly correlated with the vividness of the patient's representation of the therapist and with the tendency to use these representations for the specific purpose of continuing the therapeutic dialogue in the privacy of consciousness.

To explore the quality of difference between imagined and actual posttermination dialogue, Participants were asked to imagine the content of a conversation with their analyst were they to suddenly encounter each other. The potential "real" conversation with the analyst being imagined turned out to evoke something affective and immediate (perhaps his or her actuality) yet again. Most striking is the finding that those who had been in unsatisfactory or limited analyses often could not imagine or wanted to avoid imagining such a conversation. Thus, the sustaining function of the analyst in imaginative psychic life was aborted. In some cases, the Participant expressed the wish to withhold communication with the analyst, just as the analyst, as perceived, had withheld a helpful, communicative connection with them. In other cases, the Participant wanted to spare the dyad withheld criticism, because having it understood seemed futile. Still others wanted to spare the analyst the hurt they assumed would be inflicted if they were candid. A few did aim their anger at the analyst in imagined conversation. In contrast, those who were deeply satisfied with the analysis most often express pleasure in imagining such a conversation, a chance to communicate about the yet unexplored, to relay postanalytic developments, to express gratitude or to entertain humorously a favorite fantasy.

The following questions were posed to the Participants, and the responses grouped by the three categories of satisfaction with the analysis: If you imagine running into each other now and could talk freely, what would each of you say? What would you think and not say? What do you envision would be the effect of such a conversation for you?

In the following excerpts, some Participants are quoted twice, in relation to two analysts experienced with different degrees of satisfaction.

Deeply Satisfying Analysis

Dr. Francesca Emon: When I do run into him I am conscious of keeping what I say related to work that we have in common. I don't tell him very, very personal things, because I feel like it's not fair to him. But (in a joking voice) if I could, I'd want to know if he missed me and if he was tortured by the fact that I don't come anymore? (Laughs.) And if he longed to hear me talk about my life. (Laughs.) That's what I'd want to know.
LT: Like are you suffering for me and for my presence? (Both laugh.) What would he say? If he were without constraints?
FE: He would say, "Yes!" He would say that there was something about me that no other patient has ever been able to match. Something about my take on life that was so insightful and fascinating and funny (laughs).

Dr. Mozes Nounous: What would be the first thing? I would give myself credit first, and I would say, "I used what you gave me. Which I didn't realize fully at the time. But I realized in a very, sort of, primitive way. But it was profound, as it has shaped my life." And I would tell her that. She gave me something, like my mother gave me something, also, and to show her, "See, this is what has happened as a consequence." That's what I would say, but my main feeling would be—I'm getting all emotional here as we talk—I have strong feelings now. My main feeling would be, "We're together. And we're together because look at what I did and what you gave me" (tearful).

LT: Yes. (Pause.) And is there anything at all that you would think and not say?

MN: Well, probably that she talked too much. Sometimes I got annoyed at all the gossip. But I welcomed it, too. Because sometimes it was about people that I felt exactly the same as she did, and I would never (laughs) have thought that I was entitled to think that way. That was an interesting question.

Dr. Emma McClinton and I had just been talking about changes around termination, comparing the analyst to Prospero in *The Tempest*, willing to lay down his magic wand when he recognizes that his daughter has grown up, is ready to marry, and no longer needs him to play a magical role. She had spoken of wanting to enjoy a connection to him on a more "equal footing."

EM: With my analyst now, if I were ending with him I think it really would be what we have been saying, "Thanks for putting down the magic tools."

LT: And now we can have fun together? (Both laugh.)

EM: Yeah!

Dr. Saul Green: That's a fascinating question. I'd look at her with wide eyes and say, "Oh I love you "and she'd look at me with tears in her eyes a little bit and say, "How good you were to me at the end, before I died." I think that's all we'd say to each other. Then I'd ask her, "Was I your favorite?" And she would say, "Yeah, well, maybe, yeah." She'd say it enough that I would know, but not so much that I would wonder if there were other favorites, if they wouldn't feel betrayed. I could assume that she had more than one favorite.

LT: That's intriguing in itself. Is there a move from wanting to be the favorite to it's okay if you have more than one favorite as long as—?

SG: Yeah, as long as I'm in a bunch. I don't think I'd be so concerned about it any more as long as I know she really cared for me. She could care for a hundred others, too. And then I'd be cute and I'd say, "Should we have a dance?"

LT: And she?

SG: She would have said, "Of course, let's waltz." And then if I had some complaints I would say that, because my thought was you had to have a department of complaints, too, for it to be real. I'd say, "I think the reason I never worked out my sleep problems is because you have sleep problems too." I'd see her reading light on late at night if I passed there, so I figured that out. How am I going to work on my sleep problems if she can't work out her own?

LT: So is that a way of saying to her it was wonderful to have been so close as all the feelings of "I love you," which are really there . . . but there is also this disadvantage to having been so close that . . .

SG: That's right.

LT: I can't get a night's sleep (both laugh) because you don't?

SG: It's a problem that she had and therefore I assume had a hard time helping me overcome mine. I figure that if the analyst hasn't worked out his or her problems around a certain issue, then it's going to be very difficult to help the analysand do that kind of work. So I would have that little complaint, and she'd agree that it was right. But by and large it would be very tender, I think, and joyous, because every time I saw her after I stopped, it had that quality.

Dr. John Deere: I can't imagine anything I wouldn't say. I think I would say something about what the analysis has meant to me over the years. How valuable it was. Actually, I may have said it to him, I've certainly said it to other people, I felt it was life-saving work. Not that I was suicidal. But that it opened up my life in ways that I couldn't anticipate, I didn't see. I didn't see I was able to be a richer, fuller person. So, it liberated me. I think I would also talk about what he meant to me as a person. Who he had been to me, and how I still value that. I really liked him in the way that I knew him. I'd be curious about how his life is going. I'm interested. I care about him. He mattered to me and still matters to me. There was a way in which he felt so important to me and continues to be. I'd like to sit down with him to ask him, not so much what he thought of me, but how he put me together. Here is this person who looked at me from a vantage point different from mine, and I wondered how he put me together in the beginning, what his reactions were, how I affected him, how that changed over time, how he ended up seeing me.

Dr. Steven Zeller: My initial thought was, as if it's part of an ongoing conversation with him, I would tell him my reaction to his reading list for this new area of interest he has been pursuing and ask him what he thought of the material which I sent him a week ago. But my next thought is about the question that you asked about how would he say that I changed over those years. I just had the fantasy of telling him what I had said and asking him what he thought about that. I mean, it's something I certainly would love to know and never asked directly. And I imagine there would be something comic, because we appreciate each other's ways of being funny.

Dr. Phil Langer: My second analyst—sure! I would be interested in telling her, and I would say to her, "And how are you?" and she would say, "I'm fine." And that's all she would say. And that would be all right. That's her. And that restraint is something I've appreciated about her. And I would tell her anything she wanted to know about me. It would give her pleasure. It's not that she needs it. But it matters that it would give her pleasure and it would give me pleasure for her to know that I was doing well. That I really believe. And sometimes I hear good things about her and I'm very pleased, too.

Dr. Bob White: I'd want to catch up. I'd want him to know what's happened. And I'd want to hear what he had to say about it. I think that he [second analyst] would be astonished, he would be apprecia-tive of what had happened, to me, my wife, my kids, and, to the analy-sis. So, I think that that would be a wonderful experience. I would look forward to having a wonderful time with him, although he's very different from me. He reminds me of being with someone, like Jim or Alan [friends and colleagues], who always seems to appreciate things so much and is ready for something new and surprising. I've told you how as a kid I was forever trying to tell my mother something she didn't know, to surprise her with something new and grand, and how she would deflate me. But he would probably enjoy it.

Dr. Jack Robinson: I would like to tell her that having had many years to reflect on the experience, I felt it was very rewarding for me. Perhaps in not the most easily explainable ways. I did feel that she gave of herself to me in a very human way. And I was very grateful for that. And that was very different than my mother. There were no strings attached. No matter how much I might have, through the transference, made it out to be that way. I knew well into the analy-sis or early in the analysis that that was true and that was good. And that was very important, probably more important than any of the insights or interpretations, which I don't remember. There are many things that were right that she said, but you have to be able to accept your analyst when she's wrong too, and you have to begin to work on the fact that the person that you put up on a pedestal is your need to have her up there, and your needs can change over time, so that that person can become a human being. Anyway, I am free associating more than answering your question. So, I would like to tell her that she was very helpful to me. That it was a major experience in my life. That it was mainly registered on my emotional memory, more than my intellectual memory, and that it did me good and made me a somewhat better person, which I try to add to as time goes on.

Dr. Gary Thomas: I don't know what he would say, but I would express appreciation. I really would. Which I don't think I ever really fully did. So I wasn't sufficiently analyzed. (Laughs.) That's kind of true.

Dr. Eva Jason: If he were suddenly here and I could say anything? Once in a while, less than I used to, I still imagine what it would be like to make love and then talk—totally relaxed. Though actually I don't think that being together with him would be any less charged—that even making love wouldn't change that—because it was more the feelings than the sexual tension itself that became so charged. I don't know why that fantasy is still there once in a while—except maybe it steadies me, reminding me that my love for him actually made me more ready to love others deeply. I'm sure this is not a fantasy he shared, so he would squirm, sort of embarrassed. I can imagine the look on his face, I saw it many times. Of course, I wouldn't dream of saying any of that if we actually run into each other because doing that had to end, it would be a terrible imposition now on a sort of casual, normalish relationship, but to have the fantasy once in a while feels okay.

Analysis Moderately Satisfying

Dr. Heather Rodine: (Long pause.) She has been dead for several years. I don't know what I would say, but my image of what she would say, I think she would express a tremendous sense of deprivation in not being able to continue her life and go where she wanted. LT: Hmm—and you, meanwhile, what would you be thinking and maybe not saying?

HR: I was just going to ask you, is it fair to say I have nothing to say to her? (Both laugh.)

LT: All is fair in love and war, and both live in analysis. But I think you are saying something else. Perhaps you're saying it is finished now.

HR: It really is.

LT: Are you saying that running into her would almost be disruptive of where you are now, rather than wanted. . . . Or have no further effect—if she came and told you of being deprived and excluded from life?

HR: My first reaction to that is to invite her to continue on her own independent journey, so I think I treasure the sense of solitude and independence from her that has been so hard won.

Dr. Seymour Sonenshein: It would depend on the circumstances. If I was back in analysis with my second analyst, I certainly would bring out some of my feelings about his choices—The degree of intervention or the kinds of intervention and some of the things that maybe he didn't do that I feel might have been more helpful. I certainly would talk about some of that. I would think if I had the choice which one I would want to go to just to be with or talk more freely to, that my first analyst might be the one. Maybe because I think that there was always the feeling with the second analyst of a tremendous amount of control. There is a certain amount of warmth and availability, but whatever he's going to reveal he's going to be very much in control. My first analyst was much more spontaneous and available. He had a kind of vibrancy. The second one can be animated, but the first just had more of that kind of quality.

Dr. Harold Miller: With my first analyst, I would want to know how she was, and I would be caring and genuinely interested. And if she were still alive, would she be interested in trying to share what went on, from a very different perspective? From where I am now and where she is, when she was still alive. Even though there was so much left untouched, unworked out in that analysis, I knew her intentions were good and she was respectful, so that leads to being ready for another dialogue.

Dr. Zelda Fisher: I would say, "We need to talk. I have a lot of stuff I have to ask you, and I really need you to be my analyst, and I also need you to tell me some real things about you. I really need some additional termination time. To finish, to grow up. I need you to help me really let go here."

LT: What would you want her to say . . . that might both release you and . . . ?

ZF: I would want her to say, "I always thought you were smart. You can make a contribution." Like, what Freud said to Erickson, "You'll make it in your own way. I know you will. I don't agree with everything you're doing, but I encourage you to do it." I would want her to say, "I'm sorry I died." I'd say, "I wish you would have made plans for me, you were this powerful woman and everybody respected you, and I guess you did teach me how to do it, but somehow I feel nobody told me how to do it. And, do I have to be like you were?" I want to be different, somehow more creative. That's what I really want to do.

Dr. Horatio Encarta: I don't know, 'cause my thought was somewhat intellectual. That I would not like to get involved personally, but I think I'd want to know what she thought about what's happening to psychoanalysis and what her reaction is to it.

LT: And what would she say?

HE: She'd probably be disgusted by what's happening to psychoanalysis—the whole fragmentation, the lack of discipline, the lack of clear thinking, the erosion of standards, the whole business. Sort of the loss of what I'll call quality.

Dissatisfying Analysis

Dr. Henry Lewis: Are you talking about a social exchange or an exchange that went beyond social niceties?

LT: Beyond social niceties.

HL: It's hard to imagine. I can imagine myself saying things in fact I would never say like, "you know you're still fixed on some of these old ideas you always had. If you want to know something about development why don't you learn about development instead of making this up as you go along?" So, that's what I would think and not say because I wouldn't want to have that conversation anyway.

Dr. Phil Langer: If I ran into my first analyst, I would avoid him. I'd say hi. Because I believe in being polite. But I don't think I'd ever tell him where he failed me. And more importantly, I don't think I feel any interest in telling him where I am. I know when I run into patients,

I'm always fascinated: "What's happened? Where are you? How's the kid? How's the wife? How's the job? Did you ever get that promotion, write that book, whatever?" You want to know. At least, I want to know. Because, it's a story unfinished. And there's still a connection. But I can't imagine telling him. I wouldn't be interested. Why should I tell him? I mean, he couldn't even remember my kids' names. I hold that against him. He miscalled them. Why should I tell him anything?

Dr. Harold Miller: With the second analyst, whom I saw for therapy, that's much more complicated than the first. 'Cause I really am trying to distance that thing. I've thought about calling her and saying, "We need to meet one more time, to ask, 'Where are you on these things?'" But I think it isn't worth it. So, about her, I would be polite and I wouldn't talk to her freely. I think that comes because it's my sense that she wouldn't want that. If I thought that there was a chance that she were interested in talking more about what it was that she really meant, and that maybe we'd sort it out—not that I'm right, you're wrong, but that it's interesting that I took it this way and what did she intend? I don't think it's worth the cost of an hour, which is what it would be.

   Dr. Elizabeth Light is talking about the analyst with whom she felt deeply satisfied at termination, and who, two years later, lost his license because of multiple sexual trangressions, about which he had lied to her and to others as well. At the time of the interviews, she is highly dissatisfied with the analyst. It took several years, at high psychic cost to her, before she was able to mobilize an outpouring of her pain and anger:

LT: You talked about being ready to throttle him, to shake him into awareness or acknowledgment of some kind. I don't know what else you would imagine.
EL: I don't think I want to do that anymore. I think I'm past that. I think he's history in my life, but history like this tends to crop up again. If I hear of something else tomorrow or six months from now that inflames me, it might be different, but right now I think I would be more dismissive than anything. In my fantasies, I have said some pretty awful things to him: "How come you're still alive? You should be dead." All pretty sadistic things. I don't know what I would do. I might shake my head and say, "I hope your family isn't suffering forever because of you. I know I have, and too many other people have.

You did terrible things. Sometimes I wanted to talk to you about those but that urge has really left me pretty much." I might say, "I think you assured yourself a place in history, there will be books written about you but not the ones you pictured. You'll be remembered, but not graciously."

Dr. Jay Glenn: That would be very hard, because he would want so much for me to validate what he had done. And I think I would have to say, "I really have to say I disagree. I survived you, and I learned a lot, but, it couldn't have been much worse." I think I would do it now, though it would hurt the old man.
LT: It sounds like you have an ongoing awareness of what he wanted from you. And that you're saying you could now say, "Thanks, but no thanks."
JG: Yeah. Exactly. And I would be sorry. I really do not want to hurt him. At the same time, I think the truth is more important. And I would hold to that. I would just be sorry I had to do it. I would rather not meet him 'cause it wouldn't produce change, it would just produce sadness in him, and that I don't really need. It's clear enough.
LT: Were you saying you have managed to resolve him without him?
JG: Yeah. That's right. Which, again, I gotta say, I don't think I could have done it if I didn't have the dad I did.

Dr. Emma McClinton: If I imagine having a conversation with her now I would be angry and say, "You couldn't see who I was. Why didn't you, why couldn't you know that and just let me be."

19

CONCLUDING REFLECTIONS: THE FUTURE OF A COLLUSION

Nothing can be loved or hated unless it is first known.

—Leonardo da Vinci, *Notebooks*

To collude is to "cooperate secretly" (*Funk and Wagnall's,* 1941) or "play together" (*Oxford English Dictionary,* 1971). Although the word collusion tends to be used pejoratively, here it signifies a unique kind of collaboration. The analytic dyad colludes to rouse and maximize potentials in the analysand's inner world, as well as those lived out by him or her in the external world. This research has inquired into how the future of that collusion remained present for the Participants over time after termination. Differences emerged between those who found their analysis deeply satisfying, moderately satisfying, or dissatisfying. Such differences included the Participants' experience of freedom, within the analysis, to love and to hate, to be authentically themselves rather than automatically adaptive, to feel understood rather than unseen for who they were, to feel cared about, even loved, rather than shamed or unworthy of wanting to have some personal significance to the analyst (recall **Dr. Lewis** saying, "I don't think I'm on his radar screen").

The differences were evidenced in how the actuality of the analyst was perceived, given his or her affective communications during the analysis. The particularity of the affective dynamics within the analytic dyad has been evident for some time. In the early 1940s, Fenichel (1941) observed that "different analysts act differently and these differences influence the behavior of patients, and the personality of the therapist influences the transference" (p. 72).

A number of evocative personal accounts of analyses attest to such singularity (Knight, 1950; Wortis, 1954; H.D., 1956; Blanton, 1971;

Moser, 1974; Money-Kyrle, 1979; Bion, 1985; Little, 1990; Masson, 1990; Nakhla and Jackson, 1993; Chernin, 1995; Couch, 1995). In addition, some psychoanalysts have compared their own experiences with two or more analysts, weighing the beneficial and limiting impacts of each (Guntrip, 1975; Hurwitz, 1986; Simon, 1993), Holt (1992) reveals: While discussing the "warm and cold sides of psychoanalysis,"

> I can testify from my own experience as patient with five different analysts that there was a striking contrast among them in this aspect (warmth and coldness) of technique. One of my analysts told me directly: "Of course I love you; I never take a patient if I feel I can't love him or her." Two others would have been aghast at this violation of emotional distance, which they scrupulously maintained, one by conventional analytic neutrality, the other by a mocking, role-playing attitude. The three who really helped me all showed indirect or direct evidences of a loving, truly nurturant concern for my well-being [p. 26].

The research findings suggest that, in most cases, the analyst and the analysis continued to have profound meaning for the Participant. Repeatedly, an experience with a second analyst was described as resoundingly unlike the first, both in affective ambience and in interpretive content, although it did not entirely delete the significance of the first. The particularity of the dynamics within each analytic dyad was pivotal, because some analysts could be highly effective with one Participant and damaging with another. Strikingly similar qualities about the person of the analyst might be described by more than one analysand, yet accompanied by highly consequential differences in dynamics within the analytic dyad. In other instances, the surmised nature of the analyst emanates as steadfast signature of the analyst's approach with more than one analysand. **Dr. Veronica Clark** alludes directly to the particularity of the match with her analyst, which contributed to the depth of the analysis: "Sometimes the ways in which you match can fit too well, and therefore there are blind spots and difficulties. That's true and that happened, but I think it was because of the good fit that I was able to have the depth of the analysis that I did. I'm not sure it could have happened with someone else at that level. I think it would have been a very different analysis. Maybe it would have gotten to the same things but just as he kind of personalized it for me, it was also very personalized for him. What I'm saying is that every pair make a different analysis." If the analyst is loved, the particularity may be experienced as his irreplaceable uniqueness. As Nussbaum (2001) observes, "Love is an intense response to perceptions of the particularity, and the particular high value, of another person's body and mind. This particular specialness is impenetrably obscure to the observer; it looks like an inexplicable quirk of fortune" (p. 465).

The proportion of deeply satisfying analyses varied according to the gender combination of the analytic dyad and the social context of the times—namely, the decade during which the analysis took place. The social context is a carrier not only of what was valued in psychoanalytic technique according to the theories most prevalent in the particular Institute at the time but also indubitably of whatever unconscious reaction to his own analyst had developed in the training analyst over time. Contrary to what might be expected, Participants in the study who experienced their analyses as wounding did not transmit its harshness to the next generation of patients and candidates, whom they tended to treat with empathic care. Some, however, noted a temporary constriction in the development of their eventual analytic approach occasioned by having the need to first practice in ways that are diametrically opposed to those experienced with the wounding analyst. An objection might be raised to the conclusion that the harshness these Participants experienced is not transmitted to the next generation—namely, that there could be discrepancies between how such Participants describe their approach in research interviews and how they actually practice. And this certainly may be the case, but I noted, however, in two instances in which the Participants belonged to the "highly dissatisfied" group and subsequently were the training analyst for another Participant, the portrayals of their approach in practice by their analysands (both "deeply satisfying analyses") jibed quite closely with their own description.

It was heartening to find that the proportion of deeply satisfying analyses was large and that it significantly increased further over the last few decades. Nevertheless, the troubling minority of instances in which Participants suffered more than being helped by the analysis is haunting.

The research findings, together with other research I have cited here influenced me to revise my views about various prevailing and familiar assumptions. I believe that the transference experienced with the analyst is not an automatic displacement from objects of the past but that both its activation in memory and the quality of its eventual retranscription also reflect the affective structure of communication between analyst and analysand. Since the analyst's way of being together with, and distinct from, the analysand enter into the internal templates of the analysand, the actuality of the analyst is not deleted in psychic life. Hence, I disagree with the point of view that when the analyst's physical presence is no longer needed, the optimal relationship to the former analyst is always a progressive "out of sight, out mind"—and also with the view that detachment from the analyst signifies internalization, denoting maturity in the analysand and success of the analysis. Numerous studies have confirmed that neither transferences nor mental representations of the analyst disappear but instead can be a beneficial resource in inner life. A numbers of researchers are in accord with what was conveyed by the majority of the Participants: The more satisfying the analysis has been, the more likely that the analyst's inner presence remains vivid. Posttermination contact accrues positive or negative meanings as it further elaborates the image of the analyst. This complicates the interplay between the analyst in actual sight, and the relationship inside, as internalized. It seems important to revise the prevailing bias that if the analysand continues to desire some kind of connection with the analyst, posttermination, that it signifies an incompleteness in the analysis or a failing in the analysand. Nevertheless, the analyst must have personal freedom and choice about such wishes on the part of the analysand, since his or her responsibility as analyst has been fulfilled and pressing involvements now lie elsewhere. Furthermore, the affective charge that resided in the analytic space may not be suited for travel. Working out this asymmetry in the desire for a connection can be extraordinarily delicate.

Geller and Farber (1993) have stressed the function of the internalized therapist as benign "dialogic partner." Although such a benign dialogic partner may be most appropriately beneficial for many patients, for candidates, who are expected to come to terms with ambivalences in themselves and their patients, it may be more important to go beyond the benign to taking the more complete actuality of the analyst into account, so that the eventual affective dialogue with the analyst within is based on some tolerance of ambivalence in oneself, as well as tolerance of the ambivalence in the analyst. Most, but not all, of the Participants wanted some opportunity to synthesize their sense of the analyst as a person in "real" life with how they experienced his or her actuality during the analysis.

In groping toward an understanding of salient signifiers of satisfying or unsatisfying analyses, I continue to be impressed by the complexity inherent in the particularity of the analytic dyad and the actuality of the analyst. I have used the concept of actuality to denote those aspects of the analyst's qualities that were experienced by the analysand as evoked in relation to him. This term is not meant to comprise the analyst's character totally as it shapes his or her every relationship. The same surmised qualities may become part of an altered dynamic when directed with different affective intonation and resultant impact toward another person or in a different context.

To ponder this complexity, consider the analyst of **Drs. Noah Levy** and **Henry Lewis,** who both felt hurt and rebuffed by their interaction with him. Despite many stellar qualities, the analyst's psychic retreats in the face of intense affects directed toward him and his specific avoidance of feelings in mourning losses loomed heavily for both analysands. Among other Participants, however, there were several with whom this analyst was not in an analytic relationship, with its inherent transference–countertransference intensities, but was recalled in a different context—as seminar leader for one and consultant for another—and they recalled his positive role. Following are three further windows into aspects of his nature:

One Participant states: "I really owe a lot to him. Because, in spite of our being so different—I'm an emotional kind of person and he couldn't stand emotion very well . . . he'd come into my office . . . and start to talk, and he would just leave. If I said anything really hyper, he was out the door (laughs) without even saying good-bye. Midsentence, he was gone. But he nevertheless really encouraged, enabled, kept us in seminars together, kept us talking together. He was wonderful that way. Because unlike my analyst, he wasn't competitive with us."

Another Participant recalls: "After about two years into my struggling with this career decision and getting depressed about it, I called up Dr. X and said, 'Could I come over and talk to you? I'm feeling very uncomfortable about a professional commitment I have to decide about.' And he said, 'Sure.' And so he invited me over to his house on Sunday morning. He cleared the decks. I went over there four or five Sundays for a couple of hours and really poured out my heart about that struggle, what and where I was in regard to all that. And he was extremely helpful. I felt a lot better, I felt it was really a great thing, to have had him make himself available at the time."

The third view comes from a woman analyst who was not in the sample of Participants. She had strong positive feelings about him during the analysis. His interpretations were mostly focused on oedipal conflict. Although she had had multiple losses in early childhood, the analyst spoke much more readily about her ways of coping than her feelings about loss. Much of the time, she appreciated his comments, although she also felt that her tender and eventually erotic feelings met with formality and rebuff. This mostly took the form of quite unnecessary reiteration that any desires toward him would not be fulfilled. The decision to terminate was the analyst's, who announced during the fourth year of analysis, "This will be our last year." The analysand was happily engaged and, before the year ended, married and pregnant with her first child. Still, she felt very sad about leaving the analyst. During the last week, he mentioned that she might want to look up a paper of his, about to be published. The very last hour, while she was quite weepy, he ended 10 minutes early and said in a simultaneously brusque and friendly way, "Maybe I don't like goodbyes either."

She, of course, read his paper and was gratified to find her treatment discussed, thinly disguised. He referred to the patient as an "intelligent, sensitive, creative individual." She realized he had been more aware of the pivotal issue of loss than he had conveyed, for he wrote of her increasing tolerance of her reactions to loss during the analysis. Interestingly, at the safe remove of his writings, this analyst showed more sensitive understanding of the analysand's losses than in direct relation to her. This variation in his use of psychic retreat calls for reappraisal of its meaning. It may not signify an incapacity for mourning, but rather that the metabolism of loss could occur only in private, without the interpersonal stimulation evoked by the emergent anguish in an analysand.

What pleased this woman most about the analyst's written account was his suggestion that she had been able to surmise something about his own inner states, that in some way she knew him. He wrote: "Yet even with her love objects, situations which would have angered many people evoked in her more understanding than fury. This capacity to empathize very accurately with the mental state of the 'disappointing' love object was an outstanding feature of her process of assimilation at the time the analysis terminated. She was capable of recognizing, to an unusual extent, the feelings, motives, and significance of the behavior of other people. This could be verified in the transference situation. Her assessment was unusually precise unless she was intensely disappointed." The analysand experienced the article as his generous bequest of an emotional connection, which he had not been able to convey in his own presence.

After a period of time, her father, at age 80, suicided, and she made an appointment to see the analyst, anticipating two or three sessions to deal with her grief. At the end of the first appointment, he said that she seemed to be doing fine and saw no reason for their needing to meet again. Although he was right, she would have liked more leeway and felt rebuked. Specifically, the analyst seemed to shy away from grief about the death of a father with all three analysands (with her, **Dr. Levy**, and **Dr. Lewis**). In several later encounters with her, he remained fairly aloof and formal.

About 25 years later, she met with him once more, attempting to untangle the remnant mixture of positive feelings and rebuff. He was surprisingly direct and candid, acknowledging a central dynamic in their relationship. He said, "I always liked you, but you know how I am, I keep my distance with a 10-foot pole." When the analyst was quite aged and terminally ill, he appeared to welcome her visits, which seemed moderately comfortable for both.

One of the unexpected signifiers of satisfying analyses turned out to be the Participant's experience of the analyst as a "complete other," a person in his or her own right, with a good life of his own. Clearly, one implication for the analysand was that he need not feel pressured to fulfill the analyst's needs for recognition, admiration, or love. Another implication lay in the positive impetus to identify with the analyst's self-respect. Yet the analyst's manifestly being a person in his or her own right appears to have the additional significance of stimulating a pleasurable or anxiety-provoking (or both simultaneously) collision with Otherness. Such valuing of the "otherness" of the analyst was somewhat surprising in the contemporary ambience of psychoanalysis, for we have only fairly recently moved in the direction of acknowledging the power of empathic attunement, of "moments of meeting" emotionally to amplify the possibilities of a shared and cared about psychic reality between analysand and analyst. The Participant's emphasis on the vibrant actuality of the analyst as person did not minimize the value of such attunement, but oscillation with that attunement added the ingredient of the analyst's own inner life as active beyond reactive. Their view counters Bion's (1967) advice to the analyst to "banish memory and desire."

Loewald (1974) comments about a function of the analyst's actuality: He refers to "patient and analyst as co-authors of the play" and notes that the impact of the play "depends on its being experienced both as actuality and as a fantasy creation. This Janus-face quality is an important ingredient of the analyst's experience in the analytic situation and becomes, if things go well, an important element in the patient's experience" (p. 355). The patient is enabled to experience the transference as fantasy when it is ameliorated by the actuality of the relationship with the analyst. Transference reenactments acquire the character of fantasy play when the present actuality becomes clearly distinguishable from the past actuality.

Symington (1983) speaks of the deep and abiding patient–analyst interconnection, which he referred to as the "x-factor." The relationship between what takes place in the analyst's inner world and in the patient's is integral to the process of change. Symington wrote:

> My contention is that the inner act of freedom in the analyst causes a therapeutic shift in the patient and new insight, learning and development in the analyst. The interpretation is essential in that it gives expression to the shift that has already occurred and makes it available to consciousness. The point though is that the essential agent of change is the inner act of the analyst and that this inner act is perceived by the patient and causes change. Even the most inner mental act has some manifest correlate that is perceptible, though perception may be unconscious and probably is [cited by Bass, 2001, p. 260].

Congruent with Symington, Caper (1997) emphasizes the importance of interpretations that "make the patient simultaneously aware that he and the analyst are separate and that the analyst has a link to internal objects that are not under the patient's control" (p. 264).

Mendelsohn (2002) refreshingly lauds the analyst's "bad-enough" participation, which refers

> to the ways that all analysts inevitably cause their patients to suffer and, more specifically, within each analysis, to the ways in which the analyst's participation confirms some version of the patient's worst fears. The manifestations of "badness" as

long as they are honestly considered and creatively used, are expectable and even therapeutically essential aspects of analytic relatedness. Frequently, however, an analyst's bad-enough participation, despite its ubiquity and transformational potential is attenuated or selectively overlooked. As a result the therapeutic possibilities of analytic work may be compromised [p. 331].

A quixotic blend of the analyst's personal qualities with "good-enough" and "bad-enough" participation has been with us since the birth of psychoanalysis. But we now take more responsibility for staying aware of countertransference dynamics, as a resource to use judiciously in the treatment when we can (T. Jacobs, 1991). Gitelson was noted for his aphorism, "The analyst must have a kindly quality of evil-mindedness" (Kramer, 1967, p. 262).

To reckon with the compelling actuality of Freud as analyst, a final visit:

> Freud seemed to recognize that an intimate personal conversation could stimulate a rich vein of free association, transference, or resistance. His virtuosity centered particularly on a brilliant ability to transform a personal moment into an analytic one. Human exchanges, based in real warmth and respect, could at a moment's notice become grist for the analytic mill [S. Friedman, 1990, p. 308].

Freud was memorable to H.D. for his fervor in conveying the daring, original content of his mind. Fortunately, she was also able to become conscious of his "bad-enough participation," which she experienced in terms of the limiting qualities of his patriarchal view of women and his insistence on the correctness of his theories. Here is a glimpse of both qualities: When Freud spoke, H.D. wrote, it was

> as if he had dipped the grey web of his conventionally woven thought and with it, conventionally spoken thought, into a vat of his own brewing—or held a strip of that thought, ripped from the monotonous faded and outworn texture of the language itself, into the bubbling cauldron of his own mind in order to draw forth dyed blue, or scarlet, a new colour to the old grey mesh, a scrap of thought, even a cast-off rag, that

would become hereafter a pennant, a direction, or, fluttering aloft on a pole, to lead an army [Holland, 2002].

But she also allowed herself some private resentment of Freud's unshakeable interpretations to her of women as deficient, and the frustrating failure of her attempts to convince him that women were as complete as men. In midnight solitude she wrote: "I do not wish to be treated like a child, a weakling. . . . I was angry with the old man with his talk of the man-strength . . . I argued till day-break . . . and God will forgive me my anger" (Holland, 2002).

Controversy still reigns about how the affective availability of the object—in this case, the analyst—affects internalization and psychological structure. One point of view is that internalization, or internal psychic structure, is promoted by the unavailability of the object (Lacan, 1959; Behrends and Blatt, 1985), which then creates the motivation to convert the affective tie to an internal function. In contrast, Loewald (cited in Behrends and Blatt, 1985) argued that through intimacy or resonance, internalizations can and do occur without such disruption. However, emotional availability is not identical with a goal of constant attunement. Oscillations in the analyst's joining and being distinct from the experience of the analysand seem to augur well for the analysand's freedom, in turn, to join the analyst and to be distinct from him. In my own experience with certain analysands, I have been impressed by the power with which the analysand's unconscious resonance to distressing affective configurations surmised in the parental caretakers can be perpetuated and the specificity with which particular expectations of affective dissonance emerge in the transference and are then followed by detailed associations in memory or historical confirmation. In attempting to work through such profound early adaptations, these analysands seek to know (and often surmise more correctly than not) those aspects of the affectively organizing fantasies and impulse life of the analyst, which they view as prerequisite to being able to freely experience their own. We do not know to what extent early templates for relationships remain latent, prone to reemergence under certain affective conditions, or become permanently altered when retranscribed through analytic process. They may be recalled but slowly lose their power. I recently asked an analysand, overcome by her anxiety about ruining our relationship if she freely showed me the intensity of her need and anger, "Is that old terror indelible?" She answered, "The indelible experience was written in invisible ink. This process makes me able to read it. I have to read it with you before I can allow other feelings in."

Winnicott (1960) noted that an aspect of feeling authentic was the recognition of an outside reality that is not one's own projection. This involves not "mirroring" but the experience of contacting other minds. Developmentally, he postulates that the self-created other must be mentally destroyed to place it out of ones omnipotent control. "In these ways, the object develops its own autonomy and life, and (if it survives) contributes-in to the subject, according to its own properties. . . . From then on projective mechanisms assist in the act of noticing what is there, but they are not the reason why the object is there" (Winnicott, 1969, p. 90). The object then can belong to a "shared reality," outside the self. In this way, he viewed destructive impulses as in the service of reducing projection, paving the way for a two-person template of relatedness. As Winnicott puts it, "For this to happen, favorable conditions are necessary" (p. 91). I propose another developmental function of the distinctive individuality of the other. In the process of loving, one may be gratified that the loved person behaves differently from the way one could have imagined, that in fact his own and different reality has swept away and altered the love yearnings from the past. Because the person could not be conceived in imagination, one may feel freed from the shadow of attachments in the past and more open to the present. Deepening of the relationship further stimulates the analysand's wish to convey his or her own distinctive sensibilities and experience and to respond freely to the communications and surmised nature of the other. In this, too, pleasure is focused on the actuality of the other, outside one's projections. Then the analyst within, not born of illusion, can partake in generative collusion.

APPENDIX A

Letter to Potential Participants

An initial phone call sought to establish whether the analyst would consider participation in the project. If undecided, the following letter was sent to the potential Participant, with pronouns to fit the person's gender. If the person already agreed to participate during the phone inquiry, the first and last sentences of the letter were altered.* If the person declined during the phone inquiry, no further letter was sent.

Dear,

I am writing to give you preliminary information while you are deciding if you want to participate in some conversations about how you experienced your analyst over time after termination. I have been doing a number of interviews with analysts about this topic over the past (number) years. Time given to these interviews might be a total of anywhere between two and eight hours, according to your own choice of what there is to be said. The time could be scheduled at whatever season of the year would be most convenient for you. The interviews are strictly confidential, and I will be the only one to know the names of those interviewed or have access to the material.

The topic seems to me to have extremely rich and worthwhile potential for exploration. A few evocative personal accounts of analyses, as well as comparisons of the experience with more than one analyst, exist in the literature, including some by analysts. Numbers of

---

* "To follow up our conversation, I welcome the chance to talk with you about how you experienced your analyst over time after termination." "I very much look forward to conversations with you about these issues."

follow-up studies have concerned themselves with various aspects of analytic outcome, maintenance of gains (or lack of gains), and memories of the analysis during postanalytic life. However, the focus of the current undertaking is specifically on the place of the analyst in postanalytic psychic life and the dynamics and implications of changes in this habitation over time.

When the analysand is also an analyst, with some ongoing access to her own inner life, it seems particularly possible to explore in some depth what is involved in these changes over time as the analyst continues her own adult development, as she involves herself in analytic practice and her Institute, as she may or may not have further professional or social contact with her former analyst or be privy to further knowledge about the professional functioning, ideology, or personal life of the analyst.

At the same time, such a prospective study entails a recognition that it is fraught with special complications that pose problems, but hopefully would not be insurmountable.

One crucial dimension involves the establishment of both privacy and confidentiality. As a profound sense of privacy constitutes an essence of the analytic process, ironically I would expect some individuals to reject participation in interviews on the basis of feeling that to stay true to the spirit of that analytic interchange, introspection about it should not be extended to any one outside the analytic dyad. For others, even without this belief, the residual experience of the former analyst may simply feel too private to discuss. There appears to be considerable variation in attitude about this, however, exemplified by the casual, but meaningful, discussions of analytic experience which are not infrequent between analysts who are friends and colleagues. In our conversations, it should be clear that there is a choice of omitting whatever is too private, that "no trespassing" signs will be respected. Still, one might need to be prepared for the possibility that revisiting thoughts about the analyst may stir profoundly affecting feelings which then pose the task (or opportunity) of reassimilating them once more.

The material must be protected from identifiability of the former analysand as well as the analyst or analysts about whom she is speaking. A number of precautionary measures are involved. No one else will know that I am interviewing you unless you choose to tell them. You will be given a copy of your material to delete anything you wish, as well as to decide about whether any particular passages would be "quotable" or not. All material or quotations so included will remain anonymous. You will be asked to invent whatever code name you wish for yourself.

The interviews will be essentially open ended, but here is a list, sent to each analyst-interviewee, as preview of some of the kinds of questions to be explored.

How would you describe the inner presence of your analyst around the time of termination, how did that change over the years, how is that now . . . ?

What felt most sustaining, what felt most painful in your connection to the analyst at various periods during the analysis, around termination, afterwards, and now . . . ?

What moments, incidents, interpretations, or interchanges with your analyst remain as especially memorable, vivid, pithy, upsetting or precious?

What sort of person did you sense your analyst to be at various times during the analysis, at the time of termination, during subsequent years and now?

What are your notions about how your analyst experienced you during analysis, around termination, shortly afterwards and now?

What do you think are your analyst's beliefs about what aspects of the "transference," what aspects of the relationship to him (her), what aspects of his (her) meaning to you should be resolved by the time of termination? What do you believe might have been his (her) aim as to where the analyst would be "ideally" located in your inner life from then on? How does that fit with your actual experience? With the teachings in your Institute at the time? And now?

What forms of loving and/or hating, missing or desiring, wanting to be loved, or to be appreciated and respected by your analyst continue to have their momentum, and how? Did you and do you now have fantasies or wishes for some sort of eventual friendship with your analyst? Did you have longings to empathically know the flux of your analyst's own inner emotional life . . . and do you now? Or do you wish to be free from a sense of continuing to be influenced by feelings about him (her)?

If you imagine running into each other now and could talk freely, what would each of you say? What would you think and not say? What do you envision would be the effect of such a conversation for you?

Where is your analyst in your inner life as you practice analysis? Do you experience your own ways of being with patients as close to or very different from your analyst's, and in what ways? Do you want to pass on the "legacy," radically alter it, or have you felt it pale in relation to your own distinctive style as analyst? How did you metabolize converging influences from supervisors and from him (her) when you were doing control analyses?

If you have had a second (or second and third) analyst, how is the experience of a second (and third) analyst different in relation to all the above? If you have returned to your original analyst for further work, how is the experience of him (her) different?

What kinds of professional and/or social contact have you had with each other since the ending of analysis? Have you hoped for such contacts or wanted to avoid or minimize any encounters? Do you feel he (she) has wanted to avoid such contacts?

If you currently wanted to talk with an analyst would he (she) be the one? Why or why not?

In what ways has membership in the same Institute (if that is applicable) affected you?

If you decide to participate, I would very much look forward to conversations with you about these issues. But I also understand that there are multiple good reasons why you might want to say "no."

Best regards.

APPENDIX B

The Sampling Procedure

The sample comprises 34 psychoanalysts whose graduation from training occurred from 1 to 40 years before the interviews. Sample selection was not based on an attempt at either a random or stratified representation of variables characterizing currently practicing U.S. analysts, although it may have turned out to approximate these. Because the focus of the study revolved around the various fates of posttermination internalizations under conditions of different affective contexts affecting termination, the working premise was that the sampling should be based on those variables most likely to be relevant to those issues, rather than replicating the changing composition of a particular group. Selections were based on the intent to represent the range of decades during which the analysis took place, the four possible gender combinations, and the inclusion of both training analysts and nontraining analysts.

Because the name, number, and gender of analysts for each Participant were unknown prior to the study, I used a progressive sampling process. Once the first half of the sample had been interviewed, it became evident which decades and gender combinations were underrepresented. Sampling after this point involved an initial inquiry about these variables as a basis for selection. To explore differences between different analyst–analysand dyads, it was important that the sample include individuals with two (or more) analysts (providing material about two dyads with the analysand as the constant factor) as well as two analysands with the same analyst (providing material about two dyads, with the analyst as the constant factor). Of the 34 Participants, 28 compared their experience with two or more analysts, whereas in six instances, listed below, two Participants had shared an analyst, although mostly not at the same time. The sample also includes several narratives across "two generations," occurring because both the training analyst and the analyst trained were Participants, and, although they are not identified, they facilitated speculations about what was transmitted or transformed in analytic attitudes between generations.

Eight individuals declined participation in the study, but no common factor emerged from the reasons given. Because, by definition, the meanings of the reasons weren't further explored, speculation would be without basis.

Pairs of Participants with the Same Analyst

Drs. Raphe Lieberman and
Phil Langer   (Men with female analyst)

Drs. Henry Lewis and Noah Levy   (Men with male analyst)

Drs. Bob White and Participant
14 (record sealed)   (Men with male analyst)

Drs. John Deere and Steven Zeller   (Men with male analyst)

Drs. Eleanor Brown and Julia
Baranger   (Women with female analyst)

Drs. Heather Rodine and
Zelda Fisher   (Women with female analyst)

APPENDIX C

Tabulations of the Categories of Satisfaction, in Interaction with Gender and Decade of Analysis

Table 1. Training Analyses Only ($N = 35$; men, $n = 22$; women, $n = 13$)

Deeply Satisfying Analysis			
Decade	Gender		
	M–M	M–F	F–M	F–F
1945–1955		1		
1955–1965	1	2		1
1965–1975	1			1
1975–1985	3	1	1	
1985–1995	1		5	

Moderately Satisfying Analysis			
Decade	Gender		
	M–M	M–F	F–M	F–F
1945–1955				
1955–1965	1	2		1
1965–1975	1			1
1975–1985	2			
1985–1995				1

Dissatisfying Analysis			
Decade	Gender		
	M–M	M–F	F–M	F–F
1945–1955				
1955–1965	1			
1965–1975	5			1
1975–1985			1	
1985–1995				

Note. M–M = male analysand–male analyst; M–F = male analysand–female analyst ; F–M = female analysand–male analyst; F–F female analysand–female analyst.

Table 2. Total Analyses (N = 64; men, n = 39; women, n = 25)

	Deeply Satisfying Analysis			
Decade		*Gender*		
	M–M	*M–F*	*F–M*	*F–F*
1945–1955		1		
1955–1965	3	2		1
1965–1975	1			1
1975–1985	2	2	2	
1985–1995	3		7	

	Moderately Satisfying Analysis			
Decade		*Gender*		
	M–M	*M–F*	*F–M*	*F–F*
1945–1955	1		2	
1955–1965	3	2	2	1
1965–1975	3		1	1
1975–1985	4		1	
1985–1995	1		2	1

	Dissatisfying Analysis			
Decade		*Gender*		
	M–M	*M–F*	*F–M*	*F–F*
1945–1955				
1955–1965				
1965–1975	8	1		1
1975–1985	1		2	
1985–1995		1		

Note. M–M = male analysand–male analyst; M–F = male analysand–female analyst; F–M = female analysand–male analyst; F–F female analysand–female analyst.

SUMMARY OF TABULATIONS
Training Analyses Only
Table 3. Categories of Satisfaction.

$n = 35$ (one person had 2 training analyses):
men = 22 (63%); women = 13 (37%)

Categories of Satisfaction:
  Deeply Satisfied: 18 (51%)
  Moderately Satisfied: 9 (26%)
  Dissatisfied: 8 (23%)

| | Decade of Analysis | | |
Decade	Deeply Satisfied	Moderately Satisfied	Dissatisfied
1945–1955 (n = 1)	1 (100%)	0 (0)	0 (0%)
1955–1965 (n = 9)	4 (44.5%)	4 (44.5%)	1 (11%)
1965–1975 (n = 9)	1 (11%)	2 (22%)	6 (67%)
1975–1985 (n = 8)	5 (62.5%)	2 (25%)	1 (12.5%)
1985–1995 (n = 8)	7 (87.5%)	1 (12.5%)	0 (0%)

Note. During 1965–1975, Participants were six times more likely to be dissatisfied than deeply satisfied. During 1985–1995, it is highly likely to be deeply satisfied; seven times as likely as moderately satisfied. Since the decade 1945–1955 has an N of only 1 the percentage does not satisfy the trend.

| | Gender Combination | | |
	Deeply Satisfied	Moderately Satisfied	Dissatisfied
M–M = 16	6 (37.5%)	4 (25.0%)	6 (37.5%)
M–F = 6	4 (67%)	2 (33%)	0 (0%)
F–M = 7	6 (86%)	0 (0%)	1 (14%)
F–F = 6	2 (33%)	3 (50%)	1 (17%)

Note. The highest probability of dissatisfaction occurs for males with males. The highest probability of deep satisfaction occurs for males with females and females with males.

SUMMARY OF TABULATIONS

Total Analyses

Table 4. Categories of Satisfaction.

$n = 64$: men = 39 (61%); women = 25 (39%)

Categories of Satisfaction:
  Deeply Satisfied: 25 (39%)
  Moderately Satisfied: 25 (39%)
  Dissatisfied: 14 (22%)

Decade of Analysis

Decade	Deeply Satisfied	Moderately Satisfied	Dissatisfied
1945–1955 (n = 4)	1 (25%)	3 (75%)	0 (0%)
1955–1965 (n = 14)	6 (43%)	8 (57%)	0 (0%)
1965–1975 (n = 17)	2 (12%)	5 (29%)	10 (59%)
1975–1985 (n = 14)	6 (43%)	5 (36%)	3 (21%)
1985–1995 (n = 15)	10 (67%)	4 (26%)	1 (7%)

Note. During 1965–1975, Participants were more likely to be dissatisfied than deeply satisfied. During 1985–1995, participants were 10 times more likely to be deeply satisfied than dissatisfied.

Gender Combination

	Deeply Satisfied	Moderately Satisfied	Dissatisfied
M–M = 30	9 (30%)	12 (40%)	9 (30%)
M–F = 9	5 (56%)	2 (22%)	2 (22%)
F–M = 19	9 (47%)	8 (42%)	2 (11%)
F–F = 6	2 (33%)	3 (50%)	1 (17%)

Note. The highest probability of dissatisfaction occurs for males with males. The highest probability of deep satisfaction occurs for males with females and females with males.

REFERENCES

Balint, M. (1950). On the termination of analysis. *Internat. J. Psycho-Anal.*, 31:196–199.

Balint, M. (1952). *Primary Love and Psychoanalytic Technique*. London: Karnac Books, 1985.

Balint, M. (1954). Analytic training and training analysis: 1. *Internat. J. Psycho-Anal.*, 35:157–162.

Balint, M. (1968). *The Basic Fault*. London: Tavistock.

Bass, A. (2001). It takes one to know one: Whose unconscious is it anyway? *Psychoanal. Dial.*, 11:683–702.

Baudry, F. (1998). Kohut and Glover: The role of subjectivity in psychoanalytic theory and controversy. *The Psychoanalytic Study of the Child*, 53:3–24. New Haven, CT: Yale University Press.

Beebe, B. & Lachmann, F. (2002). *Infant Research and Adult Treatment*. Hillsdale, NJ: The Analytic Press.

Behrends, R. & Blatt, S. (1985). Internalization and psychological development throughout the life cycle. *The Psychoanalytic Study of the Child*, 40:11–39. New Haven, CT: Yale University Press.

Berenstein, I. (2001). The link and the other. *Internat. J. Psycho-Anal.*, 82:141–149.

Bergmann, M. (1988). On the fate of the intrapsychic image of the psychoanalyst after termination of the analysis. *The Psychoanalytic Study of the Child*, 43:137–153. New Haven, CT: Yale University Press.

Bergmann, M. (1997). Termination: The Achilles heel of psychoanalytic technique. *Psychoanal. Psychol.*, 14:163–174.

Bernfeld, S. (1962). On psychoanalytic training. *Psychoanal. Quart.*, 31:453–482.

Bernstein, D. (1993). *Female Identity Conflict in Clinical Practice*. Northvale, NJ: Aronson.

Bibring, G. L. (1954). The training analysis and its place in psychoanalytic training. *Internat. J. Psycho-Anal.*, 35:169–173.

Bion, W. (1967). Notes on memory and desire. In: *Classics in Psychoanalytic Technique*, ed. R. Langs. New York: Aronson, 1981, pp. 259–260.

Bion, W. (1977). *Two Papers*. Rio de Janeiro: Imago.

Bion, W. (1985). *All My Sins Remembered*. Abingdon, England: Fleetwood Press.

Bion, W. (1992). *Cogitations*. London: Karnac.

Blanck, G. & Blanck, R. (1988). The contribution of ego psychology to understanding the process of termination in psychoanalysis. *J. Amer. Psychoanal. Assn.*, 36:961–984.

Blanton, S. (1971). *Diary of My Analysis with Sigmund Freud*. New York: Hawthorn Books.

Blos, P. S. (1985). *Son and Father*. New York: Free Press.

Blum, H. P. (1989). The concept of termination and the evolution of psychoanalytic thought. *J. Amer. Psychoanal. Assn.*, 37:275–295.

Boris, H. N. (1986). Bion revisited. *Contemp. Psychoanal.*, 22:159–182.

Busch, F. (1995). Resistance analysis and object relations theory: Erroneous conceptions amidst some timely contributions. *Psychoanal. Psychol.*, 12:43–54.

Buxbaum, E. (1950). Technique of terminating analysis. *Internat. J. Psycho-Anal.*, 31:184–190.

Calef, V. & Weinshel, E. (1983). A note on consummation and termination. *J. Amer. Psychoanal. Assn.*, 31:643–650.

Caper, R. (1997). A mind of one's own. *Internat. J. Psycho-Anal.*, 78:265–278.

Chernin, K. (1995). *A Different Kind of Listening*. New York: HarperCollins.

Conway, P. S. (1999). When all is said . . . A phenomenological enquiry into post-termination experience. *Internat. J. Psychoanal.*, 80:563–574.

Cooper, A. (1985). The termination of the training analysis: Process, expectations, achievements. *Internat. J. Psycho-Anal. Monogr. Ser.*, No. 5.

Cooper, S. (2000). *Objects of Hope*. Hillsdale, NJ: The Analytic Press.

Couch, A. (1995). Anna Freud's adult psychoanalytic technique: A defence of classical analysis. *Internat. J. Psycho-Anal.*, 76:153–171.

Craige, H. (2001). Mourning analysis: The post termination. Prepublication manuscript.

Craige, H. (2002). Mourning analysis: The post-termination phase. *J. Amer. Psychoanal. Assn.*, 50:507–550.

Davies, J. M. (1994). Love in the afternoon: A relational reconsideration of desire and dread in the countertransference. *Psychoanal. Dial.*, 4:153–170.

Davies, J. M. (1998). Between the disclosure and foreclosure of erotic transference-countertransference: Can psychoanalysis find a place for adult sexuality? *Psychoanal. Dial.*, 8:747–766.

Deutsch, H. (1937). Absence of grief. *Psychoanal. Quart.*, 6:12–22.

Diamond, D. (1993). The paternal transference: A bridge to the erotic oedipal transference. *Psychoanal. Inq.*, 13:206–226.

Doolittle, H. (1956). *Tribute to Freud*. Boston: David R. Godine.

Dupont, J. (1994). Freud's analysis of Ferenczi as revealed by their correspondence. *Internat. J. Psycho-Anal.*, 75:301–320.

Edgcumbe, R. & Burgner, M. (1975). The phallic narcissistic phase: A differentiation between preodipal and oedipal aspects of phallic development. *The Psychoanalytic Study of the Child*, 30:161–180. New Haven, CT: Yale University Press.

Eissler, K. R. (1975). On possible effects of aging on the practice of psychoanalysis: An essay. *J. Phila. Assn. Psychoanal.*, 2:138–152.

Ekstein, R. (1965). Working through and termination of analysis. *J. Amer. Psychoanal. Assn.*, 13:57–78.

Elise, D. (2002a). Blocked creativity and inhibited erotic transference. *Stud. Gender & Sexual.*, 3:165–191.

Elise, D. (2002b). The primary maternal oedipal situation and female homoerotic desire. *Psychoanal. Inq.*, 22:209–228.

Etchegoyen, H. (1991). *Fundamentals of Psychoanalytic Technique*. London: Karnac Books.

Fenichel, O. (1941). *Problems of Psychoanalytic Technique*. New York: Psychoanalytic Quarterly.

Ferenczi, S. (1927). The problem of the termination of the analysis. In: *Final Contributions to the Problems and Methods of Psycho-Analysis, Vol. 3*. New York: Basic Books, 1955, pp. 77–86.

Ferenczi, S. (1933). Confusion of tongues between adults and the child (The language of tenderness and of passion). *Internat. J. Psycho-Anal.*, 30:-225–230, 1949.

Ferraro, F. (1995). Trauma and termination: 1. *Internat. J. Psycho-Anal.*, 76:51–65.

Ferraro, F. & Garella, A. (1997). Termination as a psychoanalytic event. *Internat. J. Psycho-Anal.*, 78:27–41.

Field, T. (1992). Infants of depressed mothers. *Develop. & Psychopathol.*, 4:49–66.

Firestein, S. (1969). Panel: Problems of termination in the analyses of adults. *J. Amer. Psychoanal. Assn.*, 17:222–237.

Fisher, R. S. (2002). Lesbianism: Some developmental and psychodynamic considerations. *Psychoanal. Inq.*, 22:278–295.

Fleming, J. & Weiss, S. S. (1978). Assessment of progress in a training analysis. *Internat. Rev. Psycho-Anal.*, 5:33–43.

Fonagy, P. (1999a). Memory and therapeutic action. *Internat. J. Psycho-Anal.*, 80:215–224.

Fonagy, P., ed. (1999b). *An Open Door Review of Outcome Studies in Psychoanalysis. Research Committee of the International Association of Psycho-Analysis*.

Fonagy, P., Gerber, A., Higgit, A. & Bateman, A. (1999). The comparison of intensive and non-intensive treatment of young adults. In: *An Open Door*

Review of Outcome Studies in Psychoanalysis, ed. P. Fonagy. Research Committee of the Internat. Assn. Psycho-Anal., pp. 158–160.

Fonagy, P., Gergely, G., Jurist, E. & Target, M. (2002). *Affect Regulation, Mentalization, and the Development of the Self*. New York: Other Press.

Fonagy, P., Moran, G. S., Edgcumbe, R., Kennedy, H. & Target, M. (1993). The roles of mental representations and mental processes in therapeutic action: 1. *The Psychoanalytic Study of the Child.*, 48:9–48. New Haven, CT: Yale University Press.

Fonagy, P., Steele, M., Steele, H., Leigh, T., Kennedy, R., Mattoon, G. & Target, M. (1995). Attachment, the reflective self, and borderline states. In: *Attachment Theory*, ed. S. Goldberg, R. Muir & J. Kerr. Hillsdale, NJ: The Analytic Press, pp. 253–278.

Freedman, N. & Lavender, J. (1997). On receiving the patient's transference: The symbolizing and desymbolizing countertransference. *J. Amer. Psychoanal. Assn.*, 45:79–103.

Freedman, N. & Lavender, J. (1999). On de-symbolization: The concept and observations on anorexia and bulimia (Pre-publication copy).

Freud, S. (1900). The interpretation of dreams. *Standard Edition*, 4 & 5. London: Hogarth Press, 1953.

Freud, S. (1910). The future prospects of psycho-analytic therapy. *Standard Edition*, 11:139–152. London: Hogarth Press, 1957.

Freud, S. (1912). Recommendations to physicians practicing psychoanalysis. *Standard Edition*, 12:109–120. London: Hogarth Press, 1958.

Freud, S. (1915). Observations on transference love (Further recommendations on the technique of psycho-analysis, III). *Standard Edition*, 12:159–171. London: Hogarth Press, 1958.

Freud, S. (1917). Mourning and melancholia. *Standard Edition*, 14:243–258. London: Hogarth Press, 1957.

Freud, S. (1926). The question of lay analysis. *Standard Edition*, 20:183–250. London: Hogarth Press, 1959.

Freud, S. (1937). Analysis terminable and interminable. *Standard Edition*, 23:216–253. London: Hogarth Press, 1964.

Freud, S. (1940). An outline of psychoanalysis. *Standard Edition*, 23:144–207. London: Hogarth Press, 1964.

Friedman, S. S. (1990). *Penelope's Web*. Cambridge, England: Cambridge University Press.

(1941). *Funk and Wagnall's Standard College Dictionary, Vol. 1*. New York: Funk & Wagnall's.

Furman, E. (1974). *A Child's Parent Dies*. New Haven, CT: Yale University Press.

Furman, R. (1964). Death and the young child: Some preliminary considerations. *The Psychoanalytic Study of the Child*, 19:321–328. New Haven, CT: Yale University Press.

Gabbard, G. (1994). Love and lust in the erotic transference. *J. Amer. Psychoanal. Assn.*, 42:385–404.

Gabbard, G. (2000). Disguise or consent: Problems and recommendations concerning the publication and presentation of clinical material. *Internat. J. Psychoanal.*, 81:1071–1086.

Gardner, M. R. (1989). *Self Inquiry.* Hillsdale, NJ: The Analytic Press.

Gedo, J. (1997). *Spleen and Nostalgia.* Northvale, NJ: Aronson.

Geller, J. D. & Farber, B. A. (1993). Factors influencing the process of internalization in psychotherapy. *Psychotherapy Research*, 3:166–180.

Gill, M. M. (1984). Psychoanalysis and psychotherapy: A revision. *Internat. Rev. Psycho-Anal.*, 11:161–179.

Gill, M. M. (1994). *Psychoanalysis in Transition.* Hillsdale, NJ: The Analytic Press.

Gitelson, M. (1954). Therapeutic problems in the analysis of the 'normal' candidate: 1. *Internat. J. Psycho-Anal.*, 35:174–183.

Goldberger, M. & Holmes, D. E. (1993). Transferences in male patients with female analysts: An update. *Psychoanal. Inq.*, 13:173–191.

Gornick, L. K. (1986). Developing a new narrative: The woman therapist and the male patient. *Psychoanal. Psychol.*, 3:299–325.

Gray, P. (1973). Psychoanalytic technique and the ego's capacity for viewing intrapsychic conflict. *J. Amer. Psychoanal. Assn.*, 21:474–494.

Gray, P. (1986). On helping analysands observe intrapsychic activity. In: *The Science of Mental Conflict—Essays in Honor of Charles Brenner*, ed. A. D. Richards & M. S. Willick. Hillsdale, NJ: The Analytic Press.

Gray, P. (1990). The nature of therapeutic action in psychoanalysis. *J. Amer. Psychoanal. Assn.*, 38:1083–1097.

Green, A. (1986). The dead mother. In: *On Private Madness*, ed. A. Green. London: Hogarth Press, pp. 142–173.

Greenberg, J. R. & Mitchell, S. A. (1983). *Object Relations in Psychoanalytic Theory.* Cambridge, MA: Harvard University Press.

Gumbel, E., & Heimann, P. (1970). Discussion of "the non-transference relationship in the psychoanalytic situation." *Internat. J. Psycho-Anal.*, 51:143–150.

Guntrip, H. (1975). My experience of analysis with Fairbairn and Winnicott. *Internat. Rev. Psycho-Anal.*, 2:145–156.

Hagman, G. (1995). Mourning: A review and reconsideration. *Internat. J. Psycho-Anal.*, 76:909–925.

Hagman, G. (1996). The role of the other in mourning. *Psychoanal. Quart.*, 65:327–352.

Hartlaub, G. H., Martin, G. & Rhine, M. (1986). Recontact with the analyst following termination: A survey of seventy-one cases. *J. Amer. Psychoanal. Assn.*, 34:895–910.

Haviland, J. M. & Malatesta, C. Z. (1981). The development of sex differences in nonverbal signals: Fallacies, facts and fantasies. In: *Gender and Non Verbal Behavior*, ed. C. Mayo & N. Henly. Heidelberg, NY: Springer-Verlag.

Haynal, A. (2002). *Disappearing and Reviving*. London: Karnac Books.

H.D. (1956). *Tribute to Freud: Writing on the Wall—Advent*. Boston: David R. Godine.

Heimann, P. (1954). Problems of the training analysis: 1. *Internat. J. Psycho-Anal.*, 35:163–168.

Herzog, J. M. (2001). *Father Hunger*. Hillsdale, NJ: The Analytic Press.

Hittelman, J. H. & Dickes, R. (1979). Sex differences in neonatal eye contact time. *Palmer Quart.*, 25:171–184.

Hoffer, A. (1991). The Freud–Ferenczi controversy—A living legacy. *Internat. Rev. Psycho-Anal.*, 18:465–471.

Hoffman, I. Z. (1983). The patient as interpreter of the analyst's experience. *Contemp. Psychoanal.*, 19:389–422.

Hoffman, I. Z. (1996). The intimate and ironic authority of the psychoanalyst's presence. *Psychoanal. Quart.*, 65:102–136.

Holland, N. N. (2002). H.D.'s analysis with Freud. *Psyart: A Hyperlink Journal for Psychological Study of the Arts*, Article No. 020101. http://www.clas.ufl.edu/psa/journal/2002/hollan050htm.

Holt, R. R. (1992). Freud's parental identifications as a source of some contradictions within psychoanalysis. In: *Freud and the History of Psychoanalysis*, ed. T. Gelfand & J. Kerr. Hillsdale, NJ: The Analytic Press, pp. 1–27.

Hurn, H. H. (1971). Toward a paradigm of the terminal phase: The current status of the terminal phase. *J. Amer. Psychoanal. Assn.*, 19:332–348.

Hurn, H. T. (1973). On the fate of transference after the termination of analysis [Panel]. *J. Amer. Psychoanal. Assn.*, 21:181–192.

Hurwitz, M. (1986). The analyst, his theory, and the psychoanalytic process. *The Psychoanalytic Study of the Child*, 41:439–466. New Haven, CT: Yale University Press.

Jacobs, D. (1992). Theory and its relation to early affective experience. Presented at the meetings of the Massachusetts Association for Psychoanalytic Psychology, Cambridge, MA, September.

Jacobs, T. (1991). *The Use of the Self*. Madison, CT: International Universities Press.

Jacobson, E. (1957). Normal and pathological moods: Their nature and function. *The Psychoanalytic Study of the Child*, 12:73–113. New Haven, CT: Yale University Press.

Jones, E. E. (2000). *Therapeutic Action*. Northvale, NJ: Aronson.

Joseph, B. (1981). Defense mechanism and phantasy in the psychoanalytic process. In: *Psychic Equilibrium and Psychic Change: Selected Papers of Betty Joseph*, ed. M. Feldman & E. B. Spillius. London: Routledge, 1989, pp. 116–126.

Kairys, D. (1964). The training analysis—A critical review of the literature and a controversial proposal. *Psychoanal. Quart.*, 33:485–512.

Kantrowitz, J. (1993). The uniqueness of the patient–analyst pair: Approaches for elucidating the analyst's role. *Internat. J. Psycho-Anal.*, 74:893–904.

Kantrowitz, J., Katz, A. & Paolitto, F. (1990a). Follow up of psychoanalysis five to ten years after termination. I. Stability of change. *J. Amer. Psychoanal. Assn.*, 38:471–496.

Kantrowitz, J., Katz, A. & Paolitto, F. (1990b). Follow up of psychoanalysis five to ten years after termination. II. Development of the self-analytic function. *J. Amer. Psychoanal. Assn.*, 38:637–665.

Kantrowitz, J., Katz, A. & Paolitto, F. (1990c). Follow up of psychoanalysis five to ten years after termination. III. The relation between resolution of the transference and the patient-analyst match. *J. Amer. Psychoanal. Assn.*, 38:651–678.

Karme, L. (1993). Male patients and female analysts: Erotic and other psychoanalytic encounters. *Psychoanal. Inq.*, 13:192–205.

Kernberg, O. F. (1980). *Internal World and External Reality*. New York: Aronson.

Kerr, J. (2002). *Analytic mentors are not fathers: An historical view of the origins of the training analysis*. Presented at the meetings of the American Psychoanalytic Association, Philadelphia, May.

Kirkpatrick, M. (2002). Clinical notes on the diversity in lesbian lives. *Psychoanal. Inq.*, 22:196–208.

Kirsner, D. (2000). *Unfree Associations*. London: Process Press.

Klein, M. (1950). On the criteria for the termination of an analysis. *Internat. J. Psycho-Anal.*, 31:78–80; 204.

Knight, J. (1950). *The Story of My Psychoanalysis*. New York: McGraw-Hill.

Kohon, G., ed. (1999). *The Dead Mother: The Work of Andre Green*. London: Routledge.

Kohut, H. (1994). *The Curve of Life*. Chicago: Chicago University Press.

Kramer, C. H. (1967). Maxwell Gitelson: Analytic aphorisms. *Psychoanal. Quart.*, 36:260–270.

Kramer, M. K. (1959). On the continuation of the analytic process after psycho-analysis (a self-observation). *Internat. J. Psycho-Anal.*, 40:17–25.

Kris, A. (1990). Helping patients by analyzing self-criticism. *J. Amer. Psychoanal. Assn.*, 38:605–636.

Kris, E. (1956). On some vicissitudes of insight in psycho-analysis. *Internat. J. Psycho-Analysis*, 37:445–455.

Kulish, N. (1989). Gender and transference: Conversations with female analysts. *Psychoanal. Psychol.*, 6:59–71.

Kulish, N. & Mayman, M. (1993). Gender linked determinants of transference and countertransference in psychoanalytic psychotherapy. *Pyschoanal. Inq.*, 13:286–305.

Lacan, J. (1959). The seminar of Jacques Lacan: Book 7. *The Ethics of Psychoanalysis*, ed. J. A. Miller. New York: Norton.

Lampl-De Groot, J. (1954). Problems of psycho-analytic training. *Internat. J. Psycho-Anal.*, 35:184–187.

Laplanche, J. (1992). *Seduction, Translation and the Drives*. London: Institute of Contemporary Arts.

Laplanche, J. (1997). The theory of seduction and the problem of the other. *Internat. J. Psycho-Anal.*, 78:653–666.

Lester, E. P. (1985). The female analyst and the eroticized transference. *Internat. J. Psycho-Anal.*, 66:283–293.

Leuzinger-Bohleber, M. & Pfeifer, R. (2002). Remembering a depressive primary object: Memory in the dialogue between psychoanalysis and cognitive science. *Internat. J. Psycho-Anal.*, 83:3–33.

Leuzinger-Bohleber, M. & Target, M., eds. (2002). *Outcomes of Psychoanalytic Treatment*. New York: Brunner-Routledge, pp. 1–25.

Levinson, D., Darrow, C. N., Klein, E. B., Levinson, M. H. & McKee, B. (1978). *The Seasons of a Man's Life*. New York: Knopf.

Lewin, B. (1954). Sleep, narcissistic neurosis and the analytic situation. *Psychoanal. Quart.*, 23:487–510.

Lewin, B. (1955). Dream psychology and the analytic situation. *Psychoanal. Quart.*, 24:169–199.

Liebert, R. S. (1986). Transference and countertransference issues in the treatment of women by a male analyst. In: *Between Analyst and Patient*, ed. H. C. Meyers. Hillsdale, NJ: The Analytic Press, pp. 229–236.

Lipton, S. D. (1961). The last hour. *J. Amer. Psychoanal. Assn.*, 9:325–330.

Little, M. (1990). *Psychotic Anxieties and Containment*. Northvale, NJ: Aronson.

Loewald, H. W. (1960). On the therapeutic action of psychoanalysis. In: *Papers on Psychoanalysis*. New Haven, CT: Yale University Press, 1989, pp. 221–256.

Loewald, H. W. (1962). Internalization, separation, mourning and the superego. In: *Papers on Psychoanalysis*. New Haven, CT: Yale University Press, 1989, pp. 257–276.

Loewald, H. W. (1970). Psychoanalytic theory and the psychoanalytic process. In: *Papers on Psychoanalysis*. New Haven, CT: Yale University Press, 1989, pp. 277–301.

Loewald, H. W. (1971). The transference neurosis. In: *Papers on Psychoanalysis*. New Haven, CT: Yale University Press, 1989, pp. 302–314.

Loewald, H. W. (1973). On internalization. *Internat. J. Psycho-Anal.*, 54:9–17.

Loewald, H. W. (1975). Psychoanalysis as an art and the fantasy character of the psychoanalytic situation. In: *Papers on Psychoanalysis*. New Haven, CT: Yale University Press, 1989, pp. 352–371.

Loewald, H. W. (1979). Reflections on the psychoanalytic process and its therapeutic potential. In: *Papers on Psychoanalysis*. New Haven, CT: Yale University Press, 1989, pp. 372–383.

Loewald, H.W. (1988a). Termination analyzable and unanalyzable. *The Psychoanalytic Study of the Child*, 43:155–166. New Haven, CT: Yale University Press.

Loewald, H. W. (1988b). *Sublimination*. New Haven, CT: Yale University Press.

Lohser, B. & Newton, P. M. (1996). *Unorthodox Freud*. New York: Guilford Press.

Lord, R., Ritvo, S. & Solnit, A. J. (1978). Patients' reactions to the death of the psychoanalyst. *Internat. J. Psycho-Anal.*, 59:189–197.

Masson, J., ed. (1985). *The Complete Letters of Sigmund Freud to Wilhelm Fliess*. Cambridge, MA: Harvard University Press.

Masson, J. (1990). *Final Analysis*. Reading, MA: Addison-Wesley.

Mendelsohn, E. (2002). The analyst's bad-enough participation. *Psychoanal. Dial.*, 12:331–358.

Meyers, H. (1986). Analytic work by and with women: The complexity and the challange. In: *Between Analyst and Patient*, ed. H. C. Meyers. Hillsdale, NJ: The Analytic Press, pp. 159–176.

Mitchell, S. (1988). *Relational Concepts in Psychoanalysis*. Cambridge, MA: Harvard University Press.

Mitchell, S. (1997). Psychoanalysis and the degradation of romance. *Psychoanal. Dial.*, 7:23–42.

Mitchell, S. (2000). Commentary on Freud's unconscious in the light of neurobiology. Presented at the NYU Postgraduate Program Conference, New York, December.

Mitchell, S. (2002). *Can Love Last?* New York: Norton.

Modell, A. (1984). *Psychoanalysis in a New Context*. New York: International Universities Press.

Modell, A. (1993). *The Private Self*. Cambridge, MA: Harvard University Press.

Money-Kyrle, R. E. (1979). Looking backwards—and forwards. *Internat. Rev. Psycho-Anal.*, 6:265.

Moser, T. (1974). *Years of Apprenticeship on the Couch*. New York: Urizen Books.

Nahum, J. (2002). Explicating the implicit: The local level and the microprocess of change in the analytic situation. *Internat. J. Psycho-Anal.*, 83:1051–1062.

Nakhla, F. & Jackson, G. (1993). *Picking Up the Pieces*. New Haven, CT: Yale University Press.

Norman, H. F., Blacker, K. H., Oremland, J. D. & Barrett, W. G. (1976). The fate of the transference neurosis after termination of a satisfactory analysis. *J. Amer. Psychoanal. Assn.*, 24:471–498.

Norman, J. (2001). The psychoanalyst and the baby: A new look at work with infants. *Internat. J. Psycho-Anal.*, 82:83–100.

Notman, M. T. (2002). Changes in sexual orientation and object choice in midlife in women. *Psychoanal. Inq.*, 22:182–195.

Novick, J. (1997). Termination conceivable and inconceivable. *Psychoanal. Psychol.*, 14:145–162.

Nussbaum, M. C. (2001). *Upheavals of Thought*. Cambridge, England: Cambridge University Press.

Oremland, J. D., Blacker, K. H. & Norman, H. F. (1975). Incompleteness in "successful" psychoanalysis. *J. Amer. Psychoanal. Assn.*, 23:819–944.

Orgel, S. (1982). The selection and functions of the training analyst in North American institutes. *Internat. Rev. Psycho-Anal.*, 9:417–434.

Orgel, S. (2000). Letting go: Some thoughts about termination. *J. Amer. Psychoanal. Assn.*, 48:719–738.

(1971). *Oxford English Dictionary, Vol. 1*. London: Oxford University Press.

Perez, M. B. (1985). The termination of the training analysis. The process: The expectations, the achievements, (2) The analysand's view. *Internat. J. Psycho-Anal., Monog. Ser.*, 17–33.

Person, E. (1985). The erotic transference in women and men: Differences and consequences. *J. Amer. Acad. Psychoanal.*, 13:159–180.

Pfeffer, A. (1963). The meaning of the analyst after analysis. *J. Amer. Psychoanal. Assn.*, 11:229–244.

Pfeffer, A. (1993). After the analysis: Analyst as both old and new object. *J. Amer. Psychoanal. Assn.*, 41:323–337.

Pfeffer, A. (1961). Follow-up study of a satisfactory analysis. *J. Amer. Psychoanal. Assn.*, 11:229–244.

Rangell, L. (1966). *An Overview of the Ending of an Analysis*. New York: International Universities Press.

Rangell, L. (1982). Some thoughts on termination. *Psychoanal. Inq.*, 2:367–392.

Reed, K. (2002). Listening to themes in a review of psychoanalytic literature about lesbianism. *Psychoanal. Inq.*, 22:229–258.

Reich, A. (1950). On the termination of analysis. *Internat. J. Psycho-Anal.*, 31:179–183.

Rendely, J. (1999). The death of an analyst: The loss of a real relationship. *Contemp. Psychoanal.*, 35:131–152.

Robbins, W. S. (1975). Termination: Problems and techniques [Panel]. *J. Amer. Psychoanal. Assn.*, 23:166–176.

Rohde, A., Geller, J. D. & Farber, B. A. (1992). Dreams about the therapist: Mood, interactions and themes. *Psychotherapy*, 25:536–544.

Ross, J. M. (1998). Psychoanalysis, the anxiety of influence and the sado-masochism of everyday life. Presented at the scientific meeting, Boston Psychoanalytic Society and Institute, Boston, April.

Rudolf, G. & Manz, R. (1993). Zur prognostischen bedeutung der therapeutischen arbeitsbeziehung aus der perspective von patienten und therapeuten. *Psychother. Psychosom. Med. Psychol.*, 43:193–199.

Sadow, L. (1973). Discussion of the re-analysis of the analyst. Presented at the meetings of the American Psychoanalytic Association, New York City, December.

Sagi, A. & Hoffman, M. L. (1976). Empathic distress in the newborn. *Developmental Psychol.*, 12:175–176.

Sander, L. W. (1997). Paradox and resolution. In: *Handbook of Child and Adolescent Psychiatry*, ed. J. Osofsky. New York: Wiley, pp. 153–160.

Sandler, J. (1976). Countertransference and role-responsiveness. *Internat. J. Psycho-Anal.*, 3:43–47.

Sayers, J. (1991). *Mothering Psychoanalysis*. London: Penguin Books.

Schachter, J. (1992). Concepts of termination and post-termination patient-analyst contact. *Internat. J. Psycho-Anal.*, 73:137–154.

Schacter, J. (2001). *Transference*. Hillsdale, NJ: The Analytic Press.

Schacter, J. & Brauer, L. (2001). The effect of the analyst's gender and other factors on post-termination patient-analyst contact. *Internat. J. Psychoanal.*, 82:1123–1132.

Schacter, J. & Johan, M. (1989). Evaluation of outcome of psychoanalytic treatment: Should followup by the analyst be part of the post-termination phase of analytic treatment? [Panel]. *J. Amer. Psychoanal. Assn.*, 37:813–822.

Schachter, J., Martin, G. C., Gundle, M. J. & O'Neil, M. K. (1997). Clinical experience with psychoanalytic post-termination meetings. *Internat. J. Psycho-Anal.*, 78:1183–1198.

Schlessinger, N. & Robbins, F. (1974). Assessment and follow-up in psychoanalysis. *J. Amer. Psychoanal. Assn.*, 22:542–567.

Schlessinger, N. & Robbins, F. (1975). The psychoanalytic process: Recurrent patterns of conflict and changes in ego functions. *J. Amer. Psychoanal. Assn.*, 23:761–782.

Schlessinger, N. & Robbins, F. (1983). *A Developmental View of the Psychoanalytic Process*. Madison, CT: International Universities Press.

Schmideberg, M. (1938). After the Analysis. . . . *Psychoanal. Quart.*, 7:122–142.

Shapiro, D. (1974). The training setting in training analysis: A retrospective view of the evaluative and reporting role and other 'hampering' factors. *Internat. J. Psycho-Anal.*, 55:297–306.

Shapiro, D. (1976). The analyst's own analysis. *J. Amer. Psychoanal. Assn.*, 24:5–42.

Shapiro, T. & Emde, R. E. (1993). Research in psychoanalysis: Process, development, outcome. *J. Amer. Psychoanal. Assn.*, 41 (Suppl.):424.

Silber, A. (1996). Analysis, re-analysis and self-analysis. *J. Amer. Psychoanal. Assn.*, 44:491–507.

Silverman, D. (1987). Female bonding: Some supportive findings for Melanie Klein's views. *Psychoanal. Rev.*, 74:201.

Simner, M. L. (1971). Newborns' response to the cry of another infant. *Developmental Psychol.*, 5:136–150.

Simon, B. (1993). In search of psychoanalytic technique: Perspectives from the couch and from behind the couch. *J. Amer. Psychoanal. Assn.*, 41:1051–1082.

Simon, B. (1995). Discussion of *The Tempest* by William Shakespeare. Presented at the *The Tempest*, performed at American Repertory Theater, Cambridge, MA, December.

Smith, H. (2002). Creating the psychoanalytical process incorporating three panel reports: Opening the process, being in the process and closing the process [Panel]. *Internat. J. Psycho-Anal.*, 83:211–227.

Steiner, J. (1993). *Psychic Retreats*. London: Routlege.

Steiner, J. (1996). The aim of psychoanalysis in theory and in practice. *Internat. J. Psycho-Anal.*, 77:1073–1083.

Stolorow, R. & Lachmann, F. (1984–1985). Transference: The future of an illusion. *The Annual of Psychoanalysis*, 12/13:19–37. Hillsdale, NJ: The Analytic Press.

Strachey, J. (1934). The nature of the therapeutic action in psychoanalysis. *Internat. J. Psychoanal.*, 15:127–159.

Sullivan, H. S. (1964). *The Illusion of Personal Identity*. New York: Norton.

Suomi, S. J. (1991). Early stress and adult emotional reactivity in rhesus monkeys. Presented at the Ciba Foundation Symposium 156, Childhood Environment and Adult Disease.

Suomi, S. J. (1995). Influence of attachment theory on ethological studies of biobehavioral development in nonhuman primates. In: *Attachment Theory*, ed. S. Goldberg, R. Muir & J. Kerr. Hillsdale, NJ: The Analytic Press, pp. 185–199.

Suomi, S. J. (1997). Early determinants of behavior: Evidence from primate studies. *Brit. Med. Bull.*, 53:170–184.

Symington, N. (1983). The analyst's act of freedom as agent of therapeutic change. *Internat. Rev. Psycho-Anal.*, 10:283–291.

Symington, N. (1990). The possibility of human freedom and its transmission (with particular reference to the thought of Bion). *Internat. J. Psycho-Anal.*, 71:95–105.

Tessman, L. (1978). *Children of Parting Parents*. New York: Aronson.

Tessman, L. (1982). A note on the father's contribution to the daughter's ways of loving and working. In: *Father and Child*, ed. S. Cath, A. Gurwitt & J. M. Ross. Boston: Little, Brown.

Tessman, L. (1989). Fathers and daughters: Early tones, later echoes. In: *Fathers and Their Families*, ed. S. Cath, A. Gurwitt & L. Gunsberg. Hillsdale, NJ: The Analytic Press.

Tessman, L. (1999). A cry of fire, an old flame, the matter of fireplace. In: *Female Sexuality*, ed. D. Bassin. Northvale, NJ: Aronson.

Tessman, L. (2001). Small step, giant step: A stepfather. In: *Stepparenting*, ed. S. H. Cath & M. Shopper. Hillsdale, NJ: The Analytic Press.

Ticho, G. R. (1967). On self-analysis. *Internat. J. Psycho-Anal.*, 48:308–318.

Tronick, E. Z. (1998). Dyadically expanded states of consciousness and the process of therapeutic change. *Infant Mental Health*, 19:290–299.

Viorst, J. (1982). Experiences of loss at the end of analysis: The analyst's response to termination. *Psychoanal. Inq.*, 2:399–418.

Weigert, E. (1952). Contribution to the problem of terminating psychoanalysis. *Psychoanal. Quart.*, 21:465–480.

Weigert, E. (1955). Special problems in connection with termination of training analyses. *J. Amer. Psychoanal. Assn.*, 3:630–640.

Weinberg, K. (1992). Boys and girls: Sex differences in emotional expressivity and self-regulation during early infancy. Presented at the Symposium on Early Emotional Self-Regulation: New Approaches to Understanding Developmental Change and Individual Differences, International Conference on Infant Studies, Miami, May.

Weinshel, E. M. (1992). Therapeutic technique in psychoanalysis and psychoanalytic therapy. *J. Amer. Psychoanal. Assn.*, 40:327–348.

Winnicott, D. (1960). Ego distortion in terms of true and false self. In: *The Maturational Processes and the Facilitating Environment*. New York: International Universities Press, 1965, pp. 140–152.

Winnicott, D. (1963). Communicating and not communicating leading to a study of certain opposites. In: *The Maturational Processes and the Facilitating Environment*. New York: International Universities Press, 1965, pp. 179–192.

Winnicott, D. (1969). The use of an object and relating through identifications. *Playing and Reality*. New York: Basic Books, 1971, pp. 86–94.

Wortis, J. (1954). *Fragments of an Analysis with Freud*. New York: Simon & Schuster.

Zetzel, E. (1970). *The Capacity for Emotional Growth*. New York: International Universities Press.

INDEX

absent attitude, 150
accommodation, 53
accomplishment, sense of, 40
acknowledgment, by analyst,
177–178
actuality, 314
of analyst, 8–9
adolescence, issues of, 97
affect, bearing of, 149
affective availability, 71
affective connection, 32
age, transferences and, 133–134
aggression, 47, 139
of analysand, 87
analytic responses to, 173
denial of, 221
interpreting and wrestling with,
39–40
sexuality and, 162
women candidates on, 213
aggressive freedom, 288
alliance, between analyst and
analysand, 126
aloneness, with analyst, 40
ambiguity, 218
transference and, 215
ambitions, of women, 171
ambivalence, 164, 310
American Psychoanalytic
Association, 115

analysands. *See also* Participants;
individual names, e.g., Lewis,
Dr. Henry
achieving independence, 9
autonomous personhood of, 223
data regarding, 62–64
desired connection of, 310
dialogue with analyst, 8–11
dissatisfied, 226
engagement and disengagement
with analysts, 27
experiencing self with analyst, 127
frame of mind, 183
future generations of, 54
on leave-taking, 252–253
low-disappointment analyses, 244
men with female analysts,
132–136
pairing with analysts, 2
perceptions of, 66
personhood of, 66–67
responses to leave-taking, 252–254
self-analytic capacity, 204–205
self-development of, 224–225
women with female analysts,
158–182
analysis
assumption regarding, 70
autonomy-promoting, 104–105
benefit and satisfaction with, 7

343

analysis *(continued)*
  crucial omissions from, 48
  damaging, 50–60
  deeply satisfying, 32–34, 37–45
  dialectics of, 85
  highly dissatisfying, 35–37, 50–60
  incomplete, 93
  insulated from, 109
  intrapsychic experience of, 1
  moderately satisfying, 34, 45–50
  nature of satisfying, 31
  response to bad experience, 195
  satisfaction with, 17–18
  wowing experience of, 110
analyst-analysand relationship,
    outside analysis, 100
analyst-in-training, pathology of, 208
analysts
  benign presence of, 297
  as benign superego, 172–173
  bond with, 57
  de-idealization of, 12–13
  as dialogic partner, 113
  dialogue with analysand, 8–11
  erotic love for, 42–43
  as fantasy person, 26
  feeling loved by, 59–60
  growth of during analysis, 173–174
  internalizing, 113
  match with, 31
  as model for analysand, 175
  modes of experiencing patients, 16
  patients' knowledge of, 225
  perceptions of, 66
  as person, 97–98
  personality of, 307
  personal qualities of, 315
  as real object, 239
  reporting confidential relation-
    ships, 198
  role in modeling analysand's
    style, 197
  self-respect of complete other, 313

  separation phase for, 230
  withstanding influence of,
    130–131
  wounding impact of, 309
analytic approaches, 309
  shifts in, 159
analytic birthright, 168
analytic content, ownership of,
    168–170
analytic dyad, 2
  collusion as, 307
  dynamics within, 308
analytic engagement, 38
analytic identity
  of dissatisfied Participants, 213
  Dr. Bob White on, 219–220
  Dr. Celia Laub on, 218
  Dr. Elizabeth Light on, 221–222
  Dr. Francesca Emon on, 215–216
  Dr. Horatio Encarta on, 219
  Dr. Irving Mazur on, 220–221
  Dr. Jack Robinson on, 216–217
  Dr. Julia Baranger on, 217
  Dr. Katharine Maxwell on,
    213–215
  Dr. Mozes Nounous on, 217–218
  Dr. Stuart Laraphil on, 211–212
  unconscious identification and
    time span, 217–218
analytic interactions, 33
analytic interchange, 7–8
analytic interventions, 33
analytic love, 82
analytic model, of analyst, 55
analytic modes, internalized,
    212–213
analytic process
  characteristics of, 225
  epoch of, 45
  internalization, 79
  training analysis and, 210–211
analytic relationship, sense of loss
    of, 242–244

analytic results
  developmental deprivations and, 31
  trauma and, 31
analytic situation, asymmetry of, 277
analytic stance
  caustic and deprecatory, 150
  vs. personality, 95–98
analytic theory, two-person terms in, 125
anger, 51, 166
  analytic responses to, 173
  discomfort with, 143
Angiolieri, Dr. Cecco
  homosexual panic attack, 119–120
  on leave-taking, 253
  on posttermination contact, 284
  on privacy, 21
  second analysis, 120
Anna Freud Centre, 17
anonymity, 3–4
anxiety, 51, 97, 196
association, in analytic process, 259
asymmetry, of analysis, 278–279
attachment
  core patterns of, 79
  wishes for, 54, 128
attachment avoidant, 180
attachment barrier, 176
attachment disorganized, 180–181
attachment experiences, 80
attachment studies, 79
attitude
  absent of analyst, 150
  envious and blameful, 176
  sustaining, 103
attuned moments, 79
authority issue, 146
auto-analysis, 261, 262
autonomy, 179, 251–252
  of analysand, 87
  vs. femininity, 161
  posttermination, 10

supporting, 190
avoidance, mourning and, 239

backgrounds, disparate between analyst and analysand, 137
Balint, M., 125, 200, 227
  on feeling of rebirth, 249–250
Baranger, Dr. Julia
  on analytic identity, 217
  deeply satisfying analysis, 171–175
  feelings of love for analyst, 160
  on leave taking, 252
  shared analyst, 324
Bass, A., 314
Baudry, F., 260
Beebe, B., 78–79
behavior, therapists nonverbal, 16
Behrends, R., 316
benign dialogic partner, 310
Berenstein, I., 281
Bergmann, M., 226, 227
Bernfeld, S., 201, 202, 205
Bernstein, D., 84, 161
Bibring, G.L., 206
biographic detail, 4
Bion, W., 184, 209, 258, 308, 314
birth order, 58
Blacker, K.H., 260
Blanck, G., 271
Blanck, R., 271
Blanton, S., 307
Blatt, S., 316
blind spots, 67
Blos, P.S., 115–116
Blum, H.P., on leave-taking, 250
bond, silent, good, 164
Boris, H.N., 258
Boston Change Process Study Group, 16
Boston Psychoanalytic Society and Institute, 2, 49, 62
  reporting analyst system, 198
  women analysts at, 132

boundaries, 41, 54, 94
Brauer, L., 275–276
Brown, Dr. Eleanor, 46–48
    on analytic identity, 218–219
    on female analysts, 161
    shared analyst, 324
Burgner, M., 160
Burning Patience, 94
Busch, F., 7
Buxbaum, E., 241, 273–274

Calef, V., on leave-taking, 250
candidates, reporting problem, 199
candor, modeling, 144
Caper, R., 263, 314
career progression, reporting to
        Institutes and, 198
caring, impinging and, 153
categories of satisfaction, 6
censoring, unconscious, 46
Chairman Mao, 283
challenge, negotiable, 60
change, 151
    flow of, 183
    locus of, 184
character
    problems of candidates, 199
    technique and, 215
characterologic match, 61, 199
Chernin, K., 308
children, 160
chin-up quality, 51
Clark, Dr. Veronica
    first moderately satisfying
        analysis, 95–98
    match with analyst, 308–309
    on postanalytic conversation, 278
    on privacy, 21
    response to termination,
        245–246
    second deeply satisfying analysis,
        98–102
    on solitary self-analysis, 265

    sustained erotic transference,
        94–102
    on termination, 233
    on thinking back, 24
classical analyst, 55
    response to, 95
classical theory, aberration of, 51
collaboration, 128
    by Institutes, 62
collusion, meaning of, 307
colostomy, 48–49
communication
    barriers to, 151
    between analyst and analysand,
        281
competition, 169
    with analyst, 186
    with therapist, 96
competitiveness, Dr. Encarta on, 189
compliance, 154–155
    automatic, 146
confidence, 104–105
Confidential Clerk, The (T.S. Eliot),
        38
confidentiality, 3, 198–199, 320
    lapse of, 199–200
configurations, in unsatisfactory
        analyses, 35–36
conflict, discomfort with, 143
confrontation, 214
connection, 151
    desired by analysand, 310
    inhibition and, 171
connections, 123
consciousness, dyadic expansion of,
        183
consideration, requesting, 55
constant attunement, 316
contact
    extraanalytic, 47
    vs. mirroring, 317
contemporary practice, diversity in,
        211

control case, 56
conversations
    imagined after analysis, 298–306
    interactive, 193
Conway, P.S., 260
Cooper, A., 200
Cooper, S., 9–10, 224, 241, 251, 280
core trauma, 140
Couch, A., 308
counterdependency, 36
counteridentification, by analysts, 229
countertransference, 15–16, 204
    errors, 99
    problems, 207
    rivalries, 168
Craige, H., 21, 242–243, 244, 251, 262, 273
crisis, self-analysis and, 260
critical superego, 138
criticism
    defense against, 52
    withheld, 297–298
crocodile tears, 128
crying, in newborn girls, 89

damage assessment, 53
Darrow, C.N., 116
Davies, J.M., 134, 251
dead mother
    syndrome, 85
    transference, 105–106
death
    grieving over father's, 155
    nothingness and, 41
debate, by Institutes, 62
DeBell, D.E., 239–240
    decade of analysis, 61–62
    impact of, 64
    satisfaction with gender and, 60–64
    deep analysis, 99
Deere, Dr. John

deeply satisfying analysis, 125–128
    on imagined postanalytic conversation, 300
    on intensity of feeling, 22
    on self-analysis, 266
    on self-reflections, 74–75
    on shared analyst, 324
    on termination, 246–247
defense, against criticism, 52
defense analysis, 14, 215, 216, 267
defensive shielding, 241
de-idealization, 10
    after analysis, 101–102
    individuation and, 231
    postanalytic, 34
Delphic oracle, 150
Denver Psychoanalytic Society, 274
depression
    in mothers, 81
    vs. sadness, 238
desire, for analyst, 84–85
Deutsch, H., 163, 237
developmental deprivations, analytic results and, 31
dialogue
    with analyst within, 225
    internalized, 113
Dickes, R., 89
dignity, 71
directness, 121
    modeling, 144
disagreement, leeway in, 95
disappointments, 58
    processing of, 31
disclosure, response to, 110
disgust, 52
disillusionment, in unsatisfying analyses, 68
diversity, in contemporary practice, 211
doctorhood, *vs.* personhood, 99–100

dogmatism, 49
do-it-yourself analysis, 38, 41
Doolitle, H., 15
dream analysis, 216
dream analyst, 96
dreaming, after termination, 191
dream interpretation, Dr. Jill
    Tulane, 111–112
Dupont, J., 259
dyad
    analyst-analysand, 26
    mutual influence within, 61
    negative aspects of, 129
dyadic collusion, 32–33
dyadic match, 80

early templates, latency of, 316
Edelman, G.M., 11
Edgecumbe, R., 160
Eissler, Dr. Ruth, 260
Eissler, K.R., 241–242
Ekstein, R., on leave-taking, 250
elegant analysis, 76
Eliot, T.S., *The Confidential Clerk,*
    38
Elise, D., 162
emancipation, at end of analysis, 211
Emde, R.E., 16
Emon, Dr. Francesca
    on analytic identity, 215–216
    on imagined postanalytic
        conversation, 298
    on postanalytic conversation,
        282–283
    maternal transference with male
        analyst, 102–108
    on self-reflections, 72–73
    on study discussions, 23
    on termination, 232
emotion, access to, 59–60
emotional ambience
    men with male analysts, 114
    shift in, 114

emotional availability, 316
emotional engagement, 219–220
emotional insulation, from analyst,
    35–36
emotional intimacy
    in female dyad, 164
    sustaining after analysis, 279
    wish for, 53
emotional range, 219
emotional understanding, 99
empathic communication, aborted,
    54
empathic kindness, 222
empathic presence, with patients, 182
empathy, gender and, 84
Encarta, Dr. Horatio
    analyst's evaluation of wife, 188
    on analytic identity, 219–220
    assessment of analyst's character,
        188
    family background, 187
    grandiosity, 189
    ideation of, 184
    on imagined postanalytic conver-
        sation, 304
    learning style, 185–186
    moderately satisfying analysis,
        140–141
    relationship with analyst,
        186–187
    response to analyst's death,
        189–190
    response to pain, 187
    response to termination, 185–191
    on termination, 233
enduring presence, 175
engagement, 151
    with analyst, 180
equality, 256
Erikson, E., 124
erotic fantasies, with female ana-
    lysts, 160
erotic feelings

within bounds of language, 93–94
  privacy and, 3
erotic love, 170
  in analysis, 84
  for analyst, 91–92
erotic needs, acting out, 49
erotic oedipal transference, require-
    ments, 135
erotic strivings, in analysand, 85
erotic transference
  aspects of, 86
  in female patients, 90
  male *vs.* female, 88
  men with female analysts, 133
  to old woman, 141
  reports of, 134
  resistance to, 134
  sustained, 94–102
Etchegoyen, H., 224
ethnic origins, camouflaging, 288
Evans, D., 134
evil-mindedness, 315

false-selfish, 154
fantasies
  of dancing with analyst, 156–157
  fully developed, 110
  future-oriented, 248–249
Farber, B.A., 9, 297, 310
father
  dying, 148
  idealization of, 177
  minimizing of, 167
  strong internalized, 115–116
father hunger, 116
father-son issues, 38–39
father transference, 102, 179
feelings
  capacity for wild, 42
  regressive, 178
felt experience, 98
female analysts
  age of, 132

oedipal erotic transferences and,
    135–136
  self-image and, 163
feminity
  changing models, 161
  masochism of, 163
  women with female analysts, 160
Fenichel, O., 307
Ferenczi, S., 117, 227, 229, 259
  on analyst's influences, 200–201
  on forgiveness, 116
  on homosexual libido, 116
Ferraro, F., 228
Field, T., 79
Firestein, S., 248–249
Fisher, Dr. Zelda
  competition with analyst, 159
  on imagined postanalytic
    conversation, 303–304
  moderately satisfying analysis,
    168–170
  shared analyst, 324
  on termination, 23
  on unfinished business, 24
Fisher, R.S., 162
Fleming, J., 206
flirtatiousness, 294
Fonagy, P., 7, 8, 16, 17, 67, 79
forgiveness, 116
formality, 294
  after termination, 290
free association, 40
  solitary, 259
Freedman, N., 16, 241
Freud, A., 124, 163, 201–202
  on analyst's character, 204
  on posttermination contact, 272
Freud, S., 117, 230, 236, 315
  H.D. analysis, 13–14
  Interpretation of Dreams, 259
  love of father, 116
  on love of women for male
    analyst, 90

Freud, S. *(continued)*
    on patient-analyst couple, 8
    on posttermination contact, 272
    on self-analysis and training
        analysis, 15
    talking cure, 258
Friedman, S., 315
friendship
    between analyst and analysand,
        276
    taboo of, 276–277
    tenderness and, 156
    transition to, 167
frustration, 55
Furman, E., 235
Furman, R., 235, 237

Gabbard, G., 86
    "Disguise or Consent," 4
Gang of Four, 283
Gardner, M.R., 262
Garella, A., 228
gaze aversion, 89
gazing dialogue, 89
Gedo, J., 62
Geller, J.D., 9, 297, 310
gender
    associations, choice of, 83–84
    differences observed in infants, 89
    propensities in early female
        experience, 90
    satisfaction with decade and,
        60–64
gender combinations, 2, 18, 61
    impact of, 64
gendered desires, omission in, 84
gendered transferences, therapists'
    response to, 136
generative collusion, 317
genitals, psychic representations, 90
Gergely, G., 79
German Psychoanalytic Association,
    17

ghetto, traveling in and out of, 147
Gill, M.M., 125, 259
Gitelson, M., 315
Glenn, Dr. Jay
    on feeling in analysis, 22
    forging of identity, 129–131
    on imagined postanalytic conver-
        sation, 306
    on leave-taking, 253–254
    on posttermination contact,
        291–292
    response to termination, 245
    on self-analysis, 268
    sexualized assaults, 114
    on view of analyst, 77–78
Goldberger, M., 134
good-byes, nature of, 157
good guy, need to be, 220
Gornick, 134
grandmother transference, 160
Gray, P., 7
Green, A., 85
Greenberg, J.R., 7
Green, Dr. Saul
    deeply satisfying analysis, 140
    on imagined postanalytic conver-
        sation, 299–300
    on impermanence of loving, 25
    posttermination gains, 134
    on self-analysis, 266–267
grief, 235. *See also* mourning
    analyst's response to, 313
    capacity for, 237
    inhibited states of, 237
    as opportunity, 236
    productive, 237
growth, after analysis, 140
guardedness, 221
guilt, 143
    adding to, 141
Gumbel, E., 272
Gundle, M.J., 275
Guntrip, H., 6, 308

Hagman, G., 235–237
harmonies, 76
Hartlaub, G.H., 274–275
Haviland, J.M., 89
Haynal, A., 259
H.D., 307, 315
heartburn, 189
Heimann, P., 202, 272
helplessness, intolerance of, 151
Herzog, J.M., 79, 116
Hittleman, J.H., 89
Hoffer, A., 116
Hoffman, I.Z., 7, 277
Hoffman, M.L., 89
Holland, N.N., 315–316
Holmes, D.E., 134
Holt, R.R., 308
homosexual fantasies, 114–115
homosexual transferences, 161
honesty, 128
Horney, K., 163
hostile confrontation, 130
human relationships, identity and, 80
humiliation, 52, 196
humor, 60
    sense of, 216
Hurn, H.H., 230
Hurn, H.T., 272
Hurwitz, M., 308

iatrogenic narcissism, 50, 52
idealization, 151
    by analysands, 209
    challenge of, 172
    defensiveness *vs.*, 200
    dual nature of, 209
    of training analysts, 203
idealizing transference, 52
ideas, interaction and, 193
identification, 164
    do-it-yourself, 41
    in psychoanalysis, 209
    unconscious, 26

identity, human relationships and, 80
idolization, 151
imagination, analysand's acts of, 30
impinging, caring and, 153
implicit relational knowing, 16–17
independence, 179
    achieving, 9
individuality, acceptance of, 32
individuation
    de-idealization and, 231
    evolution of, 210
indulgences, repertoire of, 53
inequality, between analyst and
        analysand, 140
infants, reactivity of female, 89
inhibitions
    connection and, 171
    prisoner of, 111
inner life, of analyst, 99
inner presence, of analyst, 214
insensitivity, of Dr. Laraphil, 194
intellectual argument, 96
interaction, nontherapeutic, 290
interconnection, patient-analyst, 314
internalization, 11, 37, 184, 224,
        241, 310
    affective availability of object
        and, 316
    of dialogue, 113
    as general phenomenon, 2
    impact on object relations,
        226–227
internalized other, conversation
        with, 193
Interpretation of Dreams (Freud), 259
interpretations
    analysand's corrections of, 166
    best, 221
    gift of wrong, 174
interventions, nonanalytic, 80
intimacy, 177
    psychic retreat from, 50
    wish for, 127–128

intrapsychic knowing, of analyst, 270
intrapsychic life, relational context
    of, 224
intrapsychic world, generating, 183
introject, 268–269
    analyst as, 130
isolating affects, 56–57
isolation, within relationship, 166
isolation induction, 70
issues, untapped, 173

Jackson, G., 308
Jacobs, D., 184
Jacobson, E., 238
Jacobs, T., 263, 315
Jason, Dr. Eva
    on imagined postanalytic conver-
        sation, 302
    on leave taking, 252
    response to termination, 245
    on self-analysis, 266
    on termination, 232
Johan, M., 271, 274
Johnson, A.M., 238
Jones, E.E., 16
Joseph, B., 7
judgmental quality, 172
judgments, Participants' subjective, 2
Jurist, E., 79

Kairys, D., 201–202
Kantrowitz, J., 16, 225–226, 260,
    262
Karme, L., 135
Katz, A., 225–226, 260
Keiser, 241
Kennedy, R., 8, 67
Kernberg, O.F., 79
Kerr, J., 116
Kirkpatrick, M., 162
Kirsner, D., 61, 62
Klein, E.B., 116
Klein, M., 163, 238

Knight, J., 307
Koestner, Dr. Harold
    on leave-taking, 254–255
    on mutual affection, 35
    as "outsider," 124–125
    on posttermination contact,
        284–285
Kohon, G., 85
Kohut, H., 260
Kramer, C.H., 315
Kramer, M.K., 261–262
Kris, A., 198
    on mourning, 236–237
Kris, E., 262
Kulish, N., 134, 136

Lacan, J., 224, 316
Lachmann, F., 78–79, 227
Lampl-de Groot, J., 204
Langer, Dr. Phil
    on caring analyst, 35
    childhood trauma, 145
    deeply satisfying analysis, 145–157
    on imagined postanalytic conver-
        sation, 300–301, 304–305
    on leave-taking, 254
    on perceptions of analysts, 70–71
    response to analyst's stance, 150
    satisfaction with female analyst,
        141
    shared analyst, 324
    termination, 151–152
language, use of, 142
Laplanche, 85
Laraphil, Dr. Stuart
    analyst's friendliness toward, 194
    on analytic identity, 211–212
    analytic motivation of, 195–197
    emotional response to analyst,
        196
    first male analyst, 117–118
    ideation of, 184Ä185
    on participation in study, 23

on posttermination contact,
293–294
response to termination, 191–197
on termination, 232–233
Laub, Dr. Celia, 91–92
on analytic identity, 218
response to termination, 245
on self-analysis, 266
Lavender, J., 16, 241
Lawrence, Dr. David
on negative feelings, 22
on posttermination contact, 278,
288–290
on self-analysis, 267
wish for paternal love from
analyst, 118–119
leave-taking
anxiety about, 255
feelings during, 251–252
feelings of analysands regarding,
252–253
halo effect of, 249
magic wand concept on, 256–257
postponed, 254–257
quality of, 249
responses to, 249–252
writers on, 248–249
Leigh, T., 8, 67
Lester, E.P., 134
letter of invitation, protective
measures in, 3
Leuzinger-Bohleber, M., 12, 17
Levinson, D., 116
Levinson, M.H., 116
Levy, Dr. Noah, 50–54
on posttermination contact,
292–293
on psychic retreats of analyst, 311
response to termination, 245
shared analyst, 324
Lewin, B., 259
Lewis, Dr. Henry, 54–60
on analyst, 307

on freshness of memory, 22
on imagined postanalytic conversation, 304
on interaction role, 24
on perceptions of analysts, 69–70
on psychic retreats of analyst, 311
response to termination, 245
shared analyst, 324
liberation, postanalytic, 45
libidinal impulse, transformation of,
90
Lieberman, Dr. Raphe
deeply satisfying analysis,
141–145
emotion of, 22
first analysis, 28–29
on perceptions of analysts, 68
on posttermination contact, 288
response to termination, 245
satisfaction with female analyst,
141
second analysis, 29
shared analyst, 324
third analysis, 29–30
third analyst, 145
transfer of analysts by, 62
Liebert, R.S., 135
Light, Dr. Elizabeth
on analytic identity, 221–222
on healing process, 25
on imagined postanalytic
conversation, 305–306
on self-analysis, 268–269
sexual boundary violations,
71–72, 93–94
linking, *vs.* identification, 263
Lionheart, Dr. Rose, 92–94
affection toward analyst, 160
deeply satisfying analysis,
164–165
on posttermination contact,
286–287
Lipton, S.D., on leave-taking, 250

listening, by analyst, 107
Little, M., 308
Loewald, H.W., 7, 11–12, 82, 211,
    223, 226, 241, 248
  on fantasy, 8
Lohser, B., 13, 14–15
Lord, R., 271
Loss, reactions to, 312
love
  particularity of, 309
  aspects of, 60
Luborsky, L., 271, 274

Malatesta, C.Z., 89
Manz, R., 16
Martin, G.C., 274, 275
masculine identification, 179
masculinity complex, 163
Masson, J., 308
maternal transference, 109, 111, 133
  age and, 138
  negative, 104
matriarch, 171–172
Mattoon, G., 8, 67
maverick, 139–140
Maxwell, Dr. Kathryn, 37, 41–45
  on analytic identity, 213–215
  on reengagement, 26–27
  response to termination, 245
Mayman, M., 136
Mazur, Dr. Irving
  on analytic identity, 220–221
  on self-analysis, 267
  on termination, 234
McClinton, Dr. Emma
  dissatisfying analysis, 175–182
  on imagined postanalytic conver-
    sation, 299, 306
  on leave-taking, 254, 255–257
  nature of termination, 181
  on perceptions of analysts, 69
  pregnancies, 160
  reciprocal love with analyst, 181
  on regressive feelings, 24
  response to termination, 245
  second analysis, 179–182
  sense of how analysts viewed her,
    179–180
  on termination, 234
McKee, B., 116
meanings, dyadic creation of, 183
memory, 11–12, 37
  analyst in, 130
  of Participants, 6
Mendelsohn, E., 314–315
mental masturbation, 104
mental processes, generation and,
    183
methodology, quandaries
    regarding, 2
myelinization, 89–90
Meyers, H., 134
Miller, Dr. Harold, 48–50
  on imagined postanalytic
    conversation, 303, 305
  posttermination gains, 134
mind, paradox of, 258
mirroring, vs. contact, 317
mismatches, 199
Mitchell, S., 7, 12, 86, 263
modeling, candor, directness, and,
    144
Modell, A., 36, 125
Money-Kyrle, R.E., 308
morale, reinforcing, 179
Moser, T., 308
mother
  as first love object, 162
  overprotective, 109
  view of self, 162
mothering, 160
mother relationship, sadistic edge
    of, 111
mother transference, 15, 130
  negative, 88
mourning, 54, 169. See also grief

capacity for, 237
content of analysand's, 235–236
delayed, 237
diversity in, 236
ego and, 240
gender differences in, 245
inability regarding, 240
internalization of, 226–227
labor of, 239
lineaments of, 240–241
pathologic, 240
potential, 54
reality and, 238
resolution in, 245
response to, 235–236
role of, 236
self-reflection and, 12
termination and, 229
multiple meanings, 148
mutuality, 166–167

Nahum, J., 16, 17
Nakhla, F., 308
narcissism, 55–56, 195
analysands berated for, 128
confrontation and, 130
institutionalized, 217
of mother, 163
narcissistic entitlement, 78
narcissistic label, 141–142
narratives, grouping of, 5
negative transference, 104, 106
negativity, 166
contagion of mood, 81
perceptions of, 67
negotiation, between analyst and
patient, 153
Neruda, Pablo, 94
neutral analyst, 70
neutrality, 179, 196
guise of, 176
in training, 199

Newton, P.M., 13–15
nonresponsiveness, 53
Norman, H.F., 79, 260
nothingness, death and, 41
Nounous, Dr. Mozes
adolescent trauma, 33
on analytic identity, 217–218
comparison with analytic siblings,
286
deeply satisfying analysis,
138–140
on free-associating, 23
on imagined postanalytic conversation, 298–299
on posttermination contact,
285–286
posttermination gains, 133–134
Novick, J., 273
Nussbaum, M.C., 236, 309

object relationships, 7
object-*See* King depression, 36
obscurity, masqueraded as
profundity, 70
oedipal age, 93
oedipal competition, 130
oedipal conflict, 95
oedipal interpretation, 57
oedipal transference, 100
oedipal victory, 92, 93
Oedipus complex, dissent and, 199
Oedipus conflict, mourning and, 239
Olympian distance, 291
O'Neil, M.K., 275
openness, 32
options, in vertical life, 43
Oremland, J.D., 260
Orgel, S., 198, 229–230, 240–241
otherness
collision with, 313
dealing with, 135
overstaying welcome, 154

pain
    attitude toward, 149
    bearing, 154
pair bonding, 88
panic, 51
Paolitto, F., 225–226, 260
parenting, 44
    analyst role in, 168–169
Parkinson's disease, 36
Participants. See also individual
        names, e.g., Clark, Dr.
        Veronica; etc.
    analytic history, 5
    analytic identity of dissatisfied, 213
    Angiolieri, Dr. Cecco. See
        Angiolieri, Dr. Cecco
    associations of, 44
    Baranger, Dr. Julia. See Baranger,
        Dr. Julia
    Brown, Dr. Eleanor. See Brown,
        Dr. Eleanor
    Clark, Dr. Veronica. See Clark,
        Dr. Veronica
    damaging perceptions, 67
    data regarding, 62–64
    Deere, Dr. John. See Deere,
        Dr. John
    Emon, Dr. Francesca. See Emon,
        Dr. Francesca
    Encarta, Dr. Horatio. See
        Encarta, Dr. Horatio
    erotic wishes of women, 87
    Fisher, Dr. Zelda. See Fisher,
        Dr. Zelda
    Glenn, Dr. Jay. See Glenn, Dr. Jay
    Green, Dr. Saul. See Green, Dr. Saul
    Jason, Dr. Eva. See Jason, Dr. Eva
    Koestner, Dr. Harold. See
        Koestner, Dr. Harold
    Langer, Dr. Phil. See Langer,
        Dr. Phil
    Laraphil, Dr. Stuart. See Laraphil,
        Dr. Stuart

    Laub, Dr. Celia. See Laub,
        Dr. Celia
    Lawrence, Dr. David. See
        Lawrence, Dr. David
    letter to potential, 319–322
    Levy, Dr. Noah. See Levy,
        Dr. Noah
    Lewis, Dr. Henry. See Lewis,
        Dr. Henry
    Lieberman, Dr. Raphe. See
        Lieberman, Dr. Raphe
    Light, Dr. Elizabeth. See Light,
        Dr. Elizabeth
    Lionheart, Dr. Rose. See
        Lionheart, Dr. Rose
    Maxwell, Dr. Kathryn. See
        Maxwell, Dr. Kathryn
    Mazur, Dr. Irving. See Mazur,
        Dr. Irving
    McClinton, Dr. Emma. See
        McClinton, Dr. Emma
    Miller, Dr. Harold. See Miller,
        Dr. Harold
    moderately satisfied, 34
    motivations of, 30
    negative self-regard of, 66
    Nounous, Dr. Mozes. See
        Nounous, Dr. Mozes
    Participant 14: record sealed, 3,
        324
    Robinson, Dr. Jack. See
        Robinson, Dr. Jack
    Rodine, Dr. Heather. See Rodine,
        Dr. Heather
    satisfaction rates of women with
        male training analysts, 87
    self-representations of, 67
    Sonenshein, Dr. Seymour. See
        Sonenshein, Dr. Seymour
    Thomas, Dr. Gary. See Thomas,
        Dr. Gary
    Tulane, Dr. Jill. See Tulane,
        Dr. Jill

views of, 44
voices of, 4
White, Dr. Bob. *See* White, Dr. Bob
wishes for postanalytic conversation, 277
women with male analysts, 91–94
Zeller, Dr. Steven. *See* Zeller, Dr. Steven
participation
bad-enough, 315
good-enough, 315
passivity, intolerance of, 151
past, memorializing, 12
paternal transference
differentiating force of, 135
negative, 104
patient-analyst interconnection, 314
patients, analysts' modes of experiencing, 16
penis envy interpretations, 95
perceptions
acting on, 146–147
damaging, 67
disputed, 178
personality, *vs.* analytic stance, 95–98
personal life, self-exclusion from intimacy in patient's, 85–86
Person, E., 88, 134
personhood, 33
vs. doctorhood, 99–100
facets of, 223
Pfeffer, A., 12, 232, 260
playfulness, 60
positive transference, 166
postanalytic contact. *See* posttermination contact
postanalytic encounters
analysts' nature pondered, 282
imagined, 303
issues of, 44–45. *See also* posttermination contact
love for analyst, 281–282

misunderstandings, 295–296
rejecting, 291
postanalytic period, 272
Postman, The, 94
posttermination
developments during, 271
sense of loss during, 273
posttermination contact, 270
alternative patterns, 287–288
ambiguities of, 279–280
content of conversations, 288–289
correlation of sex and, 274–275
in deeply satisfying analyses, 281–287
de-idealization as, 273
dissatisfying analysis, 291–294
dyad members' personal signatures, 294
effect of, 274
frequency of, 275–276
moderately satisfying analysis, 287–291
Participants wishes for, 277
reasons for, 275
rejection, 295
social, 287
value of, 271
Post-Termination Phase of Analytic Treatment (panel), 274
power
of analysts in past, 176
asymmetry of, 46–48
sexual fantasies and, 117–118
practices, authoritarian *vs.* egalitarian, 62
preoedipal transferences, 161
presence, sense of, 175
privacy, 3, 320
erotic feelings and, 3
process monitoring, 220
professional jealousy, 169–170
professional role, women with female analysts, 160

projection, taking back, 166
projective identification, 8
pseudonyms, 3
psychic life, 11–12
    aspects of, 184
psychic reality, between analysand
        and analyst, 313
psychic retreat, 36, 53–54, 241
psychoanalysis
    fragmentation of, 191
    sleeping through, 147
    warm and cold sides of, 308
Psychoanalytic Institute of New
        England, 62
psychoanalytic institutes
    ethos of, 61
    sociocultural context of, 1
psychoanalytic theorizing, change
        in, 213
psychosomatic agony, 51
psychosomatic symptom, 189
Pygmalian countertransference, 35,
        117, 211

Q-sort analysis, 16
questions, implication of raising,
        143
quotations, vetoed by Participants, 3

Rangell, L., 230, 272
Reactivity, of female infants, 89
Reality
    adapting to painful, 146
    altering, 151
    dealing with, 143
    denial of, 72
reality help, 169
reality orientation, 107
reality testing, 236
rebellion, silent, 109
reciprocal exchanges, 78
reciprocal gaze, questions
        regarding, 68

reciprocal self-inquiry, 262
reciprocal views, 75–78
Reed, K., 162
Reese, Pee Wee, 263
regression, 293
    allowing, 182
rhesus monkeys, specificity and, 80
Reich, A., 273
reinternalization, of analyst, 248
rejection, in postanalytic contact, 295
relatedness, two-person templates
        of, 317
relational templates, 116
relationships
    postanalytical, 138
    real vs. analytic, 101–102
    shift in, 256
    tolerance in, 174
    vs. transference, 129
remembered engagement, as general
        phenomenon, 2
Rendely, J., 240
repetition compulsion, 151
reporting system, 198–199
representations, reorganization and,
        78–79
repression, 111
reserve, 172
residual transference, 167
resigned compliance, 146
resilience, capacities of, 80
resistance, analysis of, 14
resolution, termination and, 245
response
    entitlement to, 106–107
    lack of, 179
Rhine, M., 274
Rickmann, 227–228
Ritvo, S., 240, 271
Robbins, F., 297
Robbins, W.S., 239–240, 241
Robinson, Dr. Jack, 263
    on analytic identity, 216–217

deeply satisfying analysis, 136–138
on imagined postanalytic conver-
    sation, 301–302
on self-observations, 23
on solitary self-analysis, 265–266
Rodine, Dr. Heather
on analyst's qualities, 76
competition with analyst, 159
on disengagement, 25–26
on imagined postanalytic conver-
    sation, 302–303
loving feelings, 160
moderately satisfying analysis,
    165–168
on regressive feelings, 24
shared analyst, 324
Rohde, A., 297
role model, female, 168
role responsiveness, gender and, 84
roles, in life vs. in analysis, 194
romantic fantasies, 133
Ross, J.M., 115
Rudolf, G., 16

sadness, vs. depression, 238
sadomasochism
in authoritarian Institutes, 116–117
Sadow, L., 207
safe space, 125
Sagi, A., 89
sampling procedure, 323–324
Sander, L.W., 9, 183
Sandler, J., 84
satisfaction
categories of, 6
with direction of trend, 64
inner presence and, 310
of interaction with gender and
    decade, 60–64
of intersects, 61
Sayers, J., 163
Schachter, J., 271, 274, 275–276
schizoid fence, 167

schizoid retreat, 77
schizoid withdrawal, 167
Schlessinger, N., 271, 274, 297
Schmideberg, M., 230
Schraft's waitresses, 77
self
freedom of, 42
views of, 66
self-acceptance, 13
analyst's regard and, 66
self-analysis, 15, 34
access to, 264
capacity for, 258
crisis and, 260
drawback of, 204
limitations of, 261
object relations view of, 263
origins of postanalytic, 260
postanalytic, 259
self-protection and, 264–265
valuing, 264
self-analytic ability, 38
self-analytic function, 225, 261
self and other
internalized representations,
    78–82
models, 79
self-criticism, 172
amelioration of, 175
self-development, of analysands,
    224–225
self-esteem, 129, 179
issues, 144
self-experience, 97
self-image, female analysts and, 163
self inquiry, 262
selflessness, of analyst, 150
self-reflection
mourning and, 12
of participants, 263
self-representations, changing,
    72–75
self-understanding, 262

sense of humor, 216
  analysand's response to, 120
sensuality, 173
separation, from mother, 148
separation anxiety, 163
sexual arousal, in analysis, 84–85
sexual desire, exploration of, 91
sexual dreams, inferred, 144
sexuality, 189
  analytic responses to, 173
sexual sensations, with female
  analysts, 160
sexual wishes, taboo, 90
Shakespeare, William, *The Tempest*,
  13
shame, 196
shaming, 55
Shapiro, D., 21, 199, 206–208, 248
Shapiro, T., 16
shared engagement, 32
sharing, in analysis, 126
shifting identifications, 111–112
shifting views, 219
Silber, A., 210
silence
  of analyst, 105–106
  vs. anonymity, 106
Silverman, D., 89
Simner, M.L., 89
Simon, B., 308
  on transformation, 13
sitting shiva, 154
Smith, H., 262, 263
Snider, Duke, 263
social position, posttermination
  contact and, 289
social relationships, postanalytic, 280
sociocultural context, female-female
  analytic dyads, 161
Socrates, 196
Solnit, A.J., 240, 271
Sonenshein, Dr. Seymour
  experience with training analyst, 121

on imagined postanalytic conversation, 303
on leave-taking, 253
moderately satisfying analysis, 121
on posttermination contact,
  290–291
on termination, 233–234
use of "jokes" in first analysis, 121
spontaneity, between analyst and
  analysand, 229
Standing, Sue, 296
standoffishness, 53
Steele, H., 8, 67
Steele, M., 8, 67
Steiner, J., 35–36, 241
Stolorow, R., 227
Strachey, J., 227
style, technique and, 215
subjectivity
  articulating states of, 195
  in training, 199
sublimation, 90–91
Sullivan, H.S., 79
Suomi, S.J., 79, 80
sweetness, 60
Symington, N., 33, 223, 314

tabulations
  categories of satisfaction,
    325–327
  decade of analysis, 325–327
  interaction with gender, 325–327
  summaries of, 328–329
  total analyses, 326–327
  training analyses only, 325–326
tailored analysis, 98
talking, thinking and, 192
talking cure, 258
Target, M., 8, 17, 67, 79
tea room coldness, 77
technique
  character and, 215
  style and, 215

tenderness, friendship and, 156
termination, 174
    analysts' challenges at, 13
    analysts' conflicts with, 241–243
    analysts' temptations during,
        230–231
    assumptions about, 9
    date of, 56
    competitive feelings during, 190
    dialogue shift in, 191
    dimensions of, 12
    Dr. Encarta's response to, 187
    feelings for analyst after, 189–191
    intrapsychic presence after,
        107–108
    knowing and, 224
    longings after, 124
    love and, 228
    memory of analyst after, 1
    mourning and, 229
    painful, 243–245
    phase, 40–41
    preemptory, 292–293
    readiness criteria, 225
    resolution and, 245
    reversion of twoness to oneness,
        183
    self-reflections after, 280
    as separation, 230
    timing of, 231
    transition at, 184
    without mourning, 273
Tessman, L., 79, 91, 134, 227, 235,
    236, 238
themes, 123
theoretical preconception, 219
thinking, nature of, 192
Thomas, Dr. Gary
    on feeling disabled, 36
    first and second analysis,
        122–124
    on imagined postanalytic conver-
        sation, 302

presence of mother, 22
    responsibility for mother's care, 123
thought
    analysands theory of, 18
    articulating, 192
    generating, 184
    meaning of, 153
threats
    internal and external, 147
    ongoing, 147
Ticho, G.R., 264
time variations, 2
training analysis, 15
    candidates and, 199
    expected achievements, 206
    focus of, 200
    problems in, 201–202
    recommended line of questions
        for, 206
    survey of problems, 206–208
    triangular relationship in,
        202–203
training analysts
    berating analysands for narcis-
        sism, 128
    challenges, 203–204
    choosing, 42
    complications deriving from, 208
    conflicts of, 129
    early tendencies, 200
    match with candidates, 208
    power of, 205
    resistance to, 203
    temptations of, 203
    wounding experiences with, 213
training complications, 198
training system, argument against,
    201
transference, 11, 224
    age and, 133
    ambiguity and, 215
    anger during, 47
    balance in, 240

transference *(continued)*
  characteristics of, 17
  cross-gender, 135
  dead mother, 105–106
  emerging in analysis, 83
  erotic wishes and, 91
  feeling of, 42
  gender and, 133–134
  limits of, 46
  maternal aspects of, 15
  nature of, 234
  in nonanalytic situation, 97
  positive and negative, 105–106
  vs. relationship, 129
  resolution of, 102, 193–194, 225,
    229
  rocky, 95–96
transference-countertransference
  impasses, 199
  interplay, 208
  shifts in configuration, 229
  unarticulated configurations, 23
transference emotions, 205
transference feelings, 176, 224
  physical, 129
transference interpretations, 43
transference issues, 214
transference neurosis, 226–227, 260
transference object, as resource, 168
transference wishes, 224
transformation, 13
transition, from analysis to friend-
    ship, 167
transitional space, 154
trauma, 33
  analytic results and, 31
trend, direction of satisfaction, 64
Tronick, E.Z., 183
trust, 71, 97
Tulane, Dr. Jill
  dream interpretation, 111–112
  emotional response to analysis, 109
  with male analyst, 108–113

maternal transference with male
    analyst, 102–108
  rebellious feeling about, 108–109
  on self-reflections, 73–74
two-person field, 218–219
two-person psychology, 227–228

unconscious life, after termination,
    191
unconscious fantasy, 45
unfinished business, 251

vaginal odor, 48
validation, analyst's need for, 292
values, acknowledging, 178
veracity, fidelity to, 295–296
vertical life, empathic, 112–113
Viorst, J., 13

Wallerstein, R.S., 274
warmth, 166
war trauma, 33
Weigert, E., 205, 238, 239, 241
Weinberg, K., 89
Weinshel, E.M., 7
  on leave-taking, 250
Weiss, S.S., 206
What About Bob?, 290–291
White, Dr. Bob, 37–41
  on analytic identity, 219–220
  on imagined postanalytic conver-
    sation, 301
  life time-line, 22
  moderately satisfying analysis,
    122
  shared analyst, 324
Winnicott, D., 4, 67, 317
withdrawal, schizoid walls of, 165
Wizard of Oz, 182
womanhood, flight from, 163
women
  issues, 159–160
  in medicine, 171

in psychiatry, 171
psychic development and
intimacy, 162
statistics with female analysts,
158–159
women candidates, on aggression,
213
Wortis, J., 307
Freud and, 14

Yiddish, 154

Zeller, Dr. Steven
analyst as father figure, 119
harmony of traits with analyst,
75–76
on imagined postanalytic conversation, 300–301
on interaction role, 24
on posttermination contact,
283–284
shared analyst, 324
Zetzel, E., 237

C. – ~~tape~~
Unseen

what ~~thought~~ you give me tape –
what expect – what if I like it or not –
– show me side of yourself
been in compet rel. with mom
so analyze what meant for
you to show it to me

– Need give authentic response
if feel trapped can't give authentic
response

Appreciate gift – but may be
something I will or won't get to